LAW, CRIME AND LAW ENFORCEMENT

U.S. DEPARTMENT OF JUSTICE ASSET FORFEITURE POLICY MANUAL AND GUIDE TO EQUITABLE SHARING

LAW, CRIME AND LAW ENFORCEMENT

Additional books in this series can be found on Nova's website
under the Series tab.

Additional E-books in this series can be found on Nova's website
under the E-book tab.

LAW, CRIME AND LAW ENFORCEMENT

U.S. DEPARTMENT OF JUSTICE ASSET FORFEITURE POLICY MANUAL AND GUIDE TO EQUITABLE SHARING

ONNI NIEMINEN
EDITOR

nova publishers
New York

For permission to use material from this book please contact us:
Telephone 631-231-7269; Fax 631-231-8175
Web Site: http://www.novapublishers.com

Library of Congress Cataloging-in-Publication Data

ISBN: 978-1-62808-226-5

Published by Nova Science Publishers, Inc. † New York

CONTENTS

PREFACE

In the nearly 25 years since the Comprehensive Crime Control Act of 1984 authorized federal officials to implement a national asset forfeiture program, asset forfeiture has become one of the most powerful tools for targeting criminals, including drug dealers and white collar criminals, who prey on the vulnerable for financial gain. Forfeiture statutes are now prevalent throughout the federal legal code and their use, along with other important anti-crime measures, has had a significant impact on crime. One of the most important provisions of asset forfeiture is the authorization to share federal forfeiture proceeds with cooperating state and local law enforcement agencies. The Department of Justice Asset Forfeiture Program serves not only to deter crime but also to provide valuable additional resources to state and local law enforcement agencies. This book examines the U.S. Department of Justice Asset Forfeiture Policy Manual and Guide to Equitable Sharing Manual, with a focus on assisting state and local law enforcement agencies participating in the program by clarifying the directives they must follow to obtain and use equitably shared funds.

Chapter 1 – This is the *Asset Forfeiture Policy Manual*, a compilation of policies governing the Justice Department's Asset Forfeiture Program. It replaces and supersedes all previous versions of the *Policy Manual* and all Policy Directives and Interim Legal Advice Memoranda.

This *Policy Manual* reflects policies that have changed since its last hardcopy publication in 2008. Some of the policies, such as the new section on *qui tam* actions in Part 4 and the new part on victim issues, were added to the electronic version in 2010 and may look familiar to readers. In addition, several parts were completely revised for the 2012 edition: Part 6 on equitable sharing includes the recent delegation to AFMLS to decide uncontested equitable sharing requests between $1 million and $5 million; and Part 9 on international forfeiture reflects recent case law and legislation, particularly concerning 28 U.S.C. § 2467. Many other parts have seen significant revision.

Some topics that require extended treatment, such as interlocutory sales and expedited settlements, are addressed at length in stand-alone publications at www.justice.gov/criminal/afmls/pubs. These additional guides supplement but do not supersede the policies set forth in the *Policy Manual*.

Chapter 2 – In the nearly 25 years since the Comprehensive Crime Control Act of 1984 authorized federal officials to implement a national asset forfeiture program, asset forfeiture has become one of the most powerful tools for targeting criminals—including drug dealers and white collar criminals— who prey on the vulnerable for financial gain. Forfeiture statutes are now prevalent throughout the federal legal code and their use, along with other important anti-crime measures, has had a significant impact on crime.

One of the most important provisions of asset forfeiture is the authorization to share federal forfeiture proceeds with cooperating state and local law enforcement agencies. The Department of Justice Asset Forfeiture Program serves not only to deter crime but also to provide valuable additional resources to state and local law enforcement agencies. As this is written, the Department of Justice has shared over $4.5 billion in forfeited assets with more than 8,000 state and local law enforcement agencies.

A Guide to Equitable Sharing for State and Local Law Enforcement Agencies serves to promote and maintain the integrity of the equitable sharing program so that it can continue to merit public confidence and support. For this reason it is supplemented with the National Code of Professional Conduct for Asset Forfeiture. All seizing and prosecutorial agencies should ensure compliance with this Code.

Most importantly, this *Guide* seeks to assist state and local law enforcement agencies participating in the program by clarifying the directives they must follow to obtain and use equitably shared funds. The goal is to make the process as clear as possible so that local communities and the nation can thrive from reduced crime and from quality law enforcement.

In: U.S. Department of Justice Asset Forfeiture …
Editor: Onni Nieminen

ISBN: 978-1-62808-226-5

Chapter 1

ASSET FORFEITURE POLICY MANUAL (2012)*

U.S. Department of Justice

FOREWORD

This is the *Asset Forfeiture Policy Manual*, a compilation of policies governing the Justice Department's Asset Forfeiture Program. It replaces and supersedes all previous versions of the *Policy Manual* and all Policy Directives and Interim Legal Advice Memoranda.

This *Policy Manual* reflects policies that have changed since its last hardcopy publication in 2008. Some of the policies, such as the new section on *qui tam* actions in Part 4 and the new part on victim issues, were added to the electronic version in 2010 and may look familiar to readers. In addition, several parts were completely revised for the 2012 edition: Part 6 on equitable sharing includes the recent delegation to AFMLS to decide uncontested equitable sharing requests between $1 million and $5 million; and Part 9 on international forfeiture reflects recent case law and legislation, particularly concerning 28 U.S.C. § 2467. Many other parts have seen significant revision.

Some topics that require extended treatment, such as interlocutory sales and expedited settlements, are addressed at length in stand-alone publications at www.justice.gov/criminal/afmls/pubs. These additional guides supplement but do not supersede the policies set forth in the *Policy Manual*.

The *Asset Forfeiture Policy Manual* sets forth the policies of the Department of Justice. It does not, however, create or confer any legal rights, privileges, or benefits that may be enforced in any way by private parties. *See United States v. Caceres*, 440 U.S. 741 (1979).

We recommend that the following format be used in citing this *Policy Manual*: *Asset Forfeiture Policy Manual* (2012), Part ___, Sec. ___.___. (e.g. Part 1, Sec. I.A).

Jennifer Shasky Calvery Chief
Asset Forfeiture and Money Laundering Section

---

* This is an edited, reformatted and augmented version of U.S. Department of Justice, U.S. Department of Justice Criminal Division, Asset Forfeiture and Money Laundering Section, dated 2012.

PART 1: SEIZURE/RESTRAINT

I. Guidelines for Pre-seizure/Restraint Planning

A. Background

These guidelines are intended to encourage practices that will minimize or avoid the possibility that the Government will unknowingly file forfeiture actions against properties leading to losses to the Assets Forfeiture Fund (AFF) and assume unnecessarily difficult or insurmountable problems in the management and disposition of seized/restrained assets.[1] In particular, they are meant to ensure that the U.S. Marshals Service (USMS) and its headquarters Asset Forfeiture Division (AFD) and other agencies with responsibility for seizing, restraining, managing, and disposing of assets are consulted before legal action is taken against forfeitable property.[2] Pre-seizure planning affords the opportunity for these agencies to conduct financial analyses to determine net equities of targeted assets and review title/ownership issues that may delay or prevent the Government from disposing of an asset in a timely manner following forfeiture. In addition, pre-seizure planning affords the USMS sufficient time to plan for the care of the assets, the opportunity to assess the level of difficulty in handling the assets and any special requirements needed to preserve the assets, and identify any special requirements needed to preserve the assets.

These guidelines direct the U.S. Attorney's Office (USAO) (or in administrative forfeitures, the agents in charge of a field office) to establish specific procedures for their respective districts or offices to ensure that critical financial and property management issues are addressed prior to seizing/restraining real property, commercial enterprises, or other types of property that may pose problems of maintenance and/or disposition (e.g., animals and aircraft). These guidelines are intended to be flexible enough to enable each USAO (or in administrative matters, the agent in charge of a field office) to establish and utilize procedures which clearly define and assign local pre-seizure/restraint planning responsibilities.

The USMS should be advised promptly prior to all seizures/restraints, the filing of civil forfeiture complaints, or the return of indictments containing forfeiture allegations to afford the USMS sufficient time to conduct ownership/title and valuation analysis, and to identify all resources necessary to effectuate seizures.

B. Scope of Assets Covered by Guidelines

These guidelines cover all assets considered for federal forfeiture, including assets seized by a state or local agency and adopted by a federal agency for purposes of federal forfeiture. The degree and nature of pre-seizure planning will vary depending upon the circumstances and complexity of each case.

In order for the USMS to best assist the USAOs and seizing agencies in a thorough, efficient, and most effective manner, the USMS must be involved in the investigation as soon as the USAO or seizing agency is aware assets will be targeted for forfeiture.[3] Formal pre-seizure planning should occur well in advance of filing a civil forfeiture complaint or the return of an indictment containing forfeiture allegations. Specifically, formal pre-seizure planning requires detailed discussion of all potential issues affecting the seizure, custody, and disposal arrangements specific to an asset targeted for forfeiture. This discussion may take place either in person, by telephone, or electronically, and may be ongoing depending on the nature of the asset and stage of the case. These pre-seizure planning discussions must take place for the asset categories listed below:

1) residential/commercial real property and vacant land[4];
2) businesses and other complex assets;
3) large quantities of assets involving potential inventory and storage or security problems (e.g., multiple vehicles, drug paraphernalia to be seized from multiple "headshops" on the same day, and the inventory of ongoing businesses such as jewelry stores);
4) assets that create difficult or unusual problems (e.g., animals, perishable items, chemicals and pharmaceuticals, leasehold agreements, intellectual property, valuable art and antiques); and
5) assets located in foreign countries.

Depending upon the complexity and scope of the case, formal pre-seizure planning may continue after this initial discussion as required by either the USAO or the USMS. In many instances, the USMS will be required to procure the professional assistance of commercial vendors during the covert stage of an investigation so that services such as inventories, appraisals, transportation, and storage will coincide with a scheduled takedown date. The USMS will take appropriate measures to protect sensitive law enforcement information while consultation occurs with the involved components. No information will be released to third-party contractors without prior USAO approval. In addition, the information provided to such contractors can be limited to that necessary to procure contractor assets (e.g., towing services and storage space for 50 vehicles required in a particular location by a certain date).

Examples of the types of services the USMS may provide upon a request by either the USAO or seizing agency (as well as the usual time it takes to obtain the requested service) include the following:

Lien search and appraisal information	3-4 weeks from date of request to return information (additional time necessary for full, non-"drive-by" appraisals)	The USMS offers these services to provide USAOs and investigative agencies information during the pre-indictment, pre-seizure planning stage of a criminal or civil investigation.
Animal care	1 month prior to seizure	Proper arrangements must be made to ensure health and daily care.
Logistics services	3-6 months prior to take-down date for unusual or complex assets	Federal contracting regulations and the time necessary to coordinate with commercial vendors make it imperative to involve the USMS' AFD as soon as such services are contemplated.
Business Recommended Action Plan	2-4 months, or longer in more complex cases	Forfeiture decisions by the USAO and the seizing agency should be made only after the USMS' AFD conducts a documentary review of the targeted business assets and financial status.

C. General Policy Guidelines

Broad pre-seizure planning policy guidelines for all agencies participating in the Department of Justice's Asset Forfeiture Program are defined below. Variations to these guidelines may be made following discussions with Asset Forfeiture and Money Laundering Section (AFMLS).

C.1. Lead Responsibility

The U.S. Attorney (or in administrative forfeiture cases, the agent in charge of a field office) is responsible for ensuring that proper and timely pre-seizure planning occurs in asset forfeiture cases within that federal judicial district. All pre-seizure planning meetings must include, at a minimum, as applicable, the Assistant U.S. Attorney (AUSA) or investigative agent in charge of the forfeiture matter (and, if applicable, the AUSA in charge of the related criminal matter), investigative agents, and the appropriate USMS representative (which should include a representative from the district where the property is to be seized and/or managed if different from the district where the action is to be filed). A federal regulatory agency representative may also attend in forfeiture cases involving federal regulatory matters as appropriate.

As a general rule, the lead agency will process all the assets. The lead agency is the agency that initiates the investigation. Another agency may be designated a lead agency if provided for in a task force agreement or memorandum of understanding. Ordinarily, assets must be processed by the lead agency only and shall not be divided among multiple agencies. For instance, a cash seizure of $800,000 may not be divided into two $400,000 seizures. Although exceptions may be made in extraordinary circumstances to permit individual seizures to be allocated to different agencies, no such allocation may be made without the express consent of the lead prosecuting office.

For asset forfeiture cases involving more than one federal judicial district, the USAO instituting the forfeiture action has the primary responsibility, in coordination with the investigative agency, to ensure that all Asset Forfeiture Program participants are notified and that proper and timely pre-seizure planning occurs in those districts where assets will be seized.

C.2. Pre-Seizure Planning Overview

The intent of pre-seizure planning is to ensure the various components of the Department of Justice work together as a team, assuring that asset forfeiture is used as an effective law enforcement tool. To that end, pre-seizure planning provides the Government with the opportunity to make informed decisions on matters regarding the financial impact of forfeiting and managing assets, and on matters affecting the Government's ability to efficiently dispose of assets after forfeiture. Specifically, pre-seizure planning consists of anticipating and making informed decisions about what property is going to be seized or restrained, how and when it is going to be seized or restrained, and, most important, whether it should be forfeited at all. Pre-seizure discussions should answer at least the following, depending on asset type and circumstance:

1) *What is being seized, who owns it, and what are the liabilities against it?* Determine the full scope of the seizure to the extent possible. For example, if a house is being seized, are the contents also to be seized? If a business is being seized, are the

building in which it operates, the property upon which it is located, the inventory of the business, and the operating or other bank accounts, accounts receivable, accounts payable, etc., also being seized? All ownership interests must be identified to the extent possible as well as existing/potential liabilities against the asset.

2) *Should the asset be seized or forfeited?* If the asset has a negative or marginal net equity at the time of seizure, should it be seized and forfeited? Over time, what is the likelihood that the asset will depreciate to a negative or marginal value? What law enforcement benefits are to be derived from seizure? Is a restraining or protective order an adequate alternative under the circumstances? Can any losses be mitigated by careful planning on the part of the participants? Will the asset require significant amounts of USMS or USAO resources and oversight, or considerable infusion of funds from the AFF?
3) *How and when is the asset going to be seized/forfeited?* Determine whether immediate seizure is necessary or if restraint of the asset is sufficient to preserve and protect the Government's interest. The type and content of the seizing instrument and authority to enter or cross private property must be communicated or provided, in advance, to both the investigative agency and the USMS to ensure that each has the necessary information and legal authority to carry out its respective seizure and post-seizure responsibilities.
4) *What management and disposition problems are anticipated, and how will they be resolved?* Any expected logistical issues involving the maintenance, management, or disposition of the asset should be discussed and resolved as early as possible.
5) *Is any negative publicity anticipated?* If publicity or public relations concerns are anticipated, appropriate public affairs personnel should be advised and consulted. How will negative publicity be handled?

D. Pre-Seizure Planning Questionnaires and Documentation

D.1. Asset-Specific Net Equity Thresholds

These guidelines set minimum net equity levels that generally must be met, preferably before property is seized and certainly before federal forfeiture actions are instituted. The net equity values are intended to decrease the number of federal seizures, thereby enhancing case quality and expediting processing of the cases we do initiate. The thresholds are also intended to encourage state and local law enforcement agencies to use state forfeiture laws. These thresholds are to be applied in direct federal and adoptive cases. In general, the minimum net equity requirements are:

1) Residential/Commercial real property and vacant land—minimum net equity must be at least 20 percent of the appraised value. For properties with appraised values less than $100,000, net equity must be at least $20,000. For example, the minimum net equity threshold on a $200,000 property is $40,000.[5]
2) Vehicles—minimum net equity must be at least $5,000. The value of multiple vehicles seized at the same time may be aggregated for purposes of meeting the minimum net equity. If the person from whom the vehicle is seized either was, or is, being criminally prosecuted by state or federal authorities for criminal activities

related to the vehicle and there is justification for a low value seizure, the minimum net equity is $2,000.[6]

3) Cash—minimum amount must be at least $5,000, unless the person from whom the cash was seized either was, or is, being criminally prosecuted by state or federal authorities for criminal activities related to the property, in which case the amount must be at least $1,000.
4) Aircraft—minimum net equity must be at least $10,000. Note that failure to obtain the log books for the aircraft will reduce the aircraft's value significantly.
5) Vessels—minimum net equity must be at least $10,000.
6) All other personal property—minimum net equity must be at least $1,000 in the aggregate.

Exceptions from the minimum net equity requirements should not be made for any individual item if it has a value of less than $1,000. Such exceptions can be made if practical considerations support the seizure (e.g., 20 items of jewelry, each valued at $500, might be seized, as the total value of the items is $10,000 and the cost of storing 20 small items of jewelry is not excessive).

The U.S. Attorneys, in consultation with local federal law enforcement agencies, may institute higher district-wide thresholds for judicial forfeiture cases as law enforcement or management needs require. Similarly, a federal law enforcement agency may institute higher thresholds for administrative forfeiture cases. Written notice of any higher thresholds shall be provided to the Chief, AFMLS, and the special agents-in-charge of the federal law enforcement agencies in the affected judicial district, as well as the local USMS office. Any threshold higher than those described above must not be the basis for failing to assist in seized property in the local district when requested to do so by another district with lower monetary thresholds if the requesting district intends to file the judicial action.

D.2. Compelling Law Enforcement Interest/Liability Forfeitures

It is understood that in some circumstances an overriding law enforcement interest may require the seizure/forfeiture of an asset that does not meet these criteria. In individual cases, these thresholds may be waived where forfeiture will serve a compelling law enforcement interest (e.g., forfeiture of a crack house, a conveyance with hidden compartments, a computer or Internet domain name seized to disrupt a major fraud scheme, or assets connected to a child pornography ring or a terrorist organization). Any downward variation from the above thresholds must be approved in writing by a supervisory-level official and an explanation of the reason for the variation noted in the case file. A copy of this approval, in either a written memorandum or an e-mail, must be provided to the USMS district office that will take custody of the asset(s).

D.3. Pre-Seizure Planning Questionnaires

The USMS' AFD has compiled a number of pre-seizure planning documents to assist stakeholders in making informed decisions when identifying assets for forfeiture. Obtaining the information required to complete these various documents will identify the concerns that must be addressed during the pre-seizure planning phase of a case, so as to reduce the chance a forfeiture may cause a loss to the AFF and to preserve the Government's ability to efficiently dispose of assets after forfeiture. Through consultation with the USMS, calculations for the storage and maintenance costs of particular assets can be determined, as well as the impact of potential liabilities against an asset. Individual offices may supplement these forms as they see fit. However, the basic information called for in these forms is required for adequate planning.

D.4. Net Equity Worksheet

When certain assets, especially residential/commercial and vacant real properties, are targeted for forfeiture, the potential net equity must be calculated as part of pre-seizure planning.[7] In cases where information relating to titles and liens cannot be acquired without compromising the investigation, the financial analysis may be completed post-seizure.[8] A written financial analysis facilitates, documents, and informs pre-seizure planning decisions. The USMS net equity worksheets provide step-by-step formulas for computing net equity—the estimated total amount of money the Government expects to recoup from the asset once the aggregate of all liens, mortgages, and management and disposal costs have been subtracted from the expected proceeds of the sale of the asset—and documents the results of this analysis. The USAO or the seizing agency are strongly encouraged to adopt the USMS net equity forms as they provide the most updated estimates for the management and disposal of properties based on current contract prices. These forms may be supplemented as conditions dictate.

D.4.A. Ownership and Encumbrances

The investigative agency is responsible for ensuring that current and accurate information on the ownership of, and any encumbrances against, personal property targeted for forfeiture is compiled and made available to the USMS and the USAO prior to seizure whenever practicable. When this is not practicable prior to the seizure, such information must be compiled and made available as soon as possible following the seizure. In instances where real property and businesses are targeted for seizure, the USMS will have primary responsibility for conducting a title search prior to seizure unless otherwise agreed in individual cases. The USMS cannot conduct a complete ownership analysis for a business unless the USAO obtains, by subpoena or otherwise, appropriate ownership documents (e.g., stock record books, stock certificates, partnership agreements, etc.).

D.4.B. Financial Analysis: Avoiding Liability Seizures

1.Pre-Seizure

If the financial analysis indicates that the aggregate of all liens (including judgment liens), mortgages, and management and disposal costs approaches or exceeds the anticipated proceeds from the sale of the property, the USAO, or in administrative forfeiture actions, the seizing agency, must either (1) determine not to go forward with the seizure,[9] or (2) acknowledge the potential financial loss and document the circumstances that warrant the seizure and institution of the forfeiture action.

2. Post-Seizure

In instances where pre-seizure planning is not possible and/or is not completed prior to seizure, the seizing agency may be responsible for custody and maintenance of the property until the USMS has had the opportunity to conduct an analysis of the assets. Upon completion and reporting of the USMS pre-seizure analysis, a pre-seizure meeting should take place to address all issues identified. If the financial assessment indicates that the aggregate of all liens, mortgages, and management and disposal costs approaches or exceeds the anticipated proceeds from the sale of the property, in administrative forfeiture cases the seizing agency must either, (1) take action to terminate the asset from the forfeiture proceeding (if any has commenced), or (2) acknowledge the potential loss and document the circumstances that warrant the continuation of the forfeiture proceeding. In judicial forfeiture cases, the USAO must either (1) take action to dismiss the forfeiture action and to void any expedited settlement agreements (if any have been entered into), or (2) acknowledge the potential loss and document the circumstances that warrant the continuation of the forfeiture action.

In deciding how to proceed with the seizure and forfeiture of potential liability seizures during the pre-seizure phase in judicial forfeitures, the USAO in consultation with the seizing agency and the USMS (and in administrative forfeitures, the agent in charge of the field office responsible for the administrative forfeiture, in consultation with the USMS) must evaluate and consider the forfeitable net equity and the law enforcement purposes to be served in light of the potential liability issues and estimated costs of post-seizure management and disposition.

D.5. Business Seizures

The complexities of seizing an ongoing business and the potential for substantial losses and other liabilities from such a seizure require that a USAO consult with AFMLS prior to initiating a forfeiture action against, seeking the seizure of, or moving to restrain an ongoing business.[10]

Deciding whether and how to restrain or seize an ongoing business is a complex and time consuming process. A comprehensive analysis of the scope of the illegal activity and what is to be achieved through seizure/restraint is necessary. AFMLS and the USMS recommend restraining a business in the least restrictive manner needed to preserve the Government's interest. Seizure of a business, and operation or closure of the business by the Government, should only be carried out where all other options have been considered and rejected.

As previously discussed, the first questions in pre-seizure planning are: What is being seized or restrained? How is the business owned? Is it a corporation, partnership, or sole proprietorship? Will the business be indicted? Will the business remain solvent if revenue tied to illegal activity is terminated? Are there innocent shareholders, payroll employees, or other third-party interests to take into consideration?

In the case of an ongoing business that has been targeted for forfeiture, it is generally desirable to utilize the least intrusive means to gain control over the business during the pendency of litigation. *See United States v. All Assets Statewide Autoparts*, 971 F.2d 896 (2d Cir. 1992) (hearing and consideration of less drastic alternatives required). AFMLS recommends civil and/or criminal restraining orders for ongoing businesses if at all possible.

There may be instances in which it will be necessary to close down a seized business prior to forfeiture, particularly if an ongoing business is engaged in substantially illegal activity and/or there are exigent circumstances, such as ongoing health and safety issues that cannot be satisfactorily addressed by other means.

Seizure of business accounts, necessary equipment, and licenses can also cause an ongoing business to fail even if the business itself is not seized. If the Government fails to achieve forfeiture and the business assets must be returned to their owner, there may be substantial financial and adverse legal ramifications for the Government if it cannot return the assets to their owner in substantially the same condition in which they were seized.

The USAO may consider simply naming the business as a defendant and/or an asset for forfeiture; often businesses shut down of their own accord once key defendants are arrested or indicted, making forfeiture of the business unnecessary and saving Government resources. This is frequently the result where the assets of the business consist primarily of inventory and goodwill. A *lis pendens* placed on the real property or restraining order on valuable equipment, with monitoring, inspection, or reporting requirements, may secure the targeted assets sufficiently without taking possession of them. Alternatively, the USAO may require, as a condition of release, that a defendant/owner maintain appropriate licenses or comply with regulatory or insurance requirements.

AFMLS recommends restraining ongoing businesses rather than seizing them prior to forfeiture wherever possible. If direct government oversight is required, the USMS has contractors available to run ongoing businesses. In rare cases, a court-appointed trustee or monitor may be required. *See* part 10. Taking over a business prior to forfeiture should be considered a last resort to occur only after the USMS has completed a thorough business review. A pre-seizure review of a business will help a USAO answer the following questions:

- Who owns the building in which the business operates?
- Who owns the land?
- What is the cash flow of the business?
- What are the monetary values of accounts receivable and payable?
- What other valuable assets does the business own?
- Are there significant liabilities?
- Are there environmental concerns?
- Is the business highly regulated? Is the business currently in compliance with its regulatory obligations?
- Will the business require capital contributions to remain viable?
- What law enforcement or regulatory methods or measures other than forfeiture may be effective?
- Is the business being seized as facilitating property or as proceeds of crime? Once the source of illegal funding and the illicit customers are gone, the business may no longer be profitable. If the business is facilitating illegal activity and also engaged in legal but unseemly activity, is the Government in a position to prevent or monitor the activity (e.g., Government operation of a strip club which attracts illegal drugs and prostitution)? The public may have an expectation that if the Government is operating the business, it will be able to prevent all illegal activity. *See* part 10, section II.J for a discussion of security measures.
- What would it cost to hire either a business monitor or trustee and necessary staff?
- How will the business be disposed of, and how long will that process take?

AFMLS and the USMS' AFD are available to organize a "business evaluation and seizure team" to conduct a business review at the request of either a USAO or a seizing agency. Business reviews take time, so the USAO or seizing agency should request a business review as early in the investigative process as possible.

The AUSA (or the agent in charge of the field office responsible for an administrative forfeiture case) is responsible for ensuring that all pre-seizure planning, questionnaires, and net equity worksheets (including those prepared by the USMS) are complete and placed in the case file.

If the net equity worksheet indicates that the property targeted for forfeiture has marginal or negative anticipated net sale proceeds, the USAO (or agency field office conducting an administrative forfeiture) must document a plan to protect innocent lienholders and to dispose of the property in a manner that will minimize potential loss to the Government (e.g., an immediate motion of interlocutory sale or stipulated sale of the property, thereby minimizing asset management costs). A copy of this plan, along with the net equity worksheet, must be sent to AFMLS.

E. Trustees and Monitors in Forfeiture Cases

See part 10 for the Department of Justice's policy on trustees and monitors in forfeiture cases.

II. General Procedures for Seizing Property

A. Notification by Seizing Agency

Most USAOs can access reports of seizures by agencies participating in the AFF in their districts from the Consolidated Asset Tracking System (CATS) database. All non-Department of Justice agencies must forward copies of seizure forms or a report of seizures to the pertinent USAO within 25 days of seizure unless an individual USAO chooses to not receive seizure notices.

B. Pre-Seizure Judicial Review

B.1. Pre-Seizure Judicial Authorization of Property Seizures

Pre-seizure judicial authorization of property seizures serves multiple purposes, including the following:

1) allowing neutral and detached judicial officers to review the basis for seizures before they occur;
2) enhancing protection for Department of Justice officers against potential civil suits claiming wrongful seizures; and
3) reducing the potential that the public will perceive property seizures to be arbitrary and capricious.

B.2. Pre-Seizure Judicial Review Favored for Seizure of Personal Property

Whenever practicable, Department of Justice officials should obtain ex parte judicial approval prior to seizing personal property.[11]

C. Forms of Process to Be Used

C.1. Warrant of Arrest in Rem

In a civil judicial case, the Government may take possession of personal property with an arrest warrant in rem. The procedure for issuing an arrest warrant in rem is set forth in Supplemental Rule G(3).

Under the Rule, no arrest warrant is needed if the property is already subject to a pretrial restraining order.[12] Obtaining jurisdiction over real property is addressed in section II.Part.3. In all other cases, however, the Government must obtain an arrest warrant in rem and serve it on the property, generally by actual or constructive seizure of the property, to ensure that the court obtains in rem jurisdiction.

The procedure for issuing the warrant differs depending on whether the property is already in the Government's custody at the time the complaint is filed. If the property is already in the Government's custody, the warrant may be issued by the clerk of the court without any finding of probable cause by a judge or magistrate judge, but if the effect of the warrant will be to take the property out of the hands of a non-government entity, the warrant must be issued by a court upon a finding of probable cause.

Once the warrant is issued, it must be delivered "to a person or organization authorized to execute it." Rule G(3)(C). *See* section II.D.

C.2. Seizure Warrant

A second form of process for seizing forfeitable property is the warrant of seizure authorized by 21 U.S.C. § 881(b) and 18 U.S.C. § 981(b)(2). This form of process requires a judicial determination of probable cause.

C.3. Seizure of Real Property

In general, real property is not seized prior to forfeiture; nor is it served with an arrest warrant in rem. Typically, a *lis pendens* is filed in the property records of the local jurisdiction. Filing a notice of *lis pendens* is not a seizure of the real property.[13] The procedures for commencing a civil forfeiture action against real property are set forth in 18 U.S.C. § 985.

D. Responsibility for Execution of Process

Generally, the USMS has primary responsibility for execution of warrants of arrest in rem, while the pertinent Department of Justice investigative agency has primary responsibility for execution of seizure warrants. It is recommended that the USMS and investigative agencies coordinate execution of process.

III. Seizures for Criminal Forfeiture

A. When Is a Seizure Warrant or Restraining Order Required?[14]

Property subject to criminal forfeiture is occasionally seized pursuant to a criminal seizure warrant issued under 21 U.S.C. § 853(f). More often, property named in a criminal indictment or information is in the custody of the Government because it was seized pursuant to a civil seizure warrant issued under section 981(b), a warrant of arrest in rem under

Supplemental Rule G(3)(b)(ii), or because it was seized as evidence in the underlying criminal investigation. The question that arises is whether it is proper for the Government to maintain possession of property subject to criminal forfeiture without obtaining a section 853(f) seizure warrant in the following situations where the property was originally seized for some other purpose:

1) Where the initial seizure was pursuant to a civil seizure warrant or warrant of arrest in rem, and the U.S. Attorney elects to pursue criminal forfeiture after someone files a claim in the administrative forfeiture proceeding.
2) Where the initial seizure was without any warrant, but was based on probable cause to believe the property was subject to forfeiture when observed in plain view in a public place or pursuant to a lawful search.
3) Where the initial seizure was for evidence, but the evidentiary basis for the continued possession of the property has terminated.
4) (4) Where the property is lawfully handed over to the federal agency for criminal forfeiture by a state court or state law enforcement agency.

B. Summary

The Government does not need to have possession of property subject to criminal forfeiture during the pendency of the criminal case, but it is perfectly appropriate for the Government to maintain possession of such property prior to the entry of a preliminary order of forfeiture as long as it has a valid basis for holding the property. The criminal forfeiture action itself is a valid basis for maintaining possession of the property only if the Government has obtained a seizure warrant pursuant to section 853(f) or a restraining order (mandating transfer of the property to Government control) pursuant to section 853(e). Absent such authority, the Government may not continue to possess property subject to criminal forfeiture unless there is an independent basis for such possession.

A seizure warrant or warrant of arrest in rem issued in a parallel civil forfeiture case provides such independent basis as long as the civil action is pending. Similarly, an administrative forfeiture action is also an independent basis for maintaining custody of an asset. Likewise, property seized for evidence may remain in Government custody as long as the evidentiary basis remains. In such cases, the Government does not need to obtain a criminal seizure warrant or restraining order to maintain possession of the property. In the absence of an administrative or civil judicial forfeiture action or if the civil forfeiture action ends, or if the evidentiary purpose for holding property terminates, then the Government must obtain either a criminal seizure warrant or a restraining order under section 853(f) or (e), respectively, to maintain custody of the property pending the outcome of the criminal case.

C. Discussion

It is not necessary for the Government to have the property subject to criminal forfeiture in its possession during the pendency of a criminal forfeiture proceeding. To the contrary, the criminal forfeiture statutes contemplate that the property will, in most cases, remain in the possession of the defendant—albeit pursuant to a pretrial restraining order—until the court enters a preliminary order of forfeiture. *See* section 853(g) ("Upon entry of an order of forfeiture under this section, the court shall authorize the Attorney General to seize all property ordered forfeited...."). Cases where the Government takes physical possession of property subject to criminal forfeiture with a criminal seizure warrant prior to the entry of a preliminary order of forfeiture are relatively rare.

But the Government frequently does have physical possession of the property subject to criminal forfeiture before any preliminary order of forfeiture is entered in the criminal case. Such possession may be the result of a seizure pursuant to a civil seizure warrant issued pursuant to section 981(b), a warrant of arrest in rem issued pursuant to Supplemental Rule G(3)(b)(ii), or a seizure for the purpose of civil forfeiture that was based on probable cause. It also could be the consequence of the seizure of the property for evidence—with or without a warrant—or the adoption of the property for the purpose of forfeiture from a state or local law enforcement agency. The question is whether such possession during the pendency of criminal forfeiture proceedings is proper absent the issuance of a criminal seizure warrant under section 853(f) or a pretrial restraining order under section 853(e).

Because the Government need not have possession of the property subject to forfeiture at all during the pendency of the criminal case, the absence of a criminal seizure warrant or pretrial restraining order is of no concern as long as the Government's possession of the property pending trial has an independent basis. The following discussion focuses on four possible independent bases for maintaining physical possession of the property pending trial.

C.1. Property Seized Pursuant to a Civil Seizure Warrant or Warrant of Arrest in Rem

The seizure of property pursuant to a civil seizure warrant issued under section 981(b) or warrant of arrest in rem under Supplemental Rule G(3)(b)(ii) provides a valid basis for the Government's physical possession of property pending the outcome of a criminal forfeiture proceeding. But this is so only as long as the civil forfeiture matter is pending, including if the civil proceeding is stayed during the pendency of the case. If someone files a claim in an administrative forfeiture proceeding, the Government has 90 days in which to (1) commence a civil forfeiture action, (2) commence a criminal forfeiture action, or (3) return the property. *See* 18 U.S.C. § 983(a)(3)(B). It is perfectly appropriate for the Government to file both a civil action and a criminal action within the 90-day period, or to file a civil action within such period and file a criminal action later. In such cases, the civil seizure warrant provides a valid basis for the Government's continued possession of the property.

But section 983(a)(3)(C) provides that if "criminal forfeiture is the only forfeiture proceeding commenced by the Government, the Government's right to continued possession of the property shall be governed by the applicable criminal forfeiture statute." In other words, if there are parallel civil and criminal proceedings, the civil seizure warrant will provide a sufficient basis for holding the property, but if there is only a criminal case, the Government must takes steps to retain possession of the property either with a criminal seizure warrant issued pursuant to 21 U.S.C. § 853(f), or with an order issued pursuant to 21 U.S.C. § 853(e).[15]

The 90-day deadline provision in CAFRA, of course, only applies to cases where the property was initially seized for the purpose of "non-judicial" (i.e., administrative) forfeiture. *See* section 981(a)(1)(A). If the property was seized pursuant to a civil forfeiture seizure warrant under section 981(b) or a warrant of arrest in rem under Supplemental Rule G(3)(b)(ii), but it was not seized for the purpose of administrative forfeiture, the prescriptions found in section 983(a)(3) regarding the 90-day deadline and the need to reseize property already in Government possession do not apply. Nevertheless, even in such cases, if the

Government proceeds only with a criminal forfeiture action, it may not lawfully maintain possession of the property pursuant to a civil seizure warrant alone, but must obtain either a criminal seizure warrant or a pretrial restraining order.

C.2. Property Seized without a Warrant

Under section 981(b), property may be seized for civil or administrative forfeiture without a warrant if there is probable cause for the seizure and an exception to the warrant requirement applies. If those conditions are satisfied, the Government may maintain physical possession of the property pursuant to the section 981(b) seizure during the pendency of a criminal forfeiture case to the same extent as it could if the property had been seized with a warrant. That is, as long as the civil or administrative forfeiture case is ongoing, the continued possession may be based on the civil seizure. But if the civil case is terminated or not filed within the statutory deadline, the Government will have to maintain physical possession pursuant to a criminal seizure warrant or pretrial restraining order.

C.3. Property Seized for Evidence

The seizure of property for evidence provides an independent basis for the continued physical possession of property during the pendency of a criminal forfeiture proceeding as long as the evidentiary value of the property persists. Thus, if property is seized for evidence, it may be named in a criminal forfeiture proceeding and held by the Government without the need to obtain a criminal seizure warrant or pretrial restraining order. However, if the evidentiary value of the property evaporates, the Government must obtain a seizure warrant or restraining order to maintain custody of the property for the purpose of forfeiture.[16] The USMS does not store property held as evidence, even when it is subject to forfeiture. Such property is retained in the custody of the seizing agency until such time as it is no longer needed for evidence.

C.4. Property Obtained from the State for Adoptive Forfeiture

A federal seizing agency may take custody of property from a state or local law enforcement agency for the purpose of administrative forfeiture. If, in such a case, someone files a claim contesting the forfeiture, the 90-day deadline provision in section 983(a)(3)(B) comes into play. Thus, the Government's obligations regarding the continued physical possession of the property during the pendency of a criminal forfeiture proceeding are the same as they would be if the property had been seized for the purpose of civil forfeiture by a federal agency in the first instance.

Alternatively, the Government may take possession of property from a state agency without any intention of proceeding with administrative or civil judicial forfeiture, but rather with the intent to seek the forfeiture of the property in a criminal case. In that instance, CAFRA does not apply, but neither does the provision in section 981(b)(2)(c) creating an exemption from the warrant requirement in adoption cases. That provision applies only to civil forfeiture proceedings. Therefore, the Government may maintain custody of the property only if it has evidentiary value, or if it obtains a criminal seizure warrant or pretrial restraining order. In such matters, the USAO must not agree to the request by a state or local agency to institute a criminal forfeiture action until a federal agency has consented to process the asset for federal seizure.

D. Proper Use of Writs of Entry in Civil and Criminal Forfeiture Cases

D.1. Summary

Writs of entry issued by the court and based upon a finding of probable cause may be used in both civil and criminal forfeiture cases by the United States in the following circumstances: (1) to enter onto the curtilage and inventory structures located thereon without entering those structures; (2) to enter onto private real property for the purpose of seizing personal property located thereon (such as an automobile) in plain view; and (3) to enter into the interior of a private structure subject to forfeiture to conduct an inventory limited to documenting the condition of the interior and inspecting for damage, and to conduct an appraisal. If a private structure is to be entered for the purpose of searching for and seizing (or inventorying) personal property located therein that is subject to forfeiture, it is recommended that a separate search warrant be obtained. Of course, warrantless seizures for forfeiture may be based on the automobile, plain view, exigent circumstances, and search incident exceptions to the Fourth Amendment.

D.2. Discussion

"Civil forfeiture of real property," 18 U.S.C. § 985, provides at (b)(2), "the filing of a *lis pendens* and the execution of a writ of entry for the purpose of conducting an inspection and inventory of the property shall not be considered a seizure under this subsection." The term *writ of entry* appears nowhere else in CAFRA, nor in any other civil or criminal forfeiture statute. Section 985 provides no guidance of any kind as to the proper use and scope of a writ of entry. Answers to those questions must be gleaned from the scant case law discussing the scope of writs of entry in the context of Fourth Amendment searches and seizures.

As an initial matter, arguments can be made that the Government may seek and a district court has the authority to issue writs of entry in both civil and criminal forfeiture cases. Despite the phrase appearing only in section 985, the use of a writ of entry is not restricted to the civil forfeiture of real property. A district court has the authority pursuant to 18 U.S.C. § 983(j)(1)[17] and 21 U.S.C. § 853(e)(1)[18] to take any action necessary to preserve the availability of property subject to forfeiture. Accordingly, the Government can make application for a writ of entry in any civil or criminal forfeiture case in order to preserve the availability of property subject to forfeiture, and the district court has the authority to issue such a writ for that purpose.

The limited case law potentially applicable to the proper use of a writ of entry is *United States v. Ladson*, 774 F.2d 436 (11th Cir. 1985) and *United States v. U.S. Currency in the amount of $324,225.00*, 726 F. Supp. 259 (W.D. Mo. 1989). The cases suggest that writs of entry based upon a finding of probable cause by the court may be used as a basis to enter, inspect, and search the interiors of structures subject to forfeiture. In *Ladson*, a civil forfeiture action was commenced against a house pursuant to 21 U.S.C. § 881(a)(6). At the time the action was commenced, the house was rented. The Government requested and received from the district court an order entitled "seizure warrant/writ of entry," which authorized the seizure of the real property and directed the preparation of a "...written inventory of the real estate and property thereon seized." Upon arriving at the home, the agent executing the seizure warrant/writ of entry, over the objection of the renters, entered the house and conducted a walk-through inventory of its contents. During the inventory, drugs were found.

The renters were indicted and moved to suppress the drugs. The district court suppressed the evidence. The Eleventh Circuit affirmed. 774 F.2d at 438.

The court of appeals found that nothing in the seizure warrant/writ of entry authorized the agents to enter the house without permission. It permitted nothing more that a cursory examination of the lot. "The warrant authorized seizure of...*real estate* and ordered an inventory of the property *seized*. It would have been a simple matter to inventory the *seized* property—that is, the real estate and improvements on it—from outside the house." *Id.* at 439. Since the contents of the house were not subject to seizure, and the seizure warrant/writ of entry did not authorize an inventory of un-seized property, the agent had no legal right to enter the house. *Id.*[19]

The Eleventh Circuit found that the writ of entry did not provide the Government with the legal authority to enter the house to inventory its contents or inspect for damage without a search warrant. The Fourth Amendment applies to searches for administrative purposes. 774 F.2d at 439-40. Absent exigent circumstances, the Government must obtain a warrant based upon probable cause to inspect a seized house and inventory its contents. 774 F.2d at 440.

The district court in United States v. U.S. Currency in the amount of $324,225.00, 726 F. Supp. 259 (W.D. Mo. 1989), disagreed with the Eleventh Circuit's analysis in Ladson. Here, a motion was filed by the Government seeking authority for the USMS to enter, inspect, inventory, and secure the defendant property.[20] 20 A magistrate judge would only grant the motion if the Government agreed not to use any contraband or evidence of a crime found inside the home against its owner. The Government appealed to the district court, which reversed the magistrate. 726 F. Supp. at 260.

> The *Ladson* decision ignores the basic purpose of the plain view doctrine which is to permit law enforcement personnel to seize evidence that is in plain view *without first obtaining a search warrant*. Under *Ladson* the government cannot protect itself by inventorying and securing a house lawfully seized without surrendering its authority to seize evidence or contraband within plain view. Just as an arrestee's person may be searched and the discovered items inventoried without probable cause or search warrant...and as an impounded vehicle may be inventoried without probable cause or search warrant...the government should be permitted to conduct a limited inventory search of a building or house *lawfully seized*. The presence of law enforcement personnel inside the house for this limited purpose is undoubtedly lawful and proper. Therefore, if such an inventory should produce contraband or evidence of crime, the plain view doctrine's first requirement of a valid prior intrusion would be met. It is the Court's judgment that the government need not first agree not to use any contraband or evidence of crime that might be found during the inventory of the house.

726 F. Supp. at 261.

The district court went on to note that in cases such as the one at issue, the Government was not conducting the inventory on a whim. Such an inventory search would only be authorized after the Government made a showing of probable cause that the property is subject to forfeiture. Moreover, the Government could not do more than conduct an inventory search. If it engaged in a broader search, it would probably violate the Fourth Amendment and any evidence or contraband discovered would be subject to the exclusionary rule. "A lawful seizure only legitimizes a limited inventory search of the seized property and not a broad search for evidence or contraband." *Id.*

See also United States v. Santiago-Lugo, 904 F. Supp. 36 (D.P.R. 1995) (inventory of seized residence permitted where civil seizure warrant expressly authorizes an inventory of the contents of the residence); *United States v. One Parcel of Real Property*, 724 F. Supp. 668 (W.D. Mo. 1989) (where Government makes an initial probable cause showing that property is subject to forfeiture, basis exists for court to issue order that authorizes the Government to enter, inspect, inventory, and secure such property at the time of arrest).

Warrantless seizures for forfeiture may be based on the automobile, plain view, exigent circumstances, and search incident exceptions to the Fourth Amendment: *Florida v. White*, 526 U.S. 559 (1999) (warrantless seizure of automobile did not violate the Fourth Amendment where there was probable cause to believe the automobile was subject to forfeiture and it was found in a public place); *United States v. Gaskin*, 364 F.3d 438 (2d Cir. 2004) (applying *Florida v. White*: if agents have probable cause to believe a vehicle was used to facilitate a drug offense, and it is in a public place, they may seize it, search it, and seize currency and evidence they find therein); *United States v. $557,933.89, More or Less, in U.S. Funds*, 287 F.3d 66 (2d Cir. 2002) (structured money orders found in plain view by airport security could be detained temporarily as a *Terry* stop and ultimately seized on probable cause to believe the items were involved in a structuring offense; the test of whether the criminal connection was "immediately apparent" is objective—the Government does not have to establish that the seizing agent was trained to understand the significance of structured money orders); *United States v. Rankin*, 261 F.3d 735 (8th Cir. 2001) (police officer's observation of defendant conducting drug deal from his car provided probable cause for seizure of car for forfeiture and subsequent inventory search); *United States v. Daccarett*, 6 F.3d 37 (2d Cir. 1993) (warrantless seizure of funds captured in middle of electronic funds transfer through intermediary bank justified by exigent circumstances); *United States v. $149,442.43 in U.S. Currency*, 965 F.2d 868, 875-76 (10th Cir. 1992) (firearms, jewelry, and vehicles may be seized as proceeds or property used to facilitate when found incident to execution of search warrant even if items were not specifically listed in the warrant); *United States v. Berry*, 2002 WL 818872 (E.D. Pa. 2002) (under statute forfeiture law, officer was entitled to make warrantless seizure of vehicle he had seen used in drug deal and was entitled to seize gun he found in plain view); *Seaborn v. Thompson*, 2002 WL 737654 (M.D.N.C. 2002) (following *Florida v.*

White: state police may seize automobile for forfeiture under state law without a warrant if they have probable cause); *United States v. Wright*, 171 F. Supp. 2d 1195 (D. Kan. 2001) (no warrant required for seizure of vehicle from public place where officer has probable cause to believe vehicle was previously used to transport drugs; lawful inventory search may follow); *United States v. Warren*, 181 F. Supp. 2d 1232 (D. Kan. 2001) (items discovered during execution of search warrant, but not named in warrant, may be seized if there is probable cause to believe they are subject to forfeiture under state law); *United States v. Medina*, 301 F. Supp. 2d 322 (S.D.N.Y. 2004) (cash found in plain view in closet during a "protective sweep" of apartment to make sure no one else is present during criminal suspect's arrest may be seized if there is probable cause); *United States v. Washington*, 1997 WL 198046 (D. Kan. 1997) (items found incident to execution of search warrant may be seized for forfeiture under section 881(b)(1)), *aff'd*, 162 F.3d 1175 (10th Cir. 1998); *but see United States v. One 1974 Learjet*, 191 F.3d 668, 672 n.2 (6th Cir. 1999) (reserving decision on whether a warrant is required to seize property for forfeiture even if the Government has probable cause); *United States v. Brookins*, 228 F. Supp. 2d 732 (E.D. Va. 2002) (*Florida v. White* permits warrantless seizure based on probable cause only when the vehicle is in a public place, not when it is on a private driveway).

D.3. Conclusion

In view of the limited and somewhat conflicting case law on this obscure writ, it is the opinion of AFMLS that writs of entry issued by the court and based upon a finding of probable cause may be used in both civil and criminal forfeiture cases by the United States in the following circumstances: (1) to enter onto the curtilage and inventory structures located thereon without entering those structures; (2) to enter onto private real property for the purpose of seizing personal property located thereon (such as an automobile) in plain view; and (3) to enter into the interior of a private structure subject to forfeiture to conduct an inventory limited to documenting the condition of the interior of the structure, inspecting for damage, and conducting an appraisal. If a private structure is to be entered for the purpose of searching for and seizing (or inventorying) personal property located therein that is subject to forfeiture, it is recommended that a separate search warrant be obtained in conjunction with or in lieu of a writ of entry. In any case where a writ of entry is being sought, the application should be accompanied by a detailed agent affidavit setting forth the facts supporting a conclusion that the Government has probable cause to believe that (1) the property being searched for, seized, and/or inventoried is subject to forfeiture; and (2) that the said property is located at or in the place to be searched.

IV. Contaminated Real Property

A. Background

Certain statutory provisions may impose liability on the United States in connection with contaminated real property that it owns—including ownership obtained through forfeiture. Moreover, even when liability is not imposed on the United States under these statutory provisions, there may be practical impediments to the sale or transfer of such properties by the United States after forfeiture. Consequentially, caution must be exercised in targeting real property for forfeiture when there are indications that the real property may be contaminated.

The most prominent of these statutory provisions include the Comprehensive Environmental Response, Compensation, and Liability Act (CERCLA), 42 U.S.C. § 9601 et seq. The liability provisions of 42 U.S.C. § 9607 are imposed upon the United States by 42 U.S.C. § 9620(a). Section 9620(h) sets forth notice and warranting requirements that apply whenever any agency, department, or instrumentality of the United States enters into a contract for the sale or other transfer of real property that is owned by the United States and on which any hazardous substance[21] either (1) has been stored for more than 1 year, (2) is known to have been released, or (3) is known to have been disposed of.

The Residential Lead-Based Paint Hazard Reduction Act of 1992 includes provisions at 42 U.S.C. § 4852(d) which require disclosure of information concerning potential lead-based paint contamination upon the transfer of residential property.[22] Further, the United States may be required to undertake certain abatement actions of lead-based paint contamination for forfeited property constructed prior to 1960.[23] Forfeited property constructed during or after

1960 but before 1978[24] may be marketed and sold after complying with certain risk assessment and lead-based paint inspection. If the sale is completed within 270 days of the final order of forfeiture, the Government is exempted from these abatement, risk assessment, and inspection requirements.[25]

In addition to federal statutory provisions, state environmental laws must be considered when targeting contaminated real property for forfeiture.[26] Even when federal statutes may allow the United States to transfer contaminated real property without continuing federal liability for cleanup, applicable state law may continue to impose liability or may make the real property unmarketable in practical terms.

B. Policy

It is the policy of the Department of Justice that real property that is contaminated or potentially contaminated with hazardous substances may in the exercise of discretion be subject to forfeiture only upon determination by the U.S. Attorney, for the district where the property is located, in consultation with the seizing agency and the USMS that such action is fiscally sound or necessary to advance a law enforcement purpose. If the U.S. Attorney chooses to delegate this authority to an AUSA, provision must be made for review by a supervisor. As part of the consultation with the seizing agency and the USMS, due consideration must be given to the disposal alternatives that may be available after forfeiture, and the impact of any cleanup costs to the AFF. Furthermore, such real property that is forfeited will only be transferred or sold with notice of the potential or actual contamination. Notice must be based on information that is available from a complete search of agency files.[27] This notice must be included in the contract of sale and the deed.

This policy is applicable regardless of the type or source of the hazardous substance(s). This policy is applicable to all cases referred to the Department of Justice by any agency of the United States.

Forfeited real property that is marketable but is contaminated, or potentially contaminated, with hazardous substances due to activities of a prior owner may be transferred or sold as is and an environmental assessment and/or remediation of the contamination need not be undertaken. Whenever possible, the USMS will obtain a commitment from the buyer to clean up the property as a part of the contract of sale.

However, the United States may bear additional responsibility and liability if the real property becomes contaminated with a hazardous substance after the United States becomes the owner. This situation normally will arise when the United States operates a business or activity on the property that results in the storage, release, or disposal of hazardous substances (e.g., gasoline stations, metal plating shops, dry cleaners, printers, etc.). Under this circumstance, the United States is responsible for (1) all costs of hazardous substances removal and/or remedial action,[28] (2) providing notice of the hazardous substance to a subsequent transferee or purchaser,[29] and (3) a warranting covenant to a subsequent transferee or purchaser. Because of the potential resulting liability and expense, the USMS' AFD shall approve the operation of such a business or activity only in unusual circumstances.

This policy envisions U.S. Attorneys exercising discretion in undertaking forfeiture action against real property that is contaminated, where the use of the property indicates contamination or where there is the potential of contamination, with hazardous substances. If such circumstances are disclosed within the period of time that the forfeiture action is being pursued, the U.S. Attorney must reevaluate the decision to continue the forfeiture. Such properties must not be forfeited unless the defendant's net equity in the property clearly exceeds the estimated cost of cleanup. *Furthermore, such properties are not to be forfeited when there is reason to believe that the property is substantially contaminated with hazardous substances and that such contamination will render the property unmarketable.* Cleanup costs can be considerable, particularly when the water table is involved. In making this determination, the USMS may order an environmental assessment that will be paid from the AFF.

If, at any point, the U.S. Attorney elects, in the exercise of discretion, not to proceed with the forfeiture because significant contamination renders the property unmarketable, the U.S. Attorney must consider the following alternatives:

1) the filing of a release of *uis pendens* (assuming a *uis pendens* had been filed) containing notice of the reason (significant contamination) for dismissal of the forfeiture action;
2) the filing of some other document in the county deed records containing notice of the significant contamination (if such filing is permitted under the law);
3) notification of a federal, state, or local environmental agency of the significant contamination for purposes of appropriate enforcement action (federal, state, or local law may require mandatory notification);
4) notification of any lienholders of the significant contamination for such action as they may want to take; and
5) consideration of prosecution, civilly or criminally, for violations of the environmental laws by the private owner—the USAO should contact ENRD).

Not all of these alternatives are mandatory. Ultimately, it is within the discretion of the U.S. Attorney to decide how best to proceed when an election not to proceed with forfeiture is made.

V. Financial Instruments

The following describes procedures and responsibilities for handling financial instruments seized for forfeiture. Consultation with the USAO is recommended.

A. Postal Money Orders

A.1. Seizing Agency

Immediately following seizure, the seizing agency should send (1) the serial numbers, (2) the amount of each money order, and (3) a statement that the Government has received the money orders and is entitled to them under forfeiture laws to the following address:

US Postal Inspection Service
Criminal Investigations Group
National Money Order Coordinator
475 L'Enfant Plaza SW, Room 3800
Washington, DC 20260-3800

The seizing agency should also provide the USMS with a copy of this letter at the time the money orders are transferred to the USMS for custody.

A.2. The USMS

Upon forfeiture of the money orders, the USMS will

(6) complete a domestic money order inquiry, PS Form 6401, for each money order; and

(7) return the form, via registered mail, with the original money order to the national money order coordinator, along with the appropriate legal documentation showing that the Government is entitled to receive the proceeds.

B. Personal and Cashier's Checks

B.1. Seizing Agency

Immediately following seizure, the seizing agency, in conjunction with the USAO, should

(1) obtain a restraining order or seizure warrant, under the applicable criminal or civil forfeiture statute, directing the financial institution upon which the check is drawn to either:

a) take necessary steps to maintain funds sufficient to cover the check, in the case of a restraining order; or
b) release funds in the amount of the check, in the case of a seizure warrant;

(2) serve the restraining order or seizure warrant on the financial institution; and

(3) provide a copy of the restraining order or seizure warrant to the USMS at the time the check is transferred for custody. In the event that a seizure warrant is obtained, the check should be voided and returned to the bank when it is no longer needed as evidence.

B.2. The USMS

The USMS will accept custody of all checks as to which the investigative agency has contacted the bank on which they were drawn and negotiate the checks after receipt of a declaration or order of forfeiture in accordance with established procedures.

C. Certificates of Deposit

C.1. Seizing Agency

Immediately following seizure or restraint, the seizing agency should (1) notify the bank that issued the certificate of deposit that it has been seized or restrained for forfeiture and (2) instruct the bank officials to take whatever steps are necessary to freeze the funds covered by the certificate so the certificate of deposit will be negotiable by the USMS after forfeiture.

C.2. The USMS

The USMS will take appropriate action, in accordance with established procedures, to liquidate the certificate of deposit after forfeiture.

D. Traveler's Checks

D.1 Seizing Agency

Immediately following seizure, the seizing agency should (1) notify the company issuing the checks that they have been seized for forfeiture and (2) determine what procedures will be required in order to redeem the checks.

If they can be redeemed prior to forfeiture, (1) take appropriate steps to liquidate the checks and (2) have the issuing company issue a cashier's check to the USMS.

If liquidation cannot occur until after forfeiture, turn the checks over to the USMS with verification that the issuing company has been notified.

D.2. The USMS

The USMS will accept custody of all traveler's checks that cannot be liquidated until after forfeiture. Upon receipt of a declaration of forfeiture, the USMS will liquidate the asset in accordance with established procedures.

E. Stocks, Bonds, and Brokerage and Other Investment Accounts

E.1. Seizing Agency

Immediately following seizure or restraint, the seizing agency should contact a certified stock broker (state and national) to establish the fair market value of the asset and determine how the instrument is traded.

Securities targeted for forfeiture that are in a brokerage account will usually be seized or restrained in place. Upon receipt of a final forfeiture order, the USMS will instruct the broker to liquidate the account. The net proceeds after commission are deposited in the AFF. Pursuant to court order, brokerage accounts may be held in a different manner in order to preserve the value of the account.

When stocks or bond certificates are seized, the USMS' AFD sends them to a USMS brokerage account at an established securities firm. Upon receipt of a final forfeiture order, the certificates are submitted to a transfer agent to change ownership to the USMS and the certificates are liquidated and deposited into the AFF.

The USMS will not accept custody of any financial instrument with a fair market value equal to $0, or any stocks or bonds that were issued by a "shell corporation" and are not traded on the open market. Consult with USMS to determine the best course of action when seeking to seize the stocks or bonds of privately or closely held corporations.

E.2. The USMS

The USMS will accept custody of all stocks and bonds for which the seizing agency can document a significant worth. As a general rule, the USMS will coordinate with the USAO to try to liquidate stocks and bonds through interlocutory sale whenever possible.

F. U.S. Savings Bonds

F.1. Seizing Agency

Immediately following seizure, the seizing agency should notify the Department of the Treasury, by certified letter, listing the following:

1) serial numbers;
2) bond denominations;
3) to whom payable; and
4) the reason for which they were seized.

The seizing agency should send the above information to the following address:

Bureau of Public Debt Savings Bond Division
Parkersburg, WV 26106

The seizing agency should provide the USMS with a copy of this letter at the time the savings bonds are transferred for custody.

F.2. The USMS

The USMS will accept custody of all savings bonds, maintain such bonds until forfeiture, and dispose of such bonds in accordance with established procedures.

VI. Seized Cash Management

The security, budgetary, and accounting problems caused by retention of large amounts of cash historically has caused great concern within the Department of Justice and Congress. In the past, agencies participating in the Department of Justice's Asset Forfeiture Program have held tens of thousands of dollars in office safes and other locations throughout the country. This raises both financial management and internal control issues. The Department of Justice must report annually to Congress on the amount of seized cash not on deposit.

The Attorney General has established the following policy on the handling of seized cash:[30]

> Seized cash, except where it is to be used as evidence, is to be deposited promptly in the Seized Asset Deposit Fund pending forfeiture. The Chief, AFMLS, may grant exceptions to this policy in extraordinary circumstances. Transfer of cash to the U.S. marshal should occur within 60 days of seizure or 10 days of indictment.

This policy applies to all cash seized for purposes of forfeiture. Therefore, all currency seized that is subject to criminal or civil forfeiture must be delivered to the USMS for deposit in the USMS Seized Asset Deposit Fund either within 60 days after seizure or 10 days after indictment, whichever occurs first.[31] Photographs or videotapes of the seized cash should be taken for use in court as evidence.

If the amount of seized cash desired to be retained for evidentiary purposes is less than $5,000, permission need not be sought from AFMLS for an exception; but any exception must be granted at a supervisory level within a USAO using the criteria below.

If the amount of seized cash to be retained for evidentiary purposes is $5,000 or greater, the request for an exemption must be forwarded to AFMLS.[32] The request should include a brief statement of the factors warranting its retention and the name, position, and phone number of the individual to contact regarding the request.

Limited exceptions to this directive are very rare. Exceptions, such as extensions of applicable time limits, will be granted, on an interim basis, only with the express written permission of the Chief of AFMLS.[33] Retention of currency will be permitted when it serves a significant independent, tangible, evidentiary purpose due to, for example, the presence of fingerprints, packaging in an incriminating fashion, or the existence of a traceable amount of narcotic residue on the bills.[34] If only a portion of the seized cash has evidentiary value, only that portion with evidentiary value should be retained. The balance should be deposited in accordance with Department of Justice policy.

The commingling of cash seized by the Government under section 881(a)(6) will not deprive the court of jurisdiction over the res. Unlike other assets seized by the Government (e.g., real property, conveyances), cash is a fungible item. Its character is not changed merely by depositing it with other cash. While it is true that the jurisdiction of the court is derived entirely from its control over the defendant res, court jurisdiction does not depend upon control over specific cash. As stated in *United States v. $57,480.05 United States Currency and Other Coins and $10,575.00 United States Currency*, 722 F.2d 1457 (9th Cir. 1984), "Jurisdiction did not depend upon control over specific bits of currency. The bank credit of fungible dollars constituted an appropriate substitute for the original res."

It has never been a requirement that the Government segregate specific cash seized for forfeiture in one case from that seized for forfeiture in another. Commingling of such assets has been the rule and not the exception.[35]

VII. General Adoption Policy and Procedure

A. Adoptive Seizures Are Encouraged

Forfeiture is one of the most effective weapons in the law enforcement arsenal and its use should be encouraged. In many areas of the nation, effective use of forfeiture requires a willingness on the part of federal law enforcement agencies to adopt state and local seizures for federal forfeiture whenever appropriate. Department of Justice personnel in the field should adopt state and local seizures in order to immobilize criminal enterprises and to enhance cooperation among federal, state, and local agencies. This does not preclude application of established monetary thresholds nor relieve approving officials of the duty to verify that the property presented for adoption is subject to seizure and forfeiture under federal law.

The policies and procedures in this section are intended to ensure consistent review and handling of state and local seizures presented for federal adoption. This section only applies to property seized exclusively through the efforts of state and local agencies where those efforts also establish a basis for federal forfeiture.[36] Where a federal law enforcement agency makes a material pre-seizure contribution to the investigation leading to a state or local seizure or post-seizure contribution establishing probable cause for the forfeiture under federal law, this section does not apply. Such seizures will be deemed the result of a joint federal investigation.

B. Federal Adoption Request

All state and local seizures presented for adoption must be reported on a form entitled *Request for Adoption of State or Local Seizure*.[37] The form should be completed by the requesting state or local agency, but federal personnel may, in their discretion, complete the form for the requesting state or local agency. Information concerning any state forfeiture proceedings instituted against the property must be detailed in the request for adoption form. A federal agency should not adopt a seizure while the property remains subject to the jurisdiction of a state court.

The state or local agency also may be required to complete the federal agency's standard seizure form as part of the adoption request. All information provided must be complete and accurate.

An estimate of fair market value must be provided for each item of seized property presented for adoption and any liens and lienholders must be identified. Copies of any investigative reports and of any affidavits in support of warrants pertinent to the seizure must be attached for review.[38]

C. Federal Law Enforcement Agency Review

The adopting federal agency must consider adoption requests promptly. Except in exceptional circumstances, the request for adoption must be approved prior to the transfer of the property to federal custody.

Only an attorney outside the chain-of-command of operational officials (e.g., the agency's office of chief counsel or other legal unit) may approve a request for adoption unless:

1) the seizure was based on a judicial seizure warrant; or
2) an arrest was made in connection with the seizure; or
3) drugs or other contraband were seized from the person from whom the property was seized.

Federal law enforcement agencies may expand the circumstances requiring attorney approval. Any attorney review shall verify that:

1) the property is subject to federal forfeiture;
2) there is probable cause to support the seizure;
3) the property is not subject to the jurisdiction of a state court; and
4) there is no other legal impediment to a successful forfeiture action.

Federal law enforcement agencies will normally secure attorney review through their own offices of chief counsel or other legal unit but may, in their discretion, request that an AUSA conduct this review. Any further review processes established in the future for federal seizures will also apply to adoptive seizures. Pre-seizure planning is an essential part of the review process. Property management issues must be addressed in consultation with the USMS prior to an adoption.

D. Minimum Monetary Thresholds

Generally, a state or local seizure may not be approved for adoption unless the equity in the property exceeds the following levels:

Conveyances	
Vehicles	$5,000
Vessels	$10,000
Aircraft	$10,000
Real Property	
Land and any improvements	For properties with appraised value less than $100,000, net equity must be at least $20,000
All other property	
Currency, bank accounts, monetary instruments, jewelry, etc.[39]	$2,000

The U.S. Attorneys, in consultation with federal law enforcement agencies and state and local law enforcement, may institute higher or lower district-wide thresholds for judicial forfeiture cases as law enforcement or management needs require. Similarly, a federal law enforcement agency may institute higher or lower thresholds for administrative forfeiture cases. Written notice of any higher or lower thresholds shall be provided to the Chief of AFMLS, the USMS, and the special agents-in-charge of the federal law enforcement agencies in the affected judicial district. Lower thresholds may not necessarily result in increased sharing with state and local law enforcement. Since sharing is always based on net proceeds, forfeiture of lower dollar-value property may result in no net proceeds to share.[40]

In individual cases, the thresholds may be waived when forfeiture of a particular asset—e.g., a crack house, a conveyance with hidden compartments, or a vehicle used in alien smuggling seized at an international border—will serve a compelling law enforcement interest. Any waiver must be approved in writing by a supervisory-level official designated by the adopting agency, and an explanation of the reason for the waiver must be noted in the case file. The fact that the owner or person in possession of the property has been arrested or will be criminally prosecuted can be an appropriate basis for a waiver.

E. Forfeitures Generally Follow the Prosecution

As discussed in part 2, section VI, when property is seized as part of an ongoing federal criminal investigation and the criminal defendants are being prosecuted in federal court, the forfeiture action, as a general rule, should be commenced administratively by a federal agency or pursued in federal court, regardless of who made the seizure. Conversely, when a state or local agency has seized property as part of an ongoing state criminal investigation and the criminal defendants are being prosecuted in state court, any forfeiture action should generally be pursued in state court assuming that state law authorizes the forfeiture.

F. 30-Day Rule for Presentation for Federal Adoption

A federal law enforcement agency may be required to commence administrative forfeiture proceedings by sending written notice "not more than 90 days after the date of seizure by the state or local law enforcement agency."[41] In order to allow ample time for federal agencies to process adoptive seizures, state and local agencies must request federal adoption within 30 calendar days of seizure. Any waiver of the 30-day rule must be approved in writing by a supervisory-level official of the adopting agency where the state or local agency requesting adoption demonstrates the existence of circumstances justifying the delay.

G. Direct Adoption by the U.S. Attorney

A U.S. Attorney may recommend in writing that a federal law enforcement agency with appropriate jurisdiction adopt a particular state or local seizure or category of seizures for federal forfeiture prior to requesting approval for a direct adoption by the USAO. If the federal agency declines to adopt the seizure, the U.S. Attorney may refer the matter to the AFMLS. AFMLS may authorize direct adoption of the seizure or category of seizures by the U.S. Attorney for judicial forfeiture under federal law where a compelling law enforcement purpose justifies such action.

In order to receive approval for a proposed direct adoption, the U.S. Attorney must send a written request to AFMLS. That request for direct adoption approval must include (1) a written summary of the investigation, (2) a written declination from the federal seizing agency, (3) a statement of whether the declining federal seizing agency objects to the proposed direct adoption, (4) the current custody status of the asset, and (5) a justification as to why the proposed direct adoption would serve a compelling law enforcement purpose. AFMLS will obtain input from the headquarters office of the seizing agency that declined to adopt the matter regarding the proposed direct adoption. All requests for direct adoption approval must be submitted to AFMLS in advance of listing the property in an indictment or forfeiture complaint.

AFMLS shall notify the U.S. Attorney and the U.S. Marshal in that district when direct adoption is authorized, at which time the U.S. Marshals Service will create a CATS ID with the agency code of STL. Where the property being adopted for federal forfeiture is a seized firearm, the state or local law enforcement agency which seized or is holding the firearm pending federal forfeiture shall perform an NCIC check and ballistic and forensic tests on the seized firearm before it is taken or transferred into federal custody.

Equitable sharing on assets approved for direct adoption shall be conducted in accordance with Part 6. In direct adoption cases, the U.S. Attorney is responsible for completing sections I, II, and III of any DAG-72 forms recommending sharing with the state or local agencies involved in the law enforcement effort. The U.S. Marshal will enter any DAG-71 forms and sections I and II of the DAG-72 into CATS, and the U.S. Attorney will enter section III of the DAG-72 into CATS.

H. Retention of Custody by State or Local Agency During Federal Forfeiture Proceedings

To minimize storage and management costs to the Department of Justice, the state or local agency requesting adoption of a conveyance should, at the discretion of the USMS, serve as the substitute custodian of the property pending forfeiture. The USMS may authorize a state or local law enforcement agency requesting adoption of other personal property, except cash and other financial instruments, to serve as the substitute custodian where appropriate. Use or disposition of the property during this period by state or local law enforcement officials or others is strictly prohibited.

I. Real Property

Following consultation with the USMS and concurrence by the USAO, a federal law enforcement agency may approve a request for federal adoption of real property seized by a state or local agency. The requirements outlined in 18 U.S.C. § 985 govern the federal seizure and civil forfeiture of real property.

J. Use of Anticipatory Seizure Warrants

If a state or local law enforcement agency commences a forfeiture action under state law, no federal forfeiture action may be commenced as long as the state court has in rem or quasi-in-rem jurisdiction over the subject property. If, however, the state or local authorities determine, for whatever reason, that the state action will be terminated before it is completed, and that the property will accordingly be released, or a federal seizing agency otherwise learns that the state court is about to order the release of property that is federally forfeitable, a federal agency may arrange to seize the property by obtaining an anticipatory seizure warrant from a federal judge or magistrate. The anticipatory seizure warrant must provide that it will be executed only after the state court has relinquished control over the property.[42]

For purposes of the notice requirements in section 983(a)(1), property seized pursuant to an anticipatory seizure warrant in these circumstances is considered the subject of a federal seizure such that the period for sending notice of the forfeiture action is 60 days, commencing on the date when the anticipatory seizure warrant is executed.

K. Concurrent Jurisdiction

As noted above, a federal agency may not approve the adoption of a seizure while the property remains subject to the in rem or quasi-in-rem jurisdiction of a state court. Depending on state law, a state court may be deemed to acquire jurisdiction over property seized by a state or local agency in a variety of ways: where a state commences forfeiture proceedings against the seized property, where a party files an action in state court seeking the return of the property, where a state or local agency seizes the property pursuant to a state search warrant or seizure warrant, or even where a state or local law enforcement officer simply seizes the property in the absence of state process. As a matter of comity, the court first assuming in rem jurisdiction over the property retains jurisdiction to the exclusion of all others. Consequently, if a state court has in rem jurisdiction over property, the state court must relinquish jurisdiction before any request for adoption may be approved. In these situations, the agency requesting adoption, with the assistance of the appropriate state or local prosecutorial office, may be required to obtain a state court turnover order relinquishing jurisdiction and authorizing the transfer of the property to a federal law enforcement agency for the purpose of federal forfeiture. Where a state search warrant or seizure warrant contains this authorization, or a state statute or controlling case law authorizes release of seized property for federal forfeiture, a subsequent turnover order is unnecessary.

The turnover order must be obtained from the state court with jurisdiction over the seized property (i.e., the state court that issued the warrant allowing the seizure or before which the state forfeiture proceedings have been commenced). The USAO should not seek such orders in state court, but may assist its state counterparts in doing so. Failure to obtain a turnover order may make it impossible for a federal court to take jurisdiction over the seized property in subsequent judicial forfeiture proceedings. In some cases, this may result in the dismissal or voiding of federal judicial forfeiture proceedings and the return of the property to the person from whom it was originally seized.

VIII. Custodial and Authority Chart

A. Department of Justice Asset Forfeiture Program

Agency/Component	Property Custodian	Statutory Jurisdiction	Seizure Authority
Asset Forfeiture Management Staff, Justice Management Division	Not applicable	• 28 U.S.C. § 524(c)(1)	• Not applicable
Criminal Division, U.S. Department of Justice	U.S. Marshals Service (USMS) for cases brought by participants in Justice Program Treasury Contractor for cases brought by participants in the Treasury Program	• All criminal and civil asset forfeiture statutes	• Not applicable
Bureau of Alcohol, Tobacco, Firearms and Explosives (ATF)	ATF, USMS, and the Treasury Contractor	• 18 U.S.C. § 981 and 982 • 28 U.S.C. § 2461 • 49 U.S.C. § 80304	• 18 U.S.C. § 3051
Department of Defense—Defense Criminal Investigation Service (DCIS)	USMS	• 22 U.S.C. § 2709, amended in 2005—all criminal and civil asset forfeiture statutes. • Primarily, but not limited to, 18 U.S.C. § 981(a)(1)(A) (civil) and 18 U.S.C. § 982(a)(6)(A) (criminal)	• 18 U.S.C. § 981(a)(1)(A) (civil) and 18 U.S.C. § 982(a)(6)(A) (criminal)
Drug Enforcement Administration (DEA)	USMS	• 18 U.S.C. §§ 981, 982 • 21 U.S.C. §§ 824, 853, and 881 • 28 U.S.C. § 2461 • 46 U.S.C. § 70507 • 49 U.S.C. § 46306	• 18 U.S.C. § 981 • 21 U.S.C. § 881 • 46 U.S.C. § 70507 • 49 U.S.C. § 46306
Executive Office for U.S. Attorneys (EOUSA)—U.S. Attorneys' Offices	USMS for cases brought by participants in Justice Program Treasury Contractor for cases brought by participants in the Treasury Program	• All criminal and civil asset forfeiture statutes	• Not applicable
Federal Bureau of Investigation (FBI)	USMS	• 28 C.F.R. § 0.85(a)—all laws not specifically assigned to the sole jurisdiction of another agency.[43]	• 28 C.F.R. § 8.2
Food and Drug Administration—Office of Criminal Investigations (FDA-OCI)	USMS and Treasury Contractor (bulk evidence only)	• Federal Food, Drug, and Cosmetic Act, 21 U.S.C. §§ 301-397 and related Title 18 and 21 statutes	• Federal Food, Drug, and Cosmetic Act, 21 U.S.C. §§ 301-397 and related Title 18 and 21 statutes
U.S. Department of Agriculture—Office of Inspector General (USDA-OIG)	The seizing agency identifies the appropriate custodian Any animal seized under warrant authorized under this section shall be held by the United States marshal or other authorized person pending disposition of the court.	• 7 U.S.C. § 2024 • 7 U.S.C. § 2270a • 7 U.S.C. § 2156	• Not applicable[44] • Not applicable[45]

(Continued)

Agency/Component	Property Custodian	Statutory Jurisdiction	Seizure Authority
U.S. Marshals Service (USMS)	USMS	Not applicable	• 28 U.S.C. § 566
U.S. Postal Inspection Service (USPIS)	USPIS—Administrative Forfeitures	• Pursuant to 18 U.S.C. § 3061—all matters relating to the Postal Service and the mails. Primary statues enforced include:	• 18 U.S.C. § 3061(a)
	USMS—Judicial Forfeitures[46]	• Child Exploitation (18 U.S.C. §§ 1470, 2251, 2252, 2253, 2254, 2422, and 2425)	
		•Controlled Substances (21 U.S.C. §§ 841, 843 and 844)	
		•Counterfeit Stamps, Money Orders and Related Crimes (18 U.S.C. §§ 500, 501, 503 and 1720)	
		•Destruction, Obstruction and Delay of Mail (18 U.S.C. §§ 1700, 1701, 1702 and 1703)	
		•Electronic Crimes (18 U.S.C. §§ 1029, 1030, 1037, 1343, and 2701)	
		•Extortion (18 U.S.C. §§ 873, 876 and 877)	
		•Forfeiture (18 U.S.C.§§ 981 and 982)	
		•Identity Fraud (18 U.S.C. § 1028)	
		•Lotteries (18 U.S.C. §§ 1301, 1302 and 1303 and 39 U.S.C. § 3005)	
		•Mail Fraud (18 U.S.C. §§ 1341, 1342 and 1345 and 39 U.S.C. §§ 3005 and 3007)	
		•Money Laundering (18 U.S.C. §§ 1956 and 1957)	
		•Obscenity and Sexually Oriented Advertising (18 U.S.C. §§ 1461, 1463 and 1735; and 39 U.S.C. § 3010)	
		•Theft of Mail (18 U.S.C. §§ 1708 & 1709)	

Agency/Component	Property Custodian	Statutory Jurisdiction	Seizure Authority
State Department, Bureau of Diplomatic Security	USMS	•22 U.S.C. § 2709, amended in 2005—all criminal and civil asset forfeiture statutes. •Primarily, but not limited to, 18 U.S.C. § 981(a) (1) (A) (civil) and 18 U.S.C. § 982(a)(6)(A) (criminal)	•18 U.S.C. § 981(a)(1) (A) (civil) and 18 U.S.C. § 982(a)(6)(A) (criminal)
Non-Justice, Non-Treasury Fund Federal Participant[47]	USMS (if proceeds eligible for deposit into the DOJ AFF)	• TBD	•TBD

B. Department of the Treasury Asset Forfeiture Program

Agency/Component	Property Custodian	Statutory Jurisdiction	Seizure Authority
Executive Office for Asset Forfeiture, Department of the Treasury	Not applicable	• 31 U.S.C. § 9703	• Not applicable
Internal Revenue Service—Criminal Investigation	Treasury Contractor	• 18 U.S.C. §§ 981 and 982 • 18 U.S.C. §§ 1956 and 1957 • 31 U.S.C. §§ 5317 and 5324	• Treasury Directive 15-42
U.S. Coast Guard	Not applicable[48]	• 14 U.S.C. § 89 • 14 U.S.C. § 141 • 14 U.S.C. § 143	• 8 U.S.C. § 1324 • 14 U.S.C. § 89 • 16 U.S.C. § 1861 • 16 U.S.C. § 3374 • 18 U.S.C. § 981-82 • 18 U.S.C. § 1028 • 18 U.S.C. §1594 • 19 U.S.C. §§ 1581, 1590, 1594, 1595, and 1595a • 19 U.S.C. § 1703 • 46 U.S.C. § 70507 • 46 U.S.C. §§ 70106 and 70118 • 50 U.S.C. §§191-92
U.S Immigration and Customs Enforcement	Treasury Contractor	• Tariff Act of 1789; as amended • Immigration & Nationality Act (1952); as amended • 18 U.S.C. §§ 981 and 982	• 8 U.S.C. §§ 1324, 1324(b) • 8 U.S.C. § 1324a • 18 U.S.C. § 545 • 18 U.S.C. § 981 and 982 • 18 U.S.C. § 1028
U.S. Customs and Border Protection		• Title 21 Memorandum of Understanding (MOU)–1994[49] • Civil Asset Forfeiture Reform Act (2000) • USA PATRIOT Act (2001) • Homeland Security Act (2002) • Patriot Act Reauthorization Act of 2006	• 18 U.S.C. § 1594 • 19 U.S.C. §§ 1581, 1590, 1594, 1595, and 1595a • 19 U.S.C. § 1703 • 31 U.S.C. §§ 5317 and 5332 • 22 U.S.C. § 401 • 50 U.S.C. § 1701, et. seq.[50]
U.S. Secret Service	Treasury Contractor	• 18 U.S.C. § 3056	• 18 U.S.C. §§ 981 and 982

PART 2: ADMINISTRATIVE AND JUDICIAL FORFEITURE

I. Interplay of Administrative and Civil Judicial Forfeiture

A. Preference for Administrative Forfeiture

Before 1990, virtually all forfeitures of properties valued at more than $100,000 were conducted judicially. In 1990, however, the law was amended to permit the administrative forfeiture of cash and monetary instruments, without regard to value, and of other property up to a value of $500,000. *See* 19 U.S.C. § 1607.

The legislative history of this law makes clear that Congress sought to increase the speed and efficiency of uncontested forfeiture actions and had confidence in the notice and other safeguards built into administrative forfeiture laws. Moreover, the due process protections enacted as part of the Civil Asset Forfeiture Reform Act (CAFRA) of 2000 ensure that the administrative forfeiture laws operate fairly. Accordingly, there is a preference for doing forfeitures administratively where it is possible to do so.

In general, properties subject to administrative forfeiture[1] must be forfeited administratively, unless one of the following exceptions applies:

1) Where several items of personal property (other than monetary instruments) are subject to civil forfeiture under the same statutory authority and on the same factual basis, and they have a common owner and a combined appraised value in excess of $500,000, the property should be forfeited judicially in a single action.
2) Where the items subject to forfeiture include some that can be forfeited administratively and others that must be forfeited judicially, the forfeitures may be combined in a single judicial action.
3) When pursuing administrative forfeiture might create the appearance that the Government is circumventing the time limits on administrative forfeiture set forth in 18 U.S.C. § 983(a), the forfeiture should be done judicially as explained in section I.D.
4) When the U.S. Attorney and the seizing agency agree that the forfeiture should proceed judicially in the first instance, administrative forfeiture is unnecessary.
5) When, as explained in section II.B, the U.S. Attorney requests that the seizing agency suspend the administrative forfeiture to allow the forfeiture to be handled criminally, and the seizing agency agrees to do so, the forfeitures may be pursued exclusively as part of the criminal case.

B. Administrative Forfeiture of Bank Accounts

Section 1607(a)(4) of Title 19 states that "monetary instruments" may be administratively forfeited without regard to dollar value. This is an exception to the $500,000 cap on the administrative forfeiture of personal property set forth in section 1607(a)(1), but it does not apply to funds in a bank account.

The term *monetary instrument* is defined in 31 U.S.C. § 5312(a)(3) to mean currency, traveler's checks, various forms of bearer paper, and "similar material." Neither this statutory definition nor the parallel definition in the applicable regulations encompasses the funds in a bank account. Moreover, the legislative history of 31 U.S.C. § 5312(a)(3) indicates that

Congress intended the term *monetary instrument* to apply only to highly liquid assets.[2] Consequently, funds in a bank account may not be considered monetary instruments for the purposes of the exception to the $500,000 cap on administrative forfeitures.[3] Seizing agencies may not invoke the exception to the $500,000 cap in 19 U.S.C. § 1607(a)(4) by waiting until funds seized from a bank account are converted to a monetary instrument such as a check, and then forfeiting the check administratively. If funds in a bank account in excess of $500,000 are seized from a bank, they must be forfeited judicially regardless of the form they take when received from the bank by the seizing agency.

Funds that were withdrawn from a bank account by the account holder and converted to currency or a monetary instrument before the seizure by a law enforcement agency took place, however, fall within the exception in section 1607(a)(4) and thus may be forfeited administratively regardless of value. Moreover, funds in a bank account of a value of $500,000 or less may be administratively forfeited pursuant to section 1607(a)(1), subject to the policy on handling forfeitures judicially if the aggregate value of two or more assets exceeds $500,000, as discussed in section I.A.

C. Conversion of Administrative Forfeitures Covered by the "Customs Carve-out" to Judicial Forfeitures Subject to 18 U.S.C. § 983

There are times when an administrative forfeiture is commenced under Title 19,[4] but the ensuing judicial forfeiture is brought under another statute. Title 19 forfeitures are exempt from the provisions of section 983, whereas most other forfeitures are not. This section discusses what action the United States should take when it converts an administrative forfeiture action under Title 19 to a civil judicial action brought under a non-Title 19 statute that is not exempt from the requirements of section 983.

C.1. Summary

The reforms enacted in 18 U.S.C. § 983 under CAFRA are applicable to all civil forfeitures taken under any provision of federal law except for those specifically exempted by 18 U.S.C. § 983(i). Forfeitures to which the provisions of section 983 are not applicable include, inter alia, forfeitures under Title 19 that are enforced by Customs and Border Protection (CBP) and U.S. Immigration and Customs Enforcement (ICE) (formerly components of the U.S. Customs Service). In instances where CBP (on its own, or on behalf of ICE) commences an administrative forfeiture action under Title 19, but the U.S. Attorney subsequently files a civil judicial forfeiture action under a non-Title 19 statute (e.g., 21 U.S.C. § 881, which is not exempt from section 983) the U.S. Attorney should comply with all CAFRA deadlines, including the 90-day filing deadline under section 983(a)(3), and CBP should return any cost bond that may have been filed.

C.2. Discussion

CAFRA governs administrative and judicial forfeitures under all civil forfeiture provisions of federal law, except for those explicitly exempted by section 983(i). Thus, the procedures governing administrative and civil judicial forfeiture in section 983 apply to nearly all federal civil forfeiture statutes, including some of the most obscure. The only forfeitures to which section 983 does not apply are those specified in section 983(i), which include, inter alia, all forfeitures under Title 19, all forfeitures under Title 26 (including forfeitures of firearms under the National Firearms Act), and certain forfeitures under other statutes enforced by CBP and ICE, or other federal agencies.[5] In those cases, the Customs laws remain in effect as if section 983 had not been enacted. Because section 983(i) exempts many forfeiture provisions enforced by CBP and ICE from application of the other provisions of section 983, it is generally referred to as the "Customs carve-out" provision.[6]

Given the Customs carve-out in section 983, a potential problem arises when a CBP or ICE officer seizes property pursuant to Title 19 authority, initiates an administrative forfeiture action, and—as CBP is required to do—refers the case to the U.S. Attorney following the filing of a claim and cost bond, but the U.S. Attorney subsequently decides to commence a civil forfeiture action under another statute that is not exempt from section 983. For example, CBP or ICE may seize property in a drug case under Title 19, but the U.S. Attorney may believe it advantageous for the Government for strategic reasons to pursue the forfeiture under section 881.

Whenever the Government chooses to pursue forfeiture under a statute subject to section 983 not designated under the Customs carve-out provision, the CAFRA-mandated procedures and deadlines become applicable to the forfeiture case. For example, section 983 changed the deadlines for filing administrative and civil judicial forfeiture actions from those required under pre-CAFRA law and abolished the cost bond.[7] In "exempted cases," such as those filed pursuant to Title 19 under the Customs carve-out provision, the Customs laws and supplemental rules require only that forfeiture proceedings be commenced "forthwith" and be prosecuted "without delay." Under section 983, by contrast, notice of administrative forfeiture generally must be sent within 60 days of the seizure, and the civil judicial complaint must be filed within 90 days of the filing of a claim contesting the administrative forfeiture. *See* section 983(a).[8]

Choosing to pursue judicial forfeiture under a statute subject to section 983, after CBP has commenced an administrative forfeiture under an exempted statute, presents a few issues: Does the 90-day period for filing a judicial forfeiture action under section 983(a)(3) run from the date the claim was filed with CBP (or ICE), or from the date the Assistant U.S. Attorney (AUSA) decided to pursue civil forfeiture under a statute subject to section 983? Does the 60-day notice requirement for administrative forfeitures apply retroactively so that a claimant who did not get notice within 60 days of the seizure may demand the return of the property pursuant to section 983(a)(1)(F) on the ground that the Government did not comply with the requirements in section 983(a)(1)(A)? Should the Government return the cost bond?

The question regarding the cost bond is the easiest to resolve. If the Government is no longer pursuing civil forfeiture under a statute exempted from section 983, it has no legal authority to continue to hold the cost bond. In such cases, the U.S. Attorney should advise CBP that the cost bond must be released. On the other hand, if the Government pursues the civil judicial forfeiture under *both* the exempted statute and a statute subject to section 983, the cost bond may be retained as long as the exempted cause of action remains part of the complaint.[9]

The question regarding the retrospective application of the 60-day notice requirement is also easy to resolve. If, at the time it seized the property and commenced administrative forfeiture proceedings, CBP or ICE was acting pursuant to an exempted statute, it is not required to send any notice within any fixed period of time. That the U.S. Attorney subsequently decides to pursue the forfeiture under a statute subject to section 983 does not change that fact. Accordingly, the U.S. Attorney's charging decision would not retroactively convert a properly conducted administrative forfeiture proceeding into one that constituted a violation of the notice requirements in section 983(a)(1).

Moreover, even if this view were mistaken, the same event that created the retrospective violation—the filing of the civil judicial action under the statute subject to section 983—would render any supposed violation of the notice requirement moot. That is because the Asset Forfeiture and Money Laundering Section (AFMLS) interprets section 983(a)(1)(F), which requires the return of the seized property if the Government fails to comply with the 60-day notice deadline "without prejudice to the right of the Government to commence a forfeiture proceeding at a later time," as allowing the Government to retain possession of the seized property if it promptly files the civil judicial action upon discovery of the missed deadline. *See Manjarrez v. United States*, 2002 WL 31870533 (N.D. Ill. 2002) (failure to send notice of an administrative forfeiture within the 60-day period prescribed by CAFRA does not bar the Government from commencing a civil judicial forfeiture action against the same property without first returning the property to the claimant). *Accord Return of Seized Property v. United States*, 625 F. Supp. 2d 949, 954-55 (C.D. Cal. 2009) (citing cases), *petition for mandamus denied sub nom In re Jordan*, 606 F. 3d 1135 (9th Cir. 2010); *United States v. $11,500.00 in United States Currency*, 797 F. Supp. 2d 1092 (D. Or. 2011). In a case where the supposed violation of the notice requirement does not even occur until the Government has decided to abandon the exempted forfeiture theory in favor of one to which the notice requirement applies, the Government will have filed the judicial action as discussed in section I.F, and maintained custody of the property pursuant to an arrest warrant in rem, before any obligation to return the seized property arises.

How to deal with the 90-day filing requirement in section 983(a)(3) presents a closer question. On the one hand, until the U.S. Attorney determines to pursue the civil judicial forfeiture under statute subject to section 983, the 90-day filing requirement simply does not apply. On the other hand, if the Government routinely seized property under an exempted statute, delayed filing any civil judicial action for more than 90 days after a claimant filed a claim and cost bond, and then filed the judicial forfeiture under a statute subject to section 983, it might create the appearance that the initial seizure under the exempted statute was merely a ruse to allow the U.S. Attorney to avoid complying with section 983 when the Government intended all along to pursue the judicial forfeiture under the statute subject to section 983. Thus, in any case referred by CBP, ICE, or another agency where the initial seizure was pursuant to an exempted statute, the U.S. Attorney should make the decision whether to switch theories to a non-exempt statute, or to include both exempt and non-exempt theories in the complaint, within 90 days of the filing of the claim and cost bond; and if the decision is made to pursue the forfeiture under the non-exempt statute, the U.S. Attorney should order return of the cost bond and either file the complaint before the 90 days expires or ask the court for an extension of time in accordance with section 983(a)(3).

D. Whether to File a Judicial Forfeiture Action When the Timeliness or Form of An Administrative Forfeiture Claim Is Disputed or Unclear

The following discussion applies only to claims filed in administrative forfeiture proceedings under statutes subject to 18 U.S.C. § 983 and not under statutes exempted from that section. *See* 18 U.S.C. § 983(i). Claims filed in administrative forfeiture proceedings under such exempted statutes should, in general terms, be handled in the same manner as set forth herein.

At times a document purporting to be a claim filed in an administrative forfeiture proceeding is facially defective or filed out of time, but the claimant disputes that characterization. This section discusses whether, in such cases, the seizing agency should enter a declaration of forfeiture or refer the case to the U.S. Attorney.

D.1. Summary

Section 983(a)(2) requires that a claim contesting an administrative forfeiture action contain certain information and be filed within a certain number of days. If the claim is not filed in accordance with the statute, the seizing agency may enter a declaration of forfeiture pursuant to 19 U.S.C. § 1609. There are times, however, when the claimant may dispute the agency's characterization of the claim as defective or untimely.

If the seizing agency ignores the claimant's protestations and proceeds with the declaration of forfeiture without referring the case to the U.S. Attorney, it runs the risk that a court may, in a future proceeding, side with the putative claimant. By that time, it is likely that the 90-day period for commencing a civil judicial forfeiture action pursuant to section 983(a)(3) will have expired, and that civil forfeiture of the property will be barred by the "death penalty" provision in section 983(a)(3)(B).

On the other hand, if the agency routinely forwards untimely or defective claims to the U.S. Attorney, and the U.S. Attorney files a civil judicial forfeiture action to toll the 90-day period, the agency's policy of insisting on strict compliance with section 983(a)(2) will be undermined, and claimants will have little incentive to adhere to the statutory requirements.

On balance, the seizing agencies should continue to adhere to the policy of strict compliance and should only refer valid claims to the U.S. Attorney. The agencies are encouraged to consult with the local U.S. Attorney if the content or timeliness of a claim filed in an administrative forfeiture proceeding is questionable before deciding to issue a declaration of forfeiture.

D.2. Discussion

Section 983(a)(2) provides that a person contesting an administrative forfeiture proceeding must file a claim with the seizing agency not later than the deadline set forth in the letter giving the person notice of the forfeiture, or not later than 30 days after the final day of publication of that notice in a newspaper, if direct notice was not received. *See* section 983(a)(2)(B). Moreover, the statute also provides that the claim must identify the property being claimed, state the claimant's interest in the property, and be made "under oath" subject to penalty of perjury. *See* section 983(a)(2)(c).[10] If no valid and timely claim is filed, the seizing agency is entitled to enter a declaration of forfeiture against the property pursuant to 19 U.S.C. § 1609.

If a claim is timely and contains the required information, however, the agency must transfer the case to the U.S. Attorney, who must either commence a civil or criminal forfeiture action in the district court or return the property within 90 days after the agency received the claim. *See* 18 U.S.C. § 983(a)(3)(A). If the U.S. Attorney does not comply with the statutory requirement, and the 90-day deadline is neither waived by the claimant nor extended by the court, the Government must release the property and the civil forfeiture of the property is forever barred. *See* section 983(a)(3)(B).

In the vast majority of cases, no one files a claim, and the seizing agency proceeds to enter the declaration of forfeiture. In most other cases, when a clearly valid and timely claim is filed, the agency transfers the case to the U.S. Attorney as required by law. When the timeliness or adequacy of the claim is in doubt (for example, if the claim asserts the notice was defective because it was sent to the wrong address), the seizing agency may—in its discretion—give the claimant additional time to perfect the claim; but if the claim was untimely, or if the defects are not corrected, the agency has the right to proceed with the administrative forfeiture.

It is clear that the U.S. Attorney's duty to file a civil or criminal forfeiture action in the district court does not arise until a claim is filed with the seizing agency in the proper form. For example, in *Manjarrez v. United States*, 2002 WL 31870533 (N.D. Ill. 2002), the district court held that a claim filed by the claimant's attorney, instead of by the claimant personally, was not under oath as the statute requires, and therefore was not a valid claim. Accordingly, the court held, the 90-day period in which the Government was required to commence a judicial forfeiture action never began to run.

There are times, however, when it is not entirely clear that the claim filed with the seizing agency is defective or untimely. For example, the agency may believe a claim is late because it was filed after the deadline set forth in the notice letter that the agency sent to the claimant; but the claimant may assert that the notice was defective because it was sent to the wrong address. If the agency is convinced that a claim is incomplete or is filed out of time, and it sticks to its guns and proceeds with the administrative forfeiture without referring the case to the U.S. Attorney, there is always the chance that a court will agree with the claimant and hold that the Government should have filed a judicial forfeiture action within the 90-day period prescribed by section 983(a)(3)(A). In that case, because there is no provision in the statute tolling the 90-day period while such disputes are resolved, it is likely that the Government will find itself outside of the 90-day period and unable to pursue the civil forfeiture of the property. *Cf. United States v. Thirty-Four Thousand Nine Hundred Twenty-Nine and 00/100 Dollars ($34,929.00) in U.S. Currency*, 2010 WL 481250, at *2-3 (S.D. Ohio, Feb. 5, 2010) (agreeing with *Manjarrez* that a claim signed only by counsel was deficient but holding that where claim signed by counsel was filed together with affidavit signed by owner-client under penalty of perjury reciting that the owner-client had reviewed the claim and found it true and accurate in every respect, the two documents together constituted a sufficient claim).

On the other hand, if the seizing agency forwarded every questionable case to the U.S. Attorney, the agency's policy of insisting on strict compliance with the terms of section 983(a)(2) would be rendered meaningless, and claimants would have little incentive to comply with those terms.

What is truly needed to resolve this problem is a provision in the statute tolling the 90-day period while any dispute as to the adequacy or timeliness of the claim filed in the administrative forfeiture proceeding is resolved by the court. But the absence of such a provision does not mean that the Government must liberally construe the otherwise strict requirements of section 983(a)(2). In fact, a recent decision by the Court of Appeals for the Third Circuit suggests that when there is a bona fide dispute as to the timeliness of a claim, the court should *equitably toll* the period for filing the judicial action to avoid any injustice to the Government.

In *Longenette v. Krusing*, 322 F.3d 758 (3d Cir. 2003), a claimant mailed his claim to the seizing agency within the statutory time period, but the agency did not receive the claim until after the time period expired. The agency assumed that the claim was untimely and entered a declaration of forfeiture, but the claimant disagreed and filed an action to recover his property in the district court. Ultimately, after protracted litigation, the court of appeals held that the claimant was correct: under pre-CAFRA law, at least, the timeliness of a claim filed in an administrative forfeiture proceeding by a prisoner was determined by the "mailbox rule." That is, the claim was deemed to have been filed when it was mailed. *Accord Karis v. United States*, 2006 WL 27085555, *6 (N.D.N.Y. Sept. 20, 2006) (applying mailbox rule to a claim filed by an incarcerated person in a case controlled by CAFRA).[11]

By this time, however, the five-year statute of limitations for filing a civil forfeiture action had expired. The claimant argued that, accordingly, the Government should be required to release the property and should be forever barred from commencing a civil forfeiture action. But the Third Circuit held that in fairness to the Government, given the novel legal issue involved, the statute of limitations would be equitably tolled. Thus, the Government was given six additional months in which to commence a new forfeiture action against the property.

While *Longenette* was a pre-CAFRA case involving the five-year statute of limitations under 19 U.S.C. § 1621, and not the 90-day filing deadline under section 983(a)(3), a similar argument may be made when the Government, in good faith, enters a declaration of forfeiture believing that the claim filed in an administrative forfeiture proceeding was inadequate or untimely, but is ultimately mistaken in that belief, the U.S. Attorney may argue that the time for filing a judicial action should be equitably tolled.

There is no guarantee, of course, that any court will agree with the Government on this point. But the availability of that remedy, coupled with the disadvantages of routinely referring all cases involving defective or untimely claims to the U.S. Attorney, militates in favor of taking the more aggressive approach on this issue.

It should be added, however, that in any case in which the legal issues regarding the adequacy or timeliness of a claim are unclear, the seizing agencies are encouraged to consult with the U.S. Attorney before deciding to go forward with the administrative forfeiture of the property. Such consultations—particularly in cases where further litigation is likely—will give the U.S. Attorney, who ultimately will have to defend the agency's action in the district court, the opportunity to advise the agency on the strengths and weaknesses of its position and the risks involved in not transferring the case for judicial forfeiture.

D.3. Conclusion

Seizing agencies should insist on strict compliance with the filing requirements of section 983(a)(2), and should not routinely refer defective claims to the U.S. Attorney just because a claimant insists that a claim contained all of the required information and was timely filed. The agencies, however, should consult with the U.S. Attorney regarding any claims in which the adequacy or the timeliness of the claim is unclear. If the agency rejects the claim and declares forfeiture, but a court ultimately decides that the claim filed in that proceeding was valid, the U.S. Attorney should argue that the 90-day period for filing a judicial forfeiture action under section 983(a)(3) should be equitably tolled.

E. 60-Day Notice Period in All Administrative Forfeiture Cases

E.1. Background

Through the many forfeiture statutes, Congress has made clear its intent that the Government be expeditious in providing notice and in initiating forfeiture actions against seized property. Further, a fundamental aspect of due process in any forfeiture proceeding is that notice be given as soon as practicable to apprise interested persons of the pendency of the action and afford them an opportunity to be heard.

Notice to owners and interested parties of the seizure and intent to forfeit in any non-judicial civil forfeiture proceeding is governed by section 983(a)(1), which requires "written notice" to all interested parties.

E.2. 60-Day Notice

Section 983(a)(1) requires that written notice of an administrative forfeiture action be sent to interested parties as soon as practicable but no later than 60 days after the date of the seizure. For interested parties determined after seizure, the written notice shall occur within 60 days after reasonably determining ownership or interest. *See* section 983(a)(1)(A)(v). Waivers of this notice deadline may be obtained in writing in exceptional circumstances from a designated official within the seizing agency. *See* section 983(a)(1)(B). The exceptional circumstances are those set forth in section 983(a)(1)(D).

If a waiver is granted, it must set forth the exceptional circumstances and be included in the administrative forfeiture case file. A waiver issued under this provision, however, is valid for no more than 30 days. If additional time is required, the waiver must be extended by a judicial officer pursuant to section 983(a)(1)(C).

F. Inadvertent Violation of 60-Day Deadline for Sending Notice

This section discusses what action the Government should take if it discovers that the seizing agency has inadvertently failed to send notice of the commencement of administrative forfeiture proceedings within 60 days of the seizure of the property as required by section 983(a)(1)(A).

F.1. Summary

Failure to comply with the 60-day deadline for sending notice precludes the Government from pursuing administrative forfeiture of the seized property and requires that the property be returned to the property owner. Section 983(a)(1)(F), however, permits the Government to file a judicial forfeiture action—civil or criminal—against the same property, and to reseize the property with either civil or criminal process. If the judicial action is commenced as soon as practicable after the discovery of the inadvertent failure to send notice, the Government may maintain custody of the property pursuant to the new civil or criminal process without having to go through the exercise of returning the property and seizing it back. References in this section to the notice deadline apply to whatever deadline may be applicable in a given case, be it the 60-day deadline, the 90-day deadline, or some other deadline established pursuant to the statutory procedure for obtaining an extension of time.

F.2. Discussion

Section 983(a)(1)(A)(i) provides that in non-judicial forfeiture proceedings,[12] the Government must send notice of the forfeiture within 60 days after the date of the seizure. Section 983(a)(1)(A)(iv) extends the deadline to 90 days in cases where the forfeiture is adopted from a state or local law enforcement agency. The statute also contains various exceptions to the notice deadlines and a procedure for obtaining extensions of time.

Congress enacted these deadlines to ensure that property owners are given timely notice of their right to contest a forfeiture and are apprised of the procedures for doing so. Hence, law enforcement agencies should endeavor at all times to adhere to the notice deadlines and obtain extensions of time for sending notice only when necessary, and only in the manner described in the statute. *See* sections 983(a)(1)(B) and (C). Intentionally ignoring a notice deadline in order to delay the sending of notice to the property owner or other interested parties is not permissible.

There are times, however, when the failure to send notice within the statutory period is purely inadvertent. The question that arises in such cases is what action the Government must take to rectify the situation.

Section 983(a)(1)(F) provides as follows:

> (F) If the Government does not send notice of a seizure of property in accordance with subparagraph (A) to the person from whom the property was seized, and no extension of time is granted, the Government shall return the property to that person *without prejudice to the right of the Government to commence a forfeiture proceeding at a later time*. The Government shall not be required to return contraband or other property that the person from whom the property was seized may not legally possess.

(Emphasis added.)

In our view, subparagraph (F) evinces Congress's intent to ensure that seized property does not indefinitely remain in the hands of the Government without the property owner having any opportunity to contest the forfeiture in a court of law. Thus, if the Government fails to send notice to the person from whom the property was seized within the statutory period for sending notice, it must return the property to that person (unless the property was contraband).

Section 983(a)(1)(F) also makes clear, however, that the Government is permitted to commence a new forfeiture proceeding. This presents two questions: Can the new proceeding be administrative, or must it be judicial? And can the Government reseize the property from the property owner when it commences the new proceeding?

While the statute does not make clear whether the new forfeiture proceeding can be administrative or must be judicial, we reject the view that section 983(a)(1)(F) permits the Government to reseize property for administrative forfeiture, thus starting the clock for sending notice all over again. The statute does not prohibit such action, but returning property to a property owner after the Government has missed the notice deadline, only to snatch the property back from the owner in order to start the clock over again, may violate the spirit of the legislation, and create the appearance that the Government is trying to circumvent the statutory requirement. Thus, it is our view that once the Government misses the notice deadline for administrative forfeiture, and has returned the property pursuant to section

983(a)(1)(F), no new administrative forfeiture should be commenced against the same property based on the violation that led to the initial seizure, unless there are extraordinary circumstances indicating that return of the property would be contrary to the public interest.

On the other hand, section 983(a)(1)(F) does permit the Government to commence either a civil or criminal forfeiture action in court. In the case of a criminal action, the Government may name the property in an indictment or information and obtain a criminal seizure warrant, a restraining order, or some other order under 21 U.S.C. § 853(e).[13] In the case of a civil judicial action, the Government may file a complaint and obtain an arrest warrant in rem for the property pursuant to Supplemental Rule G(3)(b). Like the criminal seizure warrant, the arrest warrant in rem gives the Government a lawful basis to maintain custody of the property pending the resolution of the case in court. Thus, once the Government commences a judicial forfeiture action—either civil or criminal—against the property, it may reseize the property and hold it pending the resolution of the forfeiture case.

This matter is not without some ambiguity. It is possible to read section 983(a)(1)(F) to say that once the 60-day notice deadline is missed, the property must be returned to the property owner, and must remain in the owner's possession even though a civil or criminal forfeiture action is commenced in court. AFMLS does not think, however, that this was the intent of Congress. Again, the purpose of section 983(a)(1)(F) was to ensure that the Government did not hold property indefinitely without giving the property owner a day in court. Absent extraordinary circumstances, if the notice deadline has passed, *and no forfeiture action is pending*, the property must be returned to the person from whom it was seized.[14] But once a judicial forfeiture action is filed, and the property owner is assured of a day in court, the Government can maintain the property in its possession as it would in any other forfeiture case, subject only to the "hardship" provisions in section 983(f). That, in our view, is what Congress meant by the language in section 983(a)(1)(F) providing that the return of the property is "without prejudice" to the right of the Government to commence a forfeiture proceeding at a later time.

The remaining question is whether, in cases where the Government files the criminal or civil judicial action immediately upon discovering the failure to send notice within the 60- or 90-day period, it is necessary to go through the exercise of physically returning the property to the property owner, only to reseize it immediately thereafter. AFMLS thinks that exercise is unnecessary.

Returning the property with one hand while seizing it back with the other, pursuant to an arrest warrant in rem or criminal seizure warrant, is an empty gesture that accomplishes nothing either in terms of the public interest or the private rights of the property owner. Moreover, proceeding directly to a judicial forfeiture action while maintaining custody of the property is entirely consistent with the intent of section 983(a)(1)(F). By commencing civil judicial forfeiture actions immediately upon learning of the inadvertent violation of the filing deadline, the Government will, in most cases, be placing property owners in a better position than they would have been in had the Government successfully commenced an administrative forfeiture proceeding.

As set forth in sections 983(a)(2) and (3), if the seizing agency sends notice of the administrative forfeiture action within the statutory period, the claimant has 30 days within which to file a claim to the property, after which the Government has 90 days to commence a civil or criminal forfeiture action in court. In contrast, by proceeding directly to the filing of the civil forfeiture complaint, the Government immediately places claimants in the position they would have been in if they had received the notice, filed a claim, and waited for the Government to file its complaint before the expiration of the 90-day period for doing so—assuming it did not take so long to discover the inadvertent failure to send notice that the 90-day period for filing a complaint would already have expired. Thus, filing a civil forfeiture complaint as soon as may be practicable after learning of the inadvertent violation of the notice deadline is in keeping with the intent of Congress to prevent the Government from holding on to property without giving the property owner a day in court. *See United States v. $39,480.00 in U.S. Currency*, 190 F. Supp. 2d 929 (W.D. Tex. 2002) (where the Government inadvertently filed its complaint on the 91st day because of a clerical error on the date stamp, claimant suffered no prejudice, and strict enforcement of the 90-day rule would have a "Draconian effect" on the Government's forfeiture case, the court equitably tolled the 90-day period and deemed the complaint timely filed). *Accord United States v. Thirty-Four Thousand Nine Hundred Twenty-Nine and 00/100 Dollars ($34,929.00) in U.S. Currency*, 2010 WL 481250, at *3 (S.D. Ohio Feb. 5, 2010).

F.3. Conclusion

If a seizing agency discovers that it has inadvertently failed to comply with a deadline for sending notice of the administrative forfeiture of property in a case where such deadlines apply, and the person from whom the property was seized has not waived the 60-day deadline, no further action may be taken to forfeit the property administratively based on the offense giving rise to the original seizure, and the property must be returned to the person from whom it was seized in accordance with section 983(a)(1)(F), unless the return of the property would be unlawful, or unless the Government, as soon as may be practicable, commences a judicial forfeiture proceeding by (1) naming the property in a criminal indictment or information and obtaining a judicial order pursuant to section 853(e) or (f) allowing it to hold the property; or (2) filing a civil judicial forfeiture action and retaining lawful possession of the property pursuant to an arrest warrant in rem.

G. Policy on the Deadline for Filing a Civil Forfeiture Action in Cases That Do Not Begin as Administrative Forfeiture Proceedings

G.1. Issue

In 18 U.S.C. § 983(a)(3), Congress provided that the Government must commence a judicial forfeiture proceeding within 90 days of the receipt by a seizing agency of a claim filed in an administrative forfeiture proceeding. Congress set no deadline, however, for commencing a judicial forfeiture proceeding in cases that do not start out as administrative forfeiture proceedings in the first instance. The question is what deadline applies to the commencement of a judicial forfeiture action when property is seized for forfeiture but there is no administrative forfeiture proceeding.

G.2. Summary

There are two situations in which this issue arises: when the Government could have commenced an administrative forfeiture proceeding against the seized property but, for whatever reason, opted not to do so, and when the Government is barred from forfeiting the property administratively by the limitations on such proceedings in 19 U.S.C. § 1607. The 90-day deadline in section 983(a)(3) does not apply in either situation, nor is there any other statutory deadline for commencing such actions. Nevertheless, as a matter of policy, the Department of Justice advises prosecutors that whenever administrative forfeiture is statutorily authorized but is not pursued, the U.S. Attorney should commence a judicial forfeiture action (civil or criminal) within 150 days of the seizure of the property. Moreover, the Department advises that when property is seized for forfeiture but cannot be forfeited administratively because of the limitations set forth in section 1607, the U.S. Attorney should commence a judicial forfeiture action within 90 days of the receipt of a written request for the release of the property from a potential claimant.

G.3. Discussion

G.3.A. Section 983(A)(3)

Forfeiture cases typically begin with the seizure of property and the commencement by the seizing agency of administrative forfeiture proceedings. Indeed, it is the policy of the Department of Justice that all forfeiture cases should begin as administrative forfeiture proceedings when it is possible to do so. *See* section I.A. However, in certain circumstances, cases will take different paths to final forfeitures.

When a claimant files a proper claim in an administrative forfeiture proceeding, the seizing agency must suspend the proceeding and refer the case to the U.S. Attorney. This has long been the law. Prior to the enactment of CAFRA, however, there was a widespread concern with the absence of any mechanism for forcing the Government to commence a judicial forfeiture proceeding in a timely way once a claimant had filed his claim with the seizing agency. Defense counsel complained that by filing such a claim, the claimant had done everything in his power to bring the administrative forfeiture proceeding to a halt and to demand his "day in court," yet the Government was free to sit on the case for months or years while it determined whether to proceed with the forfeiture civilly or criminally or to return the property to the claimant. In a series of cases, the Supreme Court and the lower courts had upheld this practice against constitutional challenge. *See United States v. $8,850 in U.S. Currency*, 461 U.S. 555, 565 (1983) (applying the four-part test from *Barker v. Wingo*, Supreme Court finds that 18-month delay in commencing civil forfeiture action did not violate due process).

In CAFRA, Congress responded to this concern by enacting section 983(a)(3). The statute provides that "not less than 90 days after a claim has been filed," the Government must file a civil forfeiture complaint, include the property in a criminal indictment, return the property, or obtain an extension of time from the court. Thus, it is now fairly clear what the Government must do if (1) it commences an administrative forfeiture proceeding pursuant to section 983(a)(1), and (2) a claimant files a timely claim in proper form pursuant to section 983(a)(2).

G.3.B. Cases That Do Not Begin Administratively

Congress did not consider, however, that not all forfeiture cases begin as administrative forfeitures. Notwithstanding the policy favoring administrative forfeiture, there are occasions when an AUSA may wish to by-pass the administrative forfeiture process and file a case directly as a civil forfeiture or as part of a criminal prosecution. Moreover, 19 U.S.C. § 1607, the statute that sets the boundaries for what may be forfeited administratively, expressly bars the administrative forfeiture of certain property, including all real property and most personal property having a value in excess of $500,000, except for currency. Because section 983(a)(3) applies only to cases that begin as administrative forfeitures, CAFRA contains no deadline governing when the Government must commence judicial forfeiture proceedings when it seizes property for forfeiture in those two instances.

At present, the only guidance the courts have given in this situation is that the pre-CAFRA constitutional limitations endorsed by the Supreme Court in *$8,850* still apply.

G.3.C. Policy Concerns

While no statute requires the Government to set a filing deadline for commencing a judicial forfeiture action in cases that do not begin as administrative forfeitures, there are several legal and political considerations that militate in favor of establishing a policy in that regard.

First, Congress was clearly concerned with the absence of a mechanism to force the Government to give a potential claimant timely access to the courts once his property was seized. The deadline for commencing an administrative forfeiture proceeding (generally 60 days pursuant to section 983(a)(1)), and then for commencing a judicial action once a claimant files a claim (90 days pursuant to section 983(a)(3)), reflect that. If the Government were to seize property for forfeiture in a situation where administrative forfeiture was authorized, but then ignore the 60- and 90-day deadlines in sections 983(a)(1) and (3) on the ground that it intended all along to skip over the administrative forfeiture process and proceed directly with a judicial forfeiture, courts might suspect that the Government was actually conjuring an ad hoc excuse for missing the statutory deadlines, or had decided to by-pass the administrative forfeiture proceeding for the express purpose of circumventing the statutory deadlines and the underlying congressional intent. The likely consequences of creating the appearance of trying to do an end-run around the statutory deadlines include renewed efforts by Congress to curtail the Government's ability to forfeit property administratively or civilly, and judicial decisions applying the statutory deadlines to cases where there was no administrative forfeiture, even though they were never meant to apply in that context.

Similar concerns apply to the second category of cases as well. While it cannot be denied that certain categories of cases could not be prosecuted as administrative forfeitures even if the Government wanted to do so, *see* 19 U.S.C. § 1607, the courts are reluctant to conclude that Congress would not have wanted to force the Government to be at least as timely in commencing a forfeiture action when the property is valued at more than $500,000 as it must be when the property is worth far less. Thus, there have been a number of cases in which courts have pressed prosecutors to concede that there must be a deadline for filing a judicial forfeiture action in such cases, even though no such deadline exists. By adopting a deadline for commencing a judicial action in such cases by policy or regulation, the Department of Justice may be able to relieve prosecutors of the pressure to adopt ad hoc deadlines on a case by case basis, and might forestall judicial attempts to cut back on the constitutional doctrine enshrined in the *$8,850* decision.

G.3.D. Policy on Filing a Judicial Forfeiture Action

In light of the foregoing considerations, it is the policy of the Department of Justice that prosecutors commence civil or criminal forfeiture actions in accordance with the following schedule when property is seized for forfeiture but there is no administrative forfeiture proceeding.

In cases where administrative forfeiture is possible under section 1607, but the Government has elected for whatever reason to by-pass the administrative forfeiture process, the U.S. Attorney should file a civil or criminal action for the forfeiture of the property within 150 days of the seizure of the property. This reflects the total time that the Government would have had to commence such an action if the Government had chosen to proceed in the normal way: 60 days for the commencement of an administrative forfeiture proceeding plus 90 days to file a civil forfeiture complaint or to include the property in a criminal indictment. By following this policy, the prosecutor will thus deflect any concern that the Government by-passed the administrative forfeiture process to circumvent the CAFRA deadlines.

It should be emphasized that this policy applies only in cases where the U.S. Attorney, in consultation with the seizing agency, affirmatively decides at the outset of a case that the forfeiture of the seized property will be done judicially in the first instance. It does not apply to cases where the seizure should have been handled as a routine administrative forfeiture to which the 60- or 90-day deadlines in section 983(a)(1)(A) apply, but where the notice was not sent due to inadvertence or error. The policy regarding the handling of forfeitures in that situation is set forth in section I.F.

In cases where administrative forfeiture is barred by section 1607, it is not necessary to establish a fixed deadline for commencing a judicial forfeiture action based on the date of the seizure. Congress set no deadline in this instance, and it is not necessary for the Government to adopt one. But the Government should not be free to ignore indefinitely a request made by a potential claimant for the release of his property or for the commencement of formal judicial proceedings. Accordingly, in a case where the U.S. Attorney receives such a request in writing, the prosecutor should treat the request as if it were a "claim" referred to in section 983(a)(3)(A), and should thus commence a judicial forfeiture action within 90 days of the receipt of the request.[15]

Nothing in this policy should be interpreted to allow a potential claimant to shorten the deadline for commencing an administrative forfeiture in a case where administrative forfeiture is authorized. In all events, in such cases the seizing agency will have 60 days (or 90 days in the case of adoptive forfeitures) to determine whether or not to proceed with the forfeiture proceeding. *See United States v. $200,255 in U.S. Currency*, 2006 WL 1687774, at *4 (M.D. Ga. 2006) (under the scheme set forth in section 983(a)(1), the administrative forfeiture proceeding does not begin until the seizing agency sends notice to potential claimants; then the claimant files his claim; a claim filed before the seizing agency sends notice is premature and does not start the clock running on the time to file a judicial forfeiture complaint).

II. Interplay of Administrative Forfeiture and Criminal Forfeiture

A. Starting a Case Administratively

A recurring issue concerns the interplay of criminal and administrative forfeiture. In general, there is no reason for the seizing agency not to commence administrative forfeiture proceedings against property even if the property could be included in a future criminal indictment. Therefore, in most cases, the seizing agency will commence administrative forfeiture proceedings against seized property by sending notice to potential claimants, while simultaneously the U.S. Attorney will ask the grand jury to include a forfeiture allegation against the same property in a criminal indictment. This is the proper procedure. However, if no claim is filed in the administrative forfeiture proceeding, the property will automatically be forfeited.

In cases where the property has been included in a criminal indictment but has been successfully forfeited administratively, it is necessary to file a motion with the court to dismiss the forfeiture allegation from the indictment to avoid a situation in which the court, the defendant, or the jury becomes confused and mistakenly believes that the Government abandoned the administrative forfeiture once the indictment was returned. Accordingly, in cases where administrative and criminal forfeiture proceedings are instituted simultaneously, and no one files a claim in the administrative proceeding, the agency should complete the administrative forfeiture, and the AUSA handling the criminal case should file a motion reporting the completed forfeiture and therefore striking the forfeiture from the indictment.

Once Government counsel serves the motion to dismiss the forfeiture allegation from the indictment on defense counsel, the defendant is aware of the administrative forfeiture and is not expecting to have an opportunity to contest the forfeiture in the criminal case. In that situation, the defendant would be estopped from later contesting the administrative forfeiture on the ground that the defendant never received notice of the administrative forfeiture or he or she thought the forfeiture would be handled criminally. On the other hand, if the defendant responds to the motion by stating that he or she would have contested the administrative forfeiture but for the indictment, the prosecutor should either withdraw the motion and proceed with the criminal forfeiture, or ask the court to conduct a hearing to determine if the defendant's assertion is bona fide. If the court finds that the defendant was properly notified of the administrative forfeiture and did not file a claim, it should enter an order to that effect and grant the motion to strike the forfeiture allegation. But if the court finds that the defendant may in fact have been confused regarding the status of the administrative forfeiture, the Government should proceed with the criminal forfeiture.

B. Requesting the Seizing Agency to Suspend the Administrative Forfeiture

In an extraordinary case, the U.S. Attorney may have a reason why the case should not be handled administratively and may ask the seizing agency to suspend the administrative forfeiture in favor of criminal forfeiture. Seizing agencies will generally comply with that request, but the U.S. Attorney may then have to take steps to ensure that the 60-day deadline for commencing an administrative forfeiture proceeding under section 983(a)(1)(A) is not violated. *See* section 983(a)(1)(A)(iii) (no notice of administrative forfeiture is required if, before the 60-day period expires, a grand jury returns an indictment naming the property, and the Government takes steps to preserve its right to maintain custody of the property under the criminal forfeiture laws).

C. Disposing of Administrative Forfeiture in a Plea Agreement

Criminal prosecutors cannot agree to return property that has already been forfeited administratively as part of a plea agreement in a criminal case. Once the property has been forfeited, it belongs to the Government, and may have already been liquidated, put into official use, or shared with a state or foreign law enforcement agency. Thus, the U.S. Attorney has no authority to agree to return such property as part of a plea agreement in a criminal case.

Moreover, recognizing that the seizing agencies often have put considerable resources into the administrative forfeiture of property by the time the prosecutor is negotiating a plea agreement, the U.S. Attorney should not agree to the return of property as part of a plea agreement if the property is subject to an ongoing administrative forfeiture proceeding unless (1) the seizing agency is requested to suspend the administrative forfeiture and it agrees to do so, or (2) AFMLS approves the decision to return the property.

D. Seizure Pursuant to a Criminal Warrant: Availability of Administrative Forfeiture

This section deals with the issues that arise when property is seized with a criminal seizure warrant, but the seizing agency nevertheless wants to initiate administrative forfeiture proceedings. Note: This is the reverse of the situation discussed in section II.A, which dealt with pursuing criminal forfeiture after property was seized for civil or administrative forfeiture.

D.1. Summary

There are two separate issues here. The first is whether a seizing agency can begin a forfeiture proceeding as a criminal forfeiture (i.e., by seizing the property with a criminal seizure warrant under section 853(f)) and then convert the proceeding to an administrative one without reseizing the property or taking some other action under the civil forfeiture statutes. The second is whether such an administrative forfeiture must be conducted in accordance with the 60-day deadline and other procedural requirements enacted by CAFRA.

The answer to the first question appears to be yes. Despite the common practice of commencing an administrative forfeiture only after the property has been seized pursuant to a civil warrant or valid warrantless seizure, there is no reason why property seized pursuant to a criminal warrant issued under section 853(f) cannot be forfeited administratively. There is no requirement in such cases that the Government reseize the property from itself with a civil warrant.

The second question is more difficult. The 60-day requirement in section 983(a)(1) that was enacted by CAFRA does not, by its terms, apply to criminal forfeiture proceedings. Thus, the 60-day clock never starts to tick if property is seized pursuant to a criminal seizure warrant. However, if the Government were routinely to seize property with a criminal warrant, ignore the 60-day deadline for commencing an administrative forfeiture proceeding, and then commence such a proceeding at a later date, it would create the appearance of misusing the criminal forfeiture process as a way of evading CAFRA's strict deadlines. Therefore, except in extraordinary circumstances, if the Government desires to commence administrative forfeiture proceedings against property seized pursuant to a criminal seizure warrant, it should do so within 60 days of the seizure. If the 60-day deadline has passed, and the Government still desires to pursue the forfeiture civilly instead of criminally, the case should be referred to the U.S. Attorney to commence a civil judicial proceeding.

D.2. Discussion

Most civil forfeiture statutes authorize the seizing agency to forfeit seized property administratively in accordance with the Customs laws. *See*, e.g., 18 U.S.C. § 981(d) and 21 U.S.C. § 881(d) (incorporating the provisions of 19 U.S.C. § 1602 et seq. into the civil forfeiture statutes). Nothing in the incorporated provisions of Title 19 limits administrative forfeiture to cases where the property was seized pursuant to a particular kind of seizure warrant. To the contrary, section 1603(a) provides that property may be seized for administrative forfeiture "upon process issued in the same manner as provided for a search warrant under the Federal Rules of Criminal Procedure [i.e., Rule 41], [or] any seizure authority otherwise provided by law." Thus, nothing in the Customs laws themselves would preclude the commencement of administrative forfeiture proceedings following the seizure of property pursuant to a criminal seizure warrant issued under section 853(f).

Likewise, the civil forfeiture statutes themselves do not prescribe a particular form of warrant to be used to commence a civil—and hence, an administrative—forfeiture proceeding. Section 981(b)—which governs seizures for the purpose of civil forfeiture under both that section and the drug laws[16]—provides that property may be seized either pursuant to a warrant "obtained in the same manner as provided for a search warrant under the Federal Rules of Civil Procedure" or without a warrant if (1) there is probable cause to believe the property is subject to forfeiture and an exception to the fourth amendment warrant requirement would apply, or (2) the property was seized by a state or local agency and transferred to a federal agency. *See* sections 981(b)(1) and (2).

Finally, it is now established that there is nothing improper about the Government beginning a case criminally and then deciding to proceed civilly, or vice versa. *See United States v. Leyland*, 277 F.3d 628 (2d Cir. 2002) (there is nothing improper about beginning forfeiture as an allegation in a criminal indictment and then switching to civil forfeiture); *United States v. Candelaria-Silva*, 166 F.3d 19 (1st Cir. 1999) (there is nothing improper in the Government beginning a forfeiture case with a civil seizure and switching to criminal forfeiture once an indictment is returned; it is commonplace). Moreover, CAFRA specifically authorizes parallel administrative and criminal forfeiture actions. *See* section 983(a)(1)(A)(iii)(I). Thus, administrative forfeiture under the Customs laws may be commenced in respect of any property seized by a federal law enforcement agency (including property seized by a state or local agency and transferred to a federal agency for the purpose of adoptive forfeiture) without regard to the nature of the warrant that was used to seize the property.[17]

The second question is whether such administrative forfeiture proceedings must be commenced within the 60-day deadline set forth in section 983(a)(1)(A). Section 983(a)(1)(A)(i) provides that in non-judicial forfeiture proceedings,[18] the Government must send notice of the forfeiture action within 60 days after the date of the seizure. Section 983(a)(1)(A)(iv) extends the deadline to 90 days in cases where the forfeiture is adopted from a state or local law enforcement agency. The statute also contains various exceptions to the notice deadlines and contains a procedure for obtaining extensions of time.[19]

Congress enacted these deadlines to ensure that property owners are given timely notice of their right to contest an administrative forfeiture action and are apprised of the procedures for doing so. But the statute, by its terms, only applies to *non-judicial* forfeiture proceedings, and thus cannot, and does not, apply to criminal forfeiture proceedings which must, in all cases, be judicial proceedings. Accordingly, if the Government seizes property for the purpose of criminal forfeiture and proceeds solely along the criminal forfeiture track, the 60-day deadline under section 983(a)(1)(A) never comes into play.

To be sure, there will be cases where the Government seizes property for criminal forfeiture, intending at all times that the forfeiture will be made a part of the criminal case, but then finds that the criminal forfeiture option is not viable.[20] In such cases, there is nothing in the law preventing the Government from switching to civil forfeiture, or forfeiting the property administratively. Nor would the Government be required in such circumstances to seize the property from itself with a civil seizure warrant in order to commence the civil or administrative forfeiture proceeding. CAFRA does contain an odd and burdensome procedure requiring the Government to obtain new authority to maintain custody of property already in its possession when it switches *from civil forfeiture to criminal forfeiture*. *See* section 983(a)(3)(B)(ii)(II). But as discussed above, nothing in the civil forfeiture statutes predicates administrative forfeiture proceedings on the use of a particular form of seizure warrant.

Thus, the Government may switch theories of forfeiture from criminal forfeiture to civil or administrative forfeiture at any time. At most, the deadline for commencing an administrative forfeiture would relate back to (i.e., would begin to run from) the date when the decision was made to pursue a non-judicial forfeiture, not the date of the original seizure. If, however, the Government were routinely to assert that it had originally intended to pursue a forfeiture criminally, but after 60 days had passed from the date of the seizure, it had decided to pursue administrative forfeiture instead, it would create the appearance that the criminal forfeiture process had been abused, or was a post hoc invention designed to excuse the Government from having to comply with the 60-day deadline for commencing an administrative forfeiture when the property is seized for civil forfeiture in the first instance.

To avoid such appearance of impropriety, we recommend that whenever the Government commences a criminal forfeiture action by seizing property for the purpose of criminal forfeiture, but later decides to switch theories to forfeit the property under the civil forfeiture statutes, the forfeiture action be referred to the U.S. Attorney for the purpose of filing a civil complaint in the district court unless fewer than 60 days have elapsed since the date of the seizure. Only when the decision to switch theories of forfeiture is made within 60 days of the seizure should the Government consider commencing an administrative forfeiture proceeding against the seized property. There may be other exceptions to this, but the only two that presently come to mind are (1) the extraordinary case where there is clear documentation that the decision to switch from criminal to civil forfeiture was made after the 60 days expired; and (2) a case where the claimant agrees to waive the 60-day notice requirement and allow the Government to proceed administratively (e.g., as part of a settlement or plea agreement.)

III. Form of the Claim

A. Claims Must Be Filed under Oath by the Claimant, Not by an Attorney or Agent

This section addresses the question whether claims filed by persons contesting forfeiture actions must be filed under oath by the claimants themselves instead of being verified and filed on behalf of the claimant by an attorney or other representative.

A.1. Summary

The statutes and rules governing the filing of claims in administrative, civil, and criminal forfeiture cases all require that the claim be filed under oath by the claimant, and not by his or her attorney or other representative.

A.2. Discussion

With respect to claims filed in administrative forfeiture proceedings, section 983(a)(2)(C)(iii) provides in relevant part that "A claim shall...be made under oath, subject to penalty of perjury." Moreover, section 983(h) provides that if a court finds that a "claimant's assertion of an interest in the property was frivolous, the court may impose a civil fine *on the claimant* of an amount equal to 10 percent of the value of the forfeited property." (Emphasis added.)

These provisions were included in CAFRA to address the concern that by eliminating the cost bond requirement for most forfeitures,[21] Congress would be encouraging the filing of false and frivolous claims in administrative forfeiture cases.[22] Given that context, it is clear that Congress intended that the claim be filed by the claimant personally, and that the claimant be the one to swear under oath that the assertions made in the claim are well-founded. *See Manjarrez v. United States*, 2002 WL 31870533 (N.D. Ill. 2002) (claim filed by claimant's attorney, instead of by claimant personally, is not "under oath" as the statute requires, and therefore is not a valid claim) *Cf. United States v. Thirty-Four Thousand Nine Hundred Twenty-Nine and 00/100 Dollars ($34,929.00) in U.S. Currency*, 2010 WL 481250, at *2-3 (S.D. Ohio Feb. 5, 2010) (agreeing with *Manjarrez* that a claim signed only by counsel is deficient but holding that where claim signed by counsel was filed together with affidavit signed by owner-client under penalty of perjury reciting that the owner-client had reviewed the claim and found in true and accurate in every respect, the two documents together constituted a sufficient claim).

In the case of claims (petitions) filed in the ancillary proceeding in criminal forfeiture cases, the applicable statute is 21 U.S.C. § 853(n). Subsection 853(n)(2) provides in relevant part that "any person, other than the defendant, asserting a legal interest in property which has been ordered forfeited to the United States...may...petition the court for a hearing to adjudicate the validity of his alleged interest in the property...." Subsection 853(n)(2) is qualified by subsection 853(n)(3), which mandates that "the petition shall be *signed by the petitioner under penalty of perjury* and shall set forth the nature and extent of the petitioner's right, title, or interest in the property...." (Emphasis added.) This statute appears unequivocal: if the petition must be "signed by the petitioner under penalty of perjury," there is little room to suggest that it could be filed on behalf of a claimant by his or her attorney or other representative.[23]

Prior to the enactment of Supplemental Rule G, the requirements regarding claims filed in civil judicial forfeiture cases were less clear, but the Rule has removed all ambiguity on this issue. Rule G(5)(a)(i)(C) says that the claim must identify the specific property claimed, identify the claimant, state the claimant's interest in the property, be signed by *the claimant* under penalty of perjury, and be served on the Government attorney handling the case. Accordingly, provisions of the prior law allowing claims to be verified by the claimant's attorney in some cases are no longer in effect.

A.3. Conclusion

In all federal forfeiture cases—including administrative forfeiture proceedings conducted by seizing agencies, civil judicial proceedings, and the ancillary proceedings in criminal cases—a claim filed by a person contesting the forfeiture action must be filed under oath by the claimant him or herself, and not by an attorney or other representative acting on behalf of the claimant.

IV. Criminal Forfeiture Procedure

A. Filing a Motion for Reconsideration in a Criminal Forfeiture Case

A.1. Summary

When the order of forfeiture in a criminal case contains a legal or factual error, the Government may, on certain occasions, file a motion for reconsideration. If the order was entered prior to sentencing, as contemplated by Fed. R. Crim. P. 32.2(b)(2), the filing of the motion for reconsideration is straightforward. If the order is not entered until sentencing, however, the opportunity to move to correct the order may be quite limited. That is because the filing of a motion for reconsideration in a criminal case may not suspend the time for filing an appeal under Appellate Rule 4(b), and because, in any event, the only vehicle for correcting an order of forfeiture once it becomes part of the sentence may be Rule 35(a), which requires that the motion be made, and the relief be granted, within 14 days of the sentence.[24]

Accordingly, prosecutors should always ask the court to issue a preliminary order of forfeiture as soon as possible in accordance with Rule 32.2(b)(2) so that there is ample opportunity to correct the order before it becomes final at sentencing. Prosecutors should not assume that a motion for reconsideration filed *after* the sentence will suspend the time for appeal.

A.2. Applicable Rules and Statutes

Fed. R. Crim. P. 35(a) says that motions to correct an "arithmetical, technical, or other clear error" must be filed, and ruled upon, within 14 days after sentencing. Appellate Rule 4(b)(5) says that a motion filed under Rule 35(a) does not suspend the time for filing an appeal.

A.3. The Traditional Rule Is That a Motion for Reconsideration Suspends the Time for Filing an Appeal

Prosecutors frequently find it necessary to file motions for reconsideration in criminal forfeiture cases because the court, in announcing sentence or issuing the judgment of forfeiture, has misapplied forfeiture law. The traditional rule is that a motion for reconsideration of a judgment or order may be filed at any time before the time to appeal has expired, and that the filing of such a motion suspends the time to file an appeal.[25] Indeed, the Supreme Court has applied this rule to motions for reconsideration filed by the Government in criminal cases. *See United States v. Ibarra*, 502 U.S. 1, 4-6 (1991) (noting the advantages of giving district courts the opportunity to correct their own alleged errors, and thus preventing unnecessary burdens from being placed on the courts of appeals); *United States v. Dieter*, 429 U.S. 6, 8 n.3 (1976).

A.4. Rule 35(A) Motions Do Not Suspend the Time

In contrast to the traditional rule, Rule 35(a) provides that a motion to correct an "arithmetical, technical, or other clear error" in the defendant's sentence must be filed, and ruled upon, within 14 days after sentencing.[26] Moreover, in 2002, Appellate Rule 4(b)(5) was amended to make clear that a motion filed under Rule 35(a) does not suspend the time for filing a notice of appeal. *See* Advisory Committee Note to 2002 Amendment. The question is whether motions to reconsider orders of forfeiture based on erroneous applications of forfeiture law are, in effect, Rule 35(a) motions that are subject to the seven-day rule and to the provisions of App. Rule 4(b)(5), or whether they are separate motions governed by the traditional rule that a motion for reconsideration may be filed at any time before the time for appeal has expired, and that the motion suspends the time for filing the appeal.

A.5. The Rules Applicable to Rule 35(A) Motions May Not Apply to Motions for Reconsideration of a Forfeiture Order

A strong argument could be made that Rule 35(a) relates only to motions to modify the portion of the sentence governed by the sentencing guidelines. Prior to 1987, Rule 35(a) provided that a court could "correct an illegal sentence at any time." Rule 35(a), Federal Rules of Criminal Procedure (1986). That provision was stricken by the Sentencing Reform Act as part of the effort to ensure consistency in sentencing under a guidelines system. *See* Pub. L. 98-473; 18 U.S.C. § 3582(c) (stating the narrow grounds on which a sentence of imprisonment may be modified). In 1991, however, the rule was amended to restore narrow authority to correct an "arithmetical, technical, or other clear error." This was viewed as a codification of cases holding that the courts retained inherent authority to correct such errors notwithstanding the repeal of the former rule. *See* 1991 Advisory Committee Note. But the Advisory Committee was careful to make clear that the narrow exception being created was not intended to create wholesale authority to revise the portion of the sentence governed by the sentencing guidelines. As the Committee Note states, the rule was amended to limit motions to correct the sentence to instances where there was an "obvious error or mistake," but not to give the court the opportunity "to reconsider the application or interpretation of the sentencing guidelines or for the court simply to change its mind about the appropriateness of the sentence." *Id.*

In short, the 1987 repeal of former Rule 35(a), and the 1991 amendment that restored the authority to correct certain technical errors within seven days (amended to 14 days effective December 1, 2009), were part of the sentencing reform movement that introduced the use of a guidelines system for determining the period of incarceration that could be imposed on a defendant once he or she was convicted. None of this had anything to do with the forfeiture aspects of the sentence that remain subject to the traditional rule regarding motions for reconsideration.

No court has ever held that the narrow scope of Rule 35(a) applies to a motion to correct the forfeiture aspect of a sentence. While forfeiture is part of sentencing for many purposes, it is undisputed that neither the sentencing guidelines nor the case law interpreting them apply to forfeiture, *see* U.S.S.G. § 5E1.4 and Commentary (providing that forfeiture is "automatic" upon conviction and thus not governed by the sentencing guidelines); *see United States v. Fruchter*, 411 F.3d 377 (2d Cir. 2005) (*Booker* and *Blakely* do not apply to criminal forfeiture for two reasons: because the Supreme Court expressly stated in *Booker* that its decision did not affect forfeiture under 18 U.S.C. § 3554, and because *Booker* applies only to a determinate sentencing system in which the jury's verdict mandates a sentence within a specific range; criminal forfeiture is not a determinate system).

Thus, the policy considerations that prompted the 1991 amendment to Rule 35(a) (and the 2002 amendment to App. Rule 4(b)(5))—i.e., the desire for finality in the calculation of the appropriate period of incarceration under the sentencing guidelines—have nothing to do with the forfeiture portion of the sentence. At the same time, the policy considerations that militate in favor of motions for reconsideration on other legal issues—i.e., the advantages of allowing the district court to correct its own errors—apply with full force to the complex issues that arise in applying the asset forfeiture statutes in criminal cases. For these reasons, courts may ultimately hold that a motion for reconsideration of the forfeiture aspect of a criminal sentence is not limited by the provisions relating to subject matter or time set forth in Rule 35(a), and that accordingly, such motions will suspend the time for filing an appeal in accordance with the traditional rule.

A.6. The Department's Policy, However, Is to Assume That Rule 35(A) Applies

There is no guarantee, however, that the courts will agree with this view. In the worst case, courts could hold that Rule 35(a) is the only means by which the Government can move to correct any portion of a criminal sentence, including the order of forfeiture, and that accordingly a motion must be filed, and ruled upon, within 14 days of the sentence. Moreover, if the courts were to reach that conclusion, it would follow that the filing of the motion does not suspend the time for filing an appeal. *See* App. Rule 4(b)(5).[27] Accordingly, until this issue is resolved by the courts or by Congress, in a criminal case in which the order of forfeiture is not entered until sentencing, a prosecutor who files a motion for reconsideration of the order should file the motion, and urge the court to rule on it, within 14 days of the sentence. In addition, the AUSA should not assume that the filing of the motion will extend the time for filing an appeal, but should instead file the notice of appeal before the thirtieth day under App. Rule 4(b)(1)(B) regardless of the status of a pending motion for reconsideration. As a courtesy to the district court, the prosecutor may want to advise the court of the Government's policy on this matter so that the court understands the reasons why the Government may feel compelled to file its notice of appeal—which divests the district court of jurisdiction—even though the court may have scheduled a hearing on the Government's motion.

In all cases, however, the interests of justice would be better served if the court were to enter a preliminary order of forfeiture as soon as possible after the entry of a verdict or the acceptance of a guilty plea so that the court would have a full opportunity prior to sentencing to correct any legal or factual error. A motion for reconsideration would always be appropriate if filed after the order is entered but prior to sentencing. If that practice is followed, much unnecessary litigation over the scope of Rule 35(a), and many unnecessary appeals, may be avoided.

A.7. Conclusion

Because the law regarding the application of Rule 35(a) and App. Rule 4(b)(5) to motions to reconsider orders of forfeiture in criminal cases is unclear, AUSAs should act conservatively to protect the Government's right to appeal from the forfeiture portion of a criminal sentence. Until the law on this issue becomes more clear, prosecutors should assume that any motion for reconsideration of a criminal forfeiture order should be filed and ruled upon within 14 days of sentencing in accordance with Rule 35(a), and that the filing of the motion will not suspend the time for filing an appeal under App. Rule 4(b)(1)(B). In all cases, the Government should urge the district court to comply with Rule 32.2(b)(2) in issuing a preliminary order of forfeiture as soon as possible after the entry of a verdict or the acceptance of a guilty plea so that there is ample time to correct the order prior to sentencing.

V. Publication and Direct Notice of Order of Forfeiture

A. Civil Forfeiture Cases

Upon the filing of a civil forfeiture complaint, the Government must publish notice of the forfeiture in a manner consistent with the provisions of Supplemental Rule G(4)(a) of the Supplemental Rules for Admiralty or Maritime Claims and Asset Forfeiture Actions. *See* Fed. R. Crim. P. 32.2(b)(6)(C) (eff. Dec. 1, 2009).[28] As described in Rule G(4)(a)(iv), this may include publication on the Government's forfeiture website, www.forfeiture.gov. The notice must describe the forfeited property, state the times under the applicable statute when a petition contesting the forfeiture must be filed, and the name and contact information for the government attorney to be served with the petition.

Moreover, consistent with Rule G(4)(b), the Government must send direct written notice to any person who reasonably appears to be a potential claimant with standing to contest the forfeiture. Such notice may be sent by any of the means described in Rule G(4)(b)(iii)-(v).

For the purposes of this policy, "a person who reasonably appears to be a potential claimant with standing to contest the forfeiture" includes any person who appears likely to be able to establish an ownership interest in the property within the meaning of "owner" as defined in 18 U.S.C. § 983(d)(6). As stated in that statute, an "owner" does not include a person with only a general unsecured interest in, or claim against, the property or estate of the defendant. *See United States v. Watkins*, 320 F.3d 1279, 1283-84 (11th Cir. 2003) (unsecured creditors lack standing to contest the forfeiture in the ancillary proceeding because they have no interest in the particular assets subject to forfeiture); *United States v. Phillips*, 185 F.3 d 183, 187 (4th Cir. 1999) (Government does not have to send notice to persons who lack standing to contest the forfeiture); *United States v. Carmichael,* 440 F. Supp. 2d 1280 (M.D. Ala. 2006) (Government is not required to send direct written notice to unsecured creditors in a criminal forfeiture case).

B. Criminal Forfeiture Cases

Effective December 1, 2009, Federal Rule of Criminal Procedure 32.2(b)(6) provides:

a) *Publishing and Sending Notice.* If the court orders forfeiture of specific property, the Government must publish notice of the order and send notice to any person who reasonably appears to be a potential claimant with standing to contest the forfeiture in the ancillary proceeding.

b) *Content of the Notice*. The notice must describe the forfeiture property, state the times under the applicable statute when a petition contesting the forfeiture must be filed, and state the name and contract information for the government attorney to be served with the petition.

c) *Means of Publication; Exceptions to Publication Requirement.* Publication must take place as described in Supplemental Rule G(4)(a)(iii) of the Federal Rules of Civil Procedure, and may be by any means described in Supplemental Rule G(4)(a)(iv). Publication is unnecessary if any exception in Supplemental Rule G(4)(a)(i) applies.

Thus, as soon a practical following the entry of a preliminary order of forfeiture in a criminal case, the Government should publish notice of the forfeiture in a manner consistent with the provisions of Supplemental Rule G(4)(a) of the Supplemental Rules for Admiralty or

Maritime Claims and Asset Forfeiture Actions. As described in Rule G(4)(a)(iv), this may include publication on the Government's forfeiture website on the Internet (www.forfeiture.gov). The notice must describe the forfeited property, state the times under the applicable statute when a petition contesting the forfeiture must be filed, and the name and contact information for the government attorney to be served with the petition. The Government should also send direct written notice to any person who reasonably appears to be a potential claimant with standing to contest the forfeiture of the property in the ancillary proceeding.

Rule 32.2(b)(6)(C) now specifically incorporates the exceptions to publication in Supplemental Rule G(4)(a)(i). Because Internet publication costs essentially nothing, prosecutors may determine to publish notice on the Internet in all criminal forfeiture cases rather than run the risk of challenges based on whether the value of the asset is actually below the $1,000 threshold prescribed in Rule G(4)(a)(i)(A).[29]

VI. Preference for Federal Forfeiture

As a general rule, if property is seized as part of an ongoing federal criminal investigation and the criminal defendants are being prosecuted in federal court—or it is anticipated that a federal prosecution will be pursued—the forfeiture action should be commenced administratively by a federal agency or pursued in federal court regardless of whether a local, state, or federal agency made the seizure. Forfeitures should follow the prosecution for both legal and practical reasons. Parallel state forfeitures can jeopardize the pending federal criminal investigation or prosecution and create unnecessary confusion. Where federal resources are expended on an investigation and state and local law enforcement are assisting in a federal prosecution, federal forfeiture, administrative or judicial, should be pursued absent extraordinary circumstances. The efforts of state and local law enforcement should be recognized through formal equitable sharing rather than a division of assets between state and federal forfeiture.

However, certain circumstances may make state forfeiture appropriate. These circumstances include but are not limited to the following:

1) a state forfeiture is commenced on the seized asset before the federal agency joins the investigation and has either been concluded or substantial litigation has been conducted.
2) an existing memorandum of understanding sets forth a different procedure for the handling of the seizures and forfeitures.
3) the asset was seized by a state or local agency and state law requires a turnover order. A decision not to seek the turnover order must be coordinated with agency counsel and the federal prosecuting official; if an adverse order is entered by the state court, then agency counsel, the federal prosecuting official, and the local prosecuting attorney must participate in deciding how to proceed.[30]
4) the seized asset does not meet the Department of Justice's minimum monetary thresholds.
5) the pertinent federal prosecuting official has reviewed the case, declined to initiate forfeiture proceedings, and approved a referral for state forfeiture.

When a federal agency believes a state forfeiture is appropriate, the referral of an asset for state forfeiture must be discussed with agency counsel and the federal prosecuting official responsible for asset forfeiture.

If significant assets are referred for state forfeiture, without the prior consultation discussed above, after a determination to seek federal prosecution has been made, a federal prosecuting official may then decline to go forward with the federal prosecution.

If there is a state forfeiture related to a federal criminal prosecution, federal equitable sharing requests and decisions must take into account the entire case, and seizures should be reviewed before equitable sharing recommendations or decisions are made.

VII. Firearms Forfeiture Policy Summary

This section provides a brief summary of policies bearing on the forfeiture of firearms. For further details on firearms forfeiture matters, prosecutors and law enforcement agencies should consult AFMLS.

A. Firearms Are Treated Differently

Forfeited firearms and ammunition are treated differently from other types of forfeited property in several respects. As explained below, they are not shared with state and local law enforcement, they are not sold, and most often they are destroyed.

Forfeited firearms may be placed into federal official use by the U.S. Marshals Service (USMS) and the Bureau of Alcohol, Tobacco, Firearms and Explosives (ATF) or a federal investigative agency for such purposes as federal law enforcement use, ballistics testing, or display. USMS does not equitably share firearms with non-federal law enforcement agencies, and does not sell them. USMS policy and practice in this respect are consistent with those of ATF, Drug Enforcement Administration (DEA), Federal Bureau of Investigation (FBI), and the General Services Administration (GSA). In rare cases, firearms with specific, certain, and significant historical value are placed into official use for display purposes only by a non-participating federal agency, such as the Smithsonian Institution or one of the four U.S. military museums. USMS approves this type of official use only after the subject firearms have been rendered inoperable.

Minimum value and net equity thresholds do not apply to firearms. As explained in part 1 of this *Manual*, the Department of Justice has established minimum monetary thresholds as to most types of property subject to federal seizure and forfeiture, and generally will not seize property for forfeiture, or adopt a state or local law enforcement seizure for federal forfeiture, unless the net equity in the seized property meets or exceeds these thresholds. There is an exception to the net equity thresholds where a particular forfeiture serves a compelling law enforcement interest. The Department has concluded that such a compelling interest applies to firearms and ammunition involved in crime. Therefore, unlike most forms of personal property, lawfully forfeitable firearms and ammunition may be, and should be, forfeited and adopted for forfeiture regardless of their monetary value.

There are at least two reasons for exempting firearms and ammunition from the minimum equity thresholds. Because cheap firearms, used criminally, cause harm the same as expensive ones, there is a strong law enforcement interest in removing both types from circulation. Moreover, as discussed below, the Federal Government generally destroys forfeited firearms and ammunition, and never resells them. Therefore, their potential resale value is simply irrelevant to the determination whether or not to forfeit them.

Unlike other types of forfeited property, federally forfeited firearms and ammunition *may not be sold*, except as scrap. Title 18, United States Code, section 3051(c)(3) provides, "*Notwithstanding any other provision of law*, the disposition of firearms forfeited by reason of a violation of *any law of the United States* shall be governed by the provisions of section 5872(b) of the Internal Revenue Code of 1986." 18 U.S.C. § 3051(c)(3) (emphasis added). Section 5872(b) provides that no notice of public sale is required as to forfeited firearms *and that no forfeited firearm may be sold at public sale*. 26 U.S.C. § 5872(b). Although section 5872(b) permits forfeited firearms to be retained for *federal* official use, forfeited firearms are not transferred to state or local law enforcement agencies through equitable sharing or otherwise. Although section 5872(b) indicates that GSA could sell forfeited firearms to state or local governments, GSA has determined that it will not do so. GSA's regulations provide that seized and forfeited firearms shall not be sold as firearms, but only as scrap "after total destruction." *See* 41 C.F.R. § 101-48.303, 102-42.1102-10(c) (July 2006). As a result, seized and forfeited firearms cannot be sold, and are generally destroyed.

Because sales of federally forfeited firearms are prohibited, prosecutors should take care not to enter into any agreement calling for the sale of forfeited firearms and the distribution of proceeds from any such sale. Because there can be no sale, there can be no proceeds—a fact that distinguishes forfeitures of firearms from forfeitures of most other types of property. Prosecutors should bring this prohibition on sale of forfeited firearms to the attention of the court whenever necessary to avoid entry of an order calling for such a prohibited sale. The overriding policy concern weighing against the sale or sharing of forfeited or abandoned firearms is that they may subsequently be resold and used in crime.

B. Preference for Forfeiture

Forfeiture is the preferred way to dispose of crime-related firearms and ammunition. Forfeiture is most consistent with congressional intent, as reflected in the many specific and general forfeiture statutes that apply to firearms. Forfeiture proceedings also provide the best and clearest protections for the due process rights of firearms' owners, including the rights of innocent third parties who may have a lawful interest in firearms that have been stolen or otherwise used without the owners' knowledge and consent.

Although there are other lawful ways of disposing of crime-related firearms and ammunition in cases where forfeiture is not possible, including abandonment, non-forfeiture "quiet title" actions, and other equitable proceedings, *see*, e.g., *United States v. Howell*, 425 F.3d 971 (11th Cir. 2005), it is Department of Justice policy to subject seized crime-related firearms to formal forfeiture proceedings wherever possible.

PART 3: SETTLEMENTS

I. General Policy

A. Scope

For purposes of this part, the term *settlement* includes the following:

- In a criminal forfeiture case—

1) A plea agreement with a criminal defendant that includes a criminal case in which there is an agreement regarding the forfeiture of property; or
2) An agreement to resolve a third party claim in the ancillary proceeding in a criminal case.

- In a civil forfeiture case, the resolution of a claim filed by any claimant in a civil forfeiture case, either before or after the judicial complaint is filed.

B. Principles

Settlements to forfeit property are encouraged to conserve the resources of both the United States and claimants in situations where justice will be served. The following principles must be observed when negotiating and structuring settlements.

B.1. Factual Basis

There must be a statutory basis for the forfeiture of the property and sufficient facts stated in the settlement documents to satisfy the elements of the statute.

B.2. Consultation

All settlements must be negotiated in consultation with the seizing agency[1] and the U.S. Marshals Service (USMS).[2] The seizing agency's input is essential in order to reach a settlement that is based on a common understanding of the facts and circumstances surrounding the seizure. Moreover, settlements occasionally require that administrative action be taken by the agency to implement those settlements, including, on occasion, a referral of the case back to the agency for administrative forfeiture of all or some of the seized property. Input from the USMS should always be sought to determine any current and prospective expenses to ensure that the settlement is fiscally sound from the Government's perspective and that ownership interests and title issues are adequately addressed in the settlement agreement allowing the USMS to carry out the terms of the settlement.

B.3. Recovery of Investigative and Other Costs

In general, the Government should not attempt to use a settlement to recover the costs of its investigation. It may be appropriate in unusual circumstances, however, to recover extraordinary expenditures, such as funds needed to clean up environmental damage to the forfeited property.

B.4. Status of Administrative Forfeiture

Before discussing any settlement, the Assistant U.S. Attorney (AUSA) and the investigating agent must determine what property, if any, is presently being processed for administrative forfeiture or has previously been declared administratively forfeited. AUSAs may not reach agreements with defendants or their counsel in a criminal case regarding the return of property that is the subject of a pending administrative forfeiture proceeding without first consulting the seizing agency.[3] Property that has been administratively forfeited belongs to the Government and, therefore, cannot be returned to a defendant or used to pay restitution or other obligations of the defendant as part of a plea agreement.

B.5. Disagreements

If the seizing agency or the USMS disagrees with the U.S. Attorney's recommended settlement proposal, it may refer the matter to the Chief of the Asset Forfeiture and Money Laundering Section (AFMLS) for resolution.

B.6. Property Located in Another District

To settle a forfeiture action involving property located in another judicial district, the U.S. Attorney's Office (USAO) handling the forfeiture must notify and coordinate with the USAO and the USMS in the district where the property is located. It is the responsibility of the USAO in the district that forfeits property located in another district to comply with the requirements for forfeiture in the district where the property is located. Failure to comply with such requirements may result in a cloud on the Government's title that may interfere with the disposal of assets in accordance with settlement terms; coordination will minimize this possibility.

B.7. Global Settlements

The Government may conclude a civil or administrative forfeiture action in conjunction with the resolution of the criminal charges involving the same activity that gave rise to the forfeiture of the property. The following principles should be observed in negotiating such a global settlement:

(1) The Government should *not* agree to release property subject to forfeiture (civil or criminal) in order to *coerce* a guilty plea on the substantive charges, nor should the Government agree to dismiss criminal charges in order to *coerce* a forfeiture settlement.

(2) To the maximum extent possible, the criminal plea and forfeiture should conclude the defendant's business with the Government. Delaying consideration of the forfeiture until after the conclusion of the criminal case unnecessarily extends the Government's involvement with the defendant and diminishes the effectiveness and efficiency of forfeiture enforcement.

(3) If a plea agreement in a criminal case does not resolve the criminal forfeiture or a related civil forfeiture case, express language to this effect should be included in the plea agreement so as to remove any doubt or ambiguity on this point.

(4) Where a defendant who is also a claimant in a related civil forfeiture action has negotiated a plea agreement in the criminal case and concurrently wishes to forfeit the property in the related civil forfeiture action, the plea agreement should state that the claimant/defendant is waiving any and all rights—constitutional, statutory, or otherwise—with respect to the forfeiture. Any civil settlement should be documented independently of the plea agreement and should include the following information:
   a) The claimant/defendant's interest in the property;
   b) An admission of the facts supporting forfeiture;
   c) That the claimant/defendant forfeits all rights to the property; and
   d) That he or she waives any and all right to contest the forfeiture of the property.

(5) The defendant, in the plea agreement, must admit to facts sufficient to support the forfeiture. The Government, however, should expressly reserve its right to reopen the civil forfeiture action in the event it is later determined that the settlement was based

on false information or where the defendant violates the plea agreement or the agreement is invalidated for any other reason.

B.8. Partial Payments

Settlements shall not provide for partial payments, except upon the advice and approval of AFMLS in consultation with the USMS, Headquarters Asset Forfeiture Division.[4]

B.9. Reacquiring the Property

The settlement should state that the claimant/defendant may not reacquire the forfeited property directly or indirectly through family members or any other agent. Family members who already own a partial interest in the forfeited property may, however, purchase the forfeited interest with legitimate funds.

B.10. Effect on Taxes and Other Obligations

Settlement documents should clearly state that the terms of the settlement, unless specified, do not affect the tax obligations, fines, penalties, or any other monetary obligations of the claimant/defendant owed to the Government.

USAOs are obligated pursuant to 28 U.S.C. § 547(4) to "institute and prosecute proceedings for the collection of fines, penalties, and forfeitures incurred for violation of any revenue law, unless satisfied on investigation that justice does not require the proceedings." Therefore, in order that appropriate actions may be taken when a proposed forfeiture settlement will release assets to a claimant/defendant who is known or likely to have other outstanding obligations to the United States (e.g., taxes), AUSAs should routinely notify the appropriate agency (e.g., Internal Revenue Service) of the proposed settlement.

The Debt Collection Improvement Act of 1996 (DCIA) requires the Department of the Treasury and other disbursing officials to offset federal payments to collect delinquent non-tax debts owed to the United States and to collect delinquent debts owed to states. The Treasury Offset Program (TOP) is designed to offset payments related to the DCIA. Accordingly, settlements should also notify the claimant/defendant that any funds currently on deposit in the Seized Asset Deposit Fund or Assets Forfeiture Fund will have to be processed through TOP before being returned to the claimant/defendant, with the possibility that any of the claimant/defendant's outstanding and delinquent obligations to the federal or a state government might be offset against the payment.

B.11. Settlement Authority

The authority of the U.S. Attorney to settle a forfeiture matter is circumscribed by Attorney General Order No. 1598-92, which, *inter alia*, authorizes the Assistant Attorney General for the Criminal Division to re-delegate the maximum amount of his settlement authority to U.S. Attorneys. Accordingly, the Assistant Attorney General for the Criminal Division may re-delegate to U.S. Attorneys up to $1 million to settle civil and criminal cases, subject to the approval of the Deputy Attorney General. 28 C.F.R. §§ 0.168(b), (d). Pursuant to that authority, the Assistant Attorney General for the Criminal Division has delegated, with the approval of the Deputy Attorney General, the following settlement authority to U.S. Attorneys.[5]

II. Authority of the U.S. Attorney to Enter into a Settlement

(1) Except as provided in section IX of this part, U.S. Attorneys have the authority to settle any civil or criminal forfeiture case in which the amount involved does not exceed $1 million, regardless of the amount to be released to the claimant or defendant; or

(2) Except as provided in section IX of this part, U.S. Attorneys also have the authority to settle any civil or criminal forfeiture case in which the amount involved is between $1 million and $5 million, if the amount to be released to the claimant or defendant does not exceed 15 percent of the original claim. The maximum settlement under the second scenario is at $750,000, which is 15 percent of $5 million.

(3) In all other cases, the U.S. Attorney must obtain approval of the settlement from AFMLS.

For the purposes of this provision, the term *amount involved* is defined as follows:

(1) In a civil forfeiture case, the *amount involved* is the fair market value of the interest claimed by the person with whom the Government is attempting to reach a settlement. If the person is claiming an interest in more than one asset, the amount involved is the aggregate of those interests. For example, if the defendant property is a dwelling with a fair market value of $1.2 million, and the claimant is a lienholder asserting a $400,000 lien, for purposes of reaching a settlement with the lienholder the amount involved is $400,000. In the same case, if the claimant is the owner who acknowledges the validity of the lien but is contesting the forfeiture of the equity in the property, for purposes of reaching a settlement with the owner the amount involved is $800,000. But if the claimant is the owner who is also contesting the forfeiture of three other assets with a combined value of $350,000, the amount involved would be $1.15 million.

(2) In a criminal forfeiture case, the *amount involved* is the fair market value of the defendant's interest in the aggregate value of any property that has been seized, restrained, or specifically identified as property subject to forfeiture in any forfeiture count, allegation, or bill of particulars, including substitute assets, but does not include the amount of a money judgment to the extent that there are no known assets available to satisfy the judgment. For example, if the Government has seized several assets and restrained other assets for the purpose of forfeiture in connection with a criminal prosecution, and has also alleged in the indictment that the defendant is liable for a $2 million money judgment, for purposes of negotiating a plea agreement with the defendant the amount involved is the aggregate value of the defendant's interest in all the assets that have actually been seized or restrained, but would not include the $2 million unless it appears that there are assets currently available that may be forfeited in satisfaction of the judgment.

(3) In the ancillary proceeding in a criminal case, the *amount involved* is the fair market value of the interest in the forfeited property that is claimed by the third party with whom the Government is attempting to reach a settlement.

The *amount to be released* means the value of the property that a claimant, defendant, or third party in an ancillary proceeding would recover or would be permitted to retain.

III. Authority of AFMLS to Approve a Settlement

The Chief of AFMLS[6] has the authority to approve any settlement in which the amount involved is less than $2 million and the amount being returned is less than 15 percent of the amount involved. If the amount to be released exceeds 15 percent of the amount involved *and* is more than $2 million, the settlement must be approved by the Deputy Attorney General.[7]

A. Examples

(1) The Government brings a civil forfeiture action against an asset with a market value of $1.5 million but in which the sole claimant has only $250,000 in equity. The Government agrees to abandon the forfeiture and release the entire asset to the claimant. Because the total value of the equity involved is less than $1 million, the U.S. Attorney has authority to approve the settlement.

(2) The Government files a civil forfeiture action against seized bank accounts and currency in the amount of $1.8 million, but agrees as part of a settlement to release 20 percent ($360,000) to the claimant. Because the total value of the property exceeds $1 million, the U.S. Attorney does not have authority to settle the case without approval from the Department of Justice; but because the amount to be returned does not exceed $2 million, the Chief of AFMLS would have the authority to approve the settlement without having to consult with the Deputy Attorney General, even though the amount to be returned is more than 15 percent of the total value.

(3) A criminal indictment alleges that the defendant must forfeit, upon conviction, various assets in which the defendant has a total equity of $3 million. The assets are neither seized nor restrained, but are listed in the forfeiture allegation in the indictment. As part of a plea agreement, the Government agrees not to go forward with the forfeiture of most of the assets but instead agrees to accept a lump sum payment of $750,000 in lieu of forfeiture. Because the defendant is being allowed to retain assets worth more than $2 million and representing more than 15 percent of the total value of the property subject to forfeiture, the plea agreement must be approved by the Deputy Attorney General.

IV. Using Administrative Forfeiture to Effect a Settlement

The following procedures apply to settlement agreements in civil judicial forfeiture cases and to criminal forfeiture plea agreements where an administrative forfeiture is necessary to effectuate the agreement. In such cases, the headquarters of the seizing agency involved must be consulted by the USAO prior to finalizing an agreement in order to ensure the agency can accommodate the terms of the agreement.[8] The Department of Justice's policy is to pursue an agreed upon administrative forfeiture where it is possible and economically efficient to do so.

A. Settlement of Forfeiture After a Claim Is Filed in an Administrative Forfeiture Proceeding, but Before a Judicial Complaint Is Filed

The following requirements must be met where a claim has been filed in response to a notice of administrative forfeiture and the case has been referred to the U.S. Attorney, but a settlement is reached before a civil judicial complaint is filed.

(1) The terms of the settlement should be reduced to writing by the U.S. Attorney and include the following:

a) A provision whereby the claimant/defendant identifies his or her ownership interest in the property to be forfeited;
b) A provision whereby the claimant/defendant gives up all of the right, title, and interest in the property so identified;
c) A provision whereby the claimant/defendant agrees not to contest the Government's administrative forfeiture action and waives all deadlines under 18 U.S.C. § 983(a);
d) A provision whereby the claimant/defendant agrees and states that the property to be forfeited administratively was connected to the illegal activity as proscribed by the applicable civil forfeiture statute (e.g., money to be forfeited is in fact proceeds from illegal drug trafficking);
e) Specific reference to the withdrawal of the claim; and
f) A "hold harmless" provision and a general waiver of Federal Tort Claims Act rights and *Bivens* actions, as well as a waiver of all constitutional and statutory defenses and claims.

(2) The case should promptly be referred back to the seizing agency to reinstitute the administrative process. The seizing agency shall reinstitute the administrative forfeiture process to effectuate the agreement upon receipt of a referral in compliance with this policy, consistent with its lawful authority.

Where the agreement provides for the claimant to withdraw the claim to all property subject to forfeiture, the entire case will be referred back to the agency for administrative forfeiture unless, of course, other claims have been filed as to the same property.

Where the agreement provides for the claimant to withdraw only a part of a claim, the case will be referred back to the agency for administrative forfeiture of that portion of the forfeitable property named in the agreement, and the agency may release the remainder to the claimant consistent with the settlement.

Republication of the notice or of the administrative forfeiture action is not necessary, provided publication covering the property to be forfeited occurred prior to the filing of the claim.

B. Settlement of Civil Judicial Forfeiture Without Prior Administrative Action

The following requirements must be met where the judicial action was commenced without a prior administrative forfeiture action, and a settlement agreement has been reached involving a proposed administrative forfeiture of seized property.

1) The headquarters of the seizing agency must concur in that part of the settlement that would obligate the agency to commence administrative forfeiture proceedings;
2) The complaint must be dismissed or amended so as to strike the assets to be administratively forfeited; and
3) The jurisdiction of the district court over the assets to be administratively forfeited must be relinquished before referral may be made to a seizing agency under this policy.

The seizing agency shall initiate the administrative forfeiture process to effectuate such an agreement upon receipt of a referral in compliance with this policy, consistent with its lawful authority.

C. Using Administrative Forfeiture to Settle a Criminal Forfeiture Action

In cases where property has been seized or restrained for forfeiture under criminal statutes, and an agreement relating to a proposed administrative forfeiture of the property has been reached between the U.S. Attorney and the claimant/defendant prior to entry of a preliminary order of forfeiture against the defendant's interest in the subject property,

1) The headquarters of the seizing agency must concur in that part of the settlement that would obligate the agency to commence administrative forfeiture proceedings;
2) The seizure or restraining orders must be dismissed or vacated as to the property to be administratively forfeited; and
3) The jurisdiction of the district court over the property to be administratively forfeited must be relinquished. The seizing agency shall initiate the administrative forfeiture process to effectuate such an agreement upon receipt of a referral in compliance with this policy, consistent with its lawful authority.

V. References to the Remission or Restoration Processes in Settlements

No agreement—whether a settlement in a civil judicial action, or a plea agreement resolving both criminal charges and the forfeiture of assets in a criminal case, or settlement of a claim in an ancillary proceeding—may contain any provision binding the Department of Justice and the agencies to a particular decision on a petition for remission or request for restoration, or otherwise contain terms the effectiveness of which is contingent upon the making of such a particular decision. The remission and restoration processes, like the pardon process in criminal cases, are completely independent of the litigation and case settlement process.

It is proper to include in a settlement agreement a provision that expressly leaves open or expressly forecloses the right of any party to file a petition for remission or mitigation.

VI. Settlements in Civil Judicial Forfeiture Cases

Any settlement that purports to forfeit property binds only the parties to it and forfeits only the interest in the property that the settling claimant possesses. The following procedures must be followed to ensure that a valid and complete civil judicial forfeiture of the interest occurs through the settlement occurs:

1) A civil verified complaint for forfeiture of the property must be filed in the U.S. district court to establish the court's jurisdiction. Filing an action as a "miscellaneous docket" and other attempts to shortcut the process will not be recognized as a valid forfeiture;
2) All known parties in interest must be given written notice, and notice by publication must be made;
3) If no timely claim has been filed pursuant to the Supplemental Rules for Certain Admiralty or Maritime and Asset Forfeiture Claims, a default judgment pursuant to Fed. R. Civ. P. 55 must be sought as to all interests in the property other than the interest(s) subject to the settlement agreement; and
4) Proposed orders of forfeiture that fully incorporate the terms of the settlement must be filed with the settlement agreement and include the terms of the settlement agreement.

VII. SETTLEMENTS IN CRIMINAL FORFEITURE CASES

In any plea agreement, a defendant may only consent to the forfeiture of his or her interest in the property. Forfeiture of the defendant's interest in property held by nominees can proceed criminally, but the potential for an ancillary claim by the nominee must be anticipated. A settlement that purports to forfeit the property may only bind the parties to it and transfers only the interest that the settling claimant/defendant possesses.

The following procedures must be followed to ensure that a valid forfeiture results from a plea settlement:

1) There must be a forfeiture count or allegation in the indictment or information; otherwise, forfeiture is legally impossible. To the extent property is known to be subject to forfeiture, it should be listed in the indictment, information, or in a subsequent bill of particulars. The USAO must ensure that its criminal pleadings are in compliance with Rule 32.2 of the Federal Rules of Criminal Procedure;
2) The U.S. Attorney must comply with the requirements applicable to third party interests (e.g., 21 U.S.C. §§ 853(n)(1)-(7)), and the provisions of Rule 32.2 of the Federal Rules of Criminal Procedure, including affording third parties with notice of the forfeiture and of their right to obtain an post-conviction adjudication of their interests in the property;
3) The settlement to forfeit property must be in writing, and the defendant must expressly stipulate to all facts supporting the forfeiture and waive all statutory and constitutional defenses to the forfeiture;

4) The court must issue a preliminary order of forfeiture that incorporates the settlement and must include the forfeiture order in the oral pronouncement of the sentence in the presence of the defendant and in the written judgment of conviction at sentencing; and
5) Wherever possible, in order to avoid protracted litigation of ownership issues in the context of ancillary hearings, the United States should agree to accept unencumbered property only, with the exception of valid financial institution liens, or at the very least, the plea agreement should require the defendant to convey clear title to the Government.[9] Short of this, the Government should seek to obtain from the settling defendant, as part of the plea agreement, sworn factual stipulations that may be useful against any non-pleading codefendants who might assert an interest in the same property in the "forfeiture phase" of the criminal prosecution or any claims that might be filed by third parties as to the same property in either the ancillary proceeding or any parallel civil forfeiture action.

VIII. Acceptance of a Monetary Amount in Lieu of Forfeiture of Other Tangible Property

A. Introduction

When it is in the interests of justice, and subject to the limitations described in this section, which have been imposed as a matter of policy rather than statutory requirement, the Government may accept and forfeit an agreed amount of money in lieu of seized forfeitable property. In a judicial forfeiture case, with court approval, the Government may also accept and forfeit an agreed amount of money in lieu of forfeitable property, including real estate, that has not been seized.

Accepting and forfeiting a sum of money in place of directly forfeitable property and releasing the forfeitable latter property effectively moots any unsettled forfeiture claims against the released property. It is imperative, therefore, that *all* interests in the property be resolved before the property is released.

B. Policy Considerations

The many federal forfeiture statutes reflect congressional policy that property constituting or derived from criminal proceeds and property used to commit crime should be taken away from those who took it from victims or illicit customers, committed crimes with it, or let others use it to commit crime. Forfeiting the "tainted" property itself accomplishes this goal more directly and clearly than forfeiting an agreed sum of money leaving the property in the hands of those whose acts or failures to act made it forfeitable. It is Department of Justice policy to forfeit available directly implicated property rather than a sum of money unless the interests of justice favor.

There are circumstances where accepting and forfeiting an amount of money in lieu of the property linked to an underlying offense is in the interests of justice, including cases where innocent owners own all but a small portion of the property, where forfeiture of the particular property will cause an undue hardship on innocent owners, and where, after balancing the costs and risks of continued litigation, the Government determines that settling for part of the value of allegedly forfeitable property is just and appropriate.

This discussion of accepting money in lieu of forfeitable property is limited to cases where the forfeitable property is available for forfeiture, and forfeiting a sum of money instead leaves the forfeitable property in the hands of some or all of its present owners. The policy concerns discussed in this section do not arise when the Government forfeits substitute assets under 21 U.S.C. § 853(p) because directly forfeitable property is unavailable, or sells property, either before or after forfeiture, to persons not involved in or associated with the underlying criminal activity.

C. Applicable Procedures

The following procedures must be followed when the Government accepts and forfeits money in lieu of other property:

1) **Administrative forfeitures**. 19 U.S.C. § 1613(c), as incorporated by, e.g., 18 U.S.C. § 981(d), 21 U.S.C. §§ 853(j), 881(d), permits federal seizing agencies, as a form of relief from administrative forfeiture, to accept and forfeit a sum of money in lieu of forfeitable seized property. *See also* 19 U.S.C. § 1614. As a matter of policy and discretion, however, the Drug Enforcement Administration (DEA) and the Federal Bureau of Investigation (FBI) limit their use of this authority to cases where such substitution is determined to be in the interests of justice and a timely claim for the forfeitable property has been filed pursuant to 18 U.S.C. § 983(a)(2) and referred by the seizing agency to the USAO for initiation of judicial forfeiture proceedings. After consultation with the seizing agency (*see* section I.B.2), the USAO may accept a monetary amount in lieu of forfeiture of the seized property and refer the matter back to the seizing agency to effect the settlement (*see* section IV).
2) **Judicial forfeitures**. After commencing a judicial forfeiture case, with court approval, and pursuant to an appropriate order of forfeiture, the Government may accept and forfeit an agreed sum of money in lieu of forfeitable property.

D. Discussion

When it is in the interests of justice, the Government may forfeit a sum of money in place of directly forfeitable property or a directly forfeitable partial interest in otherwise non-forfeitable property. Parties often agree to substitute forfeiture of a sum of money in place of directly forfeitable property in connection with a settlement. When courts order an interlocutory sale of forfeitable property, by agreement or otherwise, the net sale proceeds also typically become a substitute res in a civil forfeiture proceeding or a replacement for directly forfeitable property in a criminal forfeiture proceeding. Legal authority to forfeit money in lieu of other property is found in the applicable statutes, rules, regulations, and case law summarized below.

Subject to any applicable regulations[10] and the policy restrictions described herein, which have been imposed as a matter of policy, an agency in an administrative forfeiture proceeding may accept and forfeit a sum of money in lieu of directly forfeitable property that has been seized. The authority for doing this is found under 19 U.S.C. § 1613(c), which terms such replacement as a form of "relief" from the forfeiture, and under 19 U.S.C. § 1614, which authorizes agencies to release property seized for administrative forfeiture upon payment of "the value of" such property. These statutes specify that the replacement sum of money is "treated in the same manner as the proceeds of sale of a forfeited item." 19 U.S.C. § 1613(c).

The customs laws, including sections 1613(c) and 1614, are incorporated by reference into most civil and criminal forfeiture statutes. *See*, e.g., 18 U.S.C. § 981(d), 21 U.S.C. §§ 853(j), 881(d). Therefore, sections 1613(c) and 1614 also authorize forfeiture of a sum of money in place of directly forfeitable property that has been seized in most judicial forfeiture cases, although, of course, in judicial forfeiture cases, both the replacement of money for the directly forfeitable property with the sum of money and the forfeiture of the replacement sum of money require the court's approval. *See*, e.g., *United States v. Approximately 64,695 Pounds of Shark Fins*, 353 F. Supp. 2d 1095, 1098-99 (S.D. Cal. 2005) (court permitted claimant to post bond as substitute res in exchange for release of seized shark fins, which claimant was then permitted to sell).

Although section 1613(c) and section 1614 apply by their terms only to "seized" property, substituting and forfeiting an agreed amount of money in lieu of directly forfeitable property has not been so limited. Courts have recognized, generally without reference to particular statutory authority, that parties to a forfeiture case may agree to replace the directly forfeitable property with a sum of money, and then may settle or litigate the forfeiture on the same legal theory that applied to the directly forfeitable property, with the money serving as substitute res. In *Republic National Bank of Miami v. United States*, 506 U.S. 80, 82-83 (1992), the Court noted, without comment, that by agreement and with court approval, forfeitable real property had been sold and the proceeds treated as a substitute res. In *Ventura Packers, Inc. v. F/V Jeanine Kathleen*, 424 F.3d 852, 855 (9th Cir. 2005) (a private in rem action to enforce a lien on vessels), the court, like the Supreme Court in *Republic National Bank,* assumed it was proper to replace substitute money for the defendant vessels with a sum of money and a bond, and focused instead upon whether the district court lost in rem jurisdiction when the substitute replacement money and bond were transferred out of the district after the claimants prevailed in the district court.[11]

Similarly, in *United States v. Real Property Located at 22 Santa Barbara Drive*, 264 F.3d 860, 866-67 (9th Cir. 2001), the forfeitable real property was sold in 1991, the proceeds became a substitute res, and litigation over a variety of issues—but never the propriety of the substitution—continued for another ten years. In *United States v. An Article of Drug Consisting of 4,680 Pails*, 725 F.2d 976, 983 n.20 (5th Cir. 1984), which focused upon whether the district court lost jurisdiction when seized animal drug powder was mistakenly released and then removed from the district, the court of appeals described selling forfeitable property and using the sale proceeds as a "substitute *res* for jurisdictional purposes" as "an often-used and legitimate practice." *See also United States v. Twelve Pieces of Real Property*, 54 F. App'x 461, 463-64 (9th Cir. 2003) (affirming forfeiture of money that replaced facilitating real property in a drug trafficking case); *United States v. $180,893.00*, 39 F. App'x 570, 571-73 (same); *United States v. 250 Lindsay Lane*, 2005 WL 1994762 at *5 (W.D. Ky. Aug. 16, 2005) (by agreement, proceeds from sale of real property allegedly purchased with healthcare fraud proceeds became substitute res); *United States v. $1.5 Million Letter of Credit as a Substitute Res for Seized Bank Accounts*, 1992 WL 204357 at *2 (S.D.N.Y. Aug. 7, 1992) (by stipulation, parties substituted $1.5 million letter of credit for approximately $4.3 million contents of seized bank accounts); *United States v. An Article of Drug Consisting of 4,680 Pails,* 725 F.2d 976, 983 n.20 (5th Cir. 1984) (dictum describing the pre-judgment sale of forfeitable property and use of the sale proceeds as a "substitute *res* for jurisdictional purposes" as "an often-used and legitimate practice;" citation omitted).

In addition to the common law, there is statutory authority for substitution in many cases. In all criminal forfeitures, and most civil forfeitures, courts have broad power to take any action necessary to preserve the forfeitable value of property. *See* 21 U.S.C. § 853(e)(1); 18 U.S.C. § 983(j)(1). Liquidation of the property, replacing it with a sum of money, is often an effective means of preserving forfeitable value. In criminal forfeitures, substitution of money for tainted property is authorized under the substitute assets provision, 21 U.S.C. § 853(p), if the defendant has transferred or commingled interests in directly forfeitable property in a way that makes liquidation and forfeiture of the property itself difficult.

Particularly in criminal forfeiture cases, it is important that counsel refer to the replacement sum of money as "cash in lieu" and not as a "substitute asset." The phrase "substitute asset" is a term of art referring to substitute property forfeitable under 21 U.S.C. § 853(p) and 18 U.S.C. § 1963(m). "Substitute assets" are legitimate assets that are subject to forfeiture in place of directly forfeitable property that has been made unavailable for forfeiture solely because of some act or omission of the criminal defendant. Purely as a matter of statutory construction, such "substitute assets" may not be restrained or seized in most jurisdictions prior to the conviction of the criminal defendant. By contrast, "cash is lieu" is a sum of money that replaces directly forfeitable property prior to forfeiture, either by consent of the parties and/or court order, does not replace property that has been made unavailable for forfeiture by some act or omission of the defendant. Rather, it replaces directly forfeitable property that is currently available and does so by consent and/or court order; thus, the replacement sum of money should be subject to restraint and seizure the same as the directly forfeitable property it replaces.

In civil judicial forfeiture cases, interlocutory sales are specifically authorized by Supplemental Rule G(7)(b), which provides that the sale proceeds "are a substitute res subject to forfeiture in place of the property that was sold." Supp. Rule G(7)(b)(iv). Rule G(7)(b) codified preexisting law approving the practice of treating interlocutory sale proceeds as a substitute res under Supp. Rule E(9)(b). *See United States v. One Parcel Lot 41, Berryhill Farm*, 128 F.3d 1386, 1390 (10th Cir. 1997) (interlocutory sale of residence while civil case was stayed pending criminal trial avoided waste and expense and allowed Government to satisfy mortgage); *United States v. Haro-Verdugo*, 2006 WL 1990843, at *2 (D. Ariz. 2006) (magistrate judge recommended interlocutory sale under Supp. Rule E(9)(b) where transient drug dealers were using vacant property and property was deteriorating); *United States v. 2540 Chadwick Way*, 2005 WL 2124539, at *3 (N.D. Ill. 2005) (over claimant's objection, court ordered interlocutory sale of real property pursuant to section 983(j) to avoid mortgage foreclosure); *Aguilar v. United States*, 1999 WL 1067841, at *5 (D. Conn. 1999) (despite claimant's objection, exigent circumstances justified interlocutory sale of real property to prevent vandalism and to pay off mortgage). *See generally* AFMLS' *Guide to Interlocutory Sales and Expedited Settlement.*

Under many forfeiture statutes, the proceeds from sale of forfeitable property are directly forfeitable without the need for formal "substitution" because the scope of direct forfeiture under such statutes is "derived from" or "traceable to" the forfeitable property. *See, e.g.,* 18 U.S.C. § 981(a)(1)(A) (authorizing forfeiture of property traceable to property "involved in" money laundering which includes any property traceable to otherwise forfeitable property); 18 U.S.C. § 981(a)(1)(C) (property derived from "traceable to" property constituting the proceeds of any "specified unlawful activity" proceeds); 21 U.S.C. § 881(a)(6) (property traceable to drug proceeds). "Substitution" of untainted property for forfeitable property is only necessary in the interlocutory sale context where the proceeds from sale of forfeitable property are not themselves directly subject to forfeiture. *See*, e.g., 21 U.S.C. § 881(a)(7) (authorizing forfeiture of facilitating real property, but not of property derived from or traceable to such property).

In judicial forfeiture cases, the Government should request that any interlocutory order substituting money for a forfeitable asset direct the USMS or the appropriate Treasury agency or other property custodian to accept and hold the money, after paying any expenses incurred with respect to the seizure and maintenance of the asset being liquidated or released, pending further orders of the court. Once a substitute res has been forfeited, the USMS or the appropriate Treasury agency must dispose of it in the same manner as other forfeited property.

IX. Agreements to Exempt Attorneys' Fees from Forfeiture

Any agreement to exempt an asset from forfeiture so that it can be transferred to an attorney as fees must be approved by the Assistant Attorney General for the Criminal Division.[12]

PART 4: *QUI TAM* ACTIONS

I. Payment of a Relator's Share

A. Overview of the False Claims Act

The False Claims Act (FCA), 31 U.S.C. §§ 3729-3733, imposes civil liability on any person who submits a false or fraudulent claim to the Government. An action may be filed by the Attorney General, or by a private person on behalf of the United States. *Id.* § 3730(a)-(b); *Vermont Agency of Natural Resources v. United States ex rel. Stevens*, 529 U.S. 765, 769-78 (2000). An action filed by a private person is known as a *qui tam* suit, and the private party filing the action is referred to as the *relator*. The United States can intervene in and take over the litigation of a *qui tam* suit, or permit the relator to pursue the *qui tam* suit on his or her own. *Id.* § 3730(b)(4). If the *qui tam* suit is successful, the United States recovers the judgment and pays part of it to the relator. The relator's share of any recovery depends, in part, on whether the United States intervenes in the action. *Id.* § 3730(d)(1)-(2).[1]

The FCA permits the relator to object to a settlement of the relator's claim. 31 U.S.C. § 3730(c)(2)(B). However, the United States may settle notwithstanding a relator's objection if the court determines after a hearing that the settlement is "fair, adequate, and reasonable." *Id.*

In addition, the FCA provides that in *qui tam* suits the United States "may elect to pursue its claim through any alternate remedy available to the Government, including any administrative proceeding to determine a civil money penalty." *Id.* § 3730(c)(5). The FCA further provides that "the person initiating the action shall have the same rights in such proceeding as such person would have if the action had continued under this section." *Id.*

The purpose of this "alternate remedy" provision is to provide the United States with maximum flexibility to choose the best forum for pursuing its fraud claims against the defendant. *See* S. Rep. 99-345, 99th Cong., 2d Sess. 27, *reprinted in* 1986 U.S.C.C.A.N 5266, 5292. Thus, the alternate remedy provision authorizes the United States to stay the relator's FCA action, and choose instead to pursue its fraud claims against the defendant through an alternative proceeding. *Id.* Congress envisioned that the alternative proceeding would be in lieu of the relator's action under the FCA. *Id.* ("While the Government will have the opportunity to elect its remedy, it will not have an opportunity for dual recovery on the same claim or claims.") To ensure that the relator is not prejudiced in the event the United States pursues an alternate remedy, the relator is granted the same rights in the alternative proceeding that he or she would have had in her civil action under the FCA, including the right to participate in the proceedings, to object to any settlement of the proceeding, and to receive a share of any recovery.

B. Forfeiture Proceedings as Alternate Remedies

The Department's view is that a forfeiture proceeding does not qualify under the FCA as an alternate remedy giving rise to a relator share.[2] The principal basis for this view is that the alternate remedy provision encompasses only those proceedings that are properly viewed as a substitute for the relator's civil claims under the FCA. Thus, the alternate remedy provision is limited to alternative proceedings to redress the submission of false or fraudulent claims, and does not extend to forfeiture or other criminal proceedings that do not serve as a substitute for such claims.

Three district courts have considered the question of whether a criminal proceeding qualifies as an alternate remedy under the FCA. In *United States v. Lustman*, 2006 WL 1207145 (S.D. Ill. May 4, 2006), the court rejected the relators' motion to intervene in, and obtain a share of the proceeds of, a criminal proceeding instituted against one of the defendants named in their *qui tam* action. As part of that criminal proceeding, the defendant was ordered to pay restitution. The court concluded that the alternate remedy provision did not encompass criminal proceedings. The court also concluded that the relators' motion was moot, because the restitution paid by the defendant had already been disbursed.

In *United States ex rel. Oehm v. National Air Cargo, Inc. et al.*, No. 05-CV-242S (W.D.N.Y. Feb. 15, 2008), the United States executed a global settlement with the defendant that resolved the FCA claims as well as separate criminal and civil forfeiture proceedings. The court rejected the relator's request for a share of the global settlement attributable to the criminal and civil forfeiture proceedings, reasoning that "the existence of an 'alternate remedy' can be found only if the government has not pursued the [FCA] claims instituted by the relator." *Id.* at 7-8.

Finally, in *United States v. Bisig*, 2005 WL 3532554 (S.D. Ind. Dec. 21, 2005), the United States sought to freeze the defendants' assets, and then subsequently filed an indictment against the defendants, which included a criminal forfeiture allegation. One of the defendants named in the indictment was also named in a *qui tam* suit, which the United States had declined to take over. The relator in the *qui tam* suit argued that the criminal forfeiture proceeding constituted an alternate remedy to her FCA action, and the court agreed. The court noted that the relator was the first to uncover the fraud, the Government had stayed the relator's case pending a resolution of the criminal proceeding, and the Government's forfeiture action would leave the defendant without any assets. The court concluded on these facts that the United States "had made an actual monetary recovery by the relator in the *qui tam* action either impossible or futile" and thus "in effect, elected to pursue its claim through an alternate remedy under § 3730(c)(5)." The court held that the alternate proceeding in that case, however, was just the criminal forfeiture proceeding, and thus the relator's right to participate as a party was limited to that proceeding, and not the entire criminal prosecution. The court agreed that allowing a relator to participate in criminal proceedings generally "would be an undesirable result."

Although the Department disagrees with the court's ruling in *Bisig*, this case shows that the courts may be inclined to find an alternate remedy where a criminal proceeding will recover most or all of a *qui tam* defendants' assets, particularly if the Government also stayed the relator's *qui tam* suit in favor of the criminal case. Under such circumstances, the courts may conclude, as the *Bisig* court did, that the Government deprived the relator of any meaningful opportunity to pursue her *qui tam* suit, and therefore the criminal proceeding was effectively a substitute for that suit. Accordingly, in such circumstances (i.e., where the criminal proceeding will render the defendant without assets to satisfy a FCA judgment and particularly where the Government has stayed the *qui tam* case to pursue the criminal case) it may be appropriate to consider a negotiated resolution of the alternate remedy issue, provided that other bases to challenge the relator's entitlement to a share do not exist.[3]

C. The Source of the Relator's Right to Recover

To the extent that a relator is awarded a share of any forfeiture proceeds under the FCA's alternate remedy provision, the relator's entitlement to the proceeds arises strictly out of the FCA and does not constitute a claim of ownership or interest in the specific property forfeited. Consequently, a *qui tam* relator does not qualify as a third party entitled to relief pursuant to 21 U.S.C. § 853(n) or 18 U.S.C. § 983(d). *See Bisig*, 2005 WL 3532554 at *6-7 (granting relator's motions to intervene and for adjudication of relator's interest in forfeited property despite the fact that relator does not qualify for relief under section 853(n) because relator has a valid claim under the FCA). Likewise, the *qui tam* relator is not a victim or third party generally entitled to recovery pursuant to the regulations governing petitions for remission. *See* 28 C.F.R. § 9.4(b) (2011) (providing that only petitioners as defined in section 9.2(o) or attorneys and guardians on their behalf may file a petition for remission); 28 C.F.R. § 9.2(o) (2005) (defining *petitioner* to include an owner, a lienholder, or a victim as defined in other subparts of section 9.2).

D. The Relator's Share is a Percentage of the Net Forfeiture Recovery

If a court orders, or the Commercial Litigation Branch (Fraud Section) decides, that the forfeiture is an alternate proceeding and the relator is entitled to a share of the recovery, then the relator must be awarded a percentage of the net forfeiture recovery.[4] Determining the exact percentage share to be received by the relator should be determined in the FCA action by agreement of the parties or by adjudication.[5] While it is preferable for this determination to be made prior to the final disposition of the forfeited assets, this may not always occur. In fact, where the FCA action will be litigated after the forfeiture proceeding, it is unlikely that the relator's share will be determined prior to the final disposition of the forfeited assets. In such instances, the relator might request that up to 25 percent of the total forfeiture recovery be escrowed in case such funds are later needed to satisfy the relator's share.[6] Because the proceeds of the forfeiture will be deposited into the Department of Justice Assets Forfeiture Fund (AFF), an escrow is not necessary and should be opposed.

Determining the dollar value of the relator's share is more complicated. In the context of a forfeiture, "the proceeds of the action" would be the amount of money available for deposit into the AFF—i.e., the net recovery, which can be defined as the value of the forfeited property less the value of any liens and the costs associated with the seizure, forfeiture, and disposal of the property. Consequently, the dollar value of the relator's share cannot be determined until all liens and expenses are paid and the amount available for deposit into the AFF is fixed.[7]

The dollar value of the relator's share is calculated in the same fashion when the forfeiture action is resolved by settlement. Where possible, the United States should obtain the relator's agreement to the forfeiture settlement. Pursuant to 31 U.S.C. § 3730(c)(2)(B), however, the United States may settle the action with the defendant notwithstanding the objection of the relator "if the court determines, after a hearing, that the proposed settlement is fair, adequate, and reasonable under all the circumstances."

E. Procedure for Paying Relator's Share

Since the relator's share is mandated by Congress, it is a necessary expense incident to the forfeiture of the property as provided for in 28 U.S.C. § 524(c)(1)(A). Section 524(c)(1), governing the AFF, provides that the AFF "shall be available to the Attorney General...for the following law enforcement purposes—

> (A) the payment, at the discretion of the Attorney General,...of *any necessary expense incident to the* seizure, detention, *forfeiture*, or disposal of such property [forfeited pursuant to any law enforced or administered by the Department of Justice].

28 U.S.C. § 524(c)(1)(A) (2005) (emphasis added). The United States should obtain an order in the FCA action that reflects the percentage share of the net recovery to be paid to the relator. A copy of the order should be forwarded to the USMS directing the USMS to pay the relator's share.

PART 5: USE AND DISPOSITION OF SEIZED AND FORFEITED PROPERTY

I. Management and Disposal of Seized Assets

A. Role of the U.S. Marshals Service

The U.S. Marshals Service (USMS) has primary authority over the management and disposal of assets in its custody that have been seized for forfeiture or forfeited by law enforcement agencies of the Department of Justice and, by agreement, certain other federal law enforcement agencies. Arrangements for property services or commitments pertaining to the management and disposition of such property are the responsibility of the USMS. The authority of the Attorney General to dispose of forfeited real property and warrant title has been delegated to the USMS Director by 28 C.F.R. § 0.111(i).

B. Department of Treasury Property Custodians

Management and disposal of assets seized by agencies within the Department of Treasury[1] and other agencies included by agreement (including certain agencies moved from Treasury to the Department of Homeland Security) are handled by property custodians (generally contractors) operating under Treasury guidelines.[2] The Treasury agency case agent is generally the initial point of contact for issues relating to seized property custody, management, and disposal.

C. Preseizure Planning

As soon as possible after assets are identified for seizure/forfeiture in a federal case, the U.S. Attorney's Office (USAO) or agent in charge of the field office responsible for an administrative forfeiture case should contact the USMS or Treasury to discuss preseizure planning. Such discussions should address the impact that a proposed action may have on the USMS or Treasury in undertaking, continuing, or terminating custody of the property. The objective of these discussions is to ensure that informed decisions are made about what property is being seized; how and when it is going to be seized; and most importantly, whether it should be seized. In addition, due consideration should be given to alternatives to seizure (e.g., restraining orders or court-ordered monitoring of assets).

D. Coordination of Custody and Disposition Decisions

Prior to taking any action (e.g., making a commitment in a settlement or plea agreement) concerning the management or disposition of property, the USAO or agent in charge of the field office responsible for an administrative forfeiture case should contact the USMS in cases involving Department of Justice seizing agencies, or Treasury in cases involving Treasury seizing agencies, to discuss any management or disposition issues which may need to be addressed. USMS approval must be obtained prior to the execution of a settlement or plea agreement that requires the payment of a specific amount, rather than an amount determined by the proceeds received from the liquidation of the forfeited property,

II. Use of Seized Property

A. Background

Absent an order of forfeiture or declaration of administrative forfeiture affirmatively vesting title to seized property in the United States, the Government does not have title to the property. Thus, any use of property held pending forfeiture raises potential issues of liability and creates the appearance of impropriety. The following general policies govern the use of seized property pending forfeiture.

B. Use of Seized Property by Department of Justice Personnel

Property under seizure and held pending forfeiture may not be utilized for any reason by Department personnel, including for official use, until a final order of forfeiture is issued.

Likewise, Department personnel may not make such property available for use by others, including persons acting in the capacity of substitute custodians, for any purpose, prior to completion of the forfeiture. However, court authority may be sought for use of seized property, after consultation with the USMS, in situations such as the seizure of a ranch or business where use of equipment under seizure is necessary to maintain the ranch or business.

C. Use of Seized Property Where Custody Is Retained by the State or Local Seizing Agency

To minimize storage and management costs incurred by the Department of Justice or Treasury, state and local agencies that present motor vehicles or other property items for federal adoptions may be asked to serve as substitute custodians of the property, pending forfeiture, at the discretion of the USMS or Treasury, and upon consultation with the U.S. Attorney in judicial forfeiture cases. In addition, the USMS may enter into a storage and maintenance agreement with state and local agencies covering such property. Such agreements are contractual in nature and do not require district court approval. Under such an agreement the state or local agency has a responsibility to provide adequate storage, security, and maintenance for all assets in their custody.

Any use of such vehicles or other property, including official use by federal, state, and local law enforcement officials or others, is prohibited by Department of Justice and Department of Treasury policy until such time as the forfeiture is completed and an equitable transfer is made.

D. Use of Seized Real Property by Occupants

Occupants of real property that is seized for forfeiture may be permitted to remain on the property, pursuant to an occupancy agreement pending the final order of forfeiture, after consultation between the USMS or Treasury and the U.S. Attorney.

III. State and Local Real Property Taxes

A. Civil Forfeiture Cases

Notwithstanding the enactment of 18 U.S.C. § 983(d)(3), which bars assertion of the "innocent owner defense" recovery in certain civil forfeiture cases by persons who are not bona fide purchasers for value, it is the policy of the Department of Justice that the United States should pay state and local real property taxes that accrue up to the date of the entry of an order or judgment of forfeiture.[3] The reasons are two-fold. First, the refusal to pay such taxes would draw the United States into conflict with state and local authorities on matters (the collection of real property taxes) that traditionally have been left to state and local control. Second, the refusal to pay state and local real property taxes would, as a practical matter, complicate the interlocutory or post-judgment sale of real property. It would, for example, be difficult for the U.S. Marshals Service (USMS) to market and sell real property on which ad valorem property taxes had not been paid. Title insurers and escrow officers might be reluctant to provide the necessary warranties in the face of unpaid state and local property taxes, thus undermining the marketability of the property.

B. Criminal Forfeiture Cases

For the same reasons that it is the Department's policy in civil forfeiture cases to pay state and local taxes even if those tax liabilities accrue after the events giving rise to forfeiture, it is the Department's policy to also pay such taxes in criminal forfeiture cases.

C. Payment of Interest and Penalties on State and Local Real Property Taxes

The following policy is meant to ensure consistent national treatment of the payment of interest and penalties on state and local taxes on forfeited real property:

1) the United States will pay interest but not penalties on overdue taxes;
2) the formula for the rate of interest is set forth in 28 U.S.C. § 1961(a);
3) higher rates of interest may be paid where the taxing authority has incurred out-of-pocket interest expenses in excess of the rate specified by section 1961(a) (e.g., where tax certificates have been sold to private investors);
4) U.S. Attorneys, with the concurrence of AFMLS, may agree to a higher rate of interest provided that such higher rate is not punitive; and
5) taxes and interest thereon may only be paid up to the amount realized from the sale of the property.

IV. Disposition of Forfeited Property

A. Forfeiture Orders

The disposition of property forfeited to the United States is an executive branch decision and not a matter for the court. Consequently, preliminary and final orders of forfeiture should include language directing forfeiture of the property to the United States "for disposition in accordance with law."

In addition, the orders of forfeiture should specifically address any third party claims against the forfeited property that are recognized by the United States. If the interests of claimants are to be satisfied in whole or in part by payments from the proceeds of a sale of property by the USMS or Treasury, the proposed forfeiture order should provide specific guidance for the USMS or Treasury concerning such payments and, where possible, specify that such claims shall be paid only after the costs of the United States are recovered, and shall be paid only up to the amount realized from the proceeds of the forfeited property.

The comptroller general has determined that judgments in excess of the proceeds of sale are to be paid from the Judgment Fund. However, 28 U.S.C. § 524(c)(1)(D) also provides that the Assets Forfeiture Fund (AFF) is available for the payment of valid liens and mortgages "subject to the discretion of the Attorney General to determine the validity of any such lien or mortgage and the amount of payment to be made...". The USMS is authorized to pay a lien or mortgage in excess of the proceeds of sale if such payment will facilitate the liquidation of the property and, thus, reduce expenses of such property's continued custody. Requests for approval of liens and mortgages in excess of the proceeds of sale shall be submitted to AFMLS for approval.

B. Disposition of Forfeited Property in Civil and Criminal Cases

The Attorney General has been given the authority under 21 U.S.C. §§ 881(e) and 853(h) and other statutes[4] to dispose of forfeited property "by sale or any other commercially feasible means," without subsequent court approval. This is generally called a "forfeiture sale" of the property.[5] It is clear from the language of the forfeiture statutes, from their legislative history, and from the cases and other authorities that have addressed this issue that the Attorney General has complete authority to dispose of forfeited property.

Forfeiture divests an owner of property of all his or her right, title, and interest therein and vests such right, title, and interest in the Government. Accordingly, because of the property's or its owner's involvement in criminal activity, forfeiture extinguishes all of the former owner's interests in that criminally derived or criminally involved asset, and vests title in the United States.[6] While the relation back doctrine found in section 853(c) provides that all right, title, and interest in forfeitable property vests in the United States upon the commission of the criminal act giving rise to the forfeiture, the Government's ownership interest therein is not confirmed to the world until a final order of forfeiture is entered by a court.

Since the forfeiture process vests title to the property in the United States, a forfeiture sale is a sale by the Government of property it owns. The forfeiture statutes give the power to the Attorney General, on behalf of the United States as owner, to dispose of the property however he or she deems suitable. After the final order of forfeiture, the court is not involved in the sale or disposal process.

C. Disposition of Forfeited Funds

The USAO securing a forfeiture is responsible for initiating the disposal of funds forfeited to the United States, and should provide prompt notification to the USMS or Treasury custodian, which should lead to a transfer of forfeited funds to the Department of Justice AFF or Department of Treasury Forfeiture Fund. In the case of either a consent judgment or a default judgment, the forfeited cash will be immediately transferred to the appropriate forfeiture fund unless the U.S. Attorney determines that execution of the judgment should be delayed.

In the case of a judgment after trial or upon summary judgment, there is an automatic stay of execution of the judgment of 14 days, effective December 1, 2009. *See* Fed. R. Civ. P. 62(a) (prior to the 2009 amendment, the period of the automatic stay was ten days).[7] If the USAO indicates that no motions or requests for additional stays have been filed, the forfeited cash will be transferred to the appropriate forfeiture fund on the fifteenth (formerly the eleventh) day following a summary judgment or a judgment after trial.[8]

V. Attorney General's Authority to Warrant Title

A. Background

Section 2002 of the Crime Control Act of 1990, which amends 28 U.S.C. § 524(c), gives the Attorney General the authority to warrant clear title upon transfer of forfeited property. Section 524(c)(9)(A) reads as follows:

> Following the completion of procedures for the forfeiture of property pursuant to any law enforced or administered by the Department, the Attorney General is authorized, in her discretion, to warrant clear title to any subsequent purchaser or transferee of such property.

The authority to execute deeds and transfer title has been delegated to chief deputies or deputy U.S. Marshals by 28 C.F.R. § 0.156. The section 0.156 delegation predates the Asset

Forfeiture Program and applies to all court-ordered sales of property, not just forfeited property.

The preferred means to transfer forfeited real property is by special warranty deed executed by the U.S. Marshal. The special warranty deed assures the grantee/buyer that the United States, as the current seller, has done nothing to encumber the property, nor has it conveyed any right, title, or interest in the property while the Government was the owner of the property. In effect, the special warranty deed, discussed in section IV.B, warrants the forfeiture process.

Under appropriate circumstances, a quitclaim deed may be used to transfer property. The quitclaim deed makes no warranty representations. It serves only to convey whatever right, title, and interest the Government had as of the execution date. Although property may be transferred by a general warranty deed,[9] it is Department of Justice policy to use general warranty deeds only in exceptional circumstances as outlined in part IV.C.[10]

B. Use of a Special Warranty Deed and Indemnification Agreement

It is suggested that the language of the special warranty deed be as follows, with the insertion of the specifically applicable circumstances as required:

> The grantor covenants to specially warrant the title to the property hereby conveyed against any claim arising from...[insert the specifically applicable circumstances here].

Further, when such special circumstances exist, the buyer may also request that the United States provide certain indemnifications in order to obtain title insurance. These indemnification agreements establish affirmative measures to be taken by the United States, beyond the basic terms and obligations of its warranty deed, in the event that claims are later made against the property. The indemnification agreement may be included either in the terms of the special warranty deed or in a separate document that incorporates the deed by reference. In either form, indemnification agreements will be limited to the following terms:

1) The United States will specially warrant its title against defects or clouds arising out of the forfeiture process and hold the buyer harmless as a result of such defects in title or clouds involving the propriety of the forfeiture of the property.
2) In the event that a court in a final judgment rules that the United States did not acquire valid legal title to the real property through the forfeiture process and therefore was not able to convey clear title to the buyer, the United States will refund to the buyer the amount of the purchase price of the property, plus the value of any improvements made to the property by the buyer. The amount will be paid out of the AFF, plus interest on the total amount at the current rate as provided in 28 U.S.C. § 1961 from the date of the purchase of the property by the buyer to the date of the final judgment.
3) The United States, by its special warranty deed, does not warrant the title of the prior owner of the property who acquired title before the forfeiture.

C. Use of a General Warranty Deed

If the buyer of the forfeited property is still unable to procure a title insurance policy, the U.S. Marshal may be authorized to execute a general warranty deed. Any determination to transfer property by a general warranty deed must be approved by the USMS Asset Forfeiture Division.

It is Department policy that the Attorney General's discretion to warrant clear title, through the use of a general warranty deed, be exercised only in compelling circumstances where the financial advantage of offering a general warranty deed in the particular case, compared to the available alternatives, far outweighs both the potential cost of honoring the warranty in that case and the potential effect of increased purchaser demand for general warranty deeds in future sales of other forfeited properties. The USMS Asset Forfeiture Division, in the exercise of sound business judgment, shall also consider the cumulative potential liability that will accrue over time as a result of each successive use of a general warranty deed.

VI. Purchase or Personal Use of Forfeited Property by Department of Justice Employees

Under 5 C.F.R. § 3801.104, Department of Justice employees are prohibited from purchasing, either directly or indirectly, or using any property if the property has been forfeited to the Government and offered for sale by the Department of Justice or its agents. In addition, Department of Justice employees are prohibited from using such property that has been purchased, directly or indirectly, by a spouse or minor child.

This policy is intended to ensure that there is no actual or apparent use of inside information by employees wishing to purchase such property. The purpose of this policy is to protect the integrity of the Asset Forfeiture Program and avoid problems before they develop. It is important to the integrity of the Department's Asset Forfeiture Program that we preclude even the appearance of a conflict of interest that would otherwise arise should a Department employee purchase forfeited property.

A written waiver to the aforementioned restrictions may be granted by the agency designee upon a determination that, in the mind of a reasonable person with knowledge of the circumstances, purchase or use by the employee of the asset will not raise a question as to whether the employee has used his or her official position or nonpublic information to obtain or assist in an advantageous purchase or create an appearance of the loss of impartiality in the performance of the employee's duties. A copy of this waiver must be filed with the Deputy Attorney General.

Part 6: Equitable Sharing and Official Use

Federal law authorizes the Attorney General to share federally forfeited property with participating State and local law enforcement agencies.[1] Through equitable sharing, any state or local law enforcement agency that directly participates in a law enforcement effort that results in a federal forfeiture may either request to put tangible forfeited property into official use or an equitable share of the net proceeds of the forfeiture. The exercise of this authority is *discretionary*. The Attorney General is not required to share property in any case. Where the

Attorney General chooses to share forfeited property, federal law, as set forth in the Controlled Substances Act, at 21 U.S.C. §881(e)(3), for example, provides that:

The Attorney General shall assure that any property transferred to a State or local law enforcement agency...

a) has a value that bears a reasonable relationship to the degree of direct participation of the State or local agency in the law enforcement effort resulting in the forfeiture, taking into account the total value of all property forfeited and the total law enforcement effort with respect to the violation of law on which the forfeiture is based; and
b) will serve to encourage further cooperation between the recipient State or local agency and Federal law enforcement agencies.

Equitable sharing and official use requests will be granted only if forfeited property or net proceeds from the sale of forfeited property remain after all approved claims, petitions for remission, restoration/restitution requests, and international sharing have been processed and paid. Additionally, in any case with underwater asset(s) (i.e., where the asset expenses are greater than income), the deciding official must offset the negative value of the underwater asset(s) against any asset(s) with a net income prior to distribution of any approved sharing.

Funds collected to satisfy a forfeiture money judgment are not eligible for equitable sharing where no collection efforts were expended by the participants in the underlying investigation.

I. Processing Applications for Equitable Sharing

A. Eligible Participants

In order for a State or local law enforcement agency to request equitable sharing, the agency must be an eligible participant in the Equitable Sharing Program (Program). AFMLS determines the eligibility of a State or local law enforcement agency to participate in the Program.

If an agency does not appear in the Consolidated Asset Tracking System (CATS), AFMLS must be contacted in order to verify the agency's current status and/or any of its prior requests for participation in the Program. AFMLS will determine the eligibility of any law enforcement agency not currently admitted to the Program. AFMLS will assess the request according to criteria outlined in the *Guide to Equitable Sharing*. No National Crime Information Center (NCIC) code will be issued and no agency will be accepted into the Program until the determination is complete.

B. Agency Field Office

A State or local law enforcement agency participating in the Program may request official use or an equitable share of forfeited property by submitting an *Application for Transfer of Federally Forfeited Property* (Form DAG-71) to the appropriate field office of the federal investigative agency with primary responsibility for the law enforcement effort leading to the seizure and subsequent forfeiture. The requesting agency must complete the DAG-71 to include the workhours expended by agency personnel and a detailed narrative of the agency's specific role in the effort in section VI. The field office may reject an incomplete or insufficient DAG-71. Once submitted, a properly executed DAG-71 may not be changed or altered in any manner. The requesting agency may, however, submit an amended DAG-71, reflecting changes to the information reported in its original submission. The field office must enter the information reported on the DAG-71 in CATS.

Federal law enforcement agencies that participated in the effort must submit a Federal Contribution Form (FCF)[2] to the lead/processing federal agency to record participation or, where applicable, request a Fund-to-Fund transfer (*e.g.*, a transfer from the Justice Fund to the Treasury Fund or vice versa) for the assistance they provided. Effective January 25, 2010, federal agencies should no longer use the Department of Justice (DOJ) DAG-71 or the Department of the Treasury TDF for this purpose. See section VI of this part for additional information on the FCF. Once submitted, a properly executed FCF cannot be changed or altered in any manner. The requesting agency may, however, submit an amended FCF, reflecting changes to the information reported on the original submission.

Following receipt of the DAG-71 or FCF, the field office must complete section I of the *Decision Form for Transfer of Federally Forfeited Property* (Form DAG-72) and enter the information in CATS. There must be a reasonably close relationship between the field office's recommended sharing for a given agency, as reported on the DAG-72, and the degree of direct participation by the requesting agency in the total law enforcement effort leading to the forfeiture. As a general rule, the recommended equitable sharing allocation should be based on a comparison of the workhours and qualitative contributions of each and every federal, State, and local law enforcement agency that participated in the law enforcement effort resulting in the forfeiture.[3] The workhours of every agency participating in the law enforcement effort including the lead federal agency, must be reported on the DAG-71, FCF, or in a supplemental memorandum for the decision maker to review. However, equitable sharing percentages may also be awarded based on an agency's participation in a task force that has previously adopted a task force sharing arrangement consistent with Department policy.[4] The field office must forward to investigative agency headquarters all documents supporting the equitable sharing request and recommendation, including but not limited to, the DAG-71, FCF, DAG-72, and supplemental memorandum.

C. Final Decision Maker

C.1. Investigative Agency

If assets are administratively forfeited and the total appraised value of all items forfeited under a single Declaration of Administrative Forfeiture is less than $1 million, the head of the investigative agency, or designated agency headquarters official, decides the appropriate equitable share as to each item and requesting agency. The investigative agency must then complete section II of the DAG-72, and enter the decision in CATS.

C.2. United States Attorney

If the assets are judicially forfeited and the total appraised value of all of the assets forfeited in a single judicial forfeiture order is less than $1 million, the U.S. Attorney decides the appropriate equitable share as to each asset and requesting agency. The investigative agency headquarters must submit its recommendation by completing section II of the DAG-72, entering its recommendation in CATS, and forwarding all documents supporting the equitable sharing request, including, without limitation, the DAG-71, FCF, DAG-72, and supplemental memorandum to the USAO. The U.S. Attorney, or the U.S. Attorney's designee,[5] must decide the appropriate equitable share as to each asset and agency, complete section III of the DAG-72, and enter the decision in CATS.

C.3. Deputy Attorney General

Regardless of whether assets are administratively or judicially forfeited, the Deputy Attorney General (DAG), or the DAG's designee, decides the final equitable share as to each asset and requesting agency in: (1) all cases in which the total appraised value of all of the assets forfeited under a single Declaration of Administrative Forfeiture or judicial forfeiture order is $1 million or more; (2) multi-district cases; or (3) cases involving the equitable transfer of real property.[6] The appropriate decision-maker with delegated decision making authority from the DAG is generally determined by the value of the assets to be shared, as set forth below. Assets forfeited under a single declaration of administrative forfeiture or judicial forfeiture order cannot be separated so that only the individual assets having a value greater than $1 million are submitted to AFMLS, the AAG or the DAG for sharing decisions.

C.3.A Assets Valued between $1 Million and $5 Million

The DAG has delegated to the Chief of AFMLS the authority to decide equitable sharing requests for judicially or administratively forfeited assets in which (1) the property to be shared is valued between $1 million and $5 million and (2) AFMLS, the seizing agency, and the USAO agree on the sharing allocations.[7] If the seizing agency, the USAO, and AFMLS do not agree on the sharing allocations, the final decision must be made by the DAG.

C.3.B. Assets Valued over $5 Million

The Assistant Attorney General for the Criminal Division (AAG) has been delegated authority from the DAG to decide equitable sharing requests for judicially or administratively forfeited assets in which (1) the property is valued in excess of $5 million, and (2) the seizing agency, the USAO and AFMLS agree on the sharing allocations. If the seizing agency, the USAO and AFMLS do not agree on the sharing allocations, the final decision must be made by the DAG.

In all of these cases, the lead federal investigative agency for the law enforcement investigation completes section II of the DAG-72 as to each asset and the agency, must enter its recommendation in CATS, and forward all documents supporting the equitable sharing request to the USAO. The USAO then completes section III of the DAG-72 for each asset, enters its recommendation in CATS, and forwards all documents supporting the equitable sharing request to AFMLS.

Regardless of whether the final decision maker is the Chief of AFMLS, the AAG, or the DAG, AFMLS will enter the final equitable sharing decision into CATS.

D. Communication with the Requesting Agency

Federal personnel and contractors involved in making, processing, or deciding an equitable sharing request must not represent whether sharing will occur at all, what specific percentages or dollar-amounts will be awarded, or that a sharing request has been or will be approved until the final decision maker has rendered a decision. Premature projections regarding approval of a sharing request often prove unfounded, needlessly risk friction with or disappointment by a supporting law enforcement agency if the projected sharing is ultimately disapproved or substantially reduced, and demonstrate disregard and disrespect for the discretionary authority of the decision maker.

That said, federal officials should promptly advise sharing applicants whenever their requested shares are denied or reduced. DOJ seizing agencies should also inform other federal agencies that participated in the investigation of any reduction or denial of their requested shares. Prompt and accurate communication about sharing matters is of paramount importance and should occur in the first instance at the field level.

E. Reimbursement of Federal Costs and Expenses

State and local law enforcement agencies that receive real property or tangible personal property must reimburse the DOJ Assets Forfeiture Fund for any liens, accrued expenses, costs of sharing with other agencies, and the "federal share." [8] Payment must be made within 60 calendar days of notification of the total expenses. If the requesting agency is unable to pay these expenses, these costs may be offset against the requesting agency's other pending equitable sharing awards, if any. If the requesting agency has no pending sharing requests or is unable or unwilling to pay the balance within 60 calendar days, the property must be sold and the proceeds equitably distributed to the agency in lieu of transfer. The federal deciding authority shall modify the decision from item to cash/proceeds without the need for the requesting agency to submit an amended DAG-71 Form.

Payment of neither the costs and expenses nor the federal share may be waived except in cases of extreme hardship where the requesting agency lacks sufficient funds from previous equitable sharings or other available funds to pay the total costs and expenses. The requesting agency must demonstrate in writing that it is unable to pay the total reimbursement, that the payment of such reimbursement would result in an immediate and extreme financial hardship to the requesting agency, and that the benefit of receiving the property outweighs the receipt of the agency's otherwise applicable equitable share.

The decision to waive the federal share rests with the final decision maker for the overall sharing request. The decision to waive accrued expenses rests with the federal agency that incurred the expenses. The decision maker or federal agency considering waiving expenses must first contact the member of the AFMLS Agreement Certification and Audit team member who is assigned responsibility for the agency to verify the amount of sharing the State or local law enforcement agency has available prior to approving any waiver.

II. Equitable Sharing Payments

The USMS makes equitable sharing payments only after final approval of the sharing appears on the CATS Equitable Sharing Payments Authorization Report. This will not happen unless all information required to authorize the payment has been entered in CATS by the investigative agency, the USAO, and/or AFMLS.

All equitable sharing payments greater than $50.00 to State and local law enforcement agencies are electronically transferred by the USMS through its E-Share Program. Participation in the E-Share Program is mandatory for all agencies seeking funds through the DOJ Equitable Sharing Program. A recipient agency will receive an auto generated email from the E-Share Program when funds have been disbursed to their agency.

E-Share provides a fast, efficient, and secure method for making equitable sharing payments. In order to electronically receive equitable sharing payments, a State or local law enforcement agency must submit to the E-Share Helpdesk a completed Form USM-391, entitled the "ACH Vendor/Miscellaneous Payment Enrollment Form" (ACH form). This form and additional information about the E-Share Program may be obtained online at http://www.justice.gov/marshals/assets/eshare/about.htm or by e-mail to E.Share.Help @usdoj.gov.[9]

All equitable sharing payments are subject to offset under the Debt Collection Improvement Act of 1996 (DCIA). The DCIA requires the Department of the Treasury (Treasury) and other disbursing officials to offset federal payments in order to collect delinquent non-tax debts owed to the United States and certain delinquent debts owing to a State government. In addition, the Taxpayer Relief Act of 1997 includes a provision that provides for the continuous levy of federal non-tax payments to collect delinquent tax debts. The Treasury Offset Program (TOP), which is designed to offset payments related to the DCIA, requires the collection of the Taxpayer Identification Number (TIN) and banking account information for the payee on any payment.

If a delinquent debt is attributable to the TIN number provided by a requesting agency on the ACH form submitted with its sharing request, the funds the USMS would otherwise transfer to the agency will be offset—even if the delinquent debt giving rise to the offset is attributable to another governmental agency in the same governmental jurisdiction as the requesting agency. When sharing funds due to be paid to State and local law enforcement agencies are offset, the affected agency should contact the USMS E-Share helpdesk to identify the TIN that appears on its ACH form. The affected agency should then contact the TOP Help Line at 800-304-3107 to determine the amount of, and identity of the governmental agency responsible for, the delinquent debt so the requesting agency can seek repayment of the offset funds from the city, county, or State agency for which the offset was intended.

III. Compliance

In order to participate in the Program, State and local law enforcement agencies must first submit, and annually resubmit, an Equitable Sharing Agreement and Certification form[10] signed by both the head of the law enforcement agency and the head of the governing body having budgetary authority over the law enforcement agency. By signing the Equitable Sharing Agreement, the signatories agree to be bound by, and comply with, the federal statutes and DOJ policies governing the Program.

Any breach of the Sharing Agreement by a State or local law enforcement agency may render it non-compliant or ineligible to receive equitable sharing payments. Failure to annually resubmit a properly completed Equitable Sharing Agreement and Certification form may also result in the permanent extinguishment of the agency's pending equitable sharing distributions. While federal investigative agencies and U.S. Attorneys have no obligation affirmatively to monitor an agency's eligibility, they are obliged promptly to report to AFMLS any information that might affect an agency's eligibility to participate in the Program. Participation may be barred on either a temporary or permanent basis where a requesting agency has failed timely to submit an Equitable Sharing Agreement and Certification form or ACH form or to meet any other requirements as set forth in the *Guide*.

Participation may also be temporarily or permanently barred: (1) pending resolution of any audit or investigation of an agency's possible mishandling or misuse of shared funds and or property placed into official use; or (2) if applicable State laws or local ordinances prevent compliance with federal statutes and equitable sharing policies. AFMLS will ensure that non-compliant or ineligible agencies are properly identified to prevent the inclusion of their approved sharing payments on the CATS Equitable Sharing Payments Authorization Report.

There are three agency compliance statuses that appear in CATS:

(1) Compliant: An agency will be deemed compliant once all required paperwork is received by AFMLS and any discrepancies have been resolved. Compliant agencies will receive equitable sharing payments.
(2) Non-Compliant: AFMLS has the discretionary authority to designate an agency non-compliant for any of several reasons, including adverse audit findings, impermissible expenditures, or failure to submit the Equitable Sharing Agreement and Certification form within sixty (60) days from the end of an agency's fiscal year. The agency is designated to remain non-compliant until all required paperwork is received by AFMLS and/or all discrepancies and audits findings are resolved. Until AFMLS designates the agency compliant, any pending sharing distributions will be held in suspense. Federal agencies may continue accepting and processing any DAG-71(s) received from a non-compliant agency but no sharing payment will be made so long as the agency is designated non-compliant.
(3) Ineligible: AFMLS has the discretionary authority to designate an agency ineligible for equitable sharing where the agency has violated the Program's rules and regulations.[11] Any pending sharing disbursements will be suspended by the USMS until AFMLS makes a final determination regarding the agency's continued participation in the Program. Federal agencies may NOT accept or process any DAG-71 received from an ineligible agency. No seizures that occur while an agency is designated ineligible can form the basis for equitable sharing, even if the agency is rendered compliant at a later date.

IV. Equitable Sharing Ceremonies

Equitable sharing ceremonies foster goodwill and present a unique opportunity to highlight for the local community the cooperative efforts of federal, State, and local law enforcement agencies. All of the State and local law enforcement agencies involved in the law enforcement effort leading to the underlying forfeiture should be invited to participate in the ceremony. Officials from the USAO, the federal seizing agency, AFMLS, and the USMS should be included as appropriate.

On occasion and schedule permitting, the Attorney General has personally presented significant equitable sharing checks. U.S. Attorneys and federal seizing agencies must contact AFMLS as far in advance as possible of upcoming opportunities for significant sharing ceremonies to coordinate all scheduling and pertinent details.

While sharing payments are no longer made by paper checks, a sharing check template may be obtained from the E-Share Helpdesk. This template may be used to create an enlarged image of a "sharing check" suitable for the presentation ceremony.

V. Federal Contribution Form

When federal agencies work together in a joint investigation, each agency should complete the FCF to record participation and, when called for, request a transfer of funds from one forfeiture fund (e.g., AFF, TFF, USPS forfeiture funds) to the fund of the recipient agency. Any forfeited funds or proceeds from the sale or other disposition of forfeited property may only be transferred directly to the appropriate forfeiture fund of the requesting agency, not to the requesting agency itself.

When federal agencies from the same forfeiture program participate in a joint investigation, no Fund-to-Fund monetary transfers occur. In these cases, the FCF serves the important function of documenting the participation of each federal agency and also provides necessary information to the sharing decision-maker who must evaluate the overall work hour and qualitative contributions of all participating federal, State, and local agencies when determining sharing percentages for "cash/proceeds" decisions.

When a DOJ Assets Forfeiture Fund (AFF) investigative agency participates in an investigation resulting in the seizure of property processed for forfeiture by another federal investigative agency, it can record the seizure in CATS by creating a "referral asset." A referral asset is another method for capturing statistics on seizures to document participation in an investigation.

An FCF may only be completed by the following federal agencies:

NCIC/ORI CODE	Agency Name
CBPAMO000	Customs and Border Protection- Air Operations
CBPOBP000	Customs and Border Protection- Border Patrol
CBPOFO000	Customs and Border Protection- Field Operations
NCIC/ORI CODE	Agency Name
DCATF0000	Alcohol, Tobacco, Firearms and Explosives
DCDOS0000	Department of State
DCICE0000	Immigration and Customs Enforcement
DEA	Drug Enforcement Administration
FBI	Federal Bureau of Investigation
IRS	Internal Revenue Service
MDFDA03T0	Food and Drug Administration
TTB	Tax and Trade Bureau
USCG	U.S. Coast Guard
USDAIG	U.S. Department of Agriculture - Office of Inspector General
USMS	U.S. Marshals Service
USPS00000	U.S. Postal Service
USSS	U.S. Secret Service

When a Fund-to-Fund transfer occurs between agencies participating in the DOJ AFF and the Department of the Treasury Forfeiture Fund (TFF), AFMLS and TEOAF have agreed to communicate directly on the sharing at the earliest possible time to address any potential issues.

In judicial cases, TFF agencies and the USAO must communicate directly to address any concerns. In all cases involving a seizure over $1 million, the TFF agencies and AFMLS will communicate directly to address any concerns.

When a TFF agency becomes involved in an ongoing joint investigation involving a DOJ AFF agency and State or local law enforcement agencies and there is an existing MOU on sharing between the DOJ AFF agency and the participating State and local law enforcement agencies, the sharing percentages agreed upon in the MOU must be reduced to include a transfer to the TFF in recognition of the Treasury agency's participation. When a federal agency is invited to join an ongoing investigation, the agency must immediately notify the lead agency and the USAO of its involvement. Any issues that cannot be resolved through communication between case agents be submitted to the appropriate Special Agent in Charge (SAC) for the involved agencies. Agency headquarters will not become involved in the resolution of issues unless the SAC from either of the participating agencies requests assistance. Prompt and accurate communication about sharing matters is important, and should occur, in the first instance, at the field level.

VI. Federal Official Use

Section IV.D of the *Guidelines* outlines the priority scheme and approval requirements for federal retention of forfeited property. The decision maker for official use requests varies depending on the agency that submitted the request and the value of the asset.

In any instance where the property requested for federal official use is valued at over $50,000, the seizing agency and/or U.S. Marshals Service must provide AFMLS with advance notice and an opportunity to review the request.

Section IV.E of the *Guidelines* requires that each agency maintain internal guidelines governing official use requests. In addition, the AG Guidelines address how an agency must review competing official use requests and the payment of any liens on the property sought for official use.

Where one DOJ agency requests an asset for official use that was seized by another DOJ agency, the requesting agency must follow the official use request process of the seizing agency and USMS. (i.e. USDA wants to place a vehicle into official use that was seized by FBI). The FCF is not the appropriate form to request official use in this situation. The official use decision-maker, as identified in the *Guidelines*, must enter the decision in the CATS official use screen. The disposal instructions/disposal should State "retain for official use/official use."

If a non-DOJ agency wants to place an asset seized by a DOJ agency into official use, it must file an FCF with the lead seizing agency. (i.e., IRS wants to place a vehicle into official use that was seized by DEA). The seizing agency must enter the FCF in the CATS sharing request and enter a decision in the DAG-72 screen. The disposal instructions/disposal should reflect "transfer for equitable sharing." Similarly, if a DOJ agency wants to place an asset seized by a non-justice agency into official use, the Justice agency must submit a completed FCF to the seizing agency.

VII. Reverse Sharing

DOJ investigative agencies participating in an investigation resulting in the seizure of property that is processed for forfeiture by a State or local law enforcement agency or foreign jurisdiction should create a "referral asset" in CATS in order to document their participation in the investigation. If any proceeds are received from the State or law enforcement agency or foreign jurisdiction, through "reverse sharing," the agency's share will be deposited into the Assets Forfeiture Fund.

VIII. International Sharing of Forfeited Assets

DOJ encourages international asset sharing with countries that facilitate the forfeiture of assets under U.S. law. International sharing, which requires both DOJ and Department of State approval, and concurrence by the Department of the Treasury, must be either approved or pre-approved before any domestic equitable sharing can take place. The percentage granted to a foreign country is often guided by international sharing agreements or is determined based on factors which differ significantly from the "workhour and qualitative contribution" standard used in determining domestic sharing.

Department policy applicable to international sharing, as well as the forfeiture of assets located overseas, appears in part 9 of this *Manual*.

IX. Real Property Transfers

Pursuant to 18 U.S.C. § 981(e)(1) and (2) and 21 U.S.C. § 881(e)(1)(A), the Attorney General has the authority to transfer forfeited property to any federal agency or State or local law enforcement agency that participated in the seizure or forfeiture of the property. The Attorney General also may transfer forfeited property to a State or local designee, or individual State, provided that the recipient meets certain statutory requirements. *See* Pub. L. 108-199, Div. B, Title I, § 108, 118 Stat. 61 (Jan. 23, 2004) (reprinted in the "Historical and Statutory Notes" for 28 U.S.C. § 524); 21 U.S.C. § 881(e)(4)(B). Limitations and conditions regarding permissible uses of transferred property are set forth in *The Guidelines*. Listed below are several common types of real property transfers.

A. Weed and Seed

The Weed and Seed Initiative authorizes the transfer of federally forfeited real property, through State or local law enforcement agencies, to non-profit organizations. The recipient non-profit organization must agree to use the property to support the goals of the Initiative. The purpose of the Initiative is to rehabilitate and rejuvenate neighborhoods and provide specified community-based services. *See* 21 U.S.C. § 881(e)(1)(A); *Guide*, section VIII.C.2.

The proposed use of the forfeited property must support community-based drug treatment, crime prevention, education, improve housing, enhance job skills or perform other activities that will substantially further the Weed and Seed strategy. A request for a Weed and Seed transfer is initiated by the U.S. Attorney for a district in the state in which the property is located. In order for the real property to be eligible for treatment as a Weed and Seed property, it must have an appraised value of $50,000 or less, or have an appraised value of $200,000, or less if the net equity value of the property is $50,000 or less.

B. Operation Goodwill

Pursuant to Pub. L. 108-199, Div. B, Title I, § 108, 118 Stat. 61 (Jan. 23, 2004) (reprinted in the "Historical and Statutory Notes" for 28 U.S.C. § 524), the Attorney General may transfer real property of limited or marginal value to a State or local government agency, or its designated contractor or transferee, for use in support of community-based revitalization programs. Such programs include drug abuse treatment, drug and crime prevention, education, housing, job skills training, and other community-based health and safety programs.

The USMS reviews all forfeited property in its inventory to identify properties eligible for Operation Goodwill. To be eligible, the property must have an appraised value of $50,000 or less, or have an appraised value of $200,000, or less if the net equity value of the property is $50,000 or less.

C. Governor's Request for Historic and Recreational Purposes

Pursuant to 21 U.S.C. § 881(e)(4)(B), the Governor of a State in which forfeited property is located may request that the Attorney General transfer the property to the State. To be eligible for the transfer, the State must use the forfeited property as a public area reserved for recreational or historic purposes, or for the preservation of the property's natural condition.

D. Real Property Transfer to a Federal Agency

Pursuant to 21 U.S.C. § 881(e)(1)(A), the Attorney General may transfer forfeited property to a federal agency. A DOJ agency may request the authority to place the real property into official use; however, the proposed usage of such property must be consistent with a law enforcement purpose. Transfers of real property to other federal components may also be considered, however, such transfers must serve a significant and continuing federal purpose. *Guidelines*, section IV.B.

PART 7: ATTORNEYS' FEES

I. Payment of Attorneys' Fees in Civil Forfeiture Cases

A. Summary

The Civil Asset Forfeiture Reform Act (CAFRA) of 2000 amended 28 U.S.C. § 2465(b) to provide for an award of attorneys' fees and other litigation costs to any claimant in a civil forfeiture case who "substantially prevails." Such awards will be paid out of the Judgment Fund.[1]

B. Discussion

Prior to the enactment of CAFRA, there was no provision for liability for attorneys' fees and costs that applied specifically to civil forfeitures. Attorneys' fees were awarded to prevailing non-government parties pursuant to the Equal Access to Justice Act (EAJA). In EAJA, Congress provided that the non-government party could seek reimbursement of costs and legal fees if the Government's position was not substantially justified.[2]

In CAFRA, Congress amended section 2465 to provide for the mandatory award of attorneys' fees and other litigation costs to non-government parties who substantially prevail in a civil forfeiture proceeding, regardless of whether the Government was justified in bringing the forfeiture action. To be eligible for attorneys' fees, however, the claimant must pursue the claim in court and obtain a judgment that the United States is liable for attorneys' fees under section 2465.[3]

When EAJA was enacted, the primary source of funds to pay judgments against the United States was the permanent judgment appropriation. *See* 31 U.S.C. § 1304. The Judgment Fund is available, by law, to pay final adverse judgments (and certain compromise settlements) when "payment is not otherwise provided for."[4] In the past, however, citing the need to establish an aggressive use of forfeiture and considering an EAJA award as a predictable expense incident thereto, the Department of Justice used its legal authority, pursuant to 28 U.S.C. § 524(c)(1)(A), to permit the use of Assets Forfeiture Fund (AFF) monies to pay EAJA awards arising from actions related to the forfeiture, attempted forfeiture, or seizure of property for forfeiture. The Department of Justice developed a policy and three-tier test to review requests for payment of EAJA awards from the Assets Forfeiture Fund (AFF) and these requests were submitted to AFMLS for review and approval.

The enactment of CAFRA specifically provided for liability for attorneys' fees and costs for a prevailing claimant in a civil proceeding. Because the provisions of section 2465 are specific to "any civil proceeding to forfeit property under any provision of civil law," they appear to have displaced EAJA as a means for payment of attorneys' fees and costs by prevailing non-government parties in the case of civil forfeitures. Because this liability is unrelated to the strength or weakness of the Government's case and is now a routine part of civil litigation in forfeiture cases, the awards of attorneys' fees and costs will no longer come from the AFF. Although the language of the statute is silent as to the source of funding for these payments, Congressman Henry Hyde addressed this issue. Submitted in the Congressional Record on the day CAFRA was passed was the following statement:

> In addition, this act would make the federal government liable for...attorneys fees, and pre-judgment and post-judgment interest payments on certain assets to prevailing parties in civil forfeiture proceedings.... Compensation payments could come from appropriated funds or occur without further appropriation from the Judgment Fund, or both sources.[5]

Since the AFF consists of non-appropriated funds, and no funds were separately appropriated to pay obligations arising under CAFRA, it seems clear that Congress's intent is that in civil forfeiture proceedings attorneys' fees, costs, and interest should be awarded from the Judgment Fund.

C. Procedure for Requesting Payment of an Award from the Judgment Fund

When there is a judgment awarding attorneys' fees, interest, and costs in a civil forfeiture case, the U.S. Attorney's Office (USAO) should submit a request for payment of the award to the Financial Management Service (FMS), Department of the Treasury, which manages the Judgment Fund. The FMS website, found at http://www.fms.treas.gov/judgefund/forms.html, has links to procedures for submitting a request for an award of costs and fees and to the appropriate forms. In addition to the forms and instructions, the FMS Web site also contains general information about the fund. Upon submitting the appropriate forms to FMS, a courtesy copy should be forwarded to AFMLS.

II. Forfeiture of Attorneys' Fees

The policy on the forfeiture of attorneys' fees is set forth in the *U.S. Attorney's Manual.*[6] As set forth in those sources, any action to forfeit attorneys' fees in a civil or criminal case, as well as any agreement *not* to seek forfeiture of attorneys' fees in such case, requires the approval of the Assistant Attorney General (AAG) for the Criminal Division.

III. Payment of Attorneys' Fees in Criminal Forfeiture Cases

A. Defendant's Attorneys' Fees

A.1. Summary

The defendant in a criminal forfeiture action may file for an award of attorneys' fees only under the Hyde Amendment.[7] A motion for fees and costs filed in a civil forfeiture case under CAFRA cannot include fees and costs incurred in even a directly related criminal proceeding.[8] The Hyde Amendment provides that the court may award attorneys' fees to defendants in criminal actions in which the Government's position was vexatious, frivolous, or in bad faith.[9] To prevail on a Hyde Amendment claim, the defendant must prove that (1) he or she was the prevailing party on the underlying action; (2) the Government's position was vexatious, frivolous, or in bad faith; and (3) there are no special circumstances that would make the award unjust. This burden is heavier than the one the Government must meet under EAJA, 28 U.S.C. § 2412, for civil actions.[10] When a request for attorneys' fees under the Hyde Amendment is made based on the criminal prosecution, it should be submitted directly to the Hyde Amendment Committee and the Executive Office for U.S. Attorneys. If the request specifically addresses the criminal forfeiture, a copy should also be submitted to the Chief of AFMLS. Hyde Amendment claim awards are paid from the Judgment Fund.

A.2. Discussion

In articulating a standard of misconduct, the Eleventh and Fourth Circuits have relied on *Black's Law Dictionary* to define the terms "vexatious," "frivolous," and "bad faith."[11] These courts found *vexatious* to mean "without reasonable or probable cause or excuse"; *frivolous* to mean "groundless...with little prospect of success; often brought to embarrass or annoy"; and *bad faith* to mean "not simply bad judgment or negligence, but rather it implies the conscious doing of a wrong because of dishonest purpose or moral obliquity."[12]

In *United States v. Tucor Int'l, Inc.*, the court held that the language of the Hyde Amendment indicates that the test for "vexatious, frivolous, or in bad faith" is disjunctive and satisfaction of any of the three criteria is sufficient to justify an award.[13] In determining whether the Government's position during prosecution supported an award of attorneys fees under the Hyde Amendment, the court in *United States v. Sherburne*, examined the "vexatious" prong and set forth the standard to be used by courts in their analysis.[14] The court held that for the purposes of the Hyde Amendment, 1) the Government's conduct must include an element of maliciousness, or intent to harass or annoy and, 2) the suit must be objectively deficient in that lacks merit.[15] The test is whether the prosecution was unwarranted because it was intended to harass and without sufficient foundation. [16] The amendment was "targeted at prosecutorial misconduct, not prosecutorial mistake."[17]

A court recently considered a defendant's claim for attorneys fees in a criminal forfeiture case where the forfeiture, but not the conviction, was found defective.[18] In *United States v. Pease*, the defendant sought attorney fees in connection with an appeal of the criminal forfeiture. The Eleventh Circuit reversed the district court's grant of the Government's Rule 36 motion to amend the judgment post-conviction to include the necessary forfeiture language. In connection with the Hyde Amendment request, the district court found that the Government's position was not vexatious, frivolous, or in bad faith.[19] The court reasoned that the lack of clarity of the governing law regarding the use of Rule 36 to amend judgments to include previously ordered forfeitures, the legal merits of the forfeiture, and the consistency of the Government's position supported a finding that the Government's position was substantially justified—not frivolous, vexatious, or in bad faith.[20]

Although there are no reported decisions granting a Hyde Amendment claim solely with regard to a criminal forfeiture, the analysis conducted by courts in granting Hyde Amendment claims generally is instructive. In *United States v. Adkinson*, the court found that the Government acted in bad faith when they indicted a party to the Hyde Amendment action knowing at the time of the indictment that there would be insufficient evidence to convict the defendants of bank fraud conspiracy at trial.[21] Furthermore, the court found the Government's position in that case to be foreclosed by binding precedent from the start, thus making it vexatious and frivolous as well.[22]

Despite arising from a criminal action, most courts have found a Hyde Amendment action to be a civil proceeding. As a result, the Federal Rules of Civil Procedure apply to Hyde Amendment actions.[23] Moreover, the Hyde Amendment provides that the procedures and limitations for granting an award shall be derived from those set forth in EAJA.[24] In pertinent part, EAJA requires the parties seeking an award to file their claims within 30 days of final judgment of the underlying civil action.[25] EAJA also provides for the determination of reasonable attorneys; fees and other expenses.[26]

B. Third Party Petitioner's Attorneys' Fees

B.1. Summary

Since CAFRA strictly applies to civil forfeiture proceedings, the third party petitioner in an ancillary proceeding to a criminal forfeiture, pursuant to 21 U.S.C. § 853(n), must assert payment for attorneys' fees under EAJA.[27] EAJA provides for the award of attorneys' fees to prevailing parties in any civil action against the United States in which the Government's position was not substantially justified.[28] A third party claimant's ancillary proceeding to a criminal forfeiture is considered a "civil action" under EAJA.[29] Payment of attorneys' fees awarded under EAJA are paid from the AFF. The Chief of AFMLS must approve any settlement of an EAJA claim.

B.2. Discussion

EAJA requires the court to award fees upon finding (1) the applicants were the prevailing parties, (2) the Government's position was not substantially justified, and (3) no circumstances exist that would make an award unjust.[30]

The general test for determining whether an applicant is a prevailing party is if the parties "succeed on any significant issue in litigation which achieves some of the benefit the parties sought in bringing suit."[31] The Supreme Court has held that a party must secure a judgment on the merits or by judicial consent decree in order to prevail under statutes awarding attorneys' fees.[32] The court stated that these results create the "material alteration of the legal relationship of the parties' necessary to permit an award of attorneys' fees."[33] Therefore, to meet the prevailing party requirement under EAJA, a petitioner must achieve some benefit of the litigation either through a judgment on the merits or a judicial consent decree.

In *United States v. One Rural Lot*,[34] the claimants were prevailing parties where they received 60 percent of the sale proceeds from forfeited property. Likewise, the property owner in *In Re Application of Gerard Mgndichian*[35] prevailed for EAJA purposes where the district court denied his motion for return of his motorcycles, but nonetheless ordered the administrative forfeiture proceedings void,[36] giving him the right to contest the reinstated forfeiture proceedings.[37]

For the Government's position to be substantially justified, the Government must show it was "justified to a degree that could satisfy a reasonable person";[38] that is, its position had a "reasonable basis both in law and fact."[39] Relevant factors that may be considered in determining whether the Government's position was reasonable include (1) the legal merits of its position, (2) the clarity of the governing law at the time the action was instituted, (3) the stage at which the litigation was resolved, and (4) the consistency of the Government's position.[40]

PART 8: GRAND JURY

I. Disclosures of Grand Jury Information under 18 U.S.C. § 3322(a)

A. Summary

The Civil Asset Forfeiture Reform Act (CAFRA) of 2000 amended 18 U.S.C. § 3322(a) to allow criminal Assistant U.S. Attorneys (AUSAs) to disclose grand jury information to attorneys for the Government "for use in connection with any civil forfeiture provision of federal law." With this amendment, Congress legislatively overruled a portion of the holding in *United States v. Sells Engineering, Inc*, 463 U.S. 418 (1983), which interpreted Rule 6(e), Fed. R. Crim. P., to prohibit a criminal AUSA from disclosing grand jury information to a civil AUSA who was not part of the prosecution team. However, the amendment to section 3322 did not make clear whether the "use" that the civil AUSA could make of the disclosed information included further disclosure to the public in the course of the litigation of a civil forfeiture case without obtaining a court order.

One interpretation of section 3322(a) is that it only permits one AUSA to disclose grand jury information to another AUSA, but still requires the second AUSA to obtain a court order before disclosing the information to the public in the course of civil litigation. The matter is a sensitive one, as the penalty for violating the grand jury disclosure rules set forth in Rule 6(e) is contempt. For that reason, prosecutors will naturally want to act with caution in this area.

However, based on fundamental rules of statutory construction and the practice regarding the use of grand jury information in criminal cases, we conclude that the intent of section 3322 was to permit the civil AUSA not only to review and rely upon grand jury information in the preparation of civil forfeiture pleadings, but also to disclose that information in publicly filed documents and as evidence at trial.

Section 3322 does not, however, permit any AUSA to disclose grand jury information to seizing agency attorneys to use in administrative forfeiture proceedings. Seizing agency attorneys are not "attorneys for the government" as defined by Rule 1(b), of the Federal Rules of Criminal Procedure. Nor does section 3322 authorize disclosure to government contractors without a court order pursuant to Rule 6(e)(3)(E)(i) and/or 6(e)(3)(A)(ii).[1]

B. Discussion

B.1. Issue I

May an AUSA to whom grand jury information is disclosed for use in a civil forfeiture matter disclose that information to the public in the course of the civil forfeiture case without obtaining a court order?

CAFRA[2] amended section 3322(a)[3] to allow a criminal AUSA to disclose grand jury information without obtaining a judicial order to a civil AUSA for "use in connection with any civil forfeiture provision of Federal law." This amendment was intended to address the Supreme Court decision in *United States v. Sells Engineering*, which held that Rule 6(e) of the Federal Rules of Criminal Procedure does not authorize automatic disclosures of grand jury information to an attorney for the Government for use in a civil proceeding. The Supreme Court interpreted Rule 6(e) to allow automatic disclosures only to those attorneys and their supervisors who conduct the criminal matters to which the grand jury materials pertain.[4] An attorney with only civil duties, the Court said, lacks both the prosecutor's special role in supporting the grand jury and the prosecutor's own crucial need to know what occurs before the grand jury.[5] Thus, criminal AUSAs were held to have access to grand jury materials only for criminal use.

The Supreme Court refined its decision in *United States v. John Doe, Inc. I*, 481 U.S. 102 (1987), which held that civil attorneys who were members of the prosecution team may, without prior court authorization, continue to use materials or information subject to Rule 6(e) in a companion or related civil proceeding. A recent Third Circuit case, *Impounded*, 277 F.3d 407 (3d Cir. 2002), further lightened the restrictions of *Sells*. The Third Circuit, interpreting an exception to the general non-disclosure rule, allowed an AUSA from one district to disclose grand jury material to an AUSA in another district since the use of the grand jury information was a part of the performance of the recipient prosecutor's criminal law enforcement duties.

The CAFRA amendment to section 3322(a) expanded the holding in *John Doe, Inc. I* to allow disclosures of grand jury information to another "attorney for the government" without a court order for "use in connection with any civil forfeiture provision of federal law." Previously, under the version of section 3322 enacted as part of the Financial Institutions Reform and Recovery Act (FIRREA) of 1989, Congress had authorized such disclosure only in cases involving bank fraud. However, the legislative history of CAFRA indicates that Congress recognized that *all* civil forfeiture actions are law enforcement actions, and that grand jury information therefore should be available without a court order to government attorneys in all civil forfeiture cases.[6]

While it is clear that Congress intended to permit an AUSA who obtained grand jury information in connection with a criminal investigation to disclose that information to another AUSA who would be handling a related civil forfeiture matter, neither the statute nor the legislative history provides any guidance as to what the civil AUSA may do with the information once it is disclosed. In particular, it is not clear whether Congress intended to permit the civil AUSA only to review and rely upon the grand jury information while preparing a civil forfeiture case, or whether it intended that the civil AUSA would be permitted to disclose the grand jury information in publicly filed documents, such as complaints and applications for seizure warrants and restraining orders, and as evidence at trial.

A fundamental rule of statutory construction provides that the plain meaning of the words is given the greatest weight in statutory interpretation. *Browder v. United States*, 312 U.S. 335, 338 (1941). In the context of civil litigation, the plain meaning of the phrase "for use in connection with any civil forfeiture provision of federal law" would include using the information in applications for seizure warrants and court orders, in the body of the forfeiture complaint, and as evidence at trial. This comports with the dictionary definition, which suggests that information is *used* when it is "put into action or service."[7] The more limited interpretation—that one "uses" information only to inform him or herself of the facts of a case—is contrary to common sense and experience. Moreover, the broader reading of the statute is consistent with the use that a criminal AUSA typically makes of grand jury information in a criminal case. It is well established that a criminal AUSA who is privy to grand jury information may use it not only to prepare a case for trial, but may also disclose it in the indictment and in the course of the criminal trial.

Accordingly, we conclude that just as the criminal AUSA may disclose grand jury information in an indictment or other document filed in the course of a criminal prosecution, or as evidence introduced in the course of a criminal trial, so may a civil AUSA disclose grand jury information in the course of civil litigation without obtaining a judicial disclosure order.

B.2. Issue II

May an AUSA (civil or criminal) who is privy to grand jury information disclose that information to agency counsel for use in connection with an administrative proceeding, or to a government contractor who is assisting in the preparation of a civil forfeiture case?

Section 3322(a) provides for automatic disclosures of grand jury information by an AUSA who is privy to that information "to an attorney for the government...for use in connection with any civil forfeiture provision of Federal law." Rule 1(b) of the Federal Rules of Criminal Procedure defines attorney for the Government as the Attorney General, an authorized assistant of the Attorney General, a U.S. Attorney, or an authorized assistant of a U.S. Attorney. Department of Justice attorneys may conduct grand jury proceedings when authorized to do so by the Attorney General. Agency or other non-Department of Justice attorneys may not be present unless they are appointed as special assistants.[8]

In *In re Grand Jury Proceedings*,[9] the Third Circuit emphasized that the "term 'attorneys for the government' is restrictive in its application." The Court concluded that "if it had been intended that attorneys for administrative agencies were to have free access to matters occurring before the grand jury the rule would have so provided." The Sixth Circuit, addressing the definition of *attorney for the Government*, found that an attorney for the Department of Justice Tax Division was not an attorney for the Government because he was not assigned to work on a particular criminal case in any "official" capacity.[10] Seizing agency attorneys and non-Department of Justice attorneys may obtain grand jury information without a disclosure order if they are appointed under 28 U.S.C. § 515 as a Special Assistant U.S.

Attorney or Special Assistant to the Attorney General.[11] Otherwise, they are not considered "attorneys for the Government" and cannot receive grand jury information without a court order. As a result, we conclude that section 3322 does not authorize disclosure of grand jury information to a seizing agency counsel for use in connection with an administrative proceeding.

Likewise, we conclude that section 3322 does not authorize disclosure without a court order to government contractors who are assisting the civil AUSA with the preparation of the civil forfeiture case. At first glance, disclosure to the contractor paralegal or attorney who is doing the actual drafting of the document that the civil AUSA is planning to file in the civil forfeiture case would seem to fall within the scope of the use that the civil AUSA may make of the grand jury information. If the civil AUSA, for example, may disclose the grand jury information in the publicly filed civil forfeiture complaint, there would seem to be no reason he or she could not first disclose it to the contractor who is drafting the complaint. Nonetheless, the practice in criminal cases militates against this view.

Rule 6(e)(3)(A)(ii) allows for disclosure of grand jury information without judicial order to "any government personnel...that an attorney for the government considers necessary to assist in performing that attorney's duty to enforce federal criminal law." The term *government personnel* includes not only members of the prosecution support staff, such as economists, secretaries, paralegals, law clerks, and federal criminal investigators, but also employees of any federal agency who are assisting the government prosecutor.[12] However, it does not automatically include contractor personnel used in the Asset Forfeiture Program.

It is true that contract personnel have been considered government personnel for purposes of Rule 6(e) in previous instances. In *United States v. Lartey*,[13] the Second Circuit held that a retired IRS agent employed as a contractor to review financial records of the defendant, which were submitted to the grand jury, fell within the government employee exception to the grand jury secrecy rule. Relying on *In re Gruberg*[14], and legislative history,[15] the court found that the exceptions to the grand jury rules were adopted to override decisions highly restrictive of the use of government experts in grand jury investigations. In a similar case, the Tenth Circuit, relying on *Lartey*, held that an expert witness under contract with the Government was government personnel within the class of government personnel to whom disclosure is permissible.[16]

In *United States v. Pimental*,[17] the most recent case to address this issue, the court concluded that temporary employees or persons under contract, including employees of a private company, can be "government personnel" for purposes of Rule 6(e)(3)(A)(ii), where the individuals in question are directly involved in assisting government attorneys in the prosecution of cases. However, the court held that the prosecutor "must seek court authorization" prior to disclosure to such persons.[18]

Therefore, in both civil and criminal cases, the AUSA must first obtain a disclosure order pursuant to either Rule 6(e)(3)(A)(ii) or Rule 6(e)(3)(E)(i) before disclosing grand jury information to a contract employee,[19] being mindful of any required showings under these provisions.[20] Accordingly, it will remain necessary to obtain a disclosure order before a civil AUSA, who is entitled under section 3322(a) to use grand jury information in a civil forfeiture case, may disclose that information to a government contractor unless the information is first disclosed in a publicly filed document or in open court.

C. Conclusion

Under the CAFRA amendment to section 3322(a), criminal AUSAs may now disclose grand jury information to civil forfeiture AUSAs. This information may be used by the civil AUSAs in their complaints, restraining orders, and any other pleadings filed in a civil forfeiture case, and as evidence at trial, without getting a disclosure order. However, neither criminal nor civil AUSAs may disclose grand jury information to seizing agency attorneys to use in administrative forfeiture proceedings or to government contract employees who may be assisting in the preparation of a civil forfeiture case without obtaining a judicial order.

II. Presenting Forfeiture to the Grand Jury[21]

Federal Rule of Criminal Procedure 32.2(a) provides that the court may not enter a judgment of forfeiture in a criminal proceeding "unless the indictment or information contains notice to the defendant that the Government will seek the forfeiture of property as part of any sentence in accordance with the applicable statute." Fed. R. Crim. P. 32.2(a). In light of this rule and related constitutional considerations, what are the best practices for AUSAs to follow in presenting forfeiture allegations and related evidence to the grand jury, and how should the grand jury's finding of probable cause for forfeiture be memorialized and described to the district court?

A. Summary

Because forfeiture is neither an offense nor an element of an offense, but an indeterminate part of the criminal sentence not limited by any statutory maximum amount, the Constitution does not require that the grand jury find probable cause for forfeiture, either generally or with respect to particular property. In addition, the applicable statutes and rules do not mandate such a finding by the grand jury. For several reasons, however, the best practice is to present evidence to the grand jury that permits it to find probable cause to believe that the requisite nexus exists between the charged offenses and any money judgment amount and particular property alleged to be forfeitable, and to request that such a finding be made. The grand jury's finding with respect to forfeiture should be memorialized in the indictment, and may then be represented to the court, in support of pre-trial restraining orders or for other appropriate purposes, as the grand jury's probable cause finding on the forfeitability of the listed property and the specified money judgment amount.

B. Discussion

B.1. The Constitution Does Not Require a Grand Jury Finding of Probable Cause for Forfeiture

The authority to charge crimes in federal court, and the limits to that authority, derives from the Constitution. The Fifth Amendment provides, "No person shall be held to answer for a capital, or otherwise infamous crime, unless on a presentment or indictment of a Grand Jury." The grand jury clause of the Fifth Amendment serves the "dual function of determining if there is probable cause to believe that a crime has been committed, and of protecting citizens against unfounded criminal prosecutions." *Branzburg v. Hayes*, 408 U.S. 665, 686-687 (1972). Thus, elements of the criminal offense must be charged in the indictment, submitted to a jury, and proven by the Government beyond a reasonable doubt. *See*, e.g., *Jones v. United States*, 526 U.S. 227, 232 (1999); *see generally* part 11, section 1, *Federal Grand Jury Practice* (OLE February 2008).

There is no constitutional right to have the grand jury make a probable cause determination as to criminal forfeiture because forfeiture is not an element of a substantive offense. Criminal forfeiture is, instead, part of a criminal sentence. *Libretti v. United States*, 516 U.S. 29, 38-41, 48-50 (1995). Indeed, for that reason, there is no Sixth Amendment right to jury trial on criminal forfeiture. *Id.* at 49-50.[22]

Notwithstanding recent Supreme Court decisions holding that certain facts bearing upon sentencing constitute elements of separate substantive offenses, *Libretti* is apparently still good law. In *Jones v. United States*, the Court held that the federal carjacking statute, which authorized increased punishment in carjackings resulting in either serious bodily injury or death, created three separate offenses rather than one offense with additional penalty provisions. *Jones*, 526 U.S. at 251-52. In *Apprendi v. New Jersey*, 530 U.S. 466, 490 (2000), the Court held that "other than the fact of a prior conviction, any fact that increases the penalty for a crime beyond the prescribed statutory maximum must be submitted to a jury, and proved beyond a reasonable doubt."[23] In *Blakely v. Washington*, 542 U.S. 296 (2004), the Court applied the *Apprendi* rule to invalidate, under the Sixth Amendment, an upward departure under the Washington State sentencing guidelines system that was imposed on the basis of facts found by the court at sentencing.[24]

In *United States v. Messino*, 382 F.3d 704 (7th Cir. 2004), the first court of appeals to reach and decide the issue of *Blakely*'s application to criminal forfeiture, explained:

> We have previously held that *Apprendi* has no effect on criminal forfeiture proceedings because forfeiture provisions have no statutory maximum. *United States v. Vera*, 278 F.3d 672, 673 (7th Cir. 2002). *Apprendi*'s statutory maximum was supplied by the statute of conviction; *Blakely*'s is external—the statutory maximum is found not in the criminal code, but instead, the sentencing guidelines. *See [United States vj Booker*, 375 F.3d 508, 509 [(7th Cir. 2004)]. The criminal forfeiture provisions do not include a statutory maximum; they are open-ended in that *all* property representing proceeds of illegal activity is subject to forfeiture. *Vera*, 278 F.3d at 673; U.S.S.G. § 5E1.4; 21 U.S.C. § 853. Therefore, we conclude that *Blakely*, like *Apprendi*, does not apply to forfeiture proceedings.

382 F.3d at 713. The court of appeals added the following defense of the preponderance standard for criminal forfeiture:

> *Libretti* states that "the nature of criminal forfeiture as an aspect of sentencing compels the conclusion that the right to jury verdict on forfeitability does not fall within the Sixth Amendment's constitutional protection." *Libretti v. United States*, 516 U.S. 29, 49 (1995). Furthermore, the Supreme Court's decision in *Patterson* explains that, "the Due Process Clause requires the prosecution to prove beyond a reasonable doubt all of the elements included in the definition of the offense of which the defendant is charged." *Patterson v. New York*, 432 U.S. 197, 210 (1977). Since forfeiture is not a separate substantive offense, *Libretti*, 516 U.S. at 39-40, due process is also not offended by a preponderance standard.

Messino, 382 F.3d at 713-14.

Other lower courts have uniformly held that Blakely's predecessor, Apprendi, does not apply to criminal forfeiture because forfeiture has no statutory maximum amount. See United States v. Shryock, 342 F.3d 948, 991 (9th Cir. 2003); United States v. Keene, 341 F.3d 78, 85 (1st Cir. 2003); United States v. Gasanova, 332 F.3d 297, 300-01 (5th Cir. 2003); United States v. Najjar, 300 F.3d 466, 485-86 (4th Cir. 2002); United States v. Corrado, 227 F.3d 543, 550-51 (6th Cir. 2000) (Corrado I); United States v. Corrado, 286 F.3d 934, 937 (6th Cir. 2002) (Corrado II) (reaffirming, in related opinion, that forfeiture is part of the defendant's sentence); United States v. Cabeza, 258 F.3d 1256, 1257 (11th Cir. 2001).

Accordingly, a defendant has no constitutional right to have the grand jury find probable cause for forfeiture.[25]

B.2. Criminal forfeiture Statutes and the Federal Rules of Criminal Procedure Do Not Require That the Grand Jury Find Probable Cause for Forfeiture

If the Constitution does not require the grand jury to find probable cause for forfeiture, does a statute or rule require it?

Criminal forfeiture statutes typically provide that the court, "in imposing sentence on a person convicted of [the predicate] offense..., shall order that the person forfeit to the United States [specified types of property]," 18 U.S.C. § 982(a)(1), or its equivalent, "Any person convicted of a [predicate offense] shall forfeit to the United States [specified types of property]," 21 U.S.C. § 853(a). *See also* 28 U.S.C. § 2461(c) ("If a forfeiture of property is authorized in connection with a violation of an Act of Congress, and any person is charged in an indictment or information with such violation but no specific statutory provision is made for criminal forfeiture upon conviction, the government may include the forfeiture in the indictment or information in accordance with the Federal Rules of Criminal Procedure, and upon conviction, the court shall order the forfeiture of the property in accordance with...(21 U.S.C. § 853), other than subsection (d) of that section.").

Such criminal forfeiture statutes do not address grand jury process with respect to forfeiture, however, the Rules Committee determined that Rule 7(c)(2), dealing with the contents of the indictment, would only require notice of forfeiture, while Rule 31, dealing with jury verdicts at trial, required only the trial jury to return a special forfeiture verdict.[26]

B.3. Although the Constitution, Statutes, and Rules Do Not Require a Grand Jury Finding of Probable Cause for Forfeiture, the Best Practice Is to Request Such a Finding

Although neither the Constitution, nor the forfeiture statutes, nor the rules require it, it is best to ask the grand jury to find that there is probable cause to believe that the requisite nexus exists between the offenses charged in the indictment and the assets allegedly subject to criminal forfeiture, at least in cases where the indictment identifies specific forfeitable property or a specific amount due as a forfeiture money judgment.

Such a finding serves several useful purposes.

First, the finding provides a basis for restraining directly forfeitable assets identified in the indictment.[27] Section 853(e)(1)(A) provides for entry of a post-indictment restraining order "upon the filing of an indictment or information charging a violation...for which criminal forfeiture may be ordered...and alleging that the property with respect to which the order is sought would, in the event of conviction, be subject to forfeiture under this section."

Section 853(e)(1)(A). The legislative history of section 853 indicates that Congress intended for the grand jury's finding in support of forfeiture to be given considerable weight:

> For the purposes of issuing a restraining order, the probable cause established in the indictment or information is to be determinative of any issue regarding the merits of the government's case on which the forfeiture is to be based.

S. Rep. No. 225, 98th Cong., 2d Sess. 203 (1984), reprinted in 1984 U.S. Code Cong. & Administrative News 3182, 3386.

Although section 853 provides that the court "may" enter a post-indictment restraining order upon the Government's application, suggesting a certain amount of discretion, the Supreme Court in *United States v. Monsanto*, 491 U.S. 600, 612-14 (1989), made it clear that government applications for such orders should generally be granted, ruling that it was error to import "traditional principles of equity" and equitable balancing tests into the process of issuing and reviewing forfeiture restraining orders:

> This reading seriously misapprehends the nature of the provisions in question. As we have said, § 853(a) is categorical.... Under § 853(e)(1), the trial court "may" enter a restraining order if the United States requests it, but not otherwise, and it is not required to enter such an order if a bond or some other means to "preserve the availability of property described in subsection (a) of this section for forfeiture" is employed. Thus, § 853(e)(1)(A) is plainly aimed at implementing the commands of § 853(a) and cannot sensibly be construed to give the district court discretion to permit the dissipation of the very property that § 853(a) requires be forfeited upon conviction.
>
> ...Whatever discretion Congress gave the district courts in §§ 853(e) and 853(c), that discretion must be cabined by the purposes for which Congress created it: "to preserve the availability of property...for forfeiture." We cannot believe that Congress intended to permit the effectiveness of the powerful "relation-back" provision of § 853(c), and the comprehensive "any property...any proceeds" language of § 853(a), to be nullified by any other construction of the statute.
>
> This result may seem harsh, but we have little doubt that it is the one that the statute mandates. Section 853(c) states that "[a]ll right, title, and interest in [forfeitable] property...vests in the United States upon the commission of the act giving rise to forfeiture." Permitting a defendant to use assets for his private purposes that, under this provision, will become the property of the United States if a conviction occurs cannot be sanctioned.

Monsanto, 491 U.S. at 612-13.

Most circuits deciding the issue have concluded that such post-indictment restraining orders may be entered ex parte, with no pre-restraint hearing. United States v. Jones, 160 F.3d 641, 647-49 (10th Cir. 1998) (pre-trial restraints may be imposed ex parte); United States v. Jenkins, 974 F.2d 32, 35-36 (5th Cir. 1992) (no due process violation where post-indictment restraining order was entered ex parte); United States v. Monsanto, 924 F.2d 1186, 1192-93 (2d Cir. 1991) (unanimous en banc court on remand from Supreme Court) (strong Government interests and exigent circumstances in forfeiture context justify imposition of pre-trial restraints without pre-restraint hearing); United States v. Bissell, 866 F.2d 1343, 1352 (11th Cir. 1989) (no right to pre-restraint hearing, citing Calero-Toledo v. Pearson Yacht Leasing Co., 416 U.S. 663, 683 (1974) [upholding ex parte seizure of personal property]); United States v. Moya Gomez, 860 F.2d 706, 727-28 (7th Cir. 1989) (quoting legislative history to effect that post-indictment restraining order does not require prior notice or opportunity for hearing); id. at 730 (holding statutory scheme unconstitutional only to limited extent that it does not provide for post-restraint hearing before trial); United States v. Spilotro, 680 F.2d 612, 617 (9th Cir. 1982) (forfeiture under exigent circumstances creates exception to pre-deprivation hearing rule, citing Calero-Toledo); but see United States v. Melrose East Subdivision, 357 F.3d 493, 499 n.3 (5th Cir. 2004) (leaving question of pre-restraint hearing in criminal cases open, but noting authority that due process does not require pre-restraint hearing for post-indictment restraining orders); United States v. Kirschenbaum, 156 F.3d 784, 793-94 (7th Cir. 1998) (suggesting in dicta that issue whether due process requires pre-restraint hearing is "difficult" and "close," but not reaching issue); United States v. Riley, 78 F.3d 367, 370 (8th Cir. 1996) (declaring pre-conviction restraints "extreme" measures that may only be imposed where Government demonstrates "at a hearing" that defendant is likely guilty and property to be restrained will be subject to forfeiture upon conviction). Cf. United States v. Hernandez-Escarsega, 886 F.2d 1560 (9th Cir. 1989) (in deciding whether probable cause supported issuance of search warrant, magistrate judge entitled to consider that grand jury recently returned an indictment against the subjects of the search).

Second, the grand jury's finding of a probable nexus between the property and the offense may be accorded deference in subsequent proceedings where probable cause is at issue, including challenges to pre-trial restraint of assets allegedly needed to pay a defendant's attorneys' fees. One circuit views the grand jury's finding of probable cause as sufficient to satisfy the Government's burden to uphold restraints under section 853(e)(1)(A) until trial. See United States v. Bollin, 264 F.3d 391, 421 (4th Cir. 2001) (citing In re Assets of Billman, 915 F.2d 916, 919 (4th Cir. 1990)). Although "the indictment itself establishes the merits of the government's case" for purposes of post-indictment restraints, other circuits recognize that in extreme situations, due process may require inquiry even into matters decided by the grand jury. United States v. Real Property in Waterboro, 64 F.3d 752, 755-56 (1st Cir. 1995); see United States v. Monsanto, 924 F.2d at 1191 (due process requires post-restraint hearing where assets needed for attorneys' fees are involved).

The recent trend in the law is to continue post-indictment restraints based upon the grand jury's finding of probable cause unless and until the defendant establishes both (1) an actual need for the restrained assets for, among other important purposes, attorneys' fees or living expenses, and (2) that there is some substantial evidence that the assets are not forfeitable. See United States v. Jones, 160 F.3d 641, 647-48 (10th Cir. 1998) (defendant challenging pre-trial restraint of assets alleged to be forfeitable has initial burden of showing that she has no funds other than the restrained assets to hire private counsel or to pay living expenses, and that there is bona fide reason to believe restraining order should not have been entered); United States v. Farmer, 274 F.3d 800, 804-05 (4th Cir. 2001) (defendant entitled to pre-trial hearing if property is seized for civil forfeiture and defendant demonstrates no other assets are available; following Jones).

Third, the grand jury's finding of probable cause is arguably sufficient to trigger the bar on intervention by third parties set forth in section 853(k)(2). Section 853(k)(2) prevents persons claiming interest in allegedly forfeitable property from

> commenc[ing] an action at law or equity against the United States concerning the validity of his alleged interest in the property *subsequent to the filing of an indictment or information alleging that the property is subject to forfeiture* under this section.

21 U.S.C. § 853(k)(2) (emphasis added).

That the indictment alleges that property is subject to forfeiture indicates that the grand jury has made a probable cause determination. If the indictment only gives notice of forfeiture rather than alleging that particular property is forfeitable, and no explicit probable cause finding is included in the notice, then arguably the filing of the indictment would not bar collateral litigation over the property.

Fourth, that the grand jury has found probable cause to believe certain property is forfeitable, or to believe the defendant is liable for a certain forfeiture money judgment amount, increases the impact of the actual notice of forfeitability received by a hypothetical reasonable attorney or third party upon learning of the indictment. Such notice affects the ability of any such persons to continue to receive or retain forfeitable property of the defendant as "bona fide purchasers...reasonably without cause to believe that the property [is] subject to forfeiture." *See* sections 853(c) and (n)(6)(B); *United States v. McCorkle*, 321 F.3d 1292, 1295 n.4 (11th Cir. 2003) (attorney may lose bona fide purchaser status as to advance fee received from client "because the client is indicted and the attorney learns additional information about his client's guilt"); *see also Caplin & Drysdale, Chartered v. United States*, 491 U.S. 617, 633 n.10 (1989) ("the only way a lawyer could be a beneficiary of section 853(n)(6)(B)['s bona fide purchaser provision] would be to fail to read the indictment of his client").

Fifth, the grand jury's probable cause finding may help insulate case agents and prosecutors from subsequent liability under *Bivens*[28] or the Hyde Amendment.[29] The grand jury's probable cause determination is at least some evidence tending to negate any inference that an action was commenced without probable cause. *See*, e.g., *Robinson v. Cattaraugus County*, 147 F.3d 153, 163 (2d Cir. 1998) (in malicious prosecution action under 42 U.S.C. § 1983, district court did not err in instructing that grand jury's probable cause determination was evidence that trial jury could consider in deciding whether prosecution was commenced without probable cause).

Finally, the practice of presenting forfeiture evidence to the grand jury, listing particular forfeitable assets in the indictment, and requesting that the grand jury find probable cause for forfeiture of those assets should help to defend indictments against future challenge if *Blakely* is ultimately construed or extended to apply to criminal forfeiture and to require that the facts supporting forfeiture of particular assets be charged in the indictment and proven to the trial jury beyond a reasonable doubt.

For all of these reasons, prosecutors should ask the grand jury to find probable cause to believe that the requisite nexus exists between the crimes charged and any particular property or money judgment amount alleged to be forfeitable.

B.4. It Is Not Necessary to Ask the Grand Jury to Determine the Defendant's Interest in Forfeitable Property

A separate issue is whether the prosecutor should also ask the grand jury to find probable cause to believe that "the defendant (or some combination of defendants [charged] in the case) had an interest in the property that is forfeitable under the applicable statute." *See* Fed. R. Crim. P. 32.2(c)(2). Unlike the forfeiture nexus, this issue is not even presented to the *trial* jury. Indeed, the court itself only reaches the issue of the defendant's interest in forfeitable property in cases where no ancillary claims to the property are filed. Moreover, unlike the nexus finding, which serves the various useful purposes outlined above, a finding of probable cause to believe that the defendant has an interest in particular property serves no comparable purpose in most cases. Therefore, it does not make sense to present this issue to the grand jury.

Nonetheless, in cases where the defendant has attempted to conceal an interest in property subject to forfeiture, it may be important to the grand jury's understanding of the case—and its ability to make necessary findings as to elements of charged offenses—to present evidence concerning the defendant's actual, although hidden, interest in forfeitable property. For example, in a case where the defendant acquires or transfers property in such a way as to "conceal or disguise the nature, the location, the source, the ownership, or the control" of criminal proceeds in violation of 18 U.S.C. § 1956(a)(1)(B)(i), the prosecutor may be required to present evidence to the grand jury tending to show that the defendant in fact had ownership or control of the property involved in such a transaction.

In any event, because only property of the defendant can be forfeited in a criminal case, the prosecutor should make reasonable efforts to establish that any property alleged to be forfeitable, and particularly property sought to be restrained as forfeitable, is property of the defendants within the meaning of the applicable forfeiture statutes, including section 853(c), which voids purported post-crime transfers of forfeitable property other than to bona fide purchasers for value reasonably without cause to believe the property was subject to forfeiture.

B.5. Presenting Forfeiture Evidence to the Grand Jury

Just as most trial evidence relating to forfeiture is usually best, and most easily, presented as an integral part of the overall presentation of the Government's case-in-chief, most grand jury evidence bearing on forfeiture is best, and most easily, presented as an integral part of the evidence establishing probable cause to charge the underlying criminal offenses. Questions about assets and their links to criminal activity should be asked of all witnesses likely to have such knowledge, during both lengthy grand jury investigations and the more abbreviated presentations appropriate to cases investigated primarily outside of the grand jury.

When this practice is followed, a case agent or other government witness can be brought in shortly before an indictment is returned to summarize previous testimony and documentary evidence bearing on forfeiture. In addition to reminding the grand jury of such previously presented evidence, the summary witness should be prepared to present any additional documents and information necessary to calculate the amount of any proposed forfeiture money judgment and identify and describe any particular assets to be alleged as forfeitable in the proposed indictment. It is usually best to have previously marked asset-related documents—such as certified copies of public real estate, business, and vehicle registration and title records, authentic photographs of major assets, and stipulated or authenticated bank and other financial account statements—available for examination by the grand jury during its consideration of the proposed indictment, including the forfeiture allegations.

Even if forfeiture has not been an ongoing focus of the investigation, the evidence necessary to establish the required link between the charged offenses and the particular forfeitable assets to be listed in the indictment can usually be presented by a government agent witness in a simple and straightforward manner, not requiring much grand jury time. The focus in such a presentation, as in the summary presentation described above, should be upon (1) the facts that identify the assets with particularity, and (2) the facts that make the assets forfeitable under all applicable theories of forfeiture—e.g., facts indicating that the assets "constitute, or were derived from, proceeds" of the offenses; that the assets were "used, or intended to be used, in any manner or part, to commit, or to facilitate the commission" of the offenses; that the assets constitute "property, real or personal, involved in" the offenses or "property traceable to such property," etc. *See*, e.g., section 853(a) and 18 U.S.C. § 982(a)(1).

B.6. Instructing the Grand Jury on Forfeiture

If it is consistent with local practice to do so, the prosecutor may explain to the grand jury preliminarily that (1) forfeiture is not a substantive offense, or an element of an offense, but rather a required part of the punishment imposed upon conviction for certain criminal offenses; (2) the forfeiture allegations in the proposed indictment will put the defendant on notice that the Government is seeking to forfeit certain property, or types of property, upon the defendant's conviction; and (3) the Government will seek to forfeit substitute assets of the defendant if some act or omission of the defendant makes the directly forfeitable property unavailable.[30]

The prosecutor should then instruct the grand jury with respect to the links that must be found to exist between the charged offenses and the assets alleged to be forfeitable. Generally, this may be done by reading and explaining the pertinent parts of the applicable forfeiture statutes, explaining how each listed asset falls within one or more of the forfeiture provisions, and explaining the basis for calculating or estimating the amount to be alleged as a forfeiture money judgment.

Finally, if the grand jurors have no questions about the forfeiture instructions, the prosecutor should ask the grand jury, during its process of considering the entire indictment, to find probable cause to believe that the listed assets have the required links to the charged offenses and that there is a factual basis for the alleged money judgment amount.

B.7. Memorializing and Describing the Grand Jury's Probable Cause Finding

As explained in section II.B.3, there are several good reasons for asking the grand jury to find probable cause for forfeiture of particular assets. If the grand jury was actually asked to make such a finding in the course of its deliberations on the indictment, prosecutors may properly represent to the court, in connection with an application for a post-indictment restraining order or otherwise, that the grand jury has found probable cause to believe that the requisite forfeiture nexus exists with respect to the money judgment amount and any other property listed in the indictment as forfeitable.

To make the grand jury's probable cause finding readily accessible for seeking and defending pre-trial restraints and the other purposes described in section II.B.3, it is a good practice to memorialize the finding in the indictment itself. There are several ways to accomplish this.

The grand jury finding as to forfeitability may be set forth in the indictment in a way that simply parallels the presentation of the other substantive charges and allegations in the indictment as to which the grand jury also found probable cause. Practices vary from district to district with respect to whether phrases like "The grand jury charges" appear only at the beginning of the indictment or repeatedly, e.g., "The grand jury further charges", at the beginning of each count. In either case, introducing the forfeiture allegations in the same way as the substantive counts makes it reasonably plain on the face of the indictment that the grand jury has made a probable cause determination with respect to the entire indictment, including the forfeiture allegations.

In a district where there is frequent litigation over pre-trial restraints, the prosecutor may wish to give special emphasis to the grand jury's finding of probable cause for forfeiture of particular assets by making that finding explicit in the text of the indictment: "The grand jury further finds probable cause to believe that upon conviction of the offense[s] in violation of ______ set forth in Count[s] [##] of this Indictment/Information, the defendant[s], [NAME(S)], shall forfeit to the United States of America, pursuant to ___ U.S.C. ___, all [insert statutory language], including, without limitation, $______ in United States currency and the following other particular assets: ____ ." If this approach is used, it should be used consistently to avoid any negative implication that a grand jury returning an indictment with no such explicit finding did *not* find probable cause for forfeiture.

In districts that use the convention of merely giving notice of forfeiture in indictments rather than alleging forfeiture in forfeiture allegations or charging forfeiture in a forfeiture count, it is best practice to include an explicit probable cause finding of forfeitability in the notice section. Doing so will counter any possible implication or argument that the forfeiture notice was merely appended to the indictment without grand jury consideration and determination of probable cause.

PART 9: INTERNATIONAL FORFEITURE

I. Background

Federal law enforcement should give priority to pursuing forfeitable assets beyond the borders of the United States. Federal investigators and prosecutors who seek to restrain and forfeit illicit assets located abroad should seek the advice of the Asset Forfeiture and Money Laundering Section (AFMLS). It is advisable to make this contact as soon as foreign assets that might become subject to a U.S. forfeiture judgment are identified by the investigator or prosecutor. The extent and speed of forfeiture assistance can vary greatly depending upon the existence of treaty obligations and the operation of foreign law. International requests for legal assistance can touch upon diplomatically sensitive issues and may require coordination with foreign or other domestic investigations. AFMLS will help guide you through this often complicated process.

II. Importance of Reciprocal Cooperation

The Department gives high priority to requests by foreign countries for assistance in restraining, forfeiting, and repatriating assets found in the United States that are traceable to violations of foreign law. We can expect cooperation from foreign governments in our efforts to forfeit and repatriate assets found abroad in U.S. cases only if we reciprocate in a timely and effective manner. Additionally, it is important for the United States to act on these incoming requests so that it is not perceived as a haven for foreign criminal proceeds. Treaty requests to enforce foreign forfeiture orders and judgments that require AAG certification under Section 2467 of Title 28 are typically assigned to the AFMLS International Unit to handle. Other incoming forfeiture requests may be assigned to a USAO. Once the Office of International Affairs (OIA) refers a forfeiture-related request to a specific district for execution, AFMLS will advise or assist the district with the execution of that request. As a practical matter, AFMLS and OIA agree that when such foreign requests for forfeiture assistance are directed to a USAO, it should be assigned to the established forfeiture contacts in that district.

III. Policy on International Contacts

It has long been the policy of the Department of Justice that all international contacts by prosecutors in criminal justice matters be coordinated with and through OIA. OIA is the U.S. Central Authority under mutual legal assistance treaties (MLATs) and serves as the channel through which the United States must make all formal requests to foreign governments for legal assistance. The U.S. Attorney's Manual (USAM) and the Criminal Resource Manual recognize that direct communications with persons abroad may implicate Department policy. For that reason, the manuals instruct prosecutors to contact OIA prior to engaging in international contacts. Prosecutors should adhere to established procedures for international contacts and should not contact foreign officials or other persons directly on case matters unless such contacts have been approved by, are under the supervision of, or are in consultation with OIA. OIA may permit prosecutors to have direct contact with foreign officials provided that OIA is copied on or informed about all the relevant communications. Because each case is different, and the rules on direct contacts may differ depending on the countries involved, investigators and prosecutors should consult with OIA regarding such contacts in each case.

IV. Foreign Property Management Issues

Non-fungible assets located abroad may present unique property management issues. Federal prosecutors and investigators should keep in mind that although many countries are willing to restrain or seize assets in support of U.S. forfeiture efforts, some countries lack the resources, experience, or legal regime that allows for adequate property management pending the resolution of the U.S. forfeiture proceeding. Certain property located abroad may require post-seizure or post-restraint preservation or management, and this will require extensive pre-seizure planning. Foreign governments may be willing to assume responsibility of preserving assets, or they may ask the United States to do so, and the United States or the foreign government may need to hire, or legally appoint, guardians, monitors, trustees, or managers for certain assets. Prosecutors should be aware that the costs of storing, maintaining, and disposing of certain assets such as vehicles, vessels, or aircraft in a foreign country may—in protracted international forfeiture cases—exceed the value of the asset itself.

When faced with the seizure of non-fungible assets abroad that may require management, a federal prosecutor or investigator should contact the U.S. Marshals Service (USMS). The USMS, if needed, may enlist the assistance of the Diplomatic Security Services, which has been cross-designated by the USMS to provide property management services for property restrained or seized abroad. In cases where the lead law enforcement agency is a Department of Treasury or Department of Homeland Security agency, the federal prosecutor or investigator should contact the Department of Treasury, Executive Office of for Asset Forfeiture (TEOAF) at 202-622-9600. AFMLS must be consulted before the United States asks a foreign government to restrain or seize an ongoing business or its assets or to appoint or hire a guardian, monitor, trustee, or manager for same.

Finally, in order to accurately track assets restrained abroad, it is important to create a Frozen, Indicted, Restrained, Encumbered (FIRE) asset in CATS prior to requesting restraint of assets abroad. In cases where the lead law enforcement agency is a Department of Treasury or Department of Homeland Security agency and the asset is being tracked in the Asset Forfeiture Tracking and Retrieval (AFTRACK) system, the federal prosecutor or investigator should still ensure that a parallel FIRE asset is created in CATS.

V. Publication of Notice Abroad

In both civil and criminal forfeiture proceedings, the United States is required to provide notice by publication which may occur on the Government forfeiture website, www.forfeiture.gov.[1]

Publication on the Internet provides better notice than newspaper publications because it is available 24 hours a day, it is reachable by anyone throughout the globe with access to the Internet, and it is searchable. Therefore, in the absence of a compelling reason to use print publication, publication on the Internet should be considered the norm and print publication the exception.

However, depending on the facts of the case, it may be appropriate to publish notice in a newspaper of general circulation in the country where the assets are restrained or seized or via legal notices in that country where known potential claimants are located, and to do so in the appropriate foreign language. Publication abroad should be requested in the manner and format that complies with the requirements of domestic publication and, as much as is possible, in the manner requested by the foreign government providing assistance with the publication.

Some foreign governments will assist with publication, while other governments allow us to make our own arrangements. In many instances, we can rely upon U.S. law enforcement attachés stationed in foreign countries to arrange for publication. Some foreign governments will not assist the United States with publication but still require that we obtain permission before we publish in their jurisdiction. Other countries do not want publication in their country done at all. Typically, the United States pays for any publication abroad. AFMLS should be consulted to ascertain a foreign government's preferences when it comes to notice by publication in a foreign country before attempting publication in that country.

At this time, publication on www.forfeiture.gov is limited to English. AFMLS has requested a change to the system that will allow publication in other languages.

VI. Consultation with AFMLS and OIA When Seeking Repatriation of Forfeitable Assets Located Abroad

When a foreign government has restrained or seized assets based upon a formal request for assistance from the United States, the prosecutor should consult the AFMLS and OIA attorneys handling the case before seeking repatriation of those assets. The AFMLS and OIA attorneys are familiar with foreign legal constraints that apply to the repatriation of forfeitable assets, as well as sensibilities that some foreign governments have against repatriation. Consequently, prosecutors must consult AFMLS and OIA before taking any action to repatriate such assets. Repatriation of frozen assets will require that any foreign restraint order be lifted, which can only be done with the consent of the foreign country, usually, after receipt of a formal request from the United States, made by OIA. In some cases, it may not be possible to lift the foreign restraint simply by resolving the U.S. matter; for example, in jurisdictions that have mandatory prosecution laws. *See* discussion in section XI.

Federal prosecutors and investigators should always consult with an AFMLS and an OIA attorney before entering into an agreement with a defendant to repatriate criminally derived assets located abroad, even when the asset is not restrained by the foreign government. Prosecutors should also consult with AFMLS and OIA before seeking an order actually compelling the repatriation of specific assets pursuant to 21 U.S.C. § 853(e)(4). Such repatriation efforts can be controversial for a number of reasons. First, the property at issue may be subject to domestic proceedings in the foreign jurisdiction. Second, certain countries deem another government's efforts at repatriating assets located in that country's jurisdiction to be a violation of that country's sovereignty, and in rare instances, deem any persons who instigate or are involved in that process to be involved in a criminal offense such as money laundering. In addition, although many countries often do not object to a negotiated voluntary repatriation of assets and allow such transfers to occur as part of a plea or settlement agreement, these countries often will object to court-ordered repatriations because they regard such an order as a "coercive measure" that violates a person's rights under the laws of that foreign state. Other countries take the position that a failure to inform them of forfeitable assets located in their jurisdiction is a violation of specific treaty obligations. Finally, in matters where the United States previously asked a foreign government to restrain an asset, a voluntary repatriation obviously will require the lifting of the foreign restraint, which, although legally permissible, may subject the foreign jurisdiction to unintended legal liabilities under the foreign law, such as attorneys' fees.

VII. Probable Cause Finding to Seize or Restrain Assets Abroad

As the result of a federal district court case, *Kim v. Department of Justice*,[2] which held that the United States must demonstrate probable cause to seize or restrain assets located abroad before requesting another country to do so, AFMLS and OIA, in the exercise of caution, advise prosecutors seeking the seizure or restraint of property located abroad to obtain a probable cause finding regarding the property in question before asking OIA to make the request. Without conceding that the *Kim* case was correctly decided, we note that there are a number of ways listed below to obtain such a probable cause finding.[3] Nothing in this section is intended to suggest that such a probable cause finding is necessary other than as a matter of policy.

A. Civil Forfeiture Cases

In a civil forfeiture case, there are at least three options for obtaining a probable cause determination: a warrant of arrest in rem, seizure warrant, and a restraining order.

A.1. Warrant of Arrest In Rem

The preferred means of obtaining the requisite probable cause finding is to obtain an arrest warrant in rem from the district court after a civil forfeiture complaint has been filed. Supplemental Rule G(3)(b)(ii) and (c)(iv) require a probable cause finding by a judge or magistrate judge before any arrest warrant in rem is issued for property that is not already in the custody of the Government, and provide for sending the warrant to a foreign country if the property is located abroad. Obtaining an arrest warrant in rem under Rule G will be the best and easiest means of obtaining the required probable cause finding in support of MLAT requests asking another country to seize or restrain property abroad.

A.2. Civil Seizure Warrant

Another option is to obtain a civil seizure warrant for the property pursuant to 18 U.S.C. § 981(b)(2) in the same manner as provided for a search warrant under the Federal Rules of Criminal Procedure. Such a warrant requires a finding of probable cause and can be done on an *ex parte* basis. Section 981(b) applies to all property subject to civil forfeiture under section 981(a) (the general forfeiture statute for most federal crimes), and any other forfeiture statute that contains language incorporating the procedures in Part 46 of Title 18 of the U.S. Code, such as 21 U.S.C. § 881(a) (the civil forfeiture statute for drug offenses the alien smuggling provisions in 8 U.S.C. § 1324(b)).[4] Accordingly, section 981(b) is available as a means of obtaining a probable cause finding in the vast majority of federal civil forfeiture actions; however, where a statute does not incorporate section 981(b), the prosecutor will have to make sure that there is an alternative statutory basis for the pre-complaint seizure of the foreign property on a finding of probable cause.

In seeking such a warrant, it may be helpful to explain to the district court the statutory basis for its authority to order the seizure of assets in a foreign country. A court has the authority to issue seizure warrants for assets located in a foreign jurisdiction pursuant to 18 U.S.C. § 981(b)(3). Section 981(b)(3) provides that a seizure warrant may be issued by a "judicial officer in any district in which a forfeiture action against the property may be filed under [28 U.S.C. § 1355(b)], and may be executed in any district in which the property is found, or transmitted to the central authority of any foreign state for service in accordance with any treaty or other international agreement." 18 U.S.C. § 981(b)(3). Even though the property subject to forfeiture is located in a foreign jurisdiction, pursuant to 28 U.S.C. § 1355(b) a forfeiture action may be brought in any district court where some of the acts giving rise to the forfeiture occurred.

One concern about using a seizure warrant under section 981(b) is that it incorporates the rules contained in Federal Rules of Criminal Procedure 41, which requires the warrant to be executed within 14 days. However, section 981(b)(3) states that notwithstanding the provisions of Rule 41, a seizure warrant may be "transmitted to the central authority of any foreign state for service in accordance with any treaty or other international agreement."

Thus, once a seizure warrant is obtained under section 981(b) and a formal request is made through OIA to the foreign country, the requirements of section 981(b)(3) and Rule 41 should be considered to have been met.

A.3. Restraining Order

Finally, whether or not a complaint has been filed, the Government may ask the court to issue a restraining order pursuant to 18 U.S.C. § 983(j). A restraining order may be issued on an *ex parte* basis. Restraining orders may only be issued upon a showing of probable cause—usually in the form of an affidavit submitted along with the application for the order.[5] Thus, the issuance of a restraining order will constitute the probable cause finding required to support the MLAT request.

B. Criminal Cases

In a criminal forfeiture case, there are at least three options for obtaining a probable cause determination: naming the foreign-based asset in the forfeiture allegation in the indictment, obtaining a restraining order, and obtaining a criminal seizure warrant.

B.1. Indictment

If a pending indictment contains a criminal forfeiture allegation relating to property located abroad, and the grand jury has made a finding of probable cause to believe that the *specific property* listed in the indictment is subject to forfeiture, the indictment itself will serve as the necessary probable cause finding for purposes of the MLAT request.[6]

B.2. Restraining Order

Once the indictment is returned, the Government may obtain a post-indictment *ex parte* restraining order pursuant to 21 U.S.C. § 853(e). Such a restraining order requires a finding of probable cause; therefore, the issuance of the restraining order will also provide the necessary probable cause determination.

The restraining order may be obtained in either of two ways. First, if the property is specifically listed in the indictment, most courts hold that the grand jury's finding of probable cause will be sufficient to support the issuance of a restraining order without any further submission by the Government.[7] However, unless the foreign authority has requested a restraining order to use in its proceeding, it should not be necessary for purposes of complying with *Kim* to obtain such an order where the property was listed in the indictment. Second, if the property is not specifically listed in the indictment but is named in a bill of particulars, the Government may support its application for the restraining order with a probable cause affidavit.

B.3. Criminal Seizure Warrant

The legal authority for the issuance of a criminal seizure warrant against foreign-based property is not explicit. Section 853(f) authorizes an Assistant United States Attorney (AUSA) to obtain a seizure warrant from the court in the same manner as a search warrant under Rule 41, and section 853(l) provides that a federal court has "jurisdiction to enter orders as provided in this section *without regard to the location of any property which may be subject to forfeiture*" (italics added). However, section 853(f) is not as broad as the corresponding authority for civil seizure warrants under section 981(b). Criminal seizure warrants may only be obtained if it appears that a restraining order would be inadequate to preserve the availability of the property for forfeiture. The type of protective measure obtained in the United States or the fact that the Government obtained such an order is usually irrelevant to the outcome of the deliberative process for obtaining a foreign preventive measure on behalf of the United States. Thus, the Government, for the most part, will be unable to present a strong argument to a U.S. court that a Rule 41 seizure warrant will better protect the availability for forfeiture of property located abroad than will a restraining order pursuant to section 853(e), mostly because the foreign government does not execute such orders, but instead obtains and enforces orders obtained pursuant to foreign law. Refraining from using criminal seizure warrants will also avoid the question of whether or not the court has the authority to issue an extra-territorial seizure warrant under Rule 41(b) of the Federal Rules Criminal Procedure. Rule 41(b)(3) permits a federal court to issue warrants for foreign-based property, but only in domestic and international terrorism investigations, and not for any other types of investigations. Section 981(b) expressly overrides the conflicting language in Rule 41(b), whereas section 853(l) does not. For purposes of satisfying the holding in *Kim*, in criminal cases it should always be sufficient to obtain a restraining order rather than risk litigating the scope of Rule 41(b) or try satisfying the higher showing needed to get a seizure warrant under section 853(f).

C. Parallel Civil and Criminal cases

Perhaps the best option is to initiate both civil and criminal forfeiture actions and then stay the civil proceeding pursuant to 18 U.S.C. § 981(g)(1) until the conclusion of the parallel criminal proceedings. In addition to allowing you a choice of options for restraining assets abroad, you will also have preserved your options should the criminal forfeiture fail for any reason.

VIII. Approval Process for Section 981(k) Seizure from Correspondent Bank Account

Section 981(k) authorizes the United States, in a civil forfeiture action, to restrain, seize, and forfeit property held in bank accounts located outside of the United States by permitting the restraint, seizure, and forfeiture of an equivalent amount of funds from any correspondent/interbank account that the foreign financial institution holds in the United States. *See* 18 U.S.C. § 981(k). It is irrelevant for the purpose of section 981(k) whether the foreign funds to be forfeited ever transited through the foreign bank's U.S. correspondent account that is the subject of the section 981(k) forfeiture effort. Section 981(k) can be used to constructively restrain, seize, and forfeit assets abroad without having to resort to a treaty or letter rogatory request. However, use of this provision must be formally approved by AFMLS and will be approved only in extraordinary cases where the foreign government is unable or unwilling to provide assistance.

Approval to use section 981(k) rests with the Chief of AFMLS in consultation with the appropriate officials from OIA, the Department of the Treasury, and the Department of State. Because these stakeholders in the policy issues implicated by the potential use of section 981(k) need an opportunity to review the proposed section 981(k) request to consider its ramifications, formal approval to utilize section 981(k) should be sought well in advance of the intended attempt to restrain or seize assets from any foreign bank's correspondent accounts. Applications requesting approval to use section 981(k) should be submitted in writing to the Chief of AFMLS. Sample section 981(k) approval requests can be obtained from AFMLS. Prosecutors should be mindful that requests for authority to use section 981(k) as the basis for forfeiting funds on deposit in accounts located outside the United States will only be approved if there are no other viable means of effecting forfeiture of the foreign property and should be considered only as a last resort. An application will not be approved solely because it is deemed more expedient than using the treaty mechanism. Section 981(k) requests will be approved only in limited cases, such as when:

(1) There is no applicable treaty, agreement, or legal process in the foreign nation that would allow it to restrain, seize, or forfeit the target assets for the United States;
(2) There is a treaty or agreement in force, but the foreign nation does not recognize the U.S. offense that gives rise to forfeiture;
(3) There is a treaty or agreement in force, and despite its treaty obligation, in the past the foreign nation has failed to provide forfeiture assistance, or provided untimely or unsatisfactory forfeiture assistance;
(4) There is a treaty or agreement in force, but the foreign nation has no domestic enabling legislation that would permit it to fully execute U.S. forfeiture orders or judgments; or
(5) There is another significant reason that in the view of the stakeholders justifies use of section 981(k), e.g., corruption within the foreign government that may compromise the execution of a treaty request, or the inability to repatriate or return victim money to the United States after forfeiture.

Prosecutors should take special care to ensure that once permission is granted to seize funds in a correspondent account, only the amount that can be traced to the foreign bank account can be seized.

IX. Lack of Administrative Forfeiture Authority for Overseas Property

Forfeiture of assets located abroad must be initiated as part of a pending criminal case or judicial civil forfeiture action. There is no authority under federal law to initiate the administrative forfeiture of property that is not physically located in the United States or its territories or possessions. Administrative forfeiture, of course, can be pursued against property repatriated to the United States pursuant to section VI, to the extent that there is no other prohibition to forfeiting such property administratively.

X. Consultation for Civil Forfeiture of Property Located Overseas

According to section 9-13.526 of the USAM, AUSAs shall consult with OIA before filing an in rem forfeiture action based on 28 U.S.C. § 1355(b)(2). OIA and AFMLS will determine whether the foreign country where the assets are located can assist in the U.S. action.

XI. Settlements, Plea Agreements, and Attorneys' Fees

Federal prosecutors should neither agree to, nor enter into, any settlement or plea agreement affecting assets located abroad and should not make any representation about the availability of assets abroad to pay for legal fees incurred by a defendant without first speaking to AFMLS about the foreign consequences of those decisions. *See* USAM 9-111.700. In addition, prosecutors should be aware of limitations on negotiating with fugitives and persons fighting extradition. The policy considerations underlying the consultation and approval procedures that apply to settlement and plea agreements and agreements to use forfeitable funds to pay for attorneys' fees apply with even greater force in the international context, particularly in light of the problems inherent in releasing funds held abroad. *See* section VII. In some cases, a U.S. request to restrain or seize assets will precipitate the initiation of a foreign criminal investigation, as many jurisdictions lack prosecutorial discretion and are required to prosecute all criminal matters brought to their attention. Thus, it may not be possible to make commitments to defendants or claimants regarding the disposition of funds restrained or seized abroad because the funds will remain restrained or seized under foreign law, and the United States has no authority to bind a foreign jurisdiction regarding the disposal of assets made in any U.S. proceedings. In addition, all plea and settlement agreements should include broad waiver and indemnification language that protects both U.S. officials and foreign officials and their governments from any liability for seizing, restraining, or forfeiting assets located abroad. Finally, prosecutors should also get the defendant or claimant to specifically agree to waive any right to attorneys' fees under foreign law as well as agree not to oppose any legal action in any foreign jurisdiction related to U.S. forfeiture efforts or any U.S. request for related financial records.

XII. Enforcement of Judgments

A. Foreign Enforcement of U.S. Judgments

With increasing frequency, countries are able to afford full faith and credit to U.S. forfeiture judgments affecting property within their borders. Before transmitting a forfeiture judgment via OIA to another jurisdiction to be given effect, prosecutors should verify that the judgment is final under U.S. law. In other words, the judgment must be final and no longer on appeal, or, where no appeal has been filed, the time for filing an appeal must have expired. These facts should be noted in the legal assistance request to the foreign authority in the jurisdiction where such judgment is to be enforced. In criminal cases, great care should be taken to obtain a final order or judgment of forfeiture. In no case should a preliminary order of forfeiture, which is only valid as to the criminal defendant, be sent to a foreign authority for execution instead of the completed final order of forfeiture. This is particularly true in cases where an asset forfeited to the United States is not in the name of the defendant, where the defendant has a legal spouse or common law spouse, or when another person could claim a valid interest in the forfeited property even if the defendant has agreed to forfeit the asset in a plea or settlement agreement. Prosecutors should be mindful that third parties who did not appear in the U.S. proceedings may still be permitted to challenge enforcement of the U.S. forfeiture orders under foreign law. Thus, when transmitting a U.S. forfeiture judgment for execution in a foreign country, it is always advisable to show the jurisdiction that third parties were provided or sent notice of the forfeiture proceedings, had an opportunity to challenge the forfeiture, and were either unsuccessful in their challenge or failed to avail themselves of the right to contest the forfeiture.

B. U.S. Enforcement of Foreign Judgments and Restraining Orders

Pursuant to 28 U.S.C. § 2467, the United States can enforce foreign forfeiture judgments. Section 2467 was amended by the *Preserving Foreign Criminal Assets for Forfeiture Act of 2010*, Pub. L. 111-342, § 2, Dec. 22, 2010, 124 Stat. 3607. This is a technical amendment clarifying that the United States can seek the restraint of assets in the United States at the request of another jurisdiction during the pendency of the foreign proceedings. The amended statute makes clear that a final foreign forfeiture judgment is not necessary for the United States to restrain the asset. The amended statute also makes clear that the references to section 983(j) was not intended to be a literal application and references to "civil forfeiture" and U.S. judgment refer to foreign civil or criminal proceedings and foreign judgments.

XIII. International Sharing

It is the policy of the United States to encourage international asset sharing and to recognize all foreign assistance that facilitates U.S. forfeitures so far as consistent with U.S. law. International sharing is governed by 18 U.S.C. § 981(i), 21 U.S.C. § 882(e)(1)(E), and 31 U.S.C. § 9703(h)(2), and is often guided by standing international sharing agreements or the subject of a future case-specific forfeiture sharing arrangement to be negotiated by AFMLS and approved by the Department of State. The decision to share assets forfeited to the United States with a foreign government is a completely discretionary function of the Attorney General or the Secretary of the Treasury. It requires the concurrence of the Secretary of State, and, in certain circumstances, it is a decision that can be disapproved by Congress. The 1992 international sharing memorandum of understanding between the Departments of State, Justice, and Treasury expressly prohibits investigators or prosecutors from making representations to foreign officials "that assets will be transferred in a particular case, until an international agreement and commitment to transfer assets have been approved by the Secretary of State and the Attorney General or the Secretary of the Treasury." Prosecutors and federal law enforcement agencies always should be mindful that any domestic sharing occurs after all international sharing is completed, and that the domestic sharing of assets located abroad will come from the federal share, which is the amount of money that the United States has available after completion of the international sharing process. Moreover, in all cases, both international and domestic, sharing comes from the net forfeited proceeds after all case-related expenses have been deducted. Thus, federal prosecutors and investigators should take care not to make any representations about the sharing of forfeitable assets located abroad or forfeited domestically with the assistance of a foreign government to either representatives of the foreign government or any of the domestic law enforcement partners whose assistance may have contributed to the seizure and ultimate forfeiture of the assets in question.

Foreign governments are not required to follow a specific process to submit a sharing request to the United States. They may do so pursuant to a treaty, a sharing agreement, or even via other diplomatic or law enforcement channels. Prosecutors and law enforcement agencies can and should make spontaneous sharing recommendations whenever they receive foreign assistance that facilitated the forfeiture of an asset in a U.S. case, particularly when that asset is located in the United States. When the United States forfeits assets in a judicial forfeiture case with the help of a foreign state and the seizing agency is a Department of Justice component or participant in the Department of Justice Assets Forfeiture Fund, it is the responsibility of the federal prosecutor assigned to the case to send a formal sharing recommendation to AFMLS. In an administrative forfeiture matter, the seizing agency is responsible for the recommendation. In cases that implicate the Treasury forfeiture fund, the seizing agency, e.g., Internal Revenue Service, U.S. Secret Service, or Immigration and Customs Enforcement, has the responsibility to send a sharing recommendation to TEOAF. However, the seizing agency should consult the prosecutor on the case first. For Department of Justice forfeiture fund international sharing recommendations, AFMLS prepares the sharing recommendations for approval by the Deputy Attorney General. For Treasury forfeiture fund international sharing recommendations, the Director of TEOAF approves the sharing recommendations. AFMLS and TEOAF also obtain State Department and each other's concurrence for each proposed transfer to a foreign government after it is approved by their respective designees. This interagency process can be lengthy. To avoid delays, it is advisable to make the international sharing recommendation as soon as is practicable, or immediately after the final order forfeiting the foreign assets is obtained. At the earliest possible time, the seizing agency should note in any electronic asset tracking system, such as CATS or TALONS, that a particular asset might be, is, or will be subject to an international sharing request or recommendation—and definitely before that asset has been liquidated. In order to place a hold on an asset for international sharing, the seizing agency must either (1) select "international sharing anticipated" when creating the Standard Seizure Form (SSF), or (2) enter a sharing recommendation in the international sharing module. Either of these actions will prevent the asset from being shared domestically until a pre-approval or approval ruling is entered by AFMLS. Prosecutors and federal law enforcement agencies always should be mindful that domestic sharing will occur only after completion of the international sharing process, and will be taken from the federal share, which is the amount of money that the United States has available at that time.

Lastly, with increasing frequency countries are enacting laws to permit them to share domestically forfeited assets with other countries. Accordingly, if U.S. prosecutors or investigators assisted in foreign cases that resulted in a foreign forfeiture, they are encouraged to contact AFMLS to see whether it would be fruitful to submit a sharing request to that country.

PART 10: APPOINTMENT OF TRUSTEES AND MONITORS

I. Quick Points

A. Purpose

The purpose of the trustee and monitor policy is to provide guidance for the appointment of court-appointed trustees and monitors in cases involving complex assets or business enterprises in Department of Justice federal forfeiture cases.

B. Responsibilities of Trustees and Monitors

The key distinction between a monitor and a trustee is that a trustee has the authority to manage an enterprise. A monitor observes and reports findings. Note: a receiver is a fiduciary who is responsible only to the court and cannot be paid from the Assets Forfeiture Fund (AFF).

C. Circumstances in Which a Trustee or Monitor Should Be Engaged

In almost all cases, the value of an ongoing business can be preserved without appointment of a trustee or monitor. In the typical forfeiture case where property has been restrained criminally or civilly, the U.S. Marshals Service (USMS) has the capability with its own resources or with a property management contract to manage and sell property, including most businesses.

Appointment of a trustee or monitor will occur only when (1) it is plainly necessary, (2) other alternatives have been considered and rejected, and (3) there is clearly sufficient net equity in the asset to cover the cost of the trustee or monitor. The Government must avoid involvement in the management of businesses that require aggressive action, capital investment to remain competitive, or assumption of considerable risk. In rare cases, compelling law enforcement or policy considerations warrant the appointment of a trustee or monitor where there may be insufficient equity in the enterprise to cover the cost of the trustee.

D. Pre-Seizure Planning

In cases involving the appointment of trustees and monitors, prompt comprehensive pre-seizure planning with the USMS is mandatory.

E. Federal Acquisitions Regulations

All federal procurement rules and regulations must be followed in order to award a contract to a trustee or monitor. Under the federal acquisitions regulations (FAR), only the government contracting officer (CO) and contracting officer's technical representative (COTR) of record are authorized to direct the work of a trustee or monitor. All instructions to the trustee or monitor, whether from the U.S. Attorney's Office (USAO) or USMS, are communicated through the COTR.

F. Selection and Appointment of a Trustee or Monitor

The USMS Office of Procurement will award a contract to a trustee or monitor based on a court order or competitive procedures outlined in the FAR. A sole source contract, although discouraged, can be awarded to a trustee or monitor as long as an appropriate justification is provided to the CO. Typical justification includes *urgent and compelling* circumstances or where only one known source can provide the required services.

G. Payment of Monitor and Trustee Fees and Expenses

Prior to entry of a final order of forfeiture, the AFF, 28 U.S.C. § 524(c), is available under certain circumstances to pay trustee and monitor fees in cases where a Department of Justice agency is the lead law enforcement agency. Upon the entry of an order of forfeiture, payment of fees charged by a trustee ordinarily will be made from the proceeds of the business unless compelling law enforcement or policy considerations warrant payment from the AFF. Charges to the AFF for trustees and monitors are to be recovered, as a cost, from the proceeds of sale prior to the payment of restitution, restoration, remission, and equitable sharing.

H. Goals, Duties, and Powers of the Trustee or Monitor

The restraining order or other order appointing a trustee or monitor and a statement of work define the goals of the trustee or monitor. Prior to appointment, an initial assessment must be made to determine the purpose of the trusteeship or monitorship, i.e., to prevent dissipation of the asset or to prevent the enterprise from engaging in illegal activity, or both.

I. Reporting Requirements of the Trustee or Monitor

The trustee or monitor reports directly to the COTR. The USAO and USMS Asset Forfeiture Office (AFO) are encouraged to consult with and work with the trustee or monitor in carrying out the contract, but it is the COTR who directs the work of the trustee or monitor.

J. Dispute Resolution

The USAO and USMS must consult and work closely together to address issues related to the need for engaging a trustee or monitor, as well as issues related to the duties and responsibilities of a trustee or monitor. Dispute resolution must be sought from the Asset Forfeiture and Money Laundering Section (AFMLS). Timely resolution of disputes is critical.

- The USAO must consult with AFMLS before seeking the appointment of a trustee or monitor.
- The USMS field office must notify USMS headquarters when it becomes aware that a trustee or monitor may be appointed.
- The USAO or USMS must notify the Asset Forfeiture Management Staff (AFMS) when they become aware that a business is losing money, has insufficient equity, or will be sold at a loss.

II. Department of Justice Policy: Trustees and Monitors in Forfeiture Cases

A. Purpose

The purpose of the trustee and monitor policy is to provide guidance that best serves the interests of the Department of Justice components in Department of Justice federal forfeiture cases on the court appointment of trustees and monitors in diverse cases involving complex assets or business enterprises, including assets located in foreign countries. These guidelines seek to achieve the following:

(1) Preserve assets for the Government in order to achieve the ultimate goals of separating criminals from assets that are the proceeds of or have facilitated criminal activity and of dismantling criminal enterprises;

(2) Clarify our procurement obligations, while enhancing communication between USAOs and the USMS;

(3) Clarify responsibilities with respect to pre-seizure planning in any case in which there is the potential for the appointment of a trustee or monitor;
(4) Provide mechanisms for dispute resolution;
(5) Provide guidance in determining whether the AFF is an appropriate source of funding for the expenses of trustees and monitors and to promote efficient use of resources.

The following principles underlie this policy:

(1) Unless compelling circumstances exist, the United States shall seek appointment of a trustee or monitor only in cases involving complex assets and/or enterprises and where the United States will recoup its expenses.
(2) Given the labor-intensive nature and the high cost of administering a trusteeship or monitorship, and the potential for ongoing litigation or resolution of other issues even following a final order of forfeiture, trustees and monitors are appointed only when other means of protecting the United States' interests are plainly inadequate or inappropriate.
(3) The least intrusive method of operating a business (in which all or a part of the enterprise or its ownership is subject to forfeiture) should be employed, particularly prior to entry of a final order of forfeiture.

B. Statutory Authority

The authority to appoint a trustee or monitor derives from 18 U.S.C. §§ 1963(d) and (e), 21 U.S.C. §§ 853(e) and (g), and 18 U.S.C. § 983(j), which permit a court to act to preserve property. 18 U.S.C. §§ 1964(a) and (b) grant courts broad injunctive and remedial authority in RICO cases. Unless the trustee or monitor is engaged through an already existing contract, the FAR must be followed. 48 C.F.R. Part 1.000 *et seq*.

C. Definitions and Responsibilities

Historically, the terms *trustee*, *monitor*, *receiver*, and *custodian* have been used somewhat interchangeably in forfeiture cases. The key distinction between a monitor and a trustee is that only a trustee has the authority to manage an enterprise. A monitor reports findings. A receiver is a fiduciary who is responsible only to the court. *Custodian* is a very general term that refers to a fiduciary who takes custody of property.

A trustee is appointed by a court and is granted the authority to manage and/or dispose of property.[1] Trustees may be appointed before or after property has been seized or forfeited.

A monitor is appointed by the court and is responsible for examining the operations of a business or enterprise. A monitor also reports findings to the court as to whether the assets of a business or enterprise are dissipating and will be available for forfeiture to the United States. Monitors do not control the operations of a business or enterprise, but report on their findings. Similarly, monitors do not dispose of property. In some cases, a monitor may be responsible for approving payments (e.g., all payments over $10,000; payments not in the ordinary course of business) or performing other limited oversight functions.[2]

A CO is the only employee with the authority to enter into, administer, and/or terminate contracts and make related determinations and findings. The CO is responsible for ensuring that (1) the requirements of pertinent laws, regulations, etc., have been met; (2) sufficient funds are available for obligation; and (3) contractors receive impartial, fair, and equitable treatment.

The CO typically manages multiple contracts and is rarely the subject matter expert with respect to the contracted goods and services. The COTR is the individual who manages the performance of the contract from a technical perspective after it is awarded. COs appoint COTRs to be the eyes and ears of the CO. The COTR is responsible for directing the work of a trustee or monitor in consultation with the USAO and USMS AFO. While consultation with the trustee and the USMS, USAO, and other government personnel is appropriate and encouraged, only the CO and COTR may direct the work of the trustee. The COTR is given express authority by the CO and typically performs the following functions:

- Assists the contractor in interpreting technical requirements of the contract;
- Recommends changes in contract terms to the CO;
- Monitors and evaluates contractor performance;
- Reviews and approves invoices;
- Recommends corrective actions; and
- Inspects, accepts, or rejects contract deliverables.

Section II.G discusses at length procurement procedures for trustees and monitors under the FAR.

D. Determining When a Trustee or Monitor Should Be Engaged

The ultimate goal in a forfeiture case is to dismantle a criminal enterprise and to deprive a criminal of property used in or acquired as a result of illegal activity. Prior to the Government obtaining custody of an asset as a result of seizure or forfeiture, the Government has an interest in preserving the property for forfeiture and preventing further illegal activity.

Prior to forfeiture, the owners and management of an ongoing business will usually continue to operate the business unless there is probable cause to believe that the owners or management have been or are involved in criminal conduct in operating the business.

In almost all cases, the value of an ongoing business can be preserved without appointment of a trustee or monitor. In the typical forfeiture case where property has been restrained (sections 853(e), 1963(g), and 983(j)) or seized pursuant to a criminal forfeiture warrant (section 853(f) or, civilly, section 981(b)(1), etc.), the USMS has the capability with its own resources or with an existing property management contract to manage and to sell property, including most businesses.

Depending on the nature of the criminal conduct, appointment of a trustee or monitor may be appropriate. The type of oversight required depends on the stage of the case, the degree of ownership targeted for forfeiture, and the nature of the ownership interests (i.e., shares, partnerships, etc.). For example, it is usually preferable to monitor a minority partnership or stock interest. If a trustee is appointed to protect that Government's minority interest, the Government may encounter great difficulties dealing with possibly hostile majority interest holders. Similarly, if the Government has identified a majority interest for forfeiture, it must take into consideration the minority interests when fashioning a trusteeship or monitorship.

Alternatives to the appointment of a monitor or trustee must be considered to determine the least intrusive means of accomplishing and protecting the Government's goals and interests, including, but not limited to:

(1) Particularized restraining order with or without USMS oversight and consequences for violations of the order (such as the appointment of a trustee or monitor or contempt proceedings);
(2) Appointment of a business or property manager by USMS contract;
(3) Restraint or seizure of valuable assets, equipment, or inventory (restraint is preferred);
(4) Oversight and/or management by state or local regulatory agencies;
(5) Filing of a *lis pendens*;
(6) Interlocutory sale;
(7) Foreclosure by a lienholder;
(8) Retention of a professional by agreement of the business and at its own cost, to provide oversight and ensure there are no future violations;
(9) Enforcement of state or local nuisance laws;
(10) Seizure of property to satisfy outstanding tax obligations; and
(11) Performance bond, or some combination of the above.

The Department of Justice must endeavor to avoid involvement in the management of businesses that require aggressive action, capital investment to remain competitive, or assumption of considerable risk. It may be permissible to restrain or seize such a business if it is the only alternative for accomplishing the Government's objectives.

Generally, a protective order must be sought any time an ongoing business entity is targeted for forfeiture. This order should seek to restrain the owners from further encumbering the business, dissipating its assets, or selling the business. If the protective order alone, or in combination with the preceding alternatives, will not ensure the availability of the asset for forfeiture, the appointment of a manager or monitor arranged by a preexisting contract with the USMS may be appropriate. If the appointment of an outside monitor or trustee is sought, FARs must be followed. When considering a monitor or trustee, the business must be determined to be financially viable. Appointment of a trustee will occur only when it is clearly necessary and all other alternatives have been considered and rejected. In some cases, compelling law enforcement or policy considerations may warrant the appointment of a trustee or monitor even though there is not or may not be sufficient equity in the enterprises to cover the cost of the trustee or monitor. In insufficient equity cases, the USAO must thoroughly document the reasons for rejecting alternatives to the appointment of a trustee or monitor.

In addition, AFMS must be notified as soon as the USAO or USMS become aware that a business is losing money, has insufficient equity, or will be sold at a loss. Once it is determined that continued operation of the business is not financially viable, absent compelling circumstances, the USAO will seek to terminate the business as soon as practicable, with due regard for the ownership rights of the defendant/owner (prior to forfeiture) and other partners, shareholders, and third parties. Alternatively, the business could be sold by interlocutory sale, with the assets of the business sold and disposed of, even if such sale may result in a loss.

E. Prerequisites to the Selection of a Trustee or Monitor: Pre-Seizure Planning and Other Requirements

The determination of the appointment of a trustee or monitor is made only after the interested components (USAO, USMS, and investigative agencies) agree on a pre-seizure plan, as discussed below.

The USMS field office is required to notify USMS headquarters as soon as it becomes aware that a trustee or monitor appointment is being contemplated. In cases involving the sort of complex assets that may require a trustee or monitor, pre-seizure planning with the USMS is mandatory. USMS headquarters will notify the USMS Office of Procurement if preexisting contracts will likely not be suitable.

The guidelines for pre-seizure planning require that a USAO:

(1) Contact the USMS to engage in formal pre-seizure planning prior to seizing or restraining certain types of assets, including businesses and real property;
(2) Engage in timely pre-indictment coordination with the USMS in criminal forfeiture cases;
(3) Consult with the USMS prior to the submission of any proposed orders to a court that impose any restraint, seizure, property management, or financial management requirements relating to property in USMS custody;
(4) Consult with AFMLS before initiating a forfeiture action against, or seeking a temporary restraining order affecting, an ongoing business;
(5) Obtain the concurrence of AFMLS before initiating a forfeiture action under a money laundering facilitation theory; and
(6) Consult with AFMLS before seeking the appointment of a trustee or monitor.

Pre-seizure planning includes a financial assessment of the enterprise subject to forfeiture and a determination as to whether it is in the best interest of the Government to take over or to continue the operation of a business. The pre-seizure plan must develop (or include) to the extent feasible an estimate of the (1) net equity subject to forfeiture; (2) cash flow of the business; (3) fees and other costs of the trustee or monitor; and (4) likely duration of the trusteeship or monitorship.

With respect to businesses continuing in operation, once the Government obtains access to business records and other information, a business review must be developed specifically identifying the challenges faced by the business and the requirements for it to succeed. The business review must identify key historic financial data, the current operating environment (including financial activity), and projections for the next 2 years. Projections should address best and worst case scenarios for the operation of the business as well as exit strategies. If the business is likely to lose money or be sold at a loss, the business plan should include a plan to mitigate loss or a plan for liquidation. If necessary, the USMS and AFMS can provide contract services to assist in developing a business plan, and expenses may be paid from the AFF.

The need to maintain confidentiality before indictment, or while an indictment is sealed, may also be critical. Appropriate measures will be taken to ensure that sensitive law enforcement information is protected while consultation and coordination occurs among the involved components.

F. Selection and Appointment of a Trustee or Monitor

F.1. Qualifications of the Trustee or Monitor

The purpose of a trusteeship or monitorship will determine the appropriate qualifications of the trustee or monitor. The trustee or monitor (and personnel on their staff) must have expertise in the enterprise's industry. For example, if the purpose is to manage a business to prevent its dissipation, a trustee with a business and accounting background is preferred. A trustee cannot provide actual law enforcement, such as that provided by federal agents or police personnel. (The AFF is not available to fund law enforcement activities.) It may be necessary for a trustee to retain a consultant or provide personnel to address compliance and enforcement issues that would ordinarily be performed by a business.

It is required that a trustee or monitor undergo a background review to ensure that nothing in the individual's past indicates an inability to act as a trustee or monitor. A background check may be conducted by the USMS or any federal investigative agency.

F.2. Sources for Potential Trustees and Monitors

As previously discussed, the USMS may have existing contracts or access through AFMS to existing contracts with companies that provide accounting, business, and monitoring services. If those preexisting contracts are not suitable, some possible sources for potential trustees and monitors include retired Department of Justice or Treasury law enforcement agents or trustees from existing panels of private trustees utilized in U.S. bankruptcy cases. The Securities and Exchange Commission and other regulatory agencies are also sources for competent experienced trustees. Trustees and monitors are available from the private sector, particularly the local business community or accounting firms that provide business management services.

G. Procurement under FAR

G.1. Three Methods of Contracting with a Trustee or Monitor

Unless the trustee or monitor is engaged through an already existing contract, the USMS Office of Procurement will award a contract to a trustee or monitor based on a court order or competitive procedures outlined in the FAR. If the total cost of the trustee or monitor is estimated at under $100,000, a simplified process is used. A simplified acquisition typically takes 60 days to award.

If the cost of a trustee or monitor is estimated at over $100,000, the FAR requires open competition involving procedures that are lengthy, since it is necessary to perform multiple steps in order to award a contract. A typical large purchase contract takes 180 days to award. In that case a sole source acquisition may be considered.

A sole source acquisition is defined as a contract for the purchase of supplies or services that is entered into or proposed to be entered into by an agency after soliciting and negotiating with only one source. A sole source contract, although discouraged, can be awarded to a trustee or monitor as long as an appropriate justification is provided to the CO. Typical justification includes "urgent and compelling" circumstances, where only one source can provide the required services or where a court orders the appointment of a particular trustee or monitor. *See* section II.J. A sole source justification must be completed prior to the award of a sole source contract. The justification must meet the necessary requirements for the CO to approve. The sole source acquisition process can take up to 60 days or more to complete.

G.2. Statement of Work

A statement of work (SOW) sets forth the duties and responsibilities of the trustee or monitor. The SOW is an integral part of the contract with the trustee or monitor.[3] A typical example of a duty of a monitor in a SOW could be reviewing books and records of a business under restraint. Ideally, the SOW should be a part of the restraining order either as a section of the order or an attachment. The SOW should reflect the duties and responsibilities likely to be needed and should not be a laundry list addressing every potential task. A SOW can be expanded or contracted depending on the changing circumstances of the case.

G.3. Use of Staff, Consultants, and Private Counsel by Trustees and Monitors

Consultants and administrative staff are often required by trustees and monitors to support their work. The CO and COTR, in consultation with the USAO or the USMS, must approve such expenditures in advance. Staff needs, including professional and administrative staff who report directly to the trustee or monitor, and outside consultants, including private counsel, must be negotiated during the interview of the trustee or monitor and included in the SOW.

G.4. Cautionary Note

Difficulties with the execution of the contract usually occur when individuals other than the COTR interact with a trustee or monitor resulting in the failure of the Government to "speak with one voice." This can be the result of the trustee or monitor receiving contradictory or erroneous directions from unauthorized personnel. Additionally, when government personnel direct the trustee or monitor *without* the requisite authority to do so, such direction exposes the Government to claims for additional costs, adjustments to the contract schedule, and adjustments to other contract terms and conditions. Such direction may also provide the contractor an opportunity to avoid the obligation to perform under the contract. Finally, while the Government may avoid liability for an unauthorized act, the person who provided such direction may find him or herself personally liable in an action brought by the contractor.

H. Payment of Monitor and Trustee Fees and Expenses

H.1. Availability of Department of Justice Assets Forfeiture Fund

Assistant U.S. Attorneys (AUSAs) and USMS personnel must be aware that the costs of a trustee or monitor are a cost of the forfeiture action. Such costs may be paid out of the proceeds of the ongoing business or directly from the AFF (28 U.S.C. § 524(c)), as discussed above. If the costs are paid directly from the AFF, the AFF is reimbursed upon sale of the asset just as any other forfeiture cost is reimbursed (e.g., liens, maintenance, storage, etc.) prior to payment of restitution and equitable sharing. The only time the AFF would not be reimbursed is if the sale resulted in a loss, a situation which should be avoided unless compelling circumstances exist. *See* discussion below and elsewhere in this policy.

Prior to entry of a final order of forfeiture, the AFF is available to pay trustee and monitor fees when (1) an asset has been seized for forfeiture pursuant to a civil or criminal forfeiture proceeding or is subject to a criminal or civil restraining order; (2) the court declines to order payment from the proceeds of the ongoing business, or an evaluation of the business reveals there are insufficient funds available to pay the costs of the trustee or monitor, but compelling law enforcement or policy considerations warrant the appointment of a trustee or monitor; and (3) the services of a trustee or monitor are needed to protect the Government's interests and less intrusive means for accomplishing the Government's goals are unavailable. *See* section II.D.

Upon the entry of a preliminary or final order of forfeiture, payment of fees charged by a trustee ordinarily will be made from the proceeds of the business, unless compelling law enforcement or policy considerations warrant payment from the AFF. *See* section II.E, 18 U.S.C. § 1963(e), and 21 U.S.C. § 853(g).

Payment of the fees of a trustee or monitor shall be charged against the AFF by the USMS. The COTR reviews invoices from the trustee or monitor and approves payment from the AFF. (In some cases the COTR may dispute the invoice because the services were not included in the contract.)

I. Defining the Goals, Duties, and Powers of the Trustee or Monitor

I.1. Defining

The restraining order or other order appointing a trustee or monitor must define the goals of the trustee or monitor. Prior to appointment, an initial assessment must be made to determine the purpose of and need for the trusteeship or monitorship (i.e., to prevent dissipation of the asset or to prevent the enterprise from engaging in illegal activity, or both), as well as its goals.

The theory of forfeiture under which the property is seized and the nature of the business itself will inform the goals and duties of the trustee or monitor. For example, if the business subject to forfeiture was acquired with proceeds of illegal activity and is self-supporting or is subject to forfeiture as a substitute asset, the goal of the Government generally is to prevent dissipation of the business and its assets. Monitorship or trusteeship of such an asset usually requires less oversight and more often results in a profitable forfeiture than the forfeiture of an enterprise used to facilitate illegal activity.

In contrast, a business used to facilitate illegal activity often requires intense oversight to prevent further illegal activity and frequently presents difficult management, safety, or public relations issues, depending on the nature of the business. The AFF is not available to pay expenses occurred when a law enforcement function is performed. *See* section II.F.1. Additionally, when a business that is or was facilitating illegal activity is identified for forfeiture, restrained, or forfeited, the illegal funds that have supported the business typically disappear. Such businesses often have no real value when they are operated in a legitimate manner. They may also require investment of capital to meet state and local regulatory standards. Unless compelling circumstances exist, appointment of a trustee or monitor in such cases, and indeed seizure and forfeiture, should be avoided.

J. Reporting—Trustees and Monitors

The issue of to whom a trustee or monitor is responsible is complex. The trustee or monitor reports directly to the COTR. The trustee or monitor is also answerable to the appointing court and to the Government, which has appointed them to protect and prevent dissipation of the asset. They may have fiduciary responsibilities to the defendant and owners of property identified for forfeiture until the entry of a preliminary order of forfeiture and may have continuing responsibilities to non-defendant owners, partners, shareholders, and third parties. Their costs are approved by the COTR and usually paid by the AFF.

The requirement that the COTR direct the trustee or monitor does not mean that the USAO or USMS is prevented from communication or discussion with the trustee or monitor about the assets and, in fact, such discussions are important and encouraged; however, only the COTR actually directs the trustee or monitor.

An example might be where drug sales and prostitution are occurring near or in a business subject to forfeiture and a trusteeship. The trustee and AUSA may propose additional security. It is the COTR and CO's responsibility to determine that (1) additional security is required and is within the terms of the SOW; (2) the contract does not provide for additional security and modification is necessary; or (3) what is needed is law enforcement, something which the trustee cannot prove and for which the AFF is not available to pay. Preferably, the discussions about additional security would take place in a conference call or ongoing conference calls with the interested parties.

Depending on the nature of the case, personal interest, or style of the court, the court may take a greater or lesser degree of oversight of the trustee or monitor. It is not uncommon, however, for the court itself to recommend a specific trustee or monitor. In that situation, the trustee or monitor may feel a greater responsibility and accountability to the court. The COTR is ultimately responsible for directing the work of the trustee or approving payment from the AFF, but modification to the contract can be made if ordered by the court. Payment from the AFF is only available through a contract, not a court order. (*See* section II.G.)

The USAO and USMS should be aware that it is difficult to direct the trustee or monitor and to control costs in a situation where the court has appointed a trustee or monitor without input from the COTR, USAO, or USMS, or where a court wants close control over a trustee. The USAO and USMS, through the COTR, must exercise some degree of control over a trustee or monitor and their costs in order for the AFF to be a source of payment. *See* section II.G.

Any fiduciary obligation of a trustee to the defendant's interest in the enterprise ends following a preliminary order of forfeiture. An obligation to non-defendant owners and third parties continues until those interests are resolved through the ancillary hearing process and final order of forfeiture. Similarly, the court's oversight usually diminishes as the Government moves toward completion of forfeiture. Once the appellate process has ended and a final order of forfeiture has been entered, the court normally is not involved unless residual issues remain, such as final sale of the property and distribution of proceeds.

PART 11: LITIGATION ISSUES

I. Avoiding Accusations of Vindictive Prosecution

Relying primarily on the different burdens of proof applicable to criminal as opposed to civil cases, the Supreme Court has held that an acquittal in a criminal case does not bar a subsequent civil forfeiture action. *United States v. One Assortment of 89 Firearms*, 465 U.S.

354 (1984); *One Lot Emerald Cut Stones v. United States*, 409 U.S. 232 (1972). However, prosecutors initiating a civil forfeiture proceeding after a decisive event in a concurrent criminal case should be mindful of the potential for a claim of vindictiveness.

In *United States v. Goodwin*, 457 U.S. 368 (1982), the Supreme Court held that prosecutors possess wide discretion in making charging decisions. In the few cases where the Court has found it necessary to presume vindictiveness, it has done so where the defendant has exercised some right and there exists reasonable likelihood that the prosecutor acted vindictively in response to the assertion of that right.[1] The prosecutor can overcome this presumption by providing the court with objective evidence supporting the prosecutor's decision.[2]

Though it is difficult to generalize, the following considerations influence the vindictive prosecution analysis. One consideration is the timing of the prosecutorial decision at issue. Decisions made in a pre-trial setting, at a time when the prosecutor may still be discovering and assessing relevant information, are less likely to merit a presumption.[3] In contrast, a prosecutorial decision made after trial begins is more likely to merit a presumption.[4] A second consideration is the nature of the right the defendant seeks to invoke. If the defendant merely invokes pre-trial procedural rights, e.g., the right to a jury trial, to move to suppress, to plead an affirmative defense, or to challenge the sufficiency of the indictment, "it is unrealistic to assume that a prosecutor's probable response to such motions is to seek to penalize and to deter."[5] In contrast, if the defendant invokes a right to a new trial to collaterally challenge the conviction, the likelihood of vindictiveness may be greater.[6]

However, even after decisive events have occurred in the criminal case, e.g., a jury has returned a verdict of acquittal against one or more of the defendants, there are often sound reasons why a prosecutor may decide to pursue an alternative remedy such as civil forfeiture. For example, the Civil Asset Forfeiture Reform Act (CAFRA) of 2000 grants the Government 90 days after a claim is filed contesting the forfeiture of an asset in which to commence a judicial forfeiture proceeding against that same asset. A prosecutor who elects to file a forfeiture case within that 90-day period—even if a decisive event occurs in the criminal case before the expiration of the 90-day period—would not be acting vindictively.

Given these considerations, care also should be exercised to avoid the appearance that the Government has pursued criminal charges vindictively because the defendant exercised a right in the parallel civil forfeiture proceeding.[7] If the criminal charge follows a routine pre-trial event in the civil forfeiture case, e.g., the filing of an administrative or judicial claim, the risk of a court indulging a presumption of vindictiveness is negligible.[8] In contrast, if the defendant prevails on the merits of a civil judicial forfeiture case, and criminal charges come afterwards, the prosecutor should be prepared to articulate the reasons for the timing of the criminal charges.

The vindictive prosecution issue can likely be avoided altogether if the civil forfeiture action is filed (and stayed) before the criminal case is concluded. While this involves extra work, if the prosecutor can anticipate that there is a substantial chance of acquittal, and that the Government will pursue civil forfeiture in such an event, filing the civil forfeiture case before adjudication of the criminal case can be a useful method to avoid the issue of vindictiveness altogether.

II. Is a Prosecutor Bound, Ethically or Otherwise, to Forego Forfeiture in Favor of Restitution?

Forfeiture and restitution are two separate components of many criminal sentences. Both are mandatory upon conviction. In 1996, the Mandatory Victims Restitution Act (MVRA) made restitution mandatory for most federal crimes where a victim suffers a loss. *See* 18 U.S.C. § 3663A(a)(1).[9] If a court orders restitution, it must order full restitution for the victim's loss, regardless of the defendant's ability to pay. E.g., *United States v. Newman*, 144 F.3d 531 (7th Cir. 1998) ("Under the MVRA, a defendant's financial status is relevant only to fixing a payment schedule for the mandated restitution"). Likewise, courts must order forfeiture when a defendant is convicted of a statute that provides for forfeiture as part of the penalty. *See*, e.g., 18 U.S.C. § 982: "The court, in imposing sentence on a person convicted of an offense in violation of section 1956, 1957, or 1960 of this title, *shall order* that the person forfeit to the United States any property, real or personal, involved in such offense, or any property traceable to such property." (emphasis added); *United States v. Monsanto*, 491 U.S. 600, 607 (1989) ("Congress could not have chosen stronger words to express its intent that forfeiture be mandatory in cases where the statute applie[s]"); *United States v. Johnston*, 199 F.3d 1015, 1022 (9th Cir. 1999) (criminal forfeiture is mandatory and designed to ensure that a defendant does not profit from his crimes). Given the mandatory nature of the two components of a sentence, it is entirely appropriate for a defendant to pay both a forfeiture and restitution. *See United States v. Kalish*, 626 F.3d 165, 169-70 (2d Cir. 2010); *United States v. Emerson*, 128 F.3d 557, 566-67 (7th Cir. 1997); *United States v. Tencer*, 107 F.3d 1120, 1135 (5th Cir. 1997) (affirming restitution order for $451,000 to fraud victims plus criminal forfeiture of $1 million, which included the fraud proceeds plus commingled funds). And defendants have no right to a credit against a restitution order for the amount forfeited. *See United States v. Taylor*, 582 F.3d 558, 567 (5th Cir. 2009); *United States v. Bright*, 353 F.3d 1114, 1122-32 (9th Cir. 2004); *United States v. Alalade*, 204 F.3d 536 (4th Cir. 2000).

The perceived tension between forfeiture and restitution emerges when, as is often the case, a defendant lacks the financial ability to pay both the forfeiture and restitution. When a defendant lacks the resources to make full restitution, DOJ policy is to collect and marshal assets for the benefit of victims using available means. These means including discontinuance of a forfeiture before a final order and asking the court to direct the custodian to turn over liquid assets to the clerk of court to be applied to restitution; the forfeiture of the defendant's assets and the handling of victim claims through the petition for remission or mitigation process; or the completion of the forfeiture action and the restoration of forfeited assets to victims through a restoration process approved by the Asset Forfeiture and Money Laundering Section (AFMLS).

The Justice for All Act, 18 U.S.C. § 3771, obligates "officers and employees of the DOJ and other departments and agencies engaged in the detection, investigation or prosecution of crime [to] make their best efforts to see that crime victims are...accorded the rights...." under the act,[10] including the right to full and timely restitution as provided by law. Does this mean that a prosecutor should not seek forfeiture if to do so would compromise a victim's ability to collect restitution? The answer is clearly no.

At present, there is only a limited ability to restrain assets prior to trial solely for the purpose of restitution.[11] The restraint mechanisms provided by the asset forfeiture statutes are often the only effective mechanisms to prevent a criminal defendant from dissipating assets prior to sentencing. As there are at least three means whereby restrained or forfeited property may be turned over to victims, there is nothing improper in seeking forfeiture in cases where the prosecutor knows early on that a defendant is unlikely to be able to pay restitution if the assets are forfeited. Restraint and forfeiture do not preclude those same assets from being turned over to victims. Indeed, without the restraint mechanisms of the forfeiture statutes, a victim has much less chance of ever receiving restitution.

Thus, a prosecutor who uses forfeiture tools as a means to provide remission or restoration of assets to crime victims fulfills any obligation that prosecutor may have under the Justice for All Act to crime victims.[12] Various courts have acknowledged this use of the forfeiture statutes. *See United States v. O'Connor*, 321 F. Supp. 722 (E.D. Va. 2004) (although defendant has no right to use forfeited funds to satisfy a restitution order, the Government may, pursuant to 21 U.S.C. § 853(i)(1), apply the forfeited funds for benefit of the victims through restoration or remission); *United States v. Lavin*, 299 F.3d 123 (2d Cir. 2002) (instead of pursuing forfeiture, Government used seized funds to satisfy restitution order).

III. Negotiating with Fugitives

A. Summary

Absent compelling circumstances, prosecutors should not negotiate with fugitives. Before undertaking such negotiations, prosecutors should exhaust all potentially viable pre-trial motions, including any possible fugitive disentitlement motion. Even when the case cannot be resolved by pre-trial motion, prosecutors should enter into negotiations reluctantly. In many instances, the policy considerations of declining to negotiate with fugitives will outweigh the potential benefit to an individual civil forfeiture case. Only in instances where other considerations, e.g., the cost of maintaining the asset subject to forfeiture, militate towards negotiating a settlement should prosecutors entertain fugitive negotiations. In such circumstances the prosecutor handling the negotiations should consult closely with the prosecutor handling the parallel criminal case.

B. Discussion

Periodically, a situation arises where an individual has been indicted, becomes a fugitive, and seeks to challenge or negotiate with the Government regarding a civil forfeiture case. Prior to the enactment of CAFRA, a fugitive in a related criminal case was not barred from opposing the civil forfeiture of property: *Degen v. United States*, 517 U.S. 820 (1996) (fugitive disentitlement doctrine cannot be created by case law); *United States v. Funds Held in the Name of Wetterer*, 17 F. Supp. 2d 161 (E.D.N.Y. 1998) (because of *Degen*, claimant that is alter ego of fugitive may file claim challenging forfeiture of bank account held by perpetrator of mail fraud/child sex abuse scheme who is resisting extradition in Guatemala); *United States v. One 1988 Chevrolet Cheyenne Half-Ton Pickup Truck*, 357 F. Supp. 2d 1321 (S.D. Ala. 2005) (tracing the history of the fugitive disentitlement doctrine and discussing the impact of *Degen*).

CAFRA reinstated the fugitive disentitlement doctrine with the passage of 28 U.S.C. § 2466, which permits a court to "disallow a person from using the resources of the courts of the United States in furtherance of a claim in any related civil forfeiture action or a claim in third party proceedings in any criminal forfeiture action" if certain conditions are met. *See Collazos v. United States*, 368 F.3d 190 (2d Cir. 2004) (section 2466 is Congress's response to the Supreme Court's decision in *Degen*; it does not violate the claimant's constitutional right to due process); *One 1988 Chevrolet Cheyenne Half-Ton Pickup Truck*, 357 F. Supp. 2d at 1326 (section 2466 is a "forceful legislative response" to the void created by *Degen*).

While it may have made financial sense to negotiate with fugitives when they were allowed to litigate civil forfeiture actions, the Government now has less incentive to negotiate with those who are barred by the fugitive disentitlement doctrine from challenging a forfeiture. If a court agrees to apply the fugitive disentitlement doctrine, the Government should be able to obtain a default judgment, at least as to the fugitive's interest, in most cases. Thus, there would be no reason to negotiate with a party who is barred from challenging a forfeiture, and negotiation is thus discouraged in that circumstance.

Even in cases where a court may decline to apply the fugitive disentitlement doctrine, the Government may be able to prevail on a pre-trial motion.[13] For example, fugitives often will decline to appear for deposition or otherwise participate in discovery. Rule 37, Federal Rules of Civil Procedure, allows the court to order a party to comply with a discovery request, and if the party fails to comply, the court can impose sanctions that include (1) an order that certain facts shall be taken as established, (2) an order refusing to allow the disobedient party to support or oppose designated claims or defenses or introduce matters in evidence, and (3) rendering judgment by default against the disobedient party. Fed. R. Civ. P. 37(b)(2).

Where pre-trial motions are not viable or are unsuccessful, prosecutors should pursue negotiations with fugitives reluctantly, and only as a last resort. As a general matter, it is rarely in the Government's interest to negotiate with fugitives. *See In re Grand Jury Subpoenas Dated March 9, 2001*, 179 F. Supp. 2d 270, 277 (S.D.N.Y. 2001) (noting a response by the U.S. Attorney's Office (USAO) in the Southern District of New York in the Marc Rich case that "it is our firm policy not to negotiate dispositions of criminal charges with fugitives. Such negotiations would give defendants an incentive to flee, and from the Government's perspective, would provide defendants with the inappropriate leverage and luxury of remaining absent unless and until the Government agrees to their terms."). Forfeiture Assistant U.S. Attorneys (AUSAs) should be sensitive to these considerations and not take any actions that may undermine the policy considerations noted in the Rich case, and should in all circumstances coordinate closely with prosecutors handling the parallel criminal case.

In the exceptional case where negotiations with a fugitive are appropriate, prosecutors should limit the factors that influence the conduct of the negotiations. It is legitimate to take into account the Government's litigation risk at trial, or expenses the Government may incur in maintaining an asset if the case would otherwise be delayed indefinitely. For example, if the forfeiture involves tangible property that is incurring storage expenses or property where a lien is continuing to accrue and erode the equity, it may be in the Government's financial interest to resolve the forfeiture matter quickly. If a court declined to invoke the fugitive disentitlement doctrine, negotiation may be necessary in order to resolve the matter. But in no circumstances should a prosecutor agree to exchange assets for a defendant's agreement to surrender and face criminal charges.

IV. Criminal Forfeiture and *Brady* Obligations

In criminal forfeiture matters, the Government has not only an ethical but also a legal duty to disclose information favorable to the defendant as to either guilt or punishment. *See Brady v. Maryland*, 373 U.S. 83 (1963) ("suppression by the prosecution of evidence favorable to an accused upon request violates due process where the evidence is material either to guilt or to punishment irrespective of the good faith or bad faith of the prosecution").[14] Forfeiture is an element of the sentence, and thus forms part of the punishment imposed on the defendant. *Libretti v. United States*, 516 U.S. 29, 38-39 (1995). Accordingly, *Brady* requires the Government, even absent a request by the defendant, to disclose evidence favorable to the defendant that relates to criminal forfeiture.

V. Considerations Relating to Global Settlements and Dealing with Claimants and Witnesses

In situations where both a civil forfeiture proceeding and a related criminal investigation or charges are pending, forfeiture attorneys may face various ethical issues. Issues generally arise in the context of settlements and plea agreements, and in dealings with witnesses. Some of these issues are set out below, with references to certain pertinent authority; however, in addition to the materials identified here, you should consult the rules that apply in the state in which you are licensed as well as the state and court(s) in which the proceedings are pending.[15]

A. Global Settlements

The term *global settlement* is often used to describe a situation whereby criminal charges and civil forfeiture claims are resolved in a single agreement between the Government and the defendant. While such agreements are often recommended, being both effective and efficient in resolving disputed matters, they raise ethical issues that should be considered.

No settlement agreement should be used to gain an improper advantage in a related civil or criminal case: the Government should not agree to release property subject to forfeiture (civil or criminal) in order to coerce a guilty plea on the substantive charges; nor should the Government agree to dismiss criminal charges in order to coerce a forfeiture settlement.[16]

Care should be taken to avoid any plea/settlement agreement that risks undermining faith in the fairness of those who administer the criminal process, such as an agreement which appears to reduce prison time in exchange for forfeiture, or vice versa.[17]

A prudent practice followed by many government attorneys is that of not introducing or suggesting a global settlement disposition. If opposing counsel raises the issue, it may be responded to and pursued by government attorneys in close consultation with supervisors, and being mindful of the relevant ethical issues.[18]

B. Claimants and Witnesses

The same ethical considerations as those which apply in global settlements, above, also apply in situations where the Government attorney is interacting with claimants and witnesses in civil forfeiture litigation in circumstances which may raise issues of fairness and proper conduct.

These issues may occur in all situations where the line between the Government's civil litigation and prosecutorial functions may become blurred, and where there may be potential for consolidating governmental power against individuals in a way which could become abusive. While there is no ethical prohibition on conditioning the subject's status in a prosecution on that person's cooperation, care should be employed when the subject's cooperation is sought solely in connection with a civil forfeiture matter. Where, for example, a civil forfeiture action and a related criminal investigation or charges are pending at the same time, a claimant or witness may be required to take action in the civil forfeiture case, such as providing testimony in a deposition, where there is a perceived threat of criminal prosecution. In such cases care should be taken not to coerce cooperation or the providing of testimony in the civil case by threats or promises relating to the criminal proceedings.[19] Nor should civil forfeiture discovery or other proceedings be used solely to obtain information or benefit for the criminal proceeding.[20]

Ethical issues may arise in a situation where an individual, not currently charged with a crime but involved in the offense, has relevant information that would aid the Government in pursuing a civil forfeiture case. Clearly if the situation arose in a criminal case there would be nothing improper about the prosecutor advising the witness that if he did not tell the truth about what he knew, he could be charged for his own involvement in the crime, assuming there was evidence to support a prosecution. Generally, the same should be true in a civil case scenario. However, even though there is no blanket prohibition against threatening a prosecution to persuade someone to take a particular action in a civil matter, government attorneys must take care to ensure that any threat of prosecution is not solely to gain an advantage in the civil matter (i.e., to ensure that the criminal charges would be brought for some legitimate purpose in addition to gaining an advantage in the civil action), that it is related to the civil case, and that it is well-founded.

In the context of settling civil forfeiture cases, care should be taken by the government attorney handling the civil case not to harm the Government's criminal prosecution, such as in a case where, for example, we compromise a civil forfeiture case to the benefit of a defendant/witness who has already entered into a cooperation agreement with the Government. In that circumstance the civil forfeiture settlement may be viewed as a benefit to the cooperating witness which we have to disclose, and which may be used to impeach the cooperating witness on cross-examination. Prior to negotiating a civil forfeiture settlement with a cooperating witness/defendant in a pending criminal case, the government forfeiture attorney should consult with the government criminal attorney.[21] Ethical issues may also arise where government attorneys include cooperation provisions in civil forfeiture settlements. Such provisions, which may provide for assistance or cooperation by the claimant in other civil forfeitures or in related criminal proceedings, create no ethical problems so long as the settlement agreement itself stands on its merits, and if it calls for cooperation in a criminal case, does not run afoul of ethical considerations relating to the interplay of civil and criminal cases noted above.

Again, ethics rules vary from state to state, and it is strongly recommended that each attorney dealing with related civil forfeiture and criminal cases consult the rules that apply to the states in which the attorney is licensed and the action is pending, as well as consulting the ethics advisor in the USAO.

VI. Fifth Amendment Advisements in Civil Forfeiture Cases

The procedural safeguards established by the U.S. Supreme Court in *Miranda v. Arizona*, 384 U.S. 436 (1966) protect the Fifth Amendment rights of a person not to be compelled in a criminal case to be a witness against himself. The Court held that unless a suspect in a *custodial* interrogation is first warned of his or her right to remain silent, and to have an attorney, provided at no cost, if necessary, before questioning, statements made by the suspect would not be admissible at trial. *Id.* at 492. The Court's primary concern was the coercive atmosphere surrounding a person in custody who is subject to interrogation by the police. *Id.* at 457-58. Because these conditions typically are not present in the context of a deposition of a witness or claimant in a civil forfeiture case, the Constitution does not require prosecutors to warn the witness of his or her rights against self-incrimination prior to questioning in a civil deposition. *See*, e.g., *United States v. Solano-Godines*, 120 F.3d 957 (9th Cir. 1997) (*Miranda* warnings are not required before questioning in a civil deposition hearing). Consequently, statements, including those which might be self-incriminating, made in the course of a deposition in a civil forfeiture case are admissible in the proceeding even in the absence of *Miranda* warnings because deposition proceedings are civil in nature and are not criminal prosecutions.

Nonetheless, in civil forfeiture cases where the deponent is known to the Government to be a target or subject of a parallel criminal investigation or prosecution, government attorneys may wish to consider either deferring the deposition, or taking the deposition but giving an advisement that draws elements from those advisements that prosecutors routinely give targets and subjects in federal grand jury practice. For example, before taking the deposition in a civil forfeiture case of an unrepresented claimant who is a target of a parallel criminal investigation, the advisement may state simply:

> You are advised that you are a target of a parallel federal criminal investigation. You may refuse to answer any question in this proceeding if a truthful answer to the question would tend to incriminate you. Anything that you do or say may be used against you in this proceeding, in a criminal proceeding, or in any other subsequent legal proceeding.
>
> Include if applicable:
>
> If you are represented by appointed counsel in a related criminal case, you have a right to ask the court to appoint counsel for you in this proceeding.
>
> Or:
>
> If you are using the real property which this case seeks to forfeit as your primary residence, you have a right to ask the court to appoint counsel for you in this proceeding provided you show that you are financially unable to obtain counsel.

In contrast, before taking the deposition of a deponent who is a target, but who is represented and not a claimant, the advisement may simply state: "You are advised that you are a target of a parallel criminal investigation."

The suggestion that a government attorney may want to give an advisement to a deponent in certain civil forfeiture cases rests on several considerations. In grand jury practice, DOJ policy requires prosecutors to give criminal targets and subjects Fifth Amendment advisements in a target letter, and repeat those advisements on the record before the grand jury. *See* USAM 9-11.151; *Criminal Resource Manual* 160 (sample target letter). In the case of targets, the Department's policy goes further. Prosecutors must advise the person that he or she is a target of a criminal investigation. *See Grand Jury Practice Manual*, § 7.4. These policies exist notwithstanding the lack of a clear constitutional imperative requiring prosecutors to give any advisements to targets or subjects in the context of grand jury practice. *See United States Attorneys' Manual* 9-11.151; *see also Grand Jury Practice Manual*, § 7.4. While there is no constitutional right to an attorney in a civil forfeiture proceeding, certain indigent claimants may have a statutory right to counsel. The court may authorize counsel for an indigent claimant with standing to contest the forfeiture who is represented by court-appointed counsel in a related criminal case. *See* 18 U.S.C. § 983(b)(1)(A). And, upon the request of an indigent party in a civil forfeiture action brought by the Government to forfeit that person's primary residence, the court "shall ensure that the person is represented by an attorney...." *See* 18 U.S.C. § 983(b)(1)(B). An advisement also enhances the likelihood that if the testimony is offered in a criminal prosecution, it will be admitted. Finally, the advisement helps rebut a claimant's subsequent arguments that he was not aware of the Fifth Amendment right, or, in the case of certain indigent claimants, was not aware that he may have the right to counsel in the civil forfeiture case. *See* 18 U.S.C. § 983(b); *see also* 18 U.S.C. § 981(g)(2) (authorizing a claimant to move to stay a civil forfeiture proceeding based on Fifth Amendment concerns)

VII. Preservation Policy for Civil Forfeiture

A. The Legal Obligation

There is a legal duty to preserve potentially relevant evidence once a party reasonably anticipates litigation, whether the United States is the plaintiff or defendant. *Zubulake v. UBS Warburg LLC*, 220 F.R.D. 212, 218 (S.D.N.Y. 2003); Fed. R. Civ. P. 37, Advisory Committee Note, 2006 Amendments, Subdivision (f). Although a litigation hold is the primary method of preservation, reasonableness and good faith are the ultimate standards by which an alleged breach of the duty to preserve is judged. A breach of the duty to preserve may be the basis for discovery sanctions if the United States fails to produce relevant electronically stored information ("ESI") or tangible items.

Preservation should be distinguished from production under the Federal Rules of Civil Procedure that govern discovery and from admissibility under the Federal Rules of Evidence. The fact that information may be work product, otherwise privileged, or inadmissible does not obviate the duty to preserve and the fact that information is preserved does not necessarily mean it will be produced.

The practical guidance below applies equally to DOJ attorneys (including AUSAs) and to investigative agency counsel. The guidance does not apply to attorneys at independent agencies. Mentions of "the DOJ" or "a DOJ attorney" do not refer to investigative agency counsel, regardless of that fact that investigative agencies such as the DEA, FBI, and ATF, and their attorneys, fall under the DOJ umbrella. Thus, there is a distinction drawn between "the DOJ" and "agencies" or "agency counsel" for the purposes of this policy.

Except where this policy clearly addresses the particularities of a situation where a DOJ attorney is assigned to a case and he or she initiates the call for a litigation hold, agency counsel may still wish to take note of the practical guidance in Sections VII.A-D, in the event that they enact a litigation hold in the administrative context, to the extent that it does not contradict internal agency procedure relating to litigation holds.

B. The Trigger

The obligation to preserve evidence arises when a party has notice that evidence is relevant to litigation or when a party reasonably anticipates litigation and foresees that the evidence may be relevant to that future litigation. When a DOJ attorney assigned to a case determines that an event triggers the obligation, he or she should advise participating agency counsel to implement a litigation hold. In administrative forfeiture cases, relevant agency counsel should determine whether a litigation hold is necessary and appropriate and follow the guidance below, as applicable.

Where a case has been assigned to a DOJ attorney, he or she should advise the relevant agency or agencies to enact a litigation hold no later than:

(1) **Seizure/Restraint:** The time at which a seizure warrant is obtained for property that, by statute, may not be administratively forfeited or for which the seizing agency lacks administrative forfeiture authority.
(2) **Claimant Action:** Upon service or actual notice, whichever is earlier, of the filing of a complaint or other pleading; or, upon receipt of a motion for return of property or notice of other action regarding seized or forfeited property.
(3) **Reasonable Certainty:** When the DOJ attorney receives a referral to file a judicial forfeiture action, the time when it is reasonably certain that the DOJ will indeed file a complaint or a motion for extension of time to file a complaint (as opposed to declining the matter or pursuing criminal forfeiture instead).
(4) **Special Circumstances:** When the DOJ attorney advises, if he or she determines that special circumstances exist that warrant the immediate preservation of relevant information.

Administrative seizures do not often lead to litigation, and in most cases, will not trigger a litigation hold. However, there may be situations where agency counsel develops a reasonable belief that litigation will ensue. In those circumstances, agency counsel may wish to consider the propriety of a litigation hold or other method of preserving relevant information, proportional to the threat of future litigation. Events that *may* lead an agency to reasonably believe that litigation will occur include the following:

(1) The filing of a claim
(2) The investigation of a certain target and/or certain assets
   - Does anything in the pre-seizure planning stage suggest that litigation is reasonably foreseeable?
(3) Seizure
   - Were the assets seized particularly large, valuable, or rare?
   - Was there considerable publicity surrounding the seizure or the parties involved?

- Did the owner or his or her attorney make it known to agents that a claim would likely be filed, either through words or actions?
- Based on prior experience, is defense counsel known to aggressively file claims?

C. Information Subject to Preservation

C.1. Scope

The scope of the litigation hold defines what information is relevant and defines the sources (physical locations) of such documents, tangible items, and ESI. Relevant information is anything that the United States knows, or reasonably should know, relates to the foreseeable claims or defenses of any party or is likely to lead to the discovery of relevant information. There is no duty to retain every piece of paper. The DOJ attorney should determine relevance in consultation with the custodians of information, who, in an asset forfeiture matter, include persons at agencies in possession of the relevant case files. Scope is a fact-specific inquiry, the parameters of which should be explained in detail by the DOJ attorney on a case-by-case basis. The initial decision to preserve and the subsequent mechanisms chosen to fulfill the obligation should be guided by reasonableness and proportionality.

Relevant information should be preserved as it is kept in the usual course of business. Duplicates do not need to be retained. ESI should be maintained in native format.[22] Any agency advised to implement a litigation hold should ensure that all materials designated by the DOJ attorney as within the scope of the hold are, in fact, retained, and retained in the form specified.

C.2. Relevant Time Frame

All relevant information in existence at the time when the duty to preserve attaches should be retained, as well as relevant information created thereafter, until the DOJ attorney or agency counsel advises otherwise.

The starting point for information that should be captured by the litigation hold is no later than:

- the date the investigation began; or
- the date of the relevant seizure.

The point at which information will no longer require preservation under the litigation hold is no earlier than:

- the date when the forfeiture decision is final and non-appealable;
- the date upon which the time for filing an appeal or petition for a writ of certiorari expires; or,
- another date as the DOJ attorney or agency counsel advises.

D. The Litigation Hold Notice

D.1. Who Issues

The DOJ attorney or agency counsel advises the relevant agency or agencies to implement the litigation hold. The DOJ attorney should be responsible for 1) preserving documents created or received by that attorney, 2) guiding other members of his or her office, and 3) advising and monitoring preservation efforts at the agency or agencies.

The practical duty of preservation remains on agency staff, except as it relates to documents within the possession of DOJ. Proper execution of the duty to preserve includes consulting with Information Technology (IT) personnel, guiding the individual custodians of information, and following the instructions in the litigation hold notice as provided by the DOJ attorney or agency counsel.

D.2. Who Receives

All agencies should designate an attorney within the agency as the *preservation point person* to receive litigation holds from the DOJ attorney and to transmit such notices to custodians of relevant information.

Key custodians should receive the litigation hold notice from their preservation point persons at the agencies. These custodians may include, non-exclusively, counsel's office attorneys assigned to the case, case agents, and any other players who may have produced or received information relevant to the case. The list of key custodians may be amended and the hold notice should be sent to new persons as needed. The DOJ attorney should be notified of all key custodians and any changes to that list made by the agency preservation point persons.

The DOJ attorney and agency preservation point person should take particular care that the relevant documents and information are retained when key custodians leave their respective agencies or are reassigned. New employees should be apprised of existing litigation holds relevant to their assignments when they assume their positions.

D.3. Multiple Agency Situations

When more than one investigative agency works on a particular case—whether in a task force setting, through informal coordination, or under adopted seizures from state and local agencies—the DOJ attorney should consult with the lead agency to ascertain which entities, exactly, participated in the investigation. The DOJ attorney should inquire as to which other agencies may be involved and communicate with the designated preservation point persons at all additional, participating agencies. The lead agency point persons should provide the DOJ attorney with the contact information of the preservation point persons at the other agencies involved in the case no later than the date specified by the DOJ attorney so that he or she can determine the scope of the hold and send the litigation hold notice to the lead and all other participating agencies.

D.4. Format

Best practice entails a *written* litigation hold ("urgent" email is the preferred method). The DOJ attorney should attach a written (electronic) agreement to comply along with the litigation hold notice and require an affirmative response from all recipients by a certain date. In a multiple agency situation, all litigation hold recipients should be able to view the entire list of addressees. Such access enables the recipients to identify an agency that may have relevant information in its files, but was erroneously overlooked in the DOJ attorney's initial email advising the agency or agencies to implement a litigation hold.

D.5. Content

At a minimum, the litigation hold notice should contain:

- names of any foreseeable parties in the anticipated litigation
- time frame during which relevant information has been or will be created
- affirmative directions to preserve information and prohibitions on destruction/deletion
- instructions to initially separate information believed to be privileged from other preserved information
- expectations for compliance, consequences of non-compliance, and method of monitoring compliance
- instructions on how to proceed when the recipient believes the hold inadvertently excludes relevant information, sources of data, or entities likely to possess information
- an agreement to comply with the hold, to be signed and returned by a certain date
- a summary of the claims, defenses, or issues raised by the anticipated litigation and/or trigger
- scope of the hold and any limitations on it
- mechanisms for the collection of preserved ESI, tangible items, and documents
- any technological aspects of IT systems that could help/hinder preservation
- procedure for how the hold may be expanded, diminished, and terminated; and
- contact information of the advising attorney

D.6. Ongoing Duty

The DOJ attorney who advises an agency to issue a litigation hold should:

- keep a log of all steps taken to initiate and maintain a litigation hold, including a record of communication with agency point persons and a concise statement of the reason any significant decision on preservation was made;
- periodically review the litigation hold to determine whether to maintain, diminish, or expand its scope in light of the evolving claims, defenses, and issues in the case;
- document changes made to the scope of the litigation hold or list of key custodians;
- periodically review compliance with the hold, in consultation with the preservation point person at the agency(ies);
- send a reminder notice, electronically, to all recipients of the litigation hold notice, including agency preservation point persons, every 90-120 days; and
- promptly notify, electronically, all recipients of any modifications to the scope of the hold.

D.7. Removing a Hold

The advising DOJ attorney should not make the decision to lift a litigation hold until after the time for filing direct appeals in the case (and related or ancillary proceedings) or a petition for a writ of certiorari has passed. If a DOJ attorney was never assigned to the case but agency counsel issued a litigation hold independently, the hold may be removed when the time for a claimant to file a claim contesting the forfeiture has passed. The DOJ attorney or agency counsel should electronically notify all recipients of the litigation hold notice that the need for the hold has ended and that they may cease preserving information related to the case.

PART 12: FORFEITURE AND COMPENSATION FOR VICTIMS OF CRIME

Forfeiture has become a critical tool in the recovery of illicit gains arising from financial crimes such as fraud, embezzlement, and theft. Prior to the enactment of the Civil Asset Forfeiture Reform Act (CAFRA) of 2000, Pub. L. No. 106-185, 114 Stat. 202 (2000), non-owner victims of crime could recover through remission only in criminal forfeitures and civil bank fraud forfeitures. In other civil forfeitures, victims could be compensated only where they were named in a criminal restitution order arising from the prosecution of a related offense. In 2000, CAFRA amended 18 U.S.C. § 981(e) to broaden the Attorney General's authority to restore forfeited assets to the victims of any offense that gave rise to the forfeiture. Accordingly, remission authority now exists for all offenses for which a related civil or criminal forfeiture order is obtained.

In concert with this expanded remission authority, the Criminal Division initiated a procedure in 2002 called "restoration." This procedure enables the Attorney General to transfer forfeited funds to a court for satisfaction of a criminal restitution order, provided that the victim named in the order otherwise qualifies for remission under the applicable regulations. While remission and criminal restitution are not directly related, they may serve similar functions. Remission is discretionary relief intended to reduce the hardship that may arise from forfeiture for persons who have incurred a monetary loss from the offense underlying the forfeiture. Restitution is an equitable remedy that is intended to make crime victims whole and prevent unjust enrichment to the perpetrator. In many cases, restoration—the use of forfeited funds to pay restitution—is desirable, since the defendant may be left without assets to satisfy his or her restitution obligation following forfeiture.

The Treasury Forfeiture Fund (TFF) has a similar procedure for remission and restoration. Please consult the *Guidelines for Treasury Forfeiture Fund Agencies on Refunds Pursuant to Court Orders, Petitions for Remission, or Restoration Requests* ("Treasury Blue Book"), available at http://www.treasury.gov/resource-center/terrorist-illicit-finance/Asset-Forfeiture/Documents/bluebook.pd f.[1]

This part discusses the principal policies and procedures governing the return of forfeited assets to crime victims. Section I covers the basics of remission and restoration; section II discusses remission for insurers of victims; and section III discusses strategies for compensating victims of large fraud offenses within the Ninth and Eleventh Circuits.

I. Returning Forfeited Assets to Victims

A. Remission

Once assets have been judicially forfeited, the authority to distribute them to victims rests solely with the Attorney General, pursuant to the regulations governing the remission of forfeitures at 28 C.F.R. Part 9. Potential victims must be notified of the opportunity to file a petition for remission. In judicial forfeitures, notification is the responsibility of the U.S. Attorney's Office (USAO). Known victims should be notified by mail, and potential unknown victims may be notified by publication. In appropriate cases, the USAO may modify the standard notice of the Victim Notification System (VNS) to incorporate notice of the forfeiture and a model petition for remission. The notice should instruct the victims to file petitions with the USAO district that handled the civil or criminal forfeiture.

The authority to decide petitions for remission in judicial cases has been delegated to the Chief of AFMLS. 28 C.F.R. § 9.1(b)(2). Petitions are decided on the basis of written documentation; there is no right to a hearing on the petition. 28 C.F.R. § 9.4(g). Unsuccessful petitioners are entitled to one request for reconsideration, which is reviewed and decided by a different ruling official within AFMLS. 28 C.F.R. § 9.4(k)(3). Judicial review of a denial of remission is not available. *See United States v. One 1970 Buick Riviera Bearing Serial No. 494870H910774,* 463 F.2d 1168, 1170 (5th Cir.), *cert. denied*, 409 U.S. 980 (1972) (Attorney General has unreviewable discretion over remission or mitigation of forfeitures).

The determination of whether a victim is entitled to remission is governed by regulation. The breadth of options available for transfer of forfeited property to victims depends on the statute under which the property is forfeited. The options are broadest in criminal forfeiture, where the Attorney General has statutory authority not only to grant petitions for remission to victims of a violation of the offense that is the basis for the forfeiture, but also to "*take any other action to protect the rights of innocent persons which is in the interests of justice* and which is not inconsistent with the provisions of [the applicable part or section]." 21 U.S.C. § 853(i)(1), incorporated by reference in 18 U.S.C. § 982 for money laundering and other offenses (emphasis added). In civil forfeitures, the statutory authority is less broadly stated, and the Attorney General's authority to remit forfeited assets to victims does not appear to extend to other "innocent persons." *See*, e.g., 18 U.S.C. § 981(d); 21 U.S.C. § 881(d).

In administrative forfeitures, the authority to decide petitions for remission or mitigation rests with the seizing agency.[2] It is the responsibility of the agency to notify potential victims of the opportunity to file a petition for remission. The remission decision is at the discretion of the forfeiting agency and not reviewable in court. Questions regarding administrative forfeiture policies and procedures should be directed to the forfeiting agency. When petitions have been filed for both administratively and judicially forfeited assets in the same case, the seizing agency must coordinate with the forfeiture Assistant United States Attorney (AUSA) assigned to the case.

A.1. 28 C.F.R. Part 9, Standards for Victims

The factual basis and legal theory underlying the forfeiture will determine the victims under 28 C.F.R. Part 9. "The term victim means a person who has incurred a pecuniary loss as *a direct result of the commission of the offense underlying a forfeiture*." 28 C.F.R. § 9.2(v) (emphasis added). A *person* is "an individual, partnership, corporation, joint business enterprise, estate, or other legal entity capable of owning property." 28 C.F.R. § 9.2(m).

Victims may also recover losses caused by a related offense. 28 C.F.R. § 9.8(a)(1). *Related offense* means: "(1) Any predicate offense charged in a Federal Racketeer Influenced and Corrupt Organizations Act (RICO) count for which forfeiture was ordered; or (2) An offense committed as part of the same scheme or design, or pursuant to the same conspiracy, as was involved in the offense for which forfeiture was ordered." 28 C.F.R. § 9.2(s).

A.2. Qualification to File

A victim may be granted remission of the forfeiture of property if the victim satisfactorily demonstrates that:

> (1) a pecuniary loss of a specific amount has been directly caused by the criminal offense, or related offense, that was the underlying basis for the forfeiture, and the loss is supported by documentary evidence including invoices and receipts; (2) the pecuniary loss is the direct result of the illegal acts and is not the result of otherwise lawful acts that were committed in the course of the criminal offense; (3) the victim did not knowingly contribute to, participate in, benefit from, or act in a willfully blind manner towards the commission of the offense, or related offense, that was the underlying basis for the forfeiture; (4) the victim has not in fact been compensated for the wrongful loss of the property by the perpetrator or others; and (5) the victim does not have recourse reasonably available to other assets from which to obtain compensation for the wrongful loss of the property.

28 C.F.R. § 9.8(a).

"The amount of the pecuniary loss suffered by a victim for which remission may be granted is limited to the fair market value of the property of which the victim was deprived as of the date of the occurrence of the loss." 28 C.F.R. § 9.8(b). This provision presents three issues to be determined in connection with calculating a victim's loss: (1) What property did the victim lose as a direct result of the illegal activity?; (2) When was the victim deprived of it?; and (3) What was the fair market value of that property at that time? The term "fair market value" is not defined in 28 C.F.R. Part 9. When the loss is property other than money, the date of the victim's loss and the fair market value of the property on that date must be decided in order to determine the victim's recoverable loss.

A victim's pecuniary loss must be supported by documentary evidence. 28 C.F.R. § 9.8(a)(1) and (2). Losses that are secondary to the principal loss, such as "interest foregone or for collateral expenses incurred to recover lost property or to seek other recompense," are not eligible for remission. 28 C.F.R. § 9.8(b). Nor are losses from property damage or physical injuries, or from a tort, unless the tort is the illegal activity underlying the forfeiture. 28 C.F.R. § 9.8(c). Victims who "knowingly contribute to, participate in, benefit from, or act in a willfully blind manner towards the commission of the offense, or related offense, that was the underlying basis for the forfeiture" are ineligible for remission. 28 C.F.R. § 9.8(a)(3).

A victim need not show that his or her funds are among the funds that have been forfeited in order to establish eligibility for remission. Similarly, the tracing of a particular victim's funds into a forfeited account does not give that victim priority over other victims whose funds cannot be traced.

A.3. Priority of Payment

Priority in the distribution of forfeited assets is given to valid owners, lienholders, federal financial regulatory agencies, and victims (in that order), who in turn have priority over official use requests and equitable sharing requests.

A.4. Trustees

With the consultation and approval of AFMLS, the USAO may employ a trustee in large, multiple-victim cases to assist in notifying potential victims of the opportunity to seek remission, in processing the petitions, and in making decision recommendations. 28 C.F.R. § 9.9(c). The USAO must also consult with the lead seizing agency in the selection of the trustee.

A.5. Additional Grounds for Denial of Remission to Victims

Remission to victims may be denied: (1) if determination of the pecuniary loss to be paid to individual victims is too difficult; (2) if the amount to be paid to victims is small compared to the expense incurred by the Government in deciding the victims' claims; or (3) if the total number of victims is large and the amount available for payment to victims is so small as to make granting payments to victims impractical. 28 C.F.R. § 9.8(d).

A.6. Timeliness

Victims generally must file petitions for judicially forfeited assets within 30 days after receiving notice. However, when a victim fails to submit a valid petition within 30 days, exceptions may be allowed for good cause based on the particular circumstances of the case.

B. Restoration

In 2002, the Criminal Division issued new procedures designed to simplify and accelerate the return of forfeited property to victims, known as the "Restoration Procedures." The new procedures apply where: (1) both restitution to compensate victims and a related forfeiture (either civil, criminal, or administrative) have been ordered, (2) the victims and amounts listed in the restitution order essentially conform to the victims and amounts that would have been paid through the forfeiture remission process, and (3) other property is not available to satisfy the order of restitution.

The Restoration Procedures enable the United States to complete the forfeiture and recover costs. This permits victims to obtain fair compensation from the forfeited assets, in accordance with the court's restitution order, without having to file petitions for remission with the Government and await decisions. This is a standardized alternative procedure to petitions for remission, designed to accommodate victims and the courts to the furthest extent possible, while still meeting statutory requirements.

B.1. Background

Because forfeited assets are property of the United States, courts and defendants lack authority to use them to satisfy a defendant's criminal debts, including fines or restitution obligations. *See United States v. Trotter*, 912 F.2d 964 (8th Cir. 1990). In many cases, defendants are left with little or no property after the forfeiture is completed. Thus, prior to the issuance of the Restoration Procedures, the Government often seized property, and then made it available to satisfy court-ordered restitution rather than complete the forfeiture. This process, while cumbersome, worked where the seized assets were cash or bank accounts, and where there were no competing claims for the property. However, where assets needed to be maintained and sold, or where third parties claimed an interest in the property, completion of the forfeiture was necessary, and victims were generally required to take the additional step of filing petitions for remission in order to recover any part of the forfeited assets. Under the Restoration Procedures, the Government may now forfeit a defendant's property and transfer the proceeds to the court in satisfaction of an order of restitution. The Attorney General's restoration authority has been delegated to the Chief of AFMLS, pursuant to Attorney General Order No. 2088-97 (June 14, 1997).

B.2. How the Restoration Process Works

The Restoration Procedures require both a court order of restitution *and* an order of forfeiture. The Restoration Procedures also allow, when requested by the USAO, preliminary review of the expected restitution and forfeiture order by AFMLS so that AUSAs may advise the court of the Department's intended distribution of the property.

To use the Restoration Procedures, the USAO must send the Chief of AFMLS a copy of the Judgment in a Criminal Case containing the order of restitution and a copy of the forfeiture order, along with a written request signed by the U.S. Attorney, or his or her designee, that includes the representations set forth at section I.B.3. Once the Chief of AFMLS has approved the request for restoration, AFMLS notifies both the USAO and the custodian of the property. The custodian then transfers the net proceeds of the forfeiture to the clerk of court for distribution pursuant to the order of restitution.

Restoration is appropriate only when the distribution pursuant to the restitution order is essentially the same as the distribution that would be obtained through the remission process. Prosecutors wishing to use the Restoration Procedures must work with the probation officer and the court to make sure that the court's restitution order lists the names of all victims and the amount of restitution due to each. Prosecutors also should be cognizant that restitution is generally available for a much broader category of harms than may be satisfied through remission, which is allowed only for pecuniary losses caused by the offense underlying the forfeiture or a related offense. Moreover, 28 C.F.R. § 9.8(b) provides that the victim's loss is limited to the fair market value of the property of which the victim was deprived, as of the date of the loss. No allowance is made for interest forgone, lost profits, or collateral expenses incurred to recover lost property or to seek other recompense. Thus, restoration may not be used where a significant portion of the losses covered by the restitution order relate to bodily harm, injuries in tort or contract that may relate to the crime of conviction, and collateral expenses such as legal, accounting, or security expenditures incurred in trying to correct the harm caused by the crime. If the restitution order is not amenable to the restoration process, the USAO will be advised and assets may be distributed through the remission process.

B.3. Representations

The Restoration Procedures are designed to accomplish results that are consistent with the standards that apply to the remission of forfeited assets at 28 C.F.R. § 9.8. In order to ensure that such standards are met, the U.S. Attorney, or his or her designee, must inform AFMLS of the following, in writing and accompanied by a signature, as part of the request for restoration:

- all known victims have been properly notified of the restitution proceedings and are properly accounted for in the restitution order. This representation is intended to ensure that no victims have been left out of the restitution order and that all are treated fairly in the order.
- to the best of the U.S. Attorney's, or designee's, knowledge and belief after consultation with the seizing agency, the losses described in the restitution order have been verified and reflect all sources of compensation received by the victims, including returns on investments, interest payments, insurance proceeds, refunds, settlement payments, lawsuit awards, and any other sources of compensation for their losses. This is to avoid double recovery by victims who may already have been compensated for part of their losses.
- to the best of the U.S. Attorney's, or designee's, knowledge and belief after consultation with the seizing agency, reasonable efforts to locate additional assets establish that the victims do not have recourse reasonably available to obtain compensation for their losses from other assets, including those owned or controlled by the defendants.
- there is no evidence to suggest that any of the victims knowingly contributed to, participated in, benefitted from, or acted in a willfully blind manner, toward the commission of the offenses underlying the forfeiture or a related offense. This is to prevent the return of forfeited property to those who essentially took part in the conduct that led to the forfeiture.

Because restitution and forfeiture are mandatory and independent parts of a criminal sentence, the defendant may not use forfeited assets to satisfy the restitution order if other assets are available for that purpose. Typical examples of this situation might involve corporations that have extensive holdings that are not subject to forfeiture, or individuals who have property that exceeds the amount subject to forfeiture. The statutes governing restitution permit the Government to enforce the restitution order as a final judgment against almost all of the defendant's property, not just facilitating property or fraud proceeds that may be subject to forfeiture.

B.4. Timing

Civil and administrative forfeiture actions can proceed faster than the parallel criminal case. Consequently, assets might be forfeited, equitably shared, placed into official use, or remitted to victims who file petitions long before restitution is ordered, and would not be available for application to the restitution order. To avoid this outcome, the USAO must coordinate with the seizing agency to secure retention of property for restoration. In addition, the USAO should place a "hold" on the distribution of seized assets in the Consolidated Assets Tracking System (CATS). If the forfeited property has already been transferred, placed into official use, or equitably shared, CATS will not accept the hold request and will transmit an error message to the CATS user. Where appropriate, such transfers that erroneously occur before victims have received compensation may be reversed at the discretion of the Chief of AFMLS or the Director of TEOAF (for seizures by TFF member agencies) to make the property available for restoration.

Because CATS is not the TFF system of record, the USAO must request that the TFF preserve the asset in cases where restitution may be ordered or where remission or restoration may occur. To ensure the preservation of the forfeited property in judicial cases involving TFF agencies, the USAO must also notify and send a copy of the restoration request to the TFF seizing agency. *See Guidelines for Treasury Forfeiture Fund Agencies on Refunds Pursuant to Court Orders, Petitions for Remission, or Restoration Requests*, section VI.B.2.a.i.[3] In administrative forfeitures involving TFF member agencies, the USAO must obtain the written concurrence of the local and/or Headquarters TFF seizing agency before AFMLS may approve restoration of forfeited funds for purposes of criminal restitution. *See id.* at sections VI.B.2.a.ii; VI.B.3.b. TEOAF policy does not permit the release of administratively forfeited funds to crime victims without the prior approval of the TFF seizing agency. *See id.* at section VI.B.2.a.ii.2.

B.5. Payment

Payment will be made *only* in accordance with the court's restitution order. If the forfeited assets are not sufficient to fully satisfy the order, payment is made on a pro-rata basis, according to the losses listed in the restitution order. If the assets are to be restored to the victims listed in the restitution order, AFMLS will notify the USAO and property custodian in writing. The custodian will then transfer the net forfeited proceeds to the clerk of court for distribution per the restitution order.

B.6. Benefits

The Restoration Procedures are intended to assist AUSAs in their use of forfeited assets to compensate victims and to assist victims in their pursuit of compensation. Victims will not need to file petitions for remission, and the review process will be faster. The forfeiture will be completed so that costs can be recovered and third-party rights extinguished. Proceeds from civil, criminal, and DOJ administrative forfeitures can be handled together and applied to restitution. Forfeiture AUSAs and agents will get credit for their work, and assets will be distributed primarily as they would have been under the remission regulations.

C. Termination of Forfeiture and Direct Payment of Assets to Victims

In some situations, it may be preferable to move to vacate the forfeiture proceeding and request that the court direct that the property be turned over directly to the victim to be applied to restitution pursuant to 18 U.S.C. §3663A(b)(1)(A), or be transferred to the clerk of court to be paid to the victim. This approach may be preferable to remission or restoration when the victim is entitled to restitution for non-pecuniary harm or other collateral costs that are not compensable under the remission regulations. In addition, termination of forfeiture may be desirable in multiple-victim fraud cases arising in jurisdictions with unfavorable case law concerning constructive trusts. *See* "Litigation of Multiple-Victim Fraud Cases in the Ninth and Eleventh Circuits," section III. Further, victims may receive compensation faster under this approach than awaiting a final order of forfeiture and a decision from the Attorney General regarding remission or restoration. Termination of forfeiture is appropriate only if no final order of forfeiture has been entered, as once property is forfeited to the Government, the Attorney General is solely responsible for its disposition. 18 U.S.C. § 982(b)(1) (incorporating 21 U.S. C. § 853(i)). If payment is to be made to the victim through the clerk of court, the property subject to forfeiture must be liquid, as the clerk cannot liquidate real or personal property.[4]

D. Comparison of Judicial Remission and Restoration

Petition for Remission	Restoration
There is no need for a criminal conviction of person from whom property is forfeited. Judicial forfeiture orders may be criminal or civil. Seizing agencies decide petition for remission of administratively forfeited assets.	Restoration requires a criminal conviction, an Order of Restitution, and a criminal, civil, or administrative forfeiture which is related to the victim's loss.
The USAO, in cooperation with the investigative agency, sends notice to all known victims of the offense underlying the forfeiture.	The USAO works with the investigative agency and probation office to identify victims and determine their losses.
In judicial forfeitures, the victim files petition for remission with the USAO.	The victim is not required to file a petition but may be required to submit information to the investigative agency or probation office.
The USAO requests the investigative agency to prepare a report and recommendation. The USAO makes a recommendation and forwards the petition package to AFMLS.	The USAO submits a restoration request, including the four required representations, to AFMLS. See section I.B.3
The Attorney General, through AFMLS, reviews the petition and may grant remission to eligible victims.	The Attorney General, through AFMLS, reviews the restoration request and may restore forfeited property to victims identified in the restitution order.
The victim must file a petition in order to receive compensation.	The victim must be named in restitution order. "Hybrid" cases with both remission and restoration are not acceptable. All forfeited proceeds are turned over to the court for distribution to victims.
The custodian of forfeited asset distributes the net proceeds directly to victims.	The custodian of the forfeited asset transfers the net proceeds directly to the clerk of the court.

II. Remission for Insurers of Victims

AFMLS has proposed a revision to the regulatory definition of *victim* at 28 C.F.R. § 9.2(v) to include insurers of victims. Remission may be granted directly to the insurer up to the amount of the victim's pecuniary loss that was compensated. This approach recognizes an insurer's traditional right of subrogation and recovery for claims paid to victims, while preventing profits or windfalls to parties who may acquire an interest in the forfeited property from the victim *after* the loss occurred (usually for less than the full value of the victim's loss). Accordingly, remission may be granted if the insurance agreement with the victim was entered into before the offense that gave rise to the forfeiture, or before the victim's knowledge of the offense. In rare cases where the victim and the insurer both request remission, or are both named in the restitution order, the victim shall be given priority to the extent of any loss that was not compensated by the insurer (e.g., a deductible).[5]

III. Constructive Trusts in Multiple-Victim Fraud Cases

While the courts generally agree that fraud victims do not retain legal title in money paid voluntarily into a fraud scheme, the courts are increasingly recognizing constructive trusts in favor of victims. Under this equitable remedy, the perpetrator of the fraud holds title to the victim's funds in trust for the benefit of the victim. This legal theory is troublesome in forfeiture cases involving multiple victims, because it can transform the forfeiture case into a cumbersome liquidation proceeding in which all victims compete against each other and against the Government for the seized funds. The Government should generally oppose a claim of constructive trust in such cases, so that the Attorney General can return the funds to the victims through the orderly remission process.

In *United States v. $4,224,958.57* ("*Boylan*"), 392 F.3d 1002 (9th Cir. 2004), the Ninth Circuit held that victims of a large fraudulent investment scheme had established a sufficient legal interest in the seized proceeds through a constructive trust to confer upon them standing to contest the forfeiture. Under this holding, government attorneys litigating forfeiture cases may be required to identify all potential victims of the fraud, notify them of the forfeiture action, and afford them an opportunity to file claims in the judicial proceeding. A related difficulty is that a constructive trust generally requires a victim to trace his or her money to the seized funds, which may warrant extensive discovery and evidentiary hearings. Some judicial circuits have followed the holding of *Boylan* in forfeiture cases. Government attorneys should therefore consult their circuit's case law in responding to constructive trust claims in their district.

In litigating forfeiture cases in circuits that recognize constructive trusts, Government attorneys may elect to oppose victims' individual claims of constructive trust on the merits, and further argue that recognition of the trust would result in unfair priority to the claimant, contrary to the equitable principles underlying the trust. The courts should also be advised that forfeiture will enable all victims to have the opportunity to recover the funds on the *pro-rata* basis through the Attorney General's remission authority. *See* 28 C.F.R. § 9.8(a)(1), (e).

PART 13: APPROVAL, CONSULTATION AND NOTIFICATION REQUIREMENTS

Topic	Requirement	Reference
Administrative Forfeiture	*Headquarters* of seizing agency must be consulted where a civil or criminal forfeiture agreement requires an administrative forfeiture	Policy Manual part 3.IV USAM 9-113.103
Attorneys' Fees	*Assistant Attorney General* must give approval to enter into a formal or informal, written or oral agreement, to exempt from forfeiture an asset transferred to an attorney as fees for legal services, including those restrained as substitute assets	Policy Manual Part 7.II USAM 9-120.116
Attorneys' Fees	*Assistant Attorney General's* approval is required for any action to institute a criminal or civil forfeiture proceeding against an asset transferred to an attorney as a fee for legal services	Policy Manual Part. 7.II USAM 9-120.112
Business Entities	*USAO* must consult with *AFMLS* prior to seeking forfeiture of a business on the theory that it facilitated money laundering	Policy Manual Part. 1.I.D.5 USAM 9-111.124
Business Entities	*USAO* must consult with *AFMLS* prior to filing indictment, information, or complaint in any forfeiture action against, seeking the seizure of, or moving to restrain an ongoing business	Policy Manual Part. 1.I.D.5 USAM 9-105.330

Topic	*Requirement*	Reference
Business Entities	*AFMLS* must be consulted before the United States asks a foreign government to restrain or seize an ongoing business or its assets, or to appoint or hire a guardian, monitor, trustee, or manager for same.	Policy Manual Part. 9.IV USAM 9-111.700
Business Entities	*USAO* or *USMS* must notify the *Justice Management Division, Asset Forfeiture Management Staff* when they learn that a restrained or seized business is losing money, has insufficient equity, or will be sold at a loss	Policy Manual Part. 10.I.J USAM 9-111.125
Business Entities: Trustees & Monitors	*USAO* must consult with *AFMLS* before seeking appointment of a trustee, monitor, or similar fiduciary	Policy Manual Part. 10.I.J
Correspondent Accounts	*AFMLS* must give approval before serving a restraining order, seizure warrant, or warrant of arrest on a correspondent bank account under 18 U.S.C. § 981(k) (Chief of *AFMLS* will get concurrence from Director of *OIA*, Department of the Treasury and the Department of State)	Policy Manual Part. 9.VII Memorandum from AAG Chertoff USA Patriot Act, Section 319, codified at 18 U.S.C. § 981(k)
Correspondent Accounts	*AFMLS* must give approval before the *AAG* can issue summonses or subpoenas to foreign banks that maintain correspondent accounts in the United States to get records (Chief of AFMLS will get approval from *OIA* as well)	Memorandum from AAG Chertoff AG order delegating authority to AAG USA Patriot Act, Section 319, codified at 31 U.S.C. § 5318(k)
Deposit of Seized Cash	*AFMLS* must give approval for exceptions to the policy requiring prompt deposit of any seized cash into the Seized Asset Deposit Fund (delegated by AAG) unless the seized cash is less than $5,000.	Policy Manual Part. 1.VI USAM 9-111.600
EAJA Awards	*AFMLS* must give approval to use funds to pay EAJA awards arising from forfeiture actions	Policy Manual Part. 7.I.B USAM 9-117.210
Equitable Sharing/ Official Use	*Chief of AFMLS* has the authority to rule on equitable sharing requests for judicially and administratively forfeited assets in which (1) the property to be shared is valued between $1 million and $5 million and (2) AFMLS, the seizing agency and the USAO agree on the sharing.	Policy Manual Part. 6.I.C
Equitable Sharing/ Official Use	*Assistant Attorney General* has the authority to rule on equitable sharing requests if the property is over $5 million and AFMLS, the seizing agency and the USAO all agree on the sharing.	Policy Manual Part. 6.I.C
Equitable Sharing/ Official Use	*Deputy Attorney General* must approve equitable sharing in (1) cases involving multi-district cases, (2) cases involving real property transfers to a state or local agency for law enforcement related use, or (3) when the USAO, AFMLS and seizing agency do not agree on the sharing, regardless of the property value	Policy Manual Part. 6.C.3 USAM 9-116.210 USAM 9-118.540 USAM says *the Deputy Attorney General* must approve equitable sharing in cases involving (1) $1 million or more in forfeited assets,

(Continued)

Topic	*Requirement*	Reference
		(2) multi-district cases, or (3) cases involving real property transfers to a state or local agency for law enforcement related use. AFMLS is coordinating with EOUSA to update the USAM to reflect the new updated delegations.
Equitable Sharing/ Official Use	*Attorney General* and *Secretary of State* approval required before forfeited assets can be shared internationally	Policy Manual Part. 6.VIII and Part 9.XIII USAM 9-116.400
Equitable Sharing/ Official Use	*AFMLS* should be notified if seizing agency decides to place property into agency's official use and the property is valued at $50,000 or more	Policy Manual Part. 6.VI USAM 9-118.440
Forfeitable Assets Located Abroad	*AFMLS* (which will consult with *OIA*) must be consulted when seeking repatriation of forfeitable assets located abroad	Policy Manual Part. 9.VI USAM 9-111.700
Forfeitable Assets Located Abroad	*AFMLS* or *OIA* must be consulted before entering into an agreement with a defendant to repatriate criminally derived assets from abroad even when not restrained by the foreign government before seeking an order actually compelling the repatriation of specific asset pursuant to 21 U.S.C. § 853(e)(4)	Policy Manual Part. 9.VI USAM 9-111.700
Forfeitable Assets Located Abroad	*AFMLS,* in consultation with appropriate OIA, Department of the Treasury, and the Department of State officials, must approve all 18.U.S.C. § 981(k) seizures.	Policy Manual Part. 9.VIII USAM 9-111.700
Forfeitable Assets Located Abroad	*AFMLS* and *OIA* must be consulted before filing an in rem forfeiture action based on 28 U.S.C. § 1355(b)(2)	Policy Manual Part. 9.X USAM 9-13.526
Forfeitable Assets Located Abroad	*OIA* (which will consult with *AFMLS*) must be consulted before taking steps to present a foreign government for enforcement or recognition of any civil or criminal forfeiture order entered in the United States for property located within the foreign jurisdiction	Policy Manual Part. 9.XII USAM 9-13.526
Liens/Mortgages	*AFMLS* must approve any requests for payment of liens and mortgages in excess of sale proceeds	Policy Manual Part. 5.III.A *Expedited Forfeiture Settlement Policy I(B)* does not require approval, only encourages consultation with AFMLS USAM 9-113.800
Plea Agreements or Settlements	*USMS* and the seizing agency must be consulted during negotiation of settlements	Policy Manual Part. 3.I.B.2 USAM 9-113.102

Topic	*Requirement*	Reference
Plea Agreements or Settlements	*Deputy Attorney General* must approve settlements where the amount to be released exceeds $2 million and 15 percent of the amount involved	Policy Manual Part. 3.III USAM 9-113.200
Plea Agreements or Settlements	*Chief of AFMLS* has authority to approve a forfeiture settlement unless the amount to be released exceeds 15 percent of the amount involved and is greater than $2 million, and the amount involved is greater than $1 million	Policy Manual Part. 3.II–III USAM 9-113.200
Plea Agreements or Settlements	*U.S. Attorney* may approve any settlement in a criminal or civil forfeiture claim if (1) the amount involved is less than $1 million, regardless of the amount involved, or (2) the amount involved is between $1 million and $5 million, if the amount to be released does not exceed 15 percent of the amount involved	Policy Manual Part. 3.II USAM 9-113.200 USAM says cases not in excess of $500,000 and cases between $1 million and $5 million provided the amount released is not more than 15 percent of the amount involved. AFMLS is coordinating with EOUSA to update the USAM to reflect the new updated delegations.
Plea Agreements or Settlements	*Seizing agency* must be consulted before entering into plea agreements or settlements returning property that is the subject of administrative forfeiture proceedings	Policy Manual Part. 2.II.C; Part. 3.B.4 USAM 9-113.103
Plea Agreements or Settlements	*AFMLS* must give approval to return of property subject to administrative forfeiture as part of a plea agreement	Policy Manual Part. 2.II.C
Plea Agreements or Settlements	*USAO* must obtain advice and approval of *AFMLS* (in consultation with the USMS) prior to any settlement that provides for unsecured partial payment	Policy Manual Part. 3.I.B.8 USAM 9-113.107
Preseizure Planning	*USMS* must be consulted as part of the preseizure planning process prior to seizure/restraint and forfeiture of assets	Policy Manual Part. 1.I.A USAM 9-111.110
Preseizure Planning	*USAO* must give approval prior to the release of sensitive law enforcement information to third party contractors for the purpose of preseizure planning	Policy Manual Part. 1.I.B
Real property	*USMS* must be consulted prior to adoption of seizure of real property *AFMLS* may authorize direct adoption of state and local seizures by U.S. Attorneys for judicial forfeiture in appropriate circumstances	Policy Manual Part 1.VII.I USAM 9-116.190 Policy Manual Part 1.VII.G USAM 9-116.170
Real property	*USMS* must be consulted prior to seizure of contaminated real property	Policy Manual Part. 1.IV.B USAM 9-111.400 USAM says USAO should exercise its discretion
Real property	*USAO* must obtain the concurrence of *AFMLS*, prior to agreeing to pay a higher rate of interest on state and local property taxes of forfeited real property, provided that such higher rate is not punitive.	Policy Manual Part. 5.III.C

(Continued)

Topic	*Requirement*	Reference
Real property	The *Deputy Attorney General* must approve real property transfers to state or local agencies for further transfer to other government agencies or non-profit agencies for use in the Weed and Seed Program.	Policy Manual Part. 6.IX USAM 9-116.500
Real property	The *Attorney General* must approve real property transfers to state or local agencies for further transfer to non-profit agencies for use in the Operation Goodwill Program.	Policy Manual Part. 6.IX.B
Real property	The *Attorney General* must approve real property transfers to a state for use as a recreational or historic site, or for the preservation of natural conditions.	Policy Manual Part. 6.IX.C
Real property	The *Attorney General* must approve a real property transfer to a federal agency for use in fulfilling a law enforcement need, or for serving a significant and continuing federal purpose.	Policy Manual Part. 6.IX.D
Real property	The *Assistant Attorney General* must approve real property transfers to state or local agencies for use in fulfilling a compelling law enforcement need.	Policy Manual Part. 6.1.C n.6
Restraining orders	*AFMLS* review required for any proposed forfeiture restraining order in a RICO prosecution	Criminal Resource Manual 2084
Seizure Thresholds	Supervisory level approval in the *USAO* required for any downward departure from the seizing thresholds (in writing)	Policy Manual Part. 1.I.D.1 USAM 9-111.120

APPENDIX A: REDELEGATIONS OF AUTHORITY

DEPARTMENT OF JUSTICE
Office of the Attorney General
28 CFR Part 0
[A.G. Order No. 1598-92]

Redelegations of Authority to United States Attorneys, Deputy Assistant Attorneys General, Section Chiefs, and Director, Asset Forfeiture Office, in the Criminal Division.[1]

AGENCY: Department of Justice.

ACTION: Final rule.

SUMMARY: This Order is the Criminal Divisions implementation of the first increase in the settlement and compromise authority delegated to the Assistant Attorneys General since 1981. It provides a corresponding increase in the settlement and compromise authority redelegated to United States Attorneys, Deputy Assistant Attorneys General, Section Chiefs, and the Director, Asset Forfeiture Office, in the Criminal Division, to further the efficient operation of the Department of Justice.

EFFECTIVE DATE: [Insert date of publication in the FEDERAL REGISTER.]

FOR FURTHER INFORMATION CONTACT: Lee J. Radek, Director, Asset Forfeiture Office, Criminal Division, Department of Justice, Washington, D.C. 20530, 202-514-1263.

SUPPLEMENTARY INFORMATION: This Order conforms the redelegations of the Assistant Attorney General's authority to compromise civil penalties and forfeitures and close civil claims to subpart Y, part 0, title 28 of the Code of Federal Regulations (CFR), 0.160, 0.164. 0.165, and 0.168 as amended by the Attorney General (Order No. 1478-91, 56 FR 8923-24, March 4, 1991). Subject to limitations set forth in 0.160(c) and 0.168(a), 0.168(d) provides that redelegations of this authority by Assistant Attorneys General to United States Attorneys will include the authority: (1) to accept offers in compromise in cases involving original claims by the United Sates of not more than $500,000; (2) to accept offers in compromise in cases involving original claims by the United States between $500,000 and $5,000,000, so long as the difference between the original claim and the proposed settlement does not exceed 15 percent of the original claim; and (3) to accept offers in compromise of claims against the United States in cases where the principal amount of the proposed settlement does not exceed $500,000.

This Order supersedes Criminal Division Directive No. 116 (48 FR 50712-13, November 3, 1983), which contains the current redelegation of the authority of the Assistant Attorney General, Criminal Division, to compromise civil penalties and forfeitures and close civil claims.

This Order is exempt from the requirements of Executive Order 12291 as a regulation related to agency organization and management. Furthermore, this Order will not have a significant economic impact on a substantial number of small entities because its effect is internal to the Department of Justice. 5 U.S.C. 605(b).

List of Subjects in 28 CFR Part 0

Authority delegations (Government agencies), Organization and functions (Government agencies), Penalties, Seizures and forfeitures.

Accordingly, 28 CFR Part 0 is amended as follows:

PART O - ORGANIZATION OF THE DEPARTMENT OF JUSTICE

(1) The authority citation for Part 0 continues to read as follows: AUTHORITY: 5 U.S.C. 301; 28 U.S.C. 509, 510, 515-19.
(2) The Appendix to Subpart Y of Part 0 is amended by removing Criminal Division Directive No. 116.
(3) The Appendix to Subpart Y of Part 0 is further amended by adding Order No. [ ] to read as follows: [Order No.]

REDELEGATIONS OF AUTHORITY TO UNITED STATES ATTORNEYS, DEPUTY ASSISTANT ATTORNEYS GENERAL, SECTION CHIEFS, AND DIRECTOR, ASSET FORFEITURE OFFICE, IN THE CRIMINAL DIVISION

By virtue of the authority vested in me by part 0 of title 28 of the Code of Federal Regulations, as amended, particularly §§ 0.160, 0.162, 0.164, 0.168 and 0.171, it is hereby ordered as follows:

(a)(1) Each U.S. Attorney is authorized in cases delegated to the Assistant Attorney General of the Criminal Division —

(A) To accept or reject offers in compromise of —

(i) Claims in behalf of the United States in all cases (other than forfeiture cases) in which the original claim $500,000, and in all cases in which the original claim was between $500,000 and $5,000,000, so long as the difference between the gross amount of the original claim and the proposed settlement does not exceed 15 percent of the original claim; and in all civil or criminal forfeiture cases, except that the U.S. Attorney shall consult with the Asset Forfeiture Office of the Criminal Division before accepting offers in compromise or plea offers in forfeiture cases in which the original claim was $5,000,000 or more, and in forfeiture cases in which the original claim was between $500,000 and $5,000,000, when the difference between the gross amount of the original forfeiture sought and the proposed settlement exceeds 15 percent of the original claim and

(ii) Claims against the United States in all cases, or in administrative actions to settle, in which the amount of the proposed settlement does not exceed $500,000; and

(B) To close (other than by compromise or entry of judgment) claims asserted by the United States in all cases (other than forfeiture cases) in which the gross amount of the original claim does not exceed $500,000, and in all civil or criminal forfeiture cases, except that the U.S. Attorney shall consult with the Asset Forfeiture Office of the Criminal Division before closing a forfeiture case in which the gross amount of the original forfeiture sought is $500,000 or more.

(2) This subsection does not apply —

(A) When, for any reason, the compromise or closing of a particular claim (other than a forfeiture case) will, as a practical matter, control or adversely influence the disposition of other claims which, when added to the claim in question, total more than the respective amounts designated above;

(B) When the U.S. Attorney is of the opinion that because of a question of law or policy presented, or for any other reason, the matter should receive the personal attention of the Assistant Attorney General;

(C) When a settlement converts into a mandatory duty the otherwise discretionary authority of an agency or department to revise, amend, or promulgate regulations;

(D) When a settlement commits a department or agency to expend funds that Congress has not appropriated and that have not been budgeted for the action in question, or commits a department or agency to seek a particular appropriation or budget authorization; or

(E) When a settlement limits the discretion of a Secretary or agency administrator to make policy or managerial decisions committed to the Secretary or agency administrator by Congress or by the Constitution.

(b) Notwithstanding the provisions of this Order, the Assistant Attorney General of the Criminal Division may delegate to U.S. Attorneys authority to compromise or close other cases, including those involving amounts greater than as set forth in paragraph (a) above, and up to the maximum limit of his authority, where the circumstances warrant such delegation.

(c) All other authority delegated to me by §§ 0.160, 0.162,0.164 and 0.171 of title 28 of the Code of Federal Regulations not falling within the limitations of paragraph (a) of this Order is hereby redelegated to Section Chiefs in the Criminal Division, except that —

(1) The authority delegated to me by §§ 0.160, 0.162, 0.164 and 0.171 of that title relating to conducting, handling, or supervising civil and criminal forfeiture litigation (other than bail bond forfeiture), including acceptance or denial of petitions for remission or mitigation of forfeiture, is hereby redelegated to the Director of the Asset Forfeiture Office; and

(2) When a Section Chief or the Director of the Asset Forfeiture Office is of the opinion that because of a question of law or policy presented, or for any other reason, a matter described in paragraph (c) should receive the personal attention of a Deputy Assistant Attorney General or Assistant Attorney General, he shall refer the matter to the appropriate Deputy Assistant Attorney General or to the Assistant Attorney General.

(d) Notwithstanding any of the above redelegations, when the agency or agencies involved have objected in writing to the proposed closing or dismissal of a case, or to the acceptance or rejection of an offer in compromise, any such unresolved objection shall be referred to the Assistant Attorney General for resolution.

MAY 19, 1992 /s/

-- ------------------------

Date

Robert S. Mueller, III
Assistant Attorney General
Criminal Division

Approved:

June 5, 1992 /s/

-------------------------------------- --------------------------

Date

Wayne A. Budd
Associate Attorney General

APPENDIX B: OFFICE OF LEGAL COUNSEL OPINION, AG ORDER NO. 1860-94

Office of Legal Counsel Opinion[1]

You have asked us to reconsider our opinion that property seized by and forfeited to the United States is not subject to state or local taxation for the period between the commission of the offense that leads to the order of forfeiture and the entry of the order of forfeiture. *See* Liability of the United States for State and Local Taxes on Seized and Forfeited Property, 15 Op. O.L.C. 85 (1991) (preliminary print) ("Harrison Memorandum"). In light of the Supreme Court's decision in *United States v. 92 Buena Vista Ave.*, 113 S. Ct. 1126 (1993), we partially reverse our opinion.

Because states and localities may not tax federal property (absent express congressional authorization),[2] the time at which ownership of forfeited property passes to the United States and the extent of the ownership interest that passes to the United States determine whether state and local taxes are owed. In many property transactions, the time and the extent of transfer of ownership are unambiguous and independent issues. In cases of transfers of ownership under the federal forfeiture statutes, however, the answer to the question of when ownership is transferred has been a matter of dispute, and of great consequence for the extent of the interest transferred.

The Harrison Memorandum expresses the Justice Department's traditional view that title vests in the United States at the time of the offense. This view is based on an interpretation of the "relation back" doctrine, which provides that a judicial order of forfeiture retroactively vests title to the forfeited property in the United States as of the time of the offense that leads to forfeiture, not as of the time of the judicial order itself. *See* 21 U.S.C. § 881(h) ("[a]ll right, title, and interest in property [subject to forfeiture] shall vest in the United States upon commission of the act giving rise to forfeiture...."); 18 U.S.C. § 1963(c), 21 U.S.C. § 853(c) (substantially identical to quoted language from 21 U.S.C. § 881(h)). Under the Department's traditional interpretation, title in forfeited property vests in the federal government at the time of the offense. The date of the judicial order of forfeiture is not significant. From the date of the offense, states and other parties are barred from acquiring interests in the property from the owner whose interests are forfeited to the United States. *See In re One 1985 Nissan*, 889 F.2d 1317, 1319-20 (4th Cir. 1989); *Eggleston v. Colorado*, 873 F.2d 242, 245-48 (10th Cir. 1989), *cert. denied*, 493 U.S. 1070 (1990)(cases decided before *Buena Vista* and consistent with the Harrison Memorandum).

The Harrison Memorandum considers and rejects several possible grounds for limiting the operation of the relation back doctrine and requiring payment of state and local tax liens for the period between the offense and the forfeiture order. The two grounds of principal concern here are the "innocent owner" defense in the civil drug forfeiture statute, *see* 21 U.S.C. § 881(a) (6),[3] and the "bona fide purchaser" defense in the criminal drug forfeiture statute, *see* 21 U.S.C. § 853(c), and in the forfeiture provision of the RICO statute, *see* 18 U.S.C. § 1963 (c). The Harrison Memorandum concludes that these defenses do not protect a state or locality (or anyone else) who innocently acquires a property interest after the time of the offense. The Supreme Court's decision in *Buena Vista* forces us to reconsider this conclusion. We conclude that the Harrison Memorandum's conclusion concerning the innocent owner defense must be reversed, but that the Harrison Memorandum's conclusion regarding the *bona fide* purchasers defense is correct (although this latter conclusion is less certain than the Harrison Memorandum indicates and we reach it through an analysis different from that set forth in the Harrison Memorandum).

I.

The civil drug forfeiture statute provides that "no property shall be forfeited..., to the extent of the interest of an owner, by reason of any act or omission established by that owner to have been committed or omitted without the knowledge or consent of that owner." 21 U.S.C. § 881(a) (6). The Harrison Memorandum accepted that "owner" could include a state or locality holding a tax lien on the property. *See* Harrison Memorandum, 15 Op. O.L.C. at 88 (preliminary print). The Memorandum concluded, however, that this "innocent owner" provision does not apply to asserted property interests that arise after the time of the offense because, as of the moment of the offense, the property belongs (by operation of the relation back doctrine) to the United States, and not to the person from whom a third party innocently acquires an interest.

We conclude, consistent with the Harrison Memorandum, that a state or locality holding a tax lien can be an "owner" as that term is defined in the civil forfeiture statute's innocent owner provisions. The broad language of the statute—"[a]ll...things of value" and "[a]ll real property, including any right, title and interest" provides no reason to exclude a tax lien-holder from the definition of "owner." 21 U.S.C. § 881(a) (6), (7). The legislative history urges a broad reading.[4] And the courts have followed, sometimes explicitly, the path suggested by Congress.[5] The "innocence" requirement of an innocent owner defense would seem to be easy to satisfy in most cases. Like an innocent donee or purchaser, a state or locality holding a tax lien generally has obtained its interest without knowledge of the offense giving rise to the forfeiture.

The Harrison Memorandum's further conclusion with regard to the innocent owner defense, however, cannot survive the ruling in *Buena Vista*. The plurality and concurring opinions reject the interpretation of the relation back doctrine set forth in the Harrison Memorandum, and agree that the innocent owner defense is available to persons who acquire interest in forfeitable property after the commission of the offense that rendered the property subject to forfeiture. The opinions differ only as to the reading of the statute that leads to this result.

The plurality and the concurrence both analyze the common law doctrine of relation back as transferring ownership of forfeited property retroactively to the date of the offense, *but only* upon the entry of a judgment of forfeiture. Until a court issues such a judgment, this retroactive vesting of ownership in the United States does not occur, and all defenses to forfeiture that an owner of the property otherwise may invoke will remain available. Thus, a person who has acquired an interest in the property may raise any such defense in a forfeiture proceeding. If that person prevails, a judgment of forfeiture will not vest (retroactively) ownership off that property interest in the United States. *Buena Vista*, 113 S. Ct. at 1135-36, 1137 (plurality opinion), 1138-39 (Scalia, J., concurring).

The plurality and the concurrence both conclude that the federal civil forfeiture statute is fully compatible with the common law, and that the statutory innocent owner clause provides a defense for a third party who innocently acquires ownership of the property after the offense and before a judgment of forfeiture. The plurality notes that section 881(h), which sets forth the relation back doctrine for the civil forfeiture statute, applies that doctrine only to "property described in subsection (a) of this section." Subsection (a) (6) excepts, from its description of forfeitable property, the property of an innocent owner. Therefore, in the plurality's analysis, subsection (a) places the property of an innocent owner beyond the reach of the forfeiture and relation back provisions in subsection (h). *See Buena Vista*, 113 S. Ct. at 1136-37. Accordingly, an ownership interest in forfeitable property that is transferred to an innocent person (after the offense giving rise to forfeiture) does not vest in the United States as of the time of the offense. Indeed, it does not vest in the United States at all.

Interpreting the civil forfeiture statute as a more straightforward codification of common law doctrine,[6] the concurrence reads the phrase, in subsection (h), "'shall vest in the United States upon commission of the act giving rise to forfeiture'" as meaning "'shall vest in the United States upon forfeiture, effective as of commission of the act giving rise to forfeiture.'" *Buena Vista*, 113 S. Ct. at 1140 (Scalia, J., concurring).[7] The result, of course, is the same as under the plurality's analysis: a property interest innocently acquired after the offense is not forfeited to the United States if an owner asserts the interest in a proper and timely way, before the entry of a forfeiture judgment.

In sum, we reverse the Harrison Memorandum's conclusion that the innocent owner defense, set forth in 21 U.S.C. § 881(a), does not protect state and local claims for tax liabilities arising between the time of an offense rendering property subject forfeiture and the issuance of a court order of forfeiture.[8]

II.

The two federal criminal forfeiture statutes addressed in the Harrison Memorandum do not contain an innocent owner defense. Those statutes, however, do provide protection for a "transferee [who] establishes in a hearing [to 'amend' an order of forfeiture] that he is a *bona fide* purchaser for value of [the] property [subject to criminal forfeiture] who at the time of purchase was reasonably without cause to believe that the property was subject to forfeiture...." 21 U.S.C. § 853(c); 18 U.S.C. § 1963(c) (same). The Harrison Memorandum concluded that this statutory "*bona fide* purchaser" defense is not available to a state or locality asserting a lien for tax liability incurred after the offense that made the property subject to forfeiture.

We conclude, consistent with the apparent assumption of the Harrison Memorandum, that such tax liens are "property" or an "interest" in property under the two criminal forfeiture statutes. Both statutes define property broadly, as including all "real property" and all "tangible and intangible personal property, including rights, privileges, interests, claims and securities." 21 U.S.C. § 853(b); 18 U.S.C. § 1963(b) (same); *see also* 21 U.S.C. § 853(c), (n)(6); 18 U.S.C. § 1963(c), (l) (6) (forfeiture and bona fide purchaser defense provisions referring to "interest" in such property). The legislative history and the courts' application of this statutory language also suggest a definition of property interests broad enough to include state and local tax liens on real property.[9]

The Harrison Memorandum suggests two arguments—one based on the relation back doctrine and another based on the definition of *bona fide* purchaser—to support its conclusion that the *bona fide* purchaser defense does not extend to holders of property interests that consist of liens for state and local taxes for the period after the offense and before a judgment of forfeiture.

A.

The Harrison Memorandum's central argument concerning the relation back doctrine addresses the bona fide purchaser defense no less than the innocent owner defense. *See* Harrison Memorandum, 15 Op. O.L.C. at 88 (preliminary print). On the interpretation set forth in the Harrison Memorandum, the United States has owned the property since the commission of the offense giving rise to the criminal forfeiture, and no one, including a *bona fide* purchaser, can later acquire any interest from the former owner.

Although the question is a closer one than in the civil forfeiture context, we conclude that the Supreme Court's decision in *Buena Vista* rejects this argument as well.[10] We recognize that the plurality's holding is based on a reading of the civil forfeiture statute (and its innocent owner provisions) and does not address the criminal forfeiture statutes (and their *bona fide* purchaser provisions). That holding also does not require the plurality to adopt the interpretation of the common law relation back doctrine that the opinion sets forth. Nonetheless, the plurality's discussion of the common law doctrine makes clear that it agrees with the concurrence that the relation back doctrine vests ownership retroactively in the United States only upon entry of a final judgment of forfeiture. Under that reading, if a state or locality establishes that it is a "*bona fide* purchaser" of an interest in the property by virtue of a tax lien, and does so before a court orders forfeiture, the order of forfeiture will not extend to the lien-holder's interest and, therefor, will not vest title to that interest in the United States.[11]

We also recognize that the concurrence in *Buena Vista* suggests that the relation back doctrine precludes a *bona fide* purchaser defense under the criminal statutes where it allows an innocent owner defense under the civil statute. As the concurrence points out, the criminal forfeiture statutes establish a procedure by which a person asserting a *bona fide* purchaser defense raises that defense *after* the court has entered an order of forfeiture. *See* 21 U.S.C. § 853(n); 18 U.S.C. § 1963 (l). In contrast, the civil forfeiture process (on both the plurality's and the concurrence's reading) contemplates that a person asserting an innocent owner defense will do so *before* the court enters an order of forfeiture. As the concurrence sees it, in the former case, the court order already has vested title retroactively in the United States (effective as of the date of the offense) before the "transferee" asserts a claim to be a *bona fide* purchaser. In the latter case, however, the court will not yet have issued the order vesting title retroactively when the "owner" asserts an innocent owner claim. (The concurrence argues that the civil statute's use of the term "owner" and the criminal statutes' use of "transferee" reflects this distinction and suggests its significance.) On this view, if a transferee's claim to be a *bona fide* purchaser succeeds and the court amends the order of forfeiture, the amendment does not void, retroactively, the initial retroactive vesting of title in the United States. The amendment to the initial order of forfeiture simply effects a new transfer of title to the *bona fide* purchaser, leaving undisturbed the United States' ownership from the time of the offense to the time of the amendment to the forfeiture order. *See Buena Vista*, 113 S. Ct. at 1141 (Scalia, J., concurring).

The *Buena Vista* concurrence fails to establish, however, that the criminal forfeiture statutes' *bona fide* purchaser defense does not protect liens for state and local tax liabilities incurred after the offense giving rise to the forfeiture. Only the concurrence advances the argument. The plurality does not join in it, and nothing in the dissenting opinion suggests that the dissenters would adopt the concurrence's views.

Further, the concurrence's argument reads too much into the actual, multi-step procedures by which a court adjudicates a criminal forfeiture claim. It thereby overlooks—or confuses those procedures with—the more fundamental legal (and fictional) process through which a retroactive transfer of ownership occurs. The better interpretation of the criminal forfeiture statutes is that the procedures of entering an order of forfeiture, holding a hearing at which transferees assert claims to be *bona fide* purchasers, and amending the order of forfeiture upon successful presentation of such a claim are but phases in a single (if protracted) process for determining what property interest vests, retroactively, in the United States when the court enters its final, amended order of forfeiture. The entire process is the equivalent of the single order of forfeiture in the civil context.

This interpretation fits more easily with the statutory language, especially when that language is read in light of the discussion in *Buena Vista* of common law relation back doctrine. The criminal forfeiture statutes provide that title in property subject to forfeiture "shall be ordered forfeited to the United States *unless* the transferee establishes" that he is a *bona fide* purchaser for value, and that "the United States shall have clear title to [the] property" only '*following* the court's disposition of all petitions" filed by transferees asserting claims to be *bona fide* purchasers. 21 U.S.C. § 853(c), (n)(7); 18 U.S.C. § 1963(c), (l)(7) (emphasis added). Such language would seem to suggest that the United States *never obtains* title from a *bona fide* purchaser, not that the United States first obtains title and then must give it back. Only after the entry of the final, amended order of forfeiture would ownership vest retroactively in the United States.[12]

This conclusion also avoids an incongruity that the concurrence's interpretation would create: an innocent owner (under the civil statute) would owe state and local taxes from the moment he or she acquired the property, but a *bona fide* purchaser for value (under the criminal statutes) would not owe taxes from the time he or she acquired the property until the time the court amended the order of forfeiture.

Finally, the conclusion we reach also is consistent with the statutory distinction between "owner" and "transferee." A person claiming to be a *bona fide* purchaser is nothing more than a transferee until he or she establishes to the court that he or she is a *bona fide* purchaser (whether the transferee does so after an initial forfeiture order, as the statute contemplates, or at some earlier stage). Only after the transferee has made this showing is he or she recognized as an owner (indeed, an innocent owner) of a particular type. Similarly, a person claiming to be an innocent owner is recognized as an innocent owner only after he or she proves to the court that he or she meets the standards of innocent ownership. Before that, such a person is, in the eyes of the court, merely a transferee. The civil forfeiture laws simply do not address or refer explicitly to those who assert, but have not yet established, that they are innocent owners.

For these reasons, we do not believe that the concurrence's discussion of the legal significance of the differences between the civil and criminal forfeiture statutes (which, in any case, is unnecessary to its conclusions) is correct.

B.

The Harrison Memorandum also states that state and local tax authorities cannot "qualify as *bona fide* purchasers for value" under the criminal forfeiture statutes. Harrison Memorandum, 15 Op. O.L.C. at 88 (preliminary print). The Memorandum does not set forth the basis for this conclusion. The *Buena Vista* plurality and concurrence have nothing to say about this issue and, thus, do not require a reversal of the Harrison Memorandum. Although the matter is not free from doubt, we believe that the stronger argument is that state and local tax lien-holders are not "*bona fide* purchasers."

The courts have not adopted a clear and uniform view of how to interpret "*bona fide* purchaser" under the criminal forfeiture statutes. *See, e.g., United States v. Lavin*, 942 F.2d 177, 182-89 (3d Cir. 1991) (*bona fide* purchaser acquires interest through volitional, advertent and, generally, commercial transaction; victim of embezzlement acquired interest through unwitting and inadvertent tortious action of another and therefore was not a bona fide purchaser); *United States v. Reckmeyer*, 836 F.2d 200, 206-08 (4th Cir. 1987) (*bona fide* purchaser includes a general, unsecured creditor of defendant who gave value to defendant in arms'-length transaction with expectation that he would receive equivalent value in the future, and whose interest must have been in some part of the forfeited property because debtor's entire estate had been forfeited); *cf. United States v. Campos*, 859 F.2d 1233, 1237-38 (6th Cir. 1988) (general, unsecured creditor is not a *bona fide* purchaser, because he does not have a legal interest in the forfeited property); *Torres v. $36,256.80 U.S. Currency*, 1993 U.S. Dist. Lexis 9107 at *19-23 (S.D.N.Y. July 7, 1993) (similar to *Campos*; also pointing out significance, for general, unsecured creditor, of unusual circumstance in *Reckmeyer* that entire estate had been seized); *United States v. Mageean*, 649 F. Supp. 820, 824, 829 (D. Nev. 1986) (definition of *bona fide* purchaser cannot be "stretch[ed]" to include tort claimants, but "there is no reason that a good-faith provider of goods and services," although an unsecured creditor, "cannot be a bona fide purchaser"), *aff'd without opinion*, 822 F.2d 62 (9th Cir. 1987); *see also United States v. 3181 S.W. 138th Place*, 778 F. Supp. 1570, 1574-75 (S.D. Fla. 1991) (civil forfeiture case stating that locality is not *bona fide* purchaser by virtue of tax lien), *vacated on other grounds*, 996 F.2d 1141 (11th Cir. 1993); S. Rep. No. 225 at 201, 209, *reprinted in* 1984 U.S.C.C.A.N. at 3384, 3391.

We are aware of no case that has decided the precise question at issue here. We acknowledge that some of the claims that courts have rejected are weaker than those presented by tax liens, and that at least one court has pointed to a primary purpose of the criminal forfeiture statutes' relation back provisions that would not be served by denying the bona fide purchaser defense to holders of liens for state and local taxes. *See Reckmeyer*, 836 F.2d at 208 ("Congress's primary concern in adopting the relation-back provision was to make it possible for courts to void sham or fraudulent transfers that we are aimed at avoiding the consequences of forfeiture"). Nonetheless, we have found no authority that has construed *bona fide* purchaser broadly enough to encompass such a tax lien-holder.

A state or locality does provide something of value, in the form of government services, in return for the interest it acquires in property (ultimately in the form of a lien) by virtue of its taxing authority. This exchange, however, does not fit the transactional, arms'-length exchange of values contemplated in the case law and suggested by the statutory phrase "*bona fide*" purchaser for value.[13] Therefore, we do not reverse the Harrison Memorandum's conclusion that the *bona fide* purchaser provisions cannot be relied upon to require payment of state and local tax liens.[14]

III.

For the reasons set forth above, we reach the following conclusions: In civil forfeiture proceedings (under 21 U.S.C. § 881) the United States may—and, indeed, must—pay liens for state and local taxes accruing after the commission of the offense leading to forfeiture and before the entry of a judicial order of forfeiture, if the lien-holder establishes, before the court enters the order of forfeiture, that it is an innocent owner of the interest it asserts. In criminal forfeiture proceedings (under 18 U.S.C. § 1963 or 21 U.S.C. § 853), however, the United States may not pay such liens because state and local tax lien-holders are not *bona fide* purchasers for value of the interests they would assert, and therefore do not come within any applicable exception to a statute that, upon entry of a court's final order of forfeiture, vests full ownership retroactively in the United States as of the date of the offense.

A.G. ORDER NO. 1860-94[15]

Office of the Attorney General
Washington, DC 20530
ORDER NO. 1860-94

DELEGATION OF AUTHORITY TO RESTORE FORFEITED PROPERTY OR TAKE OTHER ACTION TO PROTECT THE RIGHTS OF INNOCENT PERSONS IN CRIMINAL FORFEITURES

By virtue of the authority vested in me as Attorney General of the United States, including 18 U.S.C. §§ 793(h)(3), 794(d)(3), 982(b)(1), 1467(h)(1), 1963(g)(1), 2253(h)(1), 21 U.S.C. § 853(i)(1), and 28 U.S.C. §§ 509 and 510, I hereby delegate to the Director, Asset Forfeiture Office, Criminal Division, my authority, pursuant to 18 U.S.C. §§ 793(h)(3), 794(d)(3), 982(b)(1), 1467(h)(1), 1963(g)(1), 2253(h)(1), and 21 U.S.C. § 853(i)(1), to restore forfeited property to victims or take other actions to protect the rights of innocent persons in criminal forfeitures which are in the interest of justice and which are not inconsistent with the provisions of those sections.

/s/

Date

Janet Reno
Attorney General

APPENDIX C: EQUITABLE SHARING

Delegation of Authority to Make Final Determinations
in Uncontested Equitable Sharing Requests

June 5, 1995

MEMORANDUM

TO: Assistant Attorney General, Criminal Division
United States Attorneys
Director, Federal Bureau of Investigation
Administrator, Drug Enforcement Administration
Commissioner, Immigration and Naturalization Service
Director, United States Marshals Service

FROM: Jamie S. Gorelick
Deputy Attorney General

SUBJECT: Delegation of Authority to Make Final Determinations in Uncontested Equitable Sharing Requests

Parts V.D.3 and 4 of The Attorney General's Guidelines on Seized and Forfeited Property (1990) provide that final determinations of equitable sharing (1) of forfeited property valued at $1 million or greater, (2) in multi-district cases, or (3) involving the transfer of real property are to be made by the Deputy Attorney General or her designee.

I hereby delegate to the Assistant Attorney General of the Criminal Division (or her designee) the authority to make final equitable sharing determinations that otherwise would require my approval, provided the Asset Forfeiture Office (AFO) of the Criminal Division, the United States Attorney, and the federal seizing agency agree on the allocation of judicially forfeited property or that AFO and the federal seizing agency agree on the allocation of administratively forfeited property.

I will continue to make final equitable sharing determinations where there is not complete agreement among AFO, the United States Attorney, and the federal seizing agency on the sharing of judicially forfeited property or between AFO and the federal seizing agency on the sharing of administratively forfeited property.

Recommendation:

Delegation of decision-making authority to the Assistant Attorney General of the Criminal Division (or her designee) in equitable sharing cases (1) involving property valued at $1 million or more, (2) in multi-district cases, or (3) involving the transfer of real property, provided that AFO, the United States Attorney, and the federal seizing agency agree on the allocation of judicially forfeited property or that AFO and the federal seizing agency agree on the allocation of administratively forfeited property.

APPROVE /s/ Jamie S. Gorelick

DISAPPROVE

OTHER

Delegation of Authority from the Assistant Attorney General to the Chief of the Asset Forfeiture and Money Laundering Section to Decide Uncontested Equitable Sharing Requests Between $1 Million and $5 Million

August 23, 2011

MEMORANDUM FOR THE ASSISTANT ATTORNEY GENERAL

THROUGH:	Kenneth A. Blanco /s/ Deputy Assistant Attorney General
FROM:	Jennifer Shasky Calvery, Chief /s/ Asset Forfeiture and Money Laundering Section
SUBJECT:	Delegation of Authority from the Assistant Attorney

General to the Chief of the Asset Forfeiture and Money Laundering Section to Decide Uncontested Equitable Sharing Requests Between $1 Million and $5 Million

PURPOSE: This memorandum requests the Assistant Attorney General for the Criminal Division (AAG) delegate to the Chief of the Asset Forfeiture and Money Laundering Section (AFMLS) the authority to decide equitable sharing requests for judicially or administratively forfeited assets in which: (1) the property to be shared is valued between $1 million and $5 million, and (2) AFMLS, the U.S. Attorney, and the seizing agency all agree on the sharing allocation.

TIMETABLE: As soon as practicable.

SYNOPSIS: The AAG is authorized to decide equitable sharing requests in which the value of the asset exceeds $1 million, and AFMLS, the U.S. Attorney, and the seizing agency all agree to the recommended sharing allocation. Thus memo requests that the authority to decide requests valued between $1 million and $5 million when all parties are in agreement on the sharing allocation be delegated to the Chief of AFMLS. This will streamline the approval process and relieve the AAG's office of the administrative burden of deciding what are effectively routine cases. The Chief of AFMLS is well equipped to exercise this authority given AFMLS' current involvement in the approval process for equitable sharing requests that exceed $1 million.

RECOMMENDATION: It is recommended that the AAG approve the proposed delegation.

DISCUSSION:

I. Authority to Decide Equitable Sharing Requests

The Attorney General is authorized to transfer funds from the Assets Forfeiture Fund (AFF) to federal, state, and local law enforcement agencies that participate in a seizure or forfeiture of property. See 18 U.S.C. § 981 (e) (2), 19 U.S.C. §1616a, 21 U.S.C. §881(e)(1)(A), and 28 U.S.C. § 524(c)(10). The Deputy Attorney General (DAG) or his designee is responsible for making the final determination of equitable sharing requests for forfeited property valued at $1 million or greater. *See The Attorney General's Guidelines on Seized and Forfeited Property* (July 1990), Part V.D.3. (For equitable sharing requests less than $1 million, final decision-making authority rests with the federal investigative agency in administrative forfeitures, and the U.S. Attorney in judicial forfeitures. *Id.* at V.D.l and 2.)

In 1995, the DAG delegated to the AAG, "or her designee," the authority to make final determinations on equitable sharing requests for assets that exceed $1 million in value, provided that the Asset Forfeiture Office (now AFMLS), the U.S. Attorney, and the seizing agency all agree on the allocation of the property. *See* Memorandum from DAG Gorelick, Delegation of Authority to Make Final Determinations in Uncontested Equitable Sharing Requests, June 5, 1995. (In cases of requests over $1 million in which there is no consensus among AFMLS, the seizing agency, and the U.S. Attorney, decision-making authority remains with the DAG. *Id.*) The AAG has since delegated this decision-making authority to the Deputy Assistant Attorney General for the Criminal Division (DAAG) with responsibility for AFMLS.

II. Justification for Delegation

The proposed delegation would relieve the DAAG of the administrative burden of reviewing the steadily rising amount of cases requiring his approval. From FY 2006 to FY 2010, the number of cases referred to the DAAG each year increased from 40 to 75, while in the first six months of FY 2011 there already have been 64 such cases. Of the 75 requests submitted to the DAAG in FY 2010, only seven involved property valued at more than $5 million. According to that ratio, this delegation will result in an approximate 90 percent reduction in equitable sharing requests requiring DAAG approval. Streamlining the approval process will also expedite the disbursement of equitable sharing funds to our federal, state, local partners.

Moreover, because these me uncontested cases in which AFMLS, the U.S. Attorney, and the seizing agency all agree on the allocation, approval is effectively routine. Last year, none of the recommended sharing requests submitted to the DAAG were denied, including those valued at over $5 million. The proposed delegation would apply only to a subset of such uncontested cases – those valued between $1 million mid $5 million, This formulation will ensure that high-value and contested requests continue to be subject to an elevated level of review; contested requests that exceed $1 million will go to the DAG, while uncontested requests that exceed $5 million will go to the DAAG.

The Chief of AFMLS is well equipped to exercise final decision-making authority for uncontested requests between $l million and $5 million. As the Section responsible for the oversight and policy of the Equitable Sharing Program, AFMLS is extensively involved in virtually every facet of the approval process for requests over $1 million. Most notably, in each case AFMLS must make its own assessment and recommendation of the proposed allocation of property, a process that often involves extensive negotiations with agents, prosecutors, and agency counsel. AFMLS also analyzes the proposed sharing percentages to ensure that the statutory requirements are met, reviews the requests for completeness, and prepares a recommendation memorandum for the DAAG.

RECOMMENDATION

AFMLS recommends that the AAG delegate to the Chief of AFMLS the authority to make final determinations on equitable sharing requests for judicially or administratively forfeited assets in which: (1) the property to be shared is valued between $l million and $5 million, and (2) AFMLS, the U.S. Attorney, and the seizing agency agree on the sharing allocation.

----------------------------------- --------------

APPROVE /s/ Lanny A. Breuer (Date)

----------------------------------- --------------

DISAPPROVE (Date)

------------------------------------ --------------

OTHER (Date)

Appendix D: Examples of Responsibilities of Trustees and Examples of Duties and Responsibilities of a Monitor

Examples of Responsibilities of Trustees

- Prepare periodic reports, or reports upon request, for the USAO and USMS, in a useful form.
- Manage, maintain, preserve, safeguard, and protect the interests of the Government and/or innocent third party shareholders, partners, and creditors.
- Initiate any action or claim to recover assets rightfully belonging to the Government's interest in a business or asset. This is to be done in consultation with the USAO and USMS.
- Manage and operate a specified business or revenue-producing asset and recommend changes, if needed, in the management of the business or asset.
- Arrange for the inventory of supplies, equipment, tools, furnishings, and other material resources associated with a business or property.
- Execute the powers and duties associated with the management of human resources of a business or revenue-producing asset, to include recruitment, selection, discharge, and compensation of employees.
- Responsible for bringing business into compliance with environmental and zoning laws.
- Receive, review, approve, and make all disbursements of proceeds received from a joint venture to full or limited partners. Receive, review, approve, and pay all expenses, including accounting, legal, and all other expenses related to the ongoing operations of the partnership.
- Ensure an appraisal/valuation of the business is performed.
- Set, determine, reallocate, charge, hold back, adjust, and modify distributions to any owner. Charge respective partners their appropriate share of historical, present, or future costs; distributions; reimbursements; and disbursements.
- Exercise all rights, powers, voting privileges, and authority generally conferred by law or necessity that are advisable or consistent with accomplishing the purposes of a joint venture or partnership agreement associated with a business or revenue-producing assets.
- With authorization from the USAO or USMS, employ, discharge, and fix compensation of such agents and employees, including lawyers, accountants, bankers, consultants, and other professionals, who assist in accomplishing the duties and responsibilities of the trustee.
- In executing the powers granted in performance of the duties described in a court order, the trustee may rely on any resolution, certificate, statement, instrument,

opinion, report, notice, request, consent, order, or other document believed to be genuine and signed or presented by the proper party.

- Access to and/or the right to inspect, review, audit, or request surrender of all books and records of the business, asset, or partnership as the trustee deems necessary and appropriate.
- Authority to arrange and dispose of the Government's interest in a business, joint venture, partnership, corporate holding, financial instrument, or other personal or real property asset with the approval of the USAO or USMS, as appropriate.
- Access to, and the right to inspect, review, observe, appraise, and evaluate all operations and facilities of a business, at any reasonable time and consistent with state law, as the trustee, in sole discretion, deems necessary and appropriate.
- Access to all funds contained in any and all bank accounts of the asset or those funds maintained for the purpose of operating, managing, preserving, and protecting the asset, including, but not limited to, funds designated for the payment of insurance, rent, workman's compensation, and payroll.
- Execute any and all documents on the business's behalf, either personally or as power of attorney.
- Have the right to office space and administrative services at a business that is being monitored, or has been seized or forfeited.
- Refer all media contacts to the USAO.

Examples of Duties and Responsibilities of a Monitor

- To have access to and/or the right to inspect, review, audit, or request surrender of all books and records of the business, asset, or partnership as the monitor deems necessary and appropriate.
- To have access to and the right to inspect, review, observe, appraise, and evaluate all operations and facilities of a business, at any reasonable time and consistent with state law, as the monitor, in sole discretion, deems necessary and appropriate.
- To have access to all cash receipts, check registers, deposits, bank statements, canceled checks, and payable and payroll vouchers for funds contained in any and all bank accounts of the asset or those funds maintained for the purpose of operating, managing, preserving, and protecting the asset, including, but not limited to, funds designated for the payment of insurance, rent, workman's compensation, payroll, and payroll tax deposits.
- To have the right to office space and administrative services at a business that is being monitored.
- To receive, review, and approve any disbursements above a certain dollar value specified in the order of the court (i.e., any disbursement in excess of $5,000).
- To evaluate cash management and determine the current cash position and projections. To determine if enough cash is generated from operations to cover expenses. To evaluate internal controls. To determine if the cash is properly secured and deposited regularly. To evaluate banking relationships and identify any potential problems. To verify the bank statements reconciled monthly. To

determine if controls over liquid assets prevent dissipation. To verify that excess cash is invested for interest and FDIC-insured. To identify any temporary investments, stocks, bonds, or other liquid assets.

- To evaluate the level of training and supervision of employees.
- To determine the outstanding accounts receivable balances and, if they are increasing or decreasing, to explain why. To evaluate the accounts receivable collection process and compare to other similar companies in the same industry.
- To identify all outstanding liabilities, including vendor payables, payroll payables, taxes payable, and long term liabilities such as bank loans, mortgages, long-term contractual commitments, or guarantees. To project the future balances and determine the effect on the business equity.
- To evaluate the physical and fiscal controls over the inventory and determine the inventory balance and if it is the proper amount for the business. To evaluate the ordering and receiving procedures for inventory. To identify the level of obsolete, spoiled, or damaged inventory. To determine if the company has the optimum amount of inventory at the right time to provide service to customers. To determine if any inventory is on consignment or if a floor plan or any other unique inventory arrangement exits.
- To take an inventory or verify the inventory provided of furniture, fixtures, and equipment. To determine the value, age, location, condition, and costs of all property, plants, and equipment. To identify projections for replacements or new acquisitions and how the replacements or new acquisitions are to be funded. To obtain control over all the necessary titles, deeds, registrations, etc., to assure no dissipation, if provided for in court orders. To evaluate the physical security over the fixed assets. To identify any long-term leased equipment and evaluate the ultimate liability.
- To evaluate the business's marketing and advertising program.
- To evaluate the effectiveness of operations and give an opinion as to the continued successful running of the company. To evaluate and report on any environmental issues and safety considerations.
- To determine if a budget for maintenance and repairs is used by a business, and if not, if there is a procedure in the place of reporting lighting, electrical, plumbing, air conditioning, and other problems. To report on the general appearance of the facilities upon visitation.
- To evaluate the risk management of the business and determine if the business has the proper insurance coverage for fire, flood, and general liability. To identify and assure that all patents, trademarks, licenses, and permits are maintained. To identify and assess the risks associated with employee benefit plans, retirement, insurance, or savings plans. To identify any paid-up life insurance plans, etc.
- To evaluate the quality and reliability of the business's accounting systems. To prepare a rolling 6-month comparative analysis for the businesses' balance sheet, profit and loss statement, and cash flow statement. Identify monthly changes in revenues, expenses, and the values of assets, liabilities, and owner's equity. To prepare an annual comparative analysis for the business's balance sheet, profit and loss statement, and cash flow statement identifying annual changes in

revenues, expenses, and the value of assets, liabilities, and owner's equity. To prepare a monthly and annual report with explanations of trends identified and the possible effect on the continued success of the business.

- To determine the status of all tax and compliance reports and to verify that subject reports are timely filed. Some of these reporting requirements are as follows: (1) federal income tax, (2) state income tax, (3) local income tax, (4) sales tax, (5) federal quarterly form 941, (6) state quarterly employment tax, (7) local property tax, (8) federal annual form 940, (9) state annual unemployment reports, (10) employee W-2s and W-3s, (11) federal 1099s, (12) and state income taxes withheld from the employees' paychecks along with social security and Medicare taxes and the employer-matching requirements.
- To report any extraordinary events that occur outside the normal daily operations immediately to the USMS and USAO and to the court. Some of these events may include, but are not limited to, casualty losses, employee complaints such as EEOC or sexual harassment, any accident on business property, litigation, loss of key employees, major equipment failures, and any other that seriously effects the smooth operation of the business.
- Refer all media contacts to the USAO.

End Notes for Part 1

[1] References to seizure in this part include criminal or civil restraint unless plainly not applicable or appropriate.

[2] References to USMS include other departments responsible for managing restrained and seized assets (e.g., the Department of the Treasury and the Department of Homeland Security).

[3] Assets in cases where a Department of Justice agency is not the lead agency may be handled by the independent contractors employed by non-Department of Justice agencies rather than the USMS (e.g., the Department of the Treasury or the Department of Homeland Security), and those independent contractors should participate in pre-seizure planning as appropriate.

[4] For the purposes of this manual, *commercial real property* means residential real property comprised of five or more units and other real property held for commercial purposes.

[5] As a general rule, the Department of Justice does not seize or adopt contaminated real properties. *See* discussion of contaminated real property in section IV.

[6] The arrest of the person from whom the property is taken for an offense related to the illegal use or acquisition of the property for which a forfeiture action may be brought satisfies the condition of criminal prosecution. This restriction does not apply in the case of seizures by U.S. Immigration and Customs Enforcement of vehicles used in the smuggling of aliens or in the case of vehicles modified or customized to facilitate illegal activity.

[7] *See* USMS' *Pre-Seizure Planning Guide* for examples of the net equity worksheet contained within the pre-seizure planning questionnaires.

[8] *See* discussion of post-seizure at section D.4.b(2).

[9] The USAO may consider alternatives to seizure such as a *lis pendens* or restraint of certain assets.

[10] *See U.S. Attorney's Manual* 9-111.124 ("Due to the complexities of seizing an ongoing business and the potential for substantial losses from such a seizure, a United States Attorney's Office shall obtain the concurrence of the Asset Forfeiture and Money Laundering Section prior to initiating a forfeiture action against, or seeking a temporary restraining order affecting, an ongoing business. *See* the Criminal Resource Manual at 2206 and 2207."). *See also* 9-105.330 (requiring consultation with AFMLS before the USAO seeks to forfeit, seize, or restrain a business based on its involvement in money laundering).

[11] This policy does not apply in circumstances where the owner of the property has consented to forfeiture of the property (e.g., if the owner has agreed to the forfeiture in connection with a plea agreement). Neither does it apply to the adoption for federal forfeiture of property previously seized by state or local law enforcement agencies.

[12] *See* Supplemental Rule G(3)(a)((iii).

[13] *See* 18 U.S.C. § 985(b)(2).

[14] The question of whether a seizure warrant or restraining order is required does not arise where a combination civil/criminal seizure warrant is obtained pursuant to 21 U.S.C. § 853(f) and 18 U.S.C. § 983(b).

[15] One court has held that if property is already in Government custody, the proper procedure under section 983(a)(3)(C) is not to issue a criminal seizure warrant under section 853(f), but to issue an order under section 853(e). The order need not be a restraining order or an injunction, however. Rather, the court pointed out, section 853(e) authorizes the court to issue any order that will "assure the availability of the property." *See In Re: 2000 White Mercedes ML320*, 220 F. Supp. 2d 1322, 1326 n.5 (M.D. Fla. 2001).

[16] If an AUSA declines to seek a criminal seizure warrant or a section 853(e) order on the ground that this exception applies (i.e., on the ground that the property has evidentiary value but the seizing agency feels that the evidentiary value of the property is in doubt) the agency may request that the USAO provide the agency with a letter that it may use to protect itself from liability should someone later question whether there was a lawful basis for the agency's retention of the property.

[17] 18 U.S.C. § 983, General rules for civil forfeiture proceedings, provides at (j)(1), "Upon application of the United States, the court may enter a restraining order or injunction, require the execution of satisfactory performance bonds, create receiverships, appoint conservators, custodians, appraisers, accountants, or trustees, or take any other action to seize, secure, maintain, or preserve the availability of property subject to civil forfeiture."

[18] 21 U.S.C. § 853, a criminal forfeiture statute located in the drug code, provides at (e)(1), "Upon application of the United States, the court may enter a restraining order or injunction, require the execution of a satisfactory performance bond, or take any other action to preserve the availability of property [subject to criminal forfeiture] under this section." Section 853 is applicable to the general criminal forfeiture statute found in Title 18 pursuant to 18 U.S.C. § 982(b)(2).

[19] The Eleventh Circuit did not hold that the district court could not have authorized entry into the house if presented with probable cause sufficient to support a search warrant.

[20] In addition to the cash, forfeiture was sought for 15 cars and a parcel of real estate.

[21] The term *hazardous substance* means that group of substances defined as hazardous under CERCLA (42 U.S.C. § 9601(14)) and that appear at 40 C.F.R. § 302.4. *See also* 40 C.F.R. §§ 261 and 373. The requirements for reporting hazardous substances in connection with the sale or transfer of federal property are in part 373.

[22] The regulations implementing these disclosure requirement are found at 24 C.F.R. § 35.88. Certification and acknowledgment of disclosure requirements are found at 24 C.F.R. § 35.92.

[23] 24 C.F.R. § 35.210.

[24] 24 C.F.R. § 35.215. In the case of jurisdictions that banned the sale or residential use of lead-based paint prior to 1978, an earlier date may be applicable. 24 C.F.R. § 35.115(a)(1).

[25] 24 C.F.R. § 35.115(a)(10).

[26] Section 9620(a)(4) provides that state law concerning removal and remedial action shall apply to such actions facilities owned by the United States, including property transferred by federal agencies. Section 9620(h)(3)(C).

[27] 42 U.S.C. § 9620(h)(3); 40 C.F.R. § 373.1. It is envisioned that this search will involve the investigative agency's case files(s) relating to the real property. Additionally, the search must include any documentation generated from an environmental assessment or the removal of hazardous substances from the real property.

[28] The Environmental Protection Agency's funds, to include the Superfund, are generally not available for remedial actions on federally owned property. *See* 42 U.S.C. § 9111(e)(3).

[29] The covenant must warrant that (1) all remedial action necessary to protect human health and the environment with respect to any such substance remaining on the property has been taken before the date of such transfer and (2) any additional remedial action found to be necessary after the date of such transfer shall be conducted by the United States. *See* 42 U.S.C. § 9620(h)(3)(B).

[30] *The Attorney General's Guidelines on Seized and Forfeited Property* (revised Nov. 2005), section VII(1).

[31] This policy does not apply to the recovery of buy money advanced from appropriated funds. To the extent practical, negotiable instruments and foreign currency should be converted and deposited.

[32] The criteria and procedure for obtaining exemptions remains the same for cash retained by other agencies participating in the Asset Forfeiture Program.

[33] Requests for an exemption should be filed by the USAO or Criminal Division section responsible for prosecuting, or reviewing for prosecution, a particular case.

[34] The authority to approve exceptions to the Department of Justice cash management policy requiring that all seized cash, except where it is to be used as evidence, is to be deposited promptly into the Seized Asset

Deposit Fund as set forth in section VII(1) of *The Attorney General's Guidelines on Seized and Forfeited Property* (revised Nov. 2005) was delegated by the Assistant Attorney General, Criminal Division, to the Chief, AFMLS, Criminal Division, on December 13, 1991.

[35] *See American Bank of Wage Claims v. Registry of the District Court of Guam*, 431 F.2d 1215 (9th Cir. 1970).

[36] This section does not apply to property initially seized by other federal agencies.

[37] The adoption request form is available at http://www.justice.gov/criminal/afmls/forms/pdf/request-for-adoption-form.pdf.

[38] State or local agencies may redact from investigative reports information which may disclose the identity of a confidential informant. However, disclosure ultimately may be required if information provided by the informant is needed to establish the forfeitability of the property in a subsequent judicial forfeiture proceeding.

[39] Firearms and assets related to terrorism may be forfeited regardless of value.

[40] "Net proceeds" represents the gross receipts from forfeiture or the sale of forfeited property less qualified third-party interests (e.g., liens, mortgages), federal case-related expenses (e.g., advertising costs, out-of-pocket investigation or litigation expenses), any award paid to a federal informant, and federal property management expenses (e.g., appraisal, storage, security, sale).

[41] *See* 18 U.S.C. § 983(a)(1)(A)(iv).

[42] *See United States v. $174,206.00 in U.S. Currency*, 320 F.3d 658 (6th Cir. 2003) (concurrent jurisdiction doctrine does not bar federal court from exercising in rem jurisdiction over property that state court has released to the claimants after state prosecutors failed to commence a forfeiture action within the deadlines specified by state law); *United States v. $490,920 in U.S. Currency*, 911 F. Supp. 720 (S.D.N.Y. 1996) (district court cannot exercise in rem jurisdiction until state court relinquishes it), *motion for reconsideration granted*, 937 F. Supp. 249, 252-53 (S.D.N.Y. 1996) (court may grant anticipatory seizure warrant so Government can seize property as soon as state court relinquishes it); *United States v. One Parcel Property Lot 85*, 100 F.3d 740, 743 (10th Cir. 1996) (initiation of federal civil forfeiture action does not violate concurrent jurisdiction rule as long as property is not actually seized until after state action is dismissed); *United States v. One 1987 Jeep Wrangler*, 972 F.2d 472, 478-479 (2d Cir. 1992) (federal court may exercise jurisdiction over property under federal forfeiture law once it is released by state court and reseized by federal authorities; state court's order releasing property has no effect on federal forfeiture); *United States v. One Black 1999 Ford Crown Victoria Lx*, 118 F. Supp. 2d 115, 118-19 (D. Mass. 2000) (because only one court may exercise in rem jurisdiction over property at a time, federal court may not exercise jurisdiction while state forfeiture action is pending; but once state court rules that property must be released and the order is obeyed, state jurisdiction evaporates and property may be reseized and made subject to forfeiture under federal law; following *Jeep Wrangler*); *United States v. $3,000,000 Obligation of Qatar National Bank*, 810 F. Supp. 116, 117-19 (S.D.N.Y. 1993) (federal court, though "second in time," may proceed to judgment, assert a lien that will result in seizure of the asset only upon release from state jurisdiction, but stay execution of the judgment until federal jurisdiction is perfected).

[43] A specific comprehensive list can be found in the *Outline of Forfeiture Law and Procedures* monograph published by the FBI Legal Forfeiture Unit.

[44] There is a Memorandum of Understanding (MOU) between the OIG-USDA, Justice, Treasury, and USPIS establishing OIG-USDA's participation in the Justice's Assets Forfeiture Fund (AFF). OIG-USDA submits the appropriate paperwork to the seizing agency to document OIG-USDA's participation. For cases in which Postal and Treasury are the additional parties, the MOU provides for transfers to the Justice's AFF from the Postal Fund and the Treasury Asset Forfeiture Fund in forfeitures worked with OIG-USDA.

[45] The Federal animal fighting statute allows for the forfeiture of "any animal involved in a violation of [the statute]....." 7 U.S.C. § 2156(f). Forfeiture seizure authority under the statute was granted to the United States Marshal and "any person authorized under this section to conduct investigations".

[46] There is an MOU between the USMS and the USPIS should the USPIS want to retain judicial property for Official Use, the USPIS may keep custody. *Note*: Some judicial districts get a substitute custodial agreement for this.

[47] The analysis as to whether the Fund is or is not available comes down to whether the proceeds (if any) can be deposited into the AFF. If the forfeiture statute doesn't direct the disposition proceeds to go to another entity (e.g., Secretary of the Treasury or Interior) and 28 U.S.C. § 524(c)(4) does not prohibit the deposit of the funds into the AFF, then the Fund is available and the USMS should take custody of the property. If the proceeds go elsewhere, then the USMS can still manage the property (using the Fund) but must seek a reimbursable agreement with the lead agency to ensure the costs are reimbursed. If the proceeds do not cover costs, then it must come out of the agency's appropriation.

[48] U.S. Coast Guard normally turns items seized over to other agencies, i.e., ICE, DEA, FBI, USMS. As such, those agencies would dictate the property custodian.

[49] The Title 21 MOU dated 1994 remains in effect and negotiations are underway to update the MOU. The jurisdictional authority for ICE/CBP Title 21 use includes international, border nexus, and the functional equivalent of the border. It excludes domestic enforcement and administrative forfeiture activities.

[50] The seizure authority for both ICE and CBP is extremely lengthy. The statutory authorities include administrative, criminal and civil seizure & forfeiture statutes and (some limited) abilities found in Titles 8, 12, 13, 15, 18, 21, 22, 26, 28, 31, 33, 39, 42, 46 & Appendix, 49, 50 & Appendix.

End Notes for Part 2

[1] In general, all property subject to forfeiture may be forfeited administratively except (1) real property (*see* 18 U.S.C. § 985); (2) personal property having a value of more than $500,000, except as noted in 19 U.S.C. § 1607(a); and (3) property forfeitable under a statute that does not incorporate the Customs laws (*see*, e.g., 18 U.S.C. § 492, relating to counterfeiting).

[2] H. Rep. No. 91-975, 91st Cong. 1, 2d Sess. (1970), reprinted in 1970 U.S. Code Cong. & Admin. News 4407. "It is not the intention of your committee, however, that this broadened authority be expanded any further than necessary to cover those types of bearer instruments which may substitute for currency."

[3] *See also* 31 C.F.R 1010.100(dd) (eff. Mar. 1, 2011) (formerly § 103.11(u)) (defining monetary instruments).

[4] The reference to forfeitures commenced under Title 19 is to cases in which Title 19 provides the substantive basis for the forfeiture, not cases in which the procedures in Title 19 are incorporated into other forfeiture statutes. *See*, e.g., 18 U.S.C. § 981(d).

[5] Section 983(i)(2) also exempts from the requirements of CAFRA the following provisions of law which allow for forfeiture: section 983(i)(2)(B) exempts the Internal Revenue Code of 1986; section 983(i)(2)(C) exempts the Federal Food, Drug, and Cosmetic Act (21 U.S.C. § 301 et seq.); section 983(i)(2)(D) exempts the Trading with the Enemy Act (50 U.S.C. App. § 1 et seq.) and the International Emergency Economic Powers Act (IEEPA) (50 U.S.C. § 1701 et seq.) (IEEPA provision added by the USA Patriot Act of 2001, Pub. L. 107-56, Title III, § 316(d), Oct. 26, 2001, 115 Stat. 272, 310); and section 983(i)(2)(E) exempts section 1 of Title VI of the Embargo Act of June 15, 1917 (40 Stat. 233; 22 U.S.C. § 401).

[6] Section 983(i) does not exempt all statutes enforced by CBP and ICE. The currency and monetary instrument report (CMIR) offenses in Title 31, smuggling offenses under 18 U.S.C. § 545, and other provisions are not exempted from the requirements of CAFRA.

[7] 18 U.S.C. § 983(a)(2)(E) provides that "any person may make a claim under subparagraph (A) [of section 983(a)(2)] without posting bond with respect to the property which is the subject of the claim."

[8] Section 983(a)(1) deals with notice of administrative forfeiture actions, which must, in general, be sent to interested persons within 60 days of the seizure of the property.

[9] The Asset Forfeiture and Money Laundering Section (AFMLS) notes that pursuing civil judicial forfeiture under mixed theories (i.e., under statutes subject to section 983 and statutes covered by the Customs carve-out) will be problematic and is not recommended. Among other things, the trial procedure and jury instructions would be extraordinarily complex, given that hearsay would be admissible to allow the Government initially to establish probable cause for forfeiture (outside the presence of the jury) on the exempted theory, while only admissible evidence could be used (in the presence of the jury) to establish the forfeitability of the property by a preponderance of the evidence on the non-exempt theory. Also, if the Government meets its burden under both theories, the innocent owner defense in section 983(d) would apply to the non-exempt theory, but would not apply to the exempted theory.

[10] *See* section III, regarding the "under oath" requirement.

[11] The rule seems to be otherwise for CAFRA cases and for claims filed by persons who are not prisoners. *See Sandoval v. United States*, 2001 WL 300729 (S.D.N.Y. 2001) (claim is considered filed in a civil forfeiture action when it is received by the seizing agency, not when it is mailed by the claimant); *Florez-Perez v. United States*, Case No. 3:99-cv-1230-J-20A (M.D. Fla. Sept. 1, 2000) (claim sent by Federal Express on the last day for filing a claim but not received by the DEA until the next day was not timely filed).

[12] The notice requirement in section 983(a)(1) applies to all cases where the property was seized for the purpose of forfeiture, and administrative forfeiture is permissible under 19 U.S.C. § 1608 and not barred by 18 U.S.C. § 985. Seizures that are strictly for evidence, that are undertaken only pursuant to a criminal seizure warrant (21

U.S.C. § 853(f)), or that cannot, by statute, lead to an administrative forfeiture proceeding, do not trigger the notice requirements of section 983(a)(1).

[13] *See In Re: 2000 White Mercedes ML320*, 220 F. Supp. 2d 1322, 1326 n.5 (M.D. Fla. 2001) (if property is already in Government custody, no section 853(f) seizure warrant can be issued, as an order under section 853(e) would be sufficient to preserve the property; a section 853(e) order need not be an injunction or restraining order, but can be any order that will "assure the availability of the property"), *aff'g* 174 F. Supp. 2d 1268 (M.D. Fla. 2001).

[14] If the judicial forfeiture action cannot be filed immediately, the prosecutor may want to consider obtaining a precomplaint civil restraining order under section 983(j), or a preindictment restraining order under section 853(e), to preserve the property until an action is commenced.

[15] *See United States v. $3,294.00 in U.S. Currency*, 2006 WL 1982852, at *5 (D. Utah 2006) (where property was seized for evidence, not for forfeiture, and there was no administrative forfeiture, Government's decision to delay the civil forfeiture for four years until after the criminal case was over did not violate due process under *$8,850*, but suggesting that the claimant could have triggered the 90-day deadline under section 983(a)(3) by filing a claim *sua sponte*).

[16] *See* 21 U.S.C. § 881(b) (incorporating 18 U.S.C. § 981(b)).

[17] In *United States v. Millan-Colon*, 836 F. Supp. 994 (S.D.N.Y. 1993), a district court held that it was improper for the Government to commence administrative forfeiture proceedings against property that had already been included in a criminal indictment and was subject to a pre-trial restraining order in the criminal case. As mentioned in the text, that case appears to be inconsistent with later Second Circuit law, *see Leyland, supra*, and CAFRA. Moreover, *Millan-Colon* is easily distinguished from most cases in that the pre-trial restraining order in that case may have signaled to the defendant that he did not need to respond to the notice of the administrative forfeiture proceeding. As mentioned in section II.A, such misunderstandings will be avoided if, once parallel administrative and criminal forfeiture proceedings have been commenced and the claimant fails to file a timely claim in the administrative forfeiture proceeding, the Government moves to strike the forfeiture allegation from the criminal indictment, thus giving the defendant a fair opportunity to argue that the default in the administrative proceeding was based on an assumption that the forfeiture in the criminal case could be opposed.

[18] For purposes of section 983(a)(1), a non-judicial forfeiture proceeding is any proceeding in which (1) the motive for the seizure was, at least in part, to take custody of property that the Government intended to pursue in a civil forfeiture action; and (2) administrative forfeiture is permissible under section 1608 and notwithstanding section 985. Seizures that are strictly for evidence, that are undertaken for the purpose of criminal forfeiture, or that cannot, by statute, lead to an administrative forfeiture proceeding do not trigger the notice requirements of section 983(a)(1). *See* Cassella, "The Civil Asset Forfeiture Reform Act of 2000," 27 J. Legislation 97, 127 (2001).

[19] References in this section to the notice deadline apply to whatever deadline may be applicable in a given case, be it the 60-day deadline, the 90-day deadline, or some other deadline established pursuant to the statutory procedure for obtaining an extension of time.

[20] Among other reasons, it may turn out that the defendant has died or is a fugitive, that criminal charges cannot be presented to a grand jury for strategic or evidentiary reasons, that the property subject to forfeiture belongs to a third party, or that the property was derived from or involved in an offense other than the offenses to be charged in the criminal case.

[21] Under pre-CAFRA law, a claimant had to post a bond equal to 10 percent of the value of the seized property. *See* 19 U.S.C. § 1608. This provision was repealed by 18 U.S.C. § 983(a)(2)(E), except as to forfeiture under the statutes listed in section 983(i).

[22] "The Civil Asset Forfeiture Reform Act of 2000," 27 J. Legis. 97, 142 & nn. 239-40 (2001) (quoting legislative history of the requirement that the claim be filed under oath, subject to the penalty of perjury).

[23] Courts have strictly enforced this provision. *See United States v. BCCI Holdings (Luxembourg) S.A. (Fifth Round Petition of Liquidation Comm'n for BCCI (Overseas) Macau)*, 980 F. Supp. 1 (D.D.C. 1997) (petition that is not signed under penalty of perjury and fails to identify asset in which claimant is asserting an interest and nature of that interest does not comply with 18 U.S.C. § 1963(l)(3)); *United States v. BCCI Holdings (Luxembourg) S.A. (Petition of BCCI Campaign Committee)*, 980 F. Supp. 16 (D.D.C. 1997) (petition dismissed because not signed under penalty of perjury). *Note*: section 1963(l)(3) is the RICO counterpart to section 853(n)(3).

[24] The time limit in Rule 35(a) was raised from 7 to 14 days effective December 1, 2009. The Supreme Court's Order of March 26, 2009, transmitting this amendment to Congress, recites that it "shall take effect on

December 1, 2009, and shall govern all proceedings thereafter commenced *and, insofar as just and practicable, all proceedings then pending.*" (Emphasis added). *See also* 28 U.S.C. § 2074(a). It is inconceivable that application of the 14-day time limit in a case pending on December 1, 2009, would neither be just nor practicable; thus the 14-day period will be used throughout the present discussion.

[25] 16A Charles A. Wright et al., *Wright & Miller's Federal Practice & Procedure* § 3950.10 (2005) ("It is not only those motions expressly listed in Rule 4(b) that stall the running of the time in which to appeal... A timely motion for reconsideration...postpones the appeal time."); 5 Am. Jur. 2d *Appellate Review* § 303 (2004) ("In an appeal from a District Court to the United States Supreme Court, the time for appeal does not begin to run until the court entering judgment disposes of a proper motion for...reconsideration."). *See United States v. Ibarra*, 502 U.S. 1, 6 (1991) (rejecting attempts to get around *Healy* and *Dieter*, a motion for reconsideration renders a final decision not final until the district court can rule on the motion, which suspends the time period for filing an appeal); *United States v. Dieter*, 429 U.S. 6, 8 (1976) ("consistent practice in civil and criminal cases alike has been to treat timely petitions for rehearing as rendering the original judgment nonfinal for purposes of appeal for as long as the petition is pending"); *United States v. Healy*, 376 U.S. 75, 77-78 (1964) (same); *United States v. Correa-Gomez*, 328 F.3d 297, 299 (6th Cir. 2003) (citing *Ibarra*, reiterating that a timely motion for reconsideration means that the period to file an appeal begins to run only after the district court has ruled on the motion for reconsideration).

[26] Rule 35(c) defines *sentencing* as the oral announcement of the sentence.

[27] None of this has an impact on the Government's ability to move to correct a clerical error at any time pursuant to Rule 36. For example, if the error was simply the district court's failure to make the order of forfeiture part of the judgment as required by Rule 32.2(b)(3), in most circuits the error could be corrected pursuant to Rule 36. *See United States v. Bennett*, 423 F.3d 271 (3d Cir. 2005) (if there was a preliminary order of forfeiture to which defendant did not object, the failure to include the forfeiture in both the oral pronouncement and the judgment and commitment order is a clerical error that may be corrected pursuant to Rule 36) (collecting cases); *United States v. Loe*, 248 F.3d 449, 464 (5th Cir. 2001) (if district court forgets to include forfeiture in the judgment, it may, pursuant to Rule 36, amend the judgment *nunc pro tunc*); *United States v. Hatcher*, 323 F.3d 666, 673 (8th Cir. 2003) (if there was a preliminary order of forfeiture, the failure to include the forfeiture in the judgment at sentencing is a clerical error that may be corrected at any time pursuant to Rule 36); *United States v. Thomas*, 67 F. App'x 819 (4th Cir. 2003) (amendment of the judgment pursuant to Rule 36 to include the forfeiture judgment 4 years after sentencing was appropriate as it accurately reflected the district court's intention at sentencing); *United States v. Arevalo*, 67 F App'x 589 (11th Cir. 2003), *modified* 2004 WL 1253057 (11th Cir. 2004) (failure to make the forfeiture part of the judgment is a clerical error that may be corrected pursuant to Rule 36 as long as the court apprised the defendant of the forfeiture orally at sentencing); *but see United States v. Pease*, 331 F.3d 809, 816-17 (11th Cir. 2003) (the omission of the order of forfeiture from the judgment in a criminal case is not a clerical error that can be corrected pursuant to Rule 36; if the district court does not make the order of forfeiture part of the judgment at sentencing, and the Government does not appeal, the forfeiture is void). Most errors that arise in forfeiture cases, however, are not clerical. *See*, e.g., *United States v. King*, 2005 WL 1111884 (D.S.C. 2005) (where there was no mention of forfeiture either at sentencing or in the judgment, there is a clear violation of Rule 32.2(b) that cannot be corrected as a clerical error under Rule 36).

[28] The Supreme Court's Order of March 26, 2009, transmitting this amendment to Congress, recites that it "shall take effect on December 1, 2009, and shall govern all proceedings thereafter commenced *and, insofar as just and practicable, all proceedings then pending.*" (Emphasis added.) *See also* 28 U.S.C. § 2074(a). It is inconceivable that application of the amendment in a case pending on December 1, 2009, would neither be just nor practicable; thus, the amendment would apply to all proceedings from its effective date forward.

[29] Prior to enactment of the December 1, 2009, amendments to Rule 32.2, there was an argument that the mandatory language in 21 U.S.C. §853(n)(1) stating that the government "shall publish" notice of the forfeiture did not permit the Attorney General to dispense with publication, even in cases involving property worth less than $1,000. Any argument that the mandatory language in §853(n)(1) permits no exceptions to publication is now eliminated by the specific reference in Rule 32.2(b)(6)(C) which incorporates the civil rule exceptions for low value assets. Title 28, United States Code, section 2072(b) provides, with respect to rules promulgated by the Supreme Court, "Such rules shall not abridge, enlarge or modify any substantive right. All laws in conflict with such rules shall be of no further force or effect after such rules have taken effect." Thus, the rule trumps the statute. *See United States v. Marion*, 562 F.3d 1330, 1340, n.7 (11th Cir. 2009) ("to the extent it is argued that § 853 conflicts with Rule 32.2, the rule must trump. *See* 28 U.S.C. § 2072(b) ('All laws in conflict with such rules shall be of no further force or effect after such rules have taken effect.').").

[30] *See* part 1, section VII for a full discussion of issues involving adoptive forfeitures. In particular, section E at page 40 discusses the policy favoring state forfeitures where the seizure is related to a purely state prosecution.

End Notes for Part 3

[1] The contact person at the seizing agency for the purpose of determining the agency's view of the terms of the settlement is as follows:

(1) Federal Bureau of Investigation (FBI): assistant special agent-in-charge of the respective field office or designee;
(2) Drug Enforcement Administration (DEA): assistant special agent-in-charge or resident agent-in-charge or designee;
(3) Customs and Border Protection/Immigrations and Customs Enforcement (CBP/ICE): associate/assistant chief counsel (CBP) for the respective field office or designee (note: CBP is responsible for processing all seizures for civil forfeiture made by either CBP or ICE);
(4) U.S. Postal Inspection Service (USPIS): inspector-in-charge of respective field division or designee;
(5) Internal Revenue Service (IRS): chief, criminal investigation division of the key district, or designee;
(6) U.S. Secret Service (USSS): special agent-in-charge or designee, asset forfeiture program, headquarters office; and
(7) Bureau of Alcohol, Tobacco, Firearms and Explosives (ATF): resident agent-in-charge of the respective field office or designee.

[2] In Treasury cases where the USMS is not the custodian of the property, the independent contractor will serve as the property manager, and the USMS need not be consulted. It is the responsibility of the seizing agency to contact the independent contractor and inform it of any settlement proposals.

[3] There have been instances in which AUSAs have arranged plea agreements providing for the disposition of administratively forfeitable property without consulting the appropriate seizing agency. There also have been instances in which AUSAs have agreed to return to a defendant property that has already been forfeited administratively. Such agreements are improper and arrangements cause great difficulty for the seizing agencies.

[4] In Treasury and Homeland Security cases, the advice and approval of AFMLS should also be sought.

[5] *See* Attorney General Order No. 1598-92, Appendix Subpart Y, Part O, Title 28, Code of Federal Regulations, establishing the settlement and compromise authority redelegated to the U.S. Attorneys from the Assistant Attorney General, Criminal Division, in accordance with the requirements of 28 C.F.R. § 0.168(d). Attorney General Order No. 1598-92 is reprinted in Appendix A.

[6] The authority of the Assistant Attorney General pursuant to 28 C.F.R. § 0.160 for settlement of forfeiture cases is delegated to the Chief, AFMLS, Criminal Division, by paragraph (c) of Attorney General Order No. 1598-92. *See* Appendix A.

[7] This policy is based on 28 CFR §§ 0.160 and 0.161. Section 0.160 provides that "Assistant Attorneys General are authorized, with respect to matters assigned to their respective divisions, to: (1) Accept offers in compromise of claims asserted by the United States in all cases in which the difference between the gross amount of the original claim and the proposed settlement does not exceed $2 million or 15 percent of the original claim, whichever is greater." Section 0.161 provides that matters that cannot be approved at the Criminal Division level must be approved by the Deputy Attorney General.

[8] The contact person at the seizing agency, for the purpose of determining whether the terms of any settlement requiring administrative action by the agency can be implemented, is as follows:

(1) the FBI and DEA: the forfeiture counsel;
(2) CBP/ICE: associate/assistant chief counsel (CBP) for the respective field office or designee (note: CBP is responsible for processing all seizures for civil forfeiture made by either CBP or ICE);
(3) USPIS: manager, forfeiture group, or designee;
(4) Internal Revenue Service: chief, criminal investigation division of the key district, or designee;
(5) USSS: Office of Chief Counsel or designee; and
(6) ATF: staff assistant to chief counsel, headquarters.

[9] *See also* section IV.A.

[10] Payments in lieu of forfeiture are addressed in the proposed Department of Justice regulations (28 C.F.R. § 8.12(e)).

[11] Both the Ninth Circuit in *Ventura Packers*, 424 F.3d at 864, and the Supreme Court in *Republic National Bank*, 506 U.S. at 92-93, held that transferring the "substitute res" out of the district did not deprive the district courts of in rem jurisdiction.

[12] *See United States Attorneys' Manual* § 9-120.116.

End Notes for Part 4

[1] Under the FCA, a relator is entitled to between 15 and 25 percent of the proceeds of the action if the United States intervenes in the action, and to between 25 and 30 percent of the proceeds if the United States does not intervene. 31 U.S.C. § 3730(d)(1) and (2).

[2] If a relator seeks to intervene or file a claim in any forfeiture proceeding, government counsel on the FCA action and/or the Director of the Commercial Litigation Branch (Fraud Section), Civil Division, should be consulted immediately.

[3] A threshold requirement for a relator to assert a claim under the alternate remedy provision is that the relator has filed a valid *qui tam* action. *See* Justice Department Briefs filed in *U.S. ex rel. Hefner v. Hackensack Medical Center*, No. 06-2287 (3d Cir.); *U.S. ex rel. Bledsoe v. Community Health Systems, Inc.*, No. 01-6375 (6th Cir.). One reason why the relator's suit may not be valid is that the relator's allegations are based on a "public disclosure" and the relator does not qualify as an original source of those allegations. 31 U.S.C. § 3730(e)(4). There may also be other jurisdictional and non-jurisdictional reasons (for example, where a relator is not the first to file or has failed adequately to plead a FCA claim) why a relator has failed to file a valid action. Moreover, even where a relator's action is proper, the relator may be entitled only to a reduced share. For example, even where a relator qualifies as an original source, if the relator's action is based primarily on certain disclosures as enumerated in the FCA, then the court may award no more than 10 percent of the proceeds. 31 U.S.C. § 3730(d)(1). The relator's share may also be reduced if he or she "planned or initiated the violation," unless he or she is "convicted of criminal conduct" arising from his or her role in the violation, in which case he or she is not entitled to any share. 31 U.S.C. § 3730(d)(3).

[4] Under the FCA, the percentage of the proceeds that the relator is entitled to recover varies depending on whether the United States intervenes in the relator's action, as well as other factors. 31 U.S.C. § 3730(d)(1) and (2). Assuming that the relator is not otherwise barred from claiming a share of the proceeds, determination of the relator's share will involve two related inquiries: first, the "percentage" of the proceeds of the action to be awarded to the relator, and second, the value of those "proceeds." Section 3730(c)(5) makes these inquiries applicable to a proceeding qualifying as an alternate remedy. The Civil Division has issued guidelines governing the determination of relator share percentages. The Commercial Litigation Branch (Fraud Section) of the Civil Division or government counsel in the FCA action, not forfeiture counsel, is responsible for determining or litigating the relator's share issue.

[5] Where the issue of the relator's share is addressed may well depend on the forum in which the relator chooses to pursue it; however, the Government should advocate for the determination to be made in the FCA action whenever such litigation remains viable.

[6] Relators have made similar requests regarding the escrow of funds paid toward restitution and criminal fines. Where the restitution is payable to governmental victims, the Government may consider such requests, particularly where the FCA action will not be completed. Requests for an escrow of funds due to individual victims or for criminal fines, however, always should be opposed.

[7] Upon request of the relator, the United States may provide the total expenses incurred in connection with a forfeiture action. In the Department's view, relators have no right to challenge forfeiture expenses or intervene in property management issues, and therefore, are not entitled to a detailed itemization of forfeiture expenses, even if the forfeiture action is determined to be an alternate remedy.

End Notes for Part 5

[1] For a current list of agencies participating in the Department of Treasury Forfeiture Fund, *see* 31 U.S.C. § 9703(o).

[2] Copies of these guidelines, including "Guidelines for Seized and Forfeited Property," are available at http://www.treasury.gov/resource-center/terrorist-illicit-finance/Asset-Forfeiture/pages/index.aspx, or by contacting the Executive Office for Asset Forfeiture, Department of the Treasury, 1341 G Street, N.W., Suite 900, Washington, D.C. 20220.

[3] After the Supreme Court's decision in *United States v. A Parcel of Land (92 Buena Vista)*, 507 U.S. 111 (1993), the Office of Legal Counsel (OLC) opined that the United States must pay state and local taxes on civilly forfeited real property because the innocent owner defense then in effect was broad enough to include tax liens that arose after the events giving rise to forfeiture. The rationale for the OLC opinion was undermined by the Civil Asset Forfeiture Reform Act (CAFRA) of 2000, which created a uniform innocent owner defense applicable to all civil forfeiture cases, 18 U.S.C. § 983(d). In the case of interests acquired after the events giving rise to forfeiture, only bona fide purchasers for value who acquire their interest without knowledge that the property is subject to forfeiture can maintain a meritorious innocent owner defense. 18 U.S.C. § 983(d)(3). Thus, as a matter of law, taxing authorities that acquire liens after the commission of the offense giving rise to the forfeiture would not be able to recover the value of the liens under section 983(d)(3). The OLC opinion is reprinted as Appendix B.

[4] *See* 18 U.S.C. §§ 1467(g), 1963(f), and 2253(g).

[5] The Department of Justice takes the position that 28 U.S.C. § 2001 does not apply to judicial forfeiture sales and no judicial confirmation is required.

[6] *See U.S. v. Real Property Located at 6124 Mary Lane Drive, San Diego, California*, 2008 U.S. Dist. LEXIS 57172, at *5 (W.D.N.C. July 29, 2008); *United States v. Grundy*, 7 U.S. (3 Cranch) 337, 350-351 (1806); *cf. Republic National Bank of Miami v. United States*, 506 U.S. 80, 89-92 (1992); *United States v. Real Property Located at 185 Hargraves Drive (In Re Newport Saving and Loan Association)*, 928 F.2d 472, 478 (1st Cir. 1991); 21 U.S.C. § 881(h); 21 U.S.C.§ 853(c); 18 U.S.C. § 1963(c).

[7] *See* Fed. R. Civ. P. 6(a)(1) (providing guidance in computing the length of the stay).

[8] If a losing claimant files a notice of appeal to challenge the forfeiture, but fails to move for an additional stay pending appeal pursuant to Fed. R. Civ. P. 62(d) or Fed, R, App. P. 8, the funds should nonetheless be transferred from the SADF to the AFF. The Supreme Court has held that such a transfer does not divest the courts of in rem jurisdiction over the case. See *Republic National Bank of Miami v. United States*, 506 U.S. 80, 93 (1993).

[9] A general warranty deed assures the grantee/buyer that title to the property is free and clear of any and all liens and encumbrances and insures the grantee/buyer from any future claims against the property.

[10] As used in this policy, the terms *general warranty deed* and *special warranty deed* are not intended to be limiting in their application. In some states, warranty deeds are not used (e.g., in California a "grant deed" provides limited statutory warranties). The use of such state variations equivalent to a general warranty deed is satisfactory for purposes of this policy.

End Notes for Part 6

[1] *See* 21 U.S.C. § 881(e)(1)(A) and (e)(3); 18 U.S.C. § 981(e) (2); and 19 U.S.C. § 1616a. For further details on equitable sharing, please refer to the *Guide to Equitable Sharing for State and Local Law Enforcement Agencies* (April 2009) (*Guide*) and the *Attorney General's Guidelines on Seized and Forfeited Property* (*Guidelines*) (revised Nov. 2005).

[2] The Federal Contribution Form (FCF) can be found on the CATS Information Center website and AFMLS Online.

[3] Qualitative factors that the decision maker may consider when determining a sharing percentage are outlined in Section VII.B of the *Guide to Equitable Sharing*.

[4] A formal Memorandum of Understanding (MOU) reflecting the task force sharing arrangement must be signed by all agencies participating in the task force before any sharing decisions may be made pursuant to the agreement. Such MOUs should be updated periodically to reflect material changes in the agencies constituting the task force or in any agency's contribution to forfeitures credited to the task force.

[5] Any delegation by a U.S. Attorney of authority to decide equitable sharing requests must be in writing and kept on file together with other delegations of authority by the U.S. Attorney.

[6] The transfer of real property to a State or local law enforcement agency for official use is contingent upon the agency's demonstration of a compelling law enforcement need for the property. The recipient agency must sign an MOU regarding to the use that the property is to be put and agree to pay any federal costs or expenses,

as well as the "federal share of the property's value, before the transfer will be approved. See *Guide*, section VIII.C.1. All sharing requests involving the transfer of real property must be submitted to AFMLS for processing, regardless of the value of the real property.

[7] This delegation authority is reprinted in Appendix C.

[8] The federal share is the amount retained in the Assets Forfeiture Fund which represents the percentage corresponding to the federal agency's participation in the law enforcement effort. If a State or local agency opts to take an asset for official use as opposed to receiving proceeds, the agency must pay the value of the federal share that would have been retained had the asset been sold. In these instances, the federal share is based on the most recent appraised value of the asset. In no case shall the federal share be less than 20 percent of the appraised value of the asset.

[9] Refer to the Department of the Treasury, Treasury Executive Office of Asset Forfeiture or to the U.S. Postal Inspection Service for information regarding payments from these agencies.

[10] *See* http://www.justice.gov/criminal/afmls/equitable-sharing to download a copy of the Equitable Sharing Agreement and Certification form.

[11] An agency may also be designated ineligible if its NCIC code has changed, it has disbanded or is no longer a participant in the Program or it no longer qualifies as a law enforcement agency.

End Notes for Part 7

[1] Forms for requesting payments out of the Judgment Fund are available on http://www.fms.treas.gov/judgefund /forms.html and should be submitted directly to the office that handles Judgment Fund matters.

[2] "Except as otherwise specifically provided by statute, a court shall award to a prevailing party other than the United States fees and other expenses, in addition to any costs awarded pursuant to subsection (a), incurred by that party in any civil action (other than cases sounding in tort), including proceedings for judicial review of agency action, brought by or against the United States in any court having jurisdiction of that action, unless the court finds that the position of the United States was substantially justified or that special circumstances make an award unjust." 28 U.S.C. § 2412(d)(1)(A).

[3] In civil forfeitures of firearms and ammunition pursuant to 18 U.S.C. § 924(d) where a claimant substantially prevails, CAFRA's attorneys' fees provision applies and the United States is liable for reasonable attorneys' fees and other litigation costs. 28 U.S.C. § 2465(b) (2000).

[4] 31 U.S.C. § 1304(a)(1).

[5] *Congressional Budget Office Cost Estimate: H.R. 1658 - The Civil Asset Forfeiture Reform Act of 2000, reprinted in* 146 Cong. Rec. H2040, H2047–H2049 (daily ed. Apr. 11, 2000).

[6] *See* U.S. Attorney's Manual, § 9-120.000 *et seq.*

[7] "During fiscal year 1998 and in any fiscal year thereafter, the court, in any criminal case (other than a case in which the defendant is represented by assigned counsel paid for by the public) pending on or after the date of enactment of this Act [Nov. 26, 1997], may award to the prevailing party, other than the United States, a reasonable attorney's fee and other litigation expenses, where the court finds that the position of the United States was vexatious, frivolous, or in bad faith, unless the court finds that special circumstances make such an award unjust." The Hyde Amendment to the Department of Commerce, Justice, and State, the Judiciary and Related Agencies Appropriations Act of 1998, Pub. L. No. 105-119, § 617, 111 Stat. 2440, 2519 (1997), *reprinted in* 18 U.S.C.A. § 3006A, historical and statutory notes.

[8] *See United States v. Certain Real Property, Located at 317 Nick Fitchard Road, N.W., Huntsville, AL,* 579 F.3d 1315 (11th Cir. 2009).

[9] Hyde Amendment, *supra* note 7.

[10] *See United States v. Gilbert*, 198 F.3d 1293, 1299-1302 (11th Cir. 1999) (discussing legislative history of the Hyde Amendment). In its original form, the Hyde Amendment tracked the EAJA in its burden and standard of proof, but was changed prior to enactment by switching the burden from the Government to the plaintiff and heightening the standard of misconduct that must be shown. *Id.* at 1302. *See also United States v. Wade*, 255 F.3d 833, 839 n.6 (D.D.C. 2001) (discussing in footnote that the Hyde Amendment is a heavier burden for petitioner than the EAJA standard).

[11] *Gilbert*, 198 F.3d at 1299 (11th Cir. 1999); *See also In re 1997 Grand Jury*, 215 F.3d 430, 437 (4th Cir. 2000).

[12] *Gilbert*, 198 F.3d at 1298-99 (quoting *Black's Law Dictionary* 668 (6th Ed. 1990); *In re 1997 Grand Jury*, 215 F.3d at 436 (quoting *United States v. Gilbert*, 198 F.3d 1293, 1298-99 (11th Cir. 1999)). *Accord United States*

v. Braunstein, 281 F.3d 982, 994-95 (9th Cir. 2002) (following *Gilbert* in defining the term "frivolous"). Other courts have adopted slightly different definitions of the statutory terms. *See*, e.g., *United States v. Knott*, 256 F.3d 20, (1st Cir. 2001) (vexatiousness for purposes of the Hyde Amendment requires "both a showing that the criminal case was objectively deficient, in that it lacked either legal merit or factual foundation, and a showing that the government's conduct, when viewed objectively, manifests maliciousness or an intent to harass or annoy"). *Accord United States v. Heavrin*, 330 F.3d 723, 729 (6th Cir. 2003). Thus, it is imperative to check for controlling circuit law in litigating any issues under the Hyde Amendment.

[13] *United States v. Tucor Int'l, Inc.*, 238 F.3d 1171, 1178 (9th Cir. 2001).

[14] *United States v. Sherburne*, 249 F.3d 1121, 1126-1128 (9th Cir. 2001).

[15] *Id.* at 1127.

[16] *Id.*

[17] *Gilbert*, 198 F.3d at 1304.

[18] *United States v. Pease*, 137 Fed. Appx. 220, 222-223 (11th Cir. 2005).

[19] *Id.* at 226.

[20] *Id.* at 224-226. The district court also denied the claimant's request for attorneys' fees under EAJA, finding that the Government's position was substantially justified.

[21] *United States v. Adkinson*, 247 F.3d 1289, 1293 (11th Cir. 2001).

[22] *Id.*

[23] *United States v. Braunstein*, 281 F.3d 982, 994 (9th Cir. 2002); *United States v. Holland*, 214 F.3d 523 (4th Cir. 2000); *United States v. Truesdale*, 211 F.3d 898, 902-904 (5th Cir. 2000); *United States v. Wade*, 255 F.3d 833, 839 (D.D.C. 2001). *But see United States v. Robbins*, 179 F.3d 1268, 1270 (10th Cir. 1999) (finding a Hyde Amendment action was a criminal proceeding to which the appellate rule for criminal actions applies).

[24] "Such awards shall be granted pursuant to the procedures and limitations (but not burden of proof) provided for an award under Title 28, U.S.C. § 2412." Hyde Amendment, *supra* note 7.

[25] 28 U.S.C. § 2412(d)(1)(B).

[26] 28 U.S.C. § 2412(d)(2)(A).

[27] *See United States v. Moser*, 586 F.3d 1089, 1092-96 (8th Cir. 2009) (prevailing third party in ancillary proceeding is not entitled to recover attorneys' fees under CAFRA). *Accord United States v. Nolasco*, 354 F. App'x 676, 679-81 (3d Cir. 2009).

[28] "Except as otherwise specifically provided by statute, a court shall award to a prevailing party other than the United States fees and other expenses, in addition to any costs awarded pursuant to subsection (a), incurred by that party in any civil action (other than cases sounding in tort), including proceedings for judicial review of agency action, brought by or against the United States in any court having jurisdiction of that action, unless the court finds that the position of the United States was substantially justified or that special circumstances make an award unjust." 28 U.S.C. § 2412(d)(1)(A).

[29] *United States v. Douglas*, 55 F.3d 584, 587 (11th Cir. 1995); *United States v. McAllister*, 1998 WL 855498, at *3 (E.D. Pa. 1998); *United States v. Bachner*, 877 F. Supp. 625, 627 (S.D. Fla 1995).

[30] *Jean v. Nelson*, 863 F.2d 759, 765 (11th Cir. 1988).

[31] *Hensley v. Eckerhart*, 461 U.S. 424, 433 (1983); *see also Rhoten v. Brown*, 854 F.2d 667, 669 (4th Cir. 1988); *Sims v. Apfel*, 238 F.3d 597, 600 (5th Cir. 2001).

[32] *Buckhannon Board and Care Home, Inc. v. West Va. Dept. of Health and Human Resources*, 532 U.S. 598, 604-605 (2001); *see also Select Milk Producers, Inc. v. Johanns*, 400 F.3d 939, 944-48 (D.C. Cir. 2005).

[33] *Buckhannon Board and Care Home, Inc.* at 604.

[34] *United States v. One Rural Lot*, 770 F. Supp. 66 (D.P.R. 1991).

[35] *In re Application of Gerard Mgndichian for Return of Property*, 312 F. Supp. 2d 1250 (C.D. Cal. 2003).

[36] *Id.* at 1260.

[37] *Id.* at 1257-60.

[38] *Pierce v. Underwood*, 487 U.S. 552, 565 (1988).

[39] *Id.*

[40] *Id.* at 568-70.

End Notes for Part 8

[1] Rule 6(e)(3)(A)(ii) authorizes disclosure to "government personnel," which may include contract personnel, but only upon court order as discussed below. Rule 6(e)(3)(E)(i) authorizes disclosure "preliminary to or in connection with a judicial proceeding" and also requires a court order.

[2] CAFRA applies to any forfeiture proceeding initiated on or after August 23, 2000. *See* Pub. L. No. 106-185, § 10, 114 Stat. 202, 217.

3 Section 3322(a) provides:

(a) a person who is privy to grand jury information—

(1) received in the course of duty as an attorney for the government; or

(2) disclosed under rule 6(e)(3)(A)(ii) of the Federal Rules of Criminal Procedure;

may disclose that information to an attorney for the government for use in...connection with any civil forfeiture provision of Federal law.

[4] *United States v. Sells Engineering*, 463 U.S. at 429.

[5] *Id.* at 431.

[6] H.R. Rep. 105-358(I), 105th Cong., 1st Sess. 1997.

[7] Webster's Dictionary 1301 (10th ed. 1999).

[8] *Federal Grand Jury Practice* (OLE February 2008), Part 2, Sec.12.

[9] *In re Grand Jury Proceedings*, 309 F.2d 440, 443 (3d Cir. 1962).

[10] *United States v. Forman*, 71 F.3d 1214, 1218 (6th Cir. 1995).

[11] *In re Perlin*, 589 F.2d 260, 267 (7th Cir. 1978) (Commodity Futures Trading Commission); *United States v. Bates*, 627 F.2d 349 (D.C. Cir. 1980) (Federal Maritime Commission); *Bradley v. Fairfax*, 634 F.2d 1126, 1130-32 (8th Cir. 1980) (Parole Commission hearing officer).

[12] *Federal Grand Jury Practice* (OLE February 2008), Part 3, Sec. 26.

[13] *United States v. Lartey*, 716 F.2d 955 (2d Cir. 1983).

[14] *In re Gruberg*, 453 F. Supp. 1225, 1233-34 (S.D.N.Y. 1978).

[15] S. Rep. No. 354, 95th Cong., 1st Sess. 7 (1977), reprinted in U.S. Code Cong. & Ad. News 527, 530.

[16] *United States v. Anderson*, 778 F.2d 602 (10th Cir. 1985).

[17] *United States v. Pimental*, 380 F.3d 575, 590-96 (1st Cir. 2004), *cert. denied*, 125 S. Ct. 1385 (Feb. 22, 2005),

[18] 380 F.3d at 596.

[19] The practice in a number of districts has been to obtain a standing order from the district court, under either Rule 6(e)(3)(A)(ii) or Rule 6(e)(3)(E)(i), or both, authorizing disclosure to specific contract personnel who are directly involved in assisting attorneys for the Government in the prosecution of cases. Such orders should be updated frequently to reflect any changes in conditions which were considered by the court in support of the order.

[20] *Compare In re Grand Jury Matter,* 607 F. Supp. 2d 273, 276-77 (D. Mass. 2009) (denying disclosure to contractor on grounds that the contractor was not the equivalent of government personnel and that particularized need had not been shown) *with In re Disclosure of Matters Occurring Before a Grand Jury to Litigation Technology Service Center,* 2011 WL 3837277 (D. Haw. Aug. 25, 2011) (authorizing disclosure on grounds that contractor employees are equivalent of government personnel).

[22] As explained more fully below, the Federal Rules of Criminal Procedure provide that in a case where a jury returns a guilty verdict, either the defense or the prosecution may request that the jury also determine whether the Government has established the "requisite nexus" between the property alleged to be forfeitable and the offense committed by the defendant. Fed. R. Crim. P. 32.2(b)(5).

[23] In response to *Jones* and *Apprendi*, the Criminal Division advised prosecutors "Any fact which increases the statutory maximum sentence (other than prior conviction) should be charged in the indictment and proved at trial, and the [trial] jury should be instructed that it is required to find the fact beyond a reasonable doubt." USA Book, http://dojnet.doj.gov/usao/eousa/ole/usabook/narc/apprendi/0728memo.htm.

[24] The Department of Justice has taken the position that *Blakely* does not apply to the U.S. Sentencing Guidelines, a question on which the Court has granted certiorari. *See* USA Book, http://dojnet.doj.gov/usao/eousa /ole/lakely-dagmemo.pdf.

[25] Of course, the defendant *does* have a right to indictment and a grand jury finding on the elements of the substantive offense(s) that are predicates for forfeiture. As a recent reminder of the importance of charging all applicable substantive legal theories, and the effect upon forfeiture of a failure to do so, *see United States v. Iacaboni*, 363 F.3d 1, 7 (1st Cir. 2004) (reversing forfeiture judgment based on theory that assets had facilitated money laundering with intent to conceal where indictment charged only money laundering with

intent to promote criminal activity). A fact that triggers an enhanced forfeiture penalty, greater than the penalty that would otherwise apply to a given offense, would also seem to qualify as an element of the substantive offense within the meaning of *Apprendi. See* 18 U.S.C. § 981(a)(1)(G), made applicable in criminal cases by 28 U.S.C. § 2461(c), (providing for forfeiture of *all* assets of any individual, entity, or organization engaged in certain crimes, but only if the crimes are acts of domestic or international terrorism as defined in 18 U.S.C. § 2331); *see also* 18 U.S.C. § 2332b(g)(5) (defining numerous offenses as "Federal crimes of terrorism" if they are "calculated to influence or affect the conduct of government by intimidation or coercion, or to retaliate against government conduct").

26 The decision to require a special forfeiture finding only by the trial jury was made even though the Rules Committee assumed in 1972—contrary to the holding of *Libretti* decades later—that the amount of the interest or property subject to criminal forfeiture was "an element of the offense to be alleged and proved." Advisory Committee Note to 1972 Amendment to Fed. R. Crim. P. 31(e). The reference to forfeiture was deleted from Rule 31 in 2000 in light of the creation that year of Rule 32.2, covering most aspects of criminal forfeiture procedure. Rule 32.2(b) was specifically intended to replace the special verdict requirement of Rule 31(e), a requirement that generated confusion over the scope of the determination to be made by the trial jury. Rule 32.2(b) provides instead that the court, or the jury upon a request by the Government or the defendant, must determine whether the Government has established the requisite nexus for forfeiture. *See* Advisory Committee Note to 2000 Adoption of Fed. R. Crim. P. 32.2(b).

27 Identified substitute assets may also be restrained in the Fourth Circuit. *In re Assets of Billman*, 915 F.2d 916, 919, 920-21 (4th Cir. 1990).

28 *Bivens v. Six Unknown Named Agents of Federal Bureau of Narcotics*, 403 U.S. 388 (1971).

29 Pub. L. No. 105-119, § 617, 111 Stat. 2440, 2519 (1997) (reprinted in 18 U.S.C. § 3006A, historical and statutory notes).

30 Some districts have found it useful to cover these points in an introductory presentation to the grand jury outlining forfeiture law and procedures, as part of the grand jury's orientation during the first few weeks after a new grand jury is empaneled. This can be done by the district's forfeiture AUSA, who is in the best position to cover these issues and to address the grand jurors' questions. The orientation session also provides the prosecutor with the opportunity to explain to the grand jury that forfeiting the defendant's interest in a piece of property does not end the matter, but that an ancillary proceeding is held after a preliminary order of forfeiture is entered to allow third parties who claim to have an interest in the property to petition the court to establish that interest. While that issue is of no direct concern to the grand jurors in their deliberations, it is helpful that they understand that the Government is not seeking to forfeit the property of owners with superior interests to that of the defendant or property belonging to innocent bona fide purchasers of the property.

End Notes for Part 9

1 *See* Federal Rules of Civil Procedure Supplemental Rules for Admiralty or Maritime Claims and Asset Forfeiture Actions, Rule G(4) and Federal Rules of Criminal Procedure Rule 32.2(b)(6).

2 No. CV 05-3155 ABC (FMOx) (C.D. Cal. July 11, 2005) (unpublished). *See also Collello v. Securities and Exchange Commission*, 908 F. Supp. 738 (C.D. Cal. 1995), on which the *Kim* court heavily relied.

3 OIA will consider making a formal request without a probable cause determination where the assets located in a foreign state are held by a person "with no voluntary attachment to the United States." *United States v. Verdugo-Urquidez*, 494 U.S. 259 (1990). If the facts support this conclusion, the prosecutor should discuss this possibility with OIA.

4 *See also* 18 U.S.C. § 1594 (forfeiture provisions for human trafficking).

5 *See United States v. Melrose East Subdivision,* 357 F.3d 493 (5th Cir. 2004) (applying the probable cause requirement in *United States v. Monsanto,* 491 U.S. 600 (1989), to section 983(j)(1)(A)).

6 A general description of assets, such as "all property of the defendant located in Switzerland" will likely not satisfy the particularity requirement of the Fourth Amendment.

7 *See United States v. Jamieson,* 427 F.3d 394, 405 (6th Cir. 2005) (initial issuance of restraining order may be based on grand jury's finding of probable cause); *United States v. Bollin,* 264 F.3d 391, 421 (4th Cir. 2001) (the grand jury's finding of probable cause is sufficient to satisfy the Government's burden).

End Notes for Part 10

[1] Examples of a trustee's responsibilities include, but are not limited to, those described in Appendix D.
[2] Examples of a monitor's responsibilities include, but are not limited to, those described in Appendix D.
[3] A list of possible examples or duties and responsibilities are set forth in Appendix D.

End Notes for Part 11

[1] *United States v. Goodwin*, 457 U.S. 368, 373 (1982).
[2] *Id.* at 376, n.8.
[3] *Id.* at 377.
[4] *Id.*
[5] *Id.* at 381.
[6] *See Blackledge v. Perry*, 471 U.S. 21 (1974) (defendant exercised his right to a trial de novo and consequently, during the retrial, the state increased the charge from a misdemeanor to a felony; the Court held that although there was no evidence that the prosecution acted vindictively by increasing the misdemeanor charge to a felony, the concern is the defendant's "fear of such vindictiveness" may deter him from exercising his legal right to appeal, violating due process).
[7] *See United States v. Bouler*, 799 F. Supp. 581 (W.D.N.C. 1992) ("A defendant may be able to prove vindictive prosecution in a case such as the instant one in which the Government prosecutes the defendant after he files a claim in a civil forfeiture action." However, the defendant did not pursue such a claim, and thus, the court did not address it further).
[8] *United States v. White*, 972 F.2d 16 (2d Cir. 1992) (prosecution indicted defendant after he subsequently challenged the forfeiture of his vehicle; court declined to hold that by opposing the Government's forfeiture, the Government should be precluded from bringing criminal charges).
[9] "Notwithstanding any other provision of law, when sentencing a defendant convicted of an offense described in subsection (c), the court shall order, in addition to, or in the case of a misdemeanor, in addition to or in lieu of, any other penalty authorized by law, that the defendant make restitution to the victim of the offense..."
[10] 18 U.S.C. § 3771(c)(1).
[11] Under 18 U.S.C. § 1345(a)(1), the pre-trial restraint of assets is authorized in fraud-type cases, but only in limited circumstances.
[12] Adverse court of appeals decisions from the Ninth Circuit makes the administrative and civil forfeiture of fraud proceeds impractical in cases that involve large numbers of victims and that must be filed in the Ninth Circuit. Prosecutors in the Ninth Circuit who seek to use civil or administrative forfeiture in a case involving victims should consult part 12, section III of this *Manual.*
[13] Section 2466 "'does not mandate the court to disallow the claimant,' but rather confers upon the Court discretion to determine whether or not disentitlement is warranted." 357 F. Supp. 2d at 1328.
[14] *United States v. Agurs*, 427 U.S. 97, 110-11 (1976), extended the rule announced in *Brady* to apply to evidence that "is obviously of such substantial value to the defense that elementary fairness requires it to be disclosed even without a specific request."
[15] *See* 28 U.S.C. § 530B (DOJ attorneys are "subject to State laws and rules, and local Federal court rules, governing attorneys in each State where such attorney engages in that attorney's duties, to the same extent and in the same manner as other attorneys in that State."
[16] *See* part 3, section I.B.7 of this *Manual*; *United States Attorneys' Manual* 9-113.106; *see also Grand Jury Manual* (July 2000), Part 12, "Parallel Proceedings," para. 12.16, "Global Settlements," (noting that, although *ABA Model Code of Professional Responsibility*, DR 7-105(A), which prohibited attorneys from threatening criminal prosecution solely to obtain an advantage in a civil matter, was replaced by the *ABA Model Rules of Professional Conduct* which omitted this provision (*see ABA Formal Ethics Opinion* 92-363 (1992)), many states still have ethical rules patterned after DR 7-105(A)).
[17] *See Town of Newton v. Rumery*, 480 U.S. 386, 400 (1987) (O'Connor, J., concurring).
[18] *See Grand Jury Manual* (July 2008), Part 12, "Parallel Proceedings," para. 12.12, USABook Online.
[19] A claimant or witness in a civil forfeiture proceeding who is also a defendant in a pending criminal case may want to cooperate in the civil case in the hope that such cooperation may be a factor in supporting a motion by the Government for reduction of sentence pursuant to section 5K1.1 of the Sentencing Guidelines; however, it is

not clear whether or to what extent cooperation in a civil forfeiture case would constitute a factor under section 5K1.1, though it is clear that the Guidelines expressly separate a defendant's sentence from his/her forfeiture of property. *See U.S. v. Hendrickson*, 22 F.3d 170, 175 (7th Cir.) (section 5E1.4's explicit language that "[f]orfeiture is to be imposed upon a convicted defendant as provided by statute" makes it "readily apparent that forfeiture was considered by the Sentencing Commission and was intended to be imposed in addition to, not in lieu of, incarceration") *cert. denied*, 513 U.S. 878 (1994).

[20] *See Grand Jury Manual, supra*, at. 12.10, "Abuse of Power Claims" ("person subject to parallel proceedings may raise a claim of having been manipulated or misled by the Government in a variety of contexts," including motions to suppress evidence, motions to deny enforcement of civil subpoenas, and motions to dismiss indictment (citing cases)); *see also In re Phillips, Beckwith & Hall*, 896 F. Supp. 533 (E.D. Va. 1995) (law firm moved to stay forfeiture action in view of potential criminal charges against firm personnel; court denied stay, noting that allegation of "bad faith on the Government's part by, for example, pursuing a civil lawsuit solely for the purpose of aiding a criminal investigation, or threatening or delaying bringing criminal charges in order to extract an advantage in the civil case by keeping the cloud of criminal prosecution overhead" would have produced different outcome (citing cases)).

[21] *See* part 3, section I.B.2 of this *Manual* (stating that the seizing agency must also be consulted in connection with settlement negotiations).

[22] "Native format" answers the need to produce "reasonably accessible metadata that will enable the receiving party to have the same ability to access, search, and display the information as the producing party where appropriate or necessary in light of the nature of the information and the needs of the case." *See The Sedona Conference Commentary on Legal Holds: The Trigger and the Process*, 11 SEDONA CONFERENCE JOURNAL 265, 278 (2010), *available at* http://www.thesedonaconference.org/content/miscFiles /publications_html.

End Notes for Part 12

[1] Treasury Forfeiture Fund member agencies include the Internal Revenue Service (IRS), U.S. Immigration and Customs Enforcement (ICE), U.S. Customs and Border Protection (CBP), U.S. Secret Service (USSS), and U.S. Coast Guard.

[2] *See*, e.g., 19 C.F.R. Parts 171 and 172.2; 26 C.F.R. Part 403, Subpart D; 28 C.F.R. § 9.1(b)(1).

[3] *Available at* http://www.treasury.gov/resource-center/terrorist-illicit-finance/Asset-Forfeiture/Documents /blue book.pdf.

[4] *See also* part 11, section II of this *Manual*, "Is a Prosecutor Bound, Ethically or Otherwise, to Forego Forfeiture in Favor of Restitution?"

[5] *See generally* 18 U.S.C. § 3664(j)(1).

End Note for Appendix A

[1] The following is a reprint of Attorney General Order No. 1598-92.

End Notes for Appendix B

[1] The following is a reprint of the Office of Legal Counsel Opinion.

[2] *See, e.g., United States v. City of Detroit*, 355 U.S. 466, 469 (1958) ("[A] [s]tate cannot constitutionally levy a tax directly against the Government of the United States or its property without the consent of Congress."); *M'Culloch v. Maryland*, 17 U.S. (4 Wheat.) 316 (1819).

[3] The conclusions with regard to section 881(a) (6), the innocent owner provision immediately at issue in *Buena Vista* and applicable to all "things of value" traceable to an exchange for a controlled substance, also apply to section 881(a) (7), which contains a nearly identical innocent owner provision applicable to real property used in a drug offense. *See* n.2, *supra*, and n.6, *infra*.

[4] *See* Joint Explanatory Statement of Titles II and III, 95th Cong., 2d Sess. (1978), *reprinted in* 1978 U.S. Code Cong. & Admin. News 9522 (in section 881(a) (6), "[t]he term 'owner' should be broadly interpreted to include any person with a recognizable legal or equitable interest in the property seized"); *see also* S. Rep. No. 225, 98th Cong., 2d Sess. 195, 215 (1984), *reprinted in* 1984 U.S. Code Cong.& Admin. News 3182, 3378, 3398 (describing section 881(a) (7) as, in effect, extending section 881(a) (6) to cover real property used in a drug offense but not acquired with proceeds of prohibited drug transactions).

[5] *See, e.g., United States v. 717 S. Woodward St.*, 1993 U.S. App. Lexis 21051 at *15 (3d Cir. Aug. 20, 1993) (citing legislative history); *United States v. 6960 Miraflores Ave.*, 995 F.2d 1558, 1561 (11th Cir. 1993) ("Lienholders have the right to assert their claims of innocent ownership" under section 881(a), as interpreted in *Buena Vista*); *United States v. 6109 Grubb Rd.*, 886 F.2d 618, 625 n.4 (3d Cir. 1989) (cited in *Buena Vista* and citing legislative history); *see also United States v. 2350 N.W. 187 St.*, 996 F.2d 1141 (11th Cir. 1993) (*Buena Vista* analysis of section 881(a) innocent owner provisions assumed to apply where purported innocent owner is local tax lien holder).

[6] The concurrence specifically rejects the plurality's reading of the phrase, in subsection (h), "property described in subsection (a)" as meaning, in effect, "property forfeitable under subsection (a)." The concurrence stresses that subsection (h) refers to "property *described* in subsection (a)," not property deemed forfeitable under subsection (a). Since subsection (a) describes property generally and does not declare that property that cannot be forfeited is not "property," the "property described in subsection (a)" refers to all relevant property interests, including those of innocent owners. *Buena Vista*, 113 S. Ct. at 1139 (Scalia, J., concurring).

[7] The concurrence "acknowledge[s] that there is some textual difficulty with th[is] interpretation," but argues, first, that the imprecision imputed to the quoted language in subsection (h) is to be expected "in a legal culture familiar with retroactive forfeiture" and, second, that the civil forfeiture statute as a whole, including subsection (d) and its adoption of forfeiture procedures applicable under 19 U.S.C. § 1602 *et seq.*, does not make sense if one rejects the concurrence's reading of subsection (h) (and the plurality's reading of subsections (a) and (h)). *Buena Vista*, 113 S. Ct. at 1140 (Scalia, J., concurring).

[8] The local tax lien cases decided by lower courts since the Supreme Court's decision in *Buena Vista* do not alter our conclusion. In *2350 N.W. 187 St.*, 996 F.2d 1141, the court vacated the judgments in two cases in which the district courts had relied on the interpretation of the relation back doctrine described in the Harrison Memorandum, and had granted summary judgment against a county invoking the innocent owner defense in 21 U.S.C. § 881(a) (6), (7) to assert liens for property taxes owed for some of the period between an offense giving rise to forfeiture and the entry of a judgment of forfeiture. The appellate court remanded the cases for further consideration in light of the Supreme Court's decision in *Buena Vista*.

[9] *See* S. Rep. No. 225 at 193, *reprinted in* 1984 U.S. Code Cong. & Admin. News at 3376 (section enacting current 18 U.S.C. § 1963(c) and 21 U.S.C. § 853(c) "allows the use of criminal forfeiture as an alternative to civil forfeiture in all drug felony cases"); *id.* at 211, *reprinted in* 1984 U.S. Code Cong. & Admin. News at 3394 (property defined as subject to criminal forfeiture under 18 U.S.C. § 1963(a) and 21 U.S.C. § 853(a) is equivalent to property subject to civil forfeiture under 21 U.S.C. § 881(a)); *United States v. Reckmeyer*, 836 F.2d 200, 205 (4th Cir. 1987) (unsecured creditor who has reduced his claim to judgment and acquired a lien could seek an amendment to a forfeiture order under 21 U.S.C. § 853(n)); *United States v. Robinson*, 721 F. Supp. 1541, 1545 (D.R.I. 1989) (a leasehold interest ordinarily is a real property interest within the definition in 21 U.S.C. § 853(b)); *see also United States v. Monsanto*, 491 U.S. 600, 606-09 (1989) (noting breadth of forfeitable property under 21 U.S.C. § 853 (a)).

[10] *Cf. United States v. Harry*, 1993 U.S. Dist. Lexis 11999 at *21-27 (E.D. Iowa May 6, 1993) (drawing on *Buena Vista* discussion of innocent owners to resolve *bona fide* purchaser issue under the criminal forfeiture statute).

[11] This conclusion would follow rather simply from the court's analysis in *Buena Vista* when the state or locality asserts its *bona fide* purchaser defense at or before the proceedings in which the court issues an order of forfeiture. The conclusion is less certain under the procedure set forth in the criminal forfeiture statutes, which provides for assertion of *bona fide* purchaser claims at a hearing held after the court issues an initial order of forfeiture. The remainder of this subsection addresses this issue.

[12] Although the statutory language does not fit perfectly with the interpretation adopted here, somewhat imprecise drafting concerning the sequence of events leading to a retroactive vesting of title is, as the *Buena Vista* concurrence points out, perhaps to be expected in a legal culture familiar with retroactive vesting. *See Buena Vista*, 113 S. Ct. at 1140 (Scalia, J., concurring).

[13] *See, e.g., Lavin*, 942 F.2d at 185-86 (Congress derived *bona fide* purchaser exception "from hornbook commercial law" principle of protecting the "innocent purchaser for valuable consideration" which had developed at common law "in order to promote finality in commercial transactions and thus to...foster

commerce"); *Reckmeyer*, 836 F.2d at 208 (scope of *bona fide* purchaser provision "construed liberally" is to protect "all persons who give value to the defendant in an arms'-length transaction with the expectation that they would receive equivalent value in return").

[14] The Harrison Memorandum also found that payment of liens for state and local taxes, accruing after the offense, was not within the Attorney General's discretionary authority under 28 U.S.C. § 524(c) (1) (D) ("payment of valid liens...against property that has been forfeited") or 28 U.S.C. § 524(c) (1) (E) (payments "in connection with remission or mitigation procedures relating to property forfeited"). We reach the same conclusion through a different analysis. A tax lien-holder who establishes that he or she is an innocent owner under the civil forfeiture statute or a *bona fide* purchaser under the criminal statutes is protected from the operation of the relation back doctrine, and need not rely on the Attorney General's discretionary payment of a valid lien or remission or mitigation of a forfeiture that has not occurred with respect to the lienholder's interest. *See* S. Rep. No. 225 at 207-08, 217, *reprinted in* 1984 U.S. Code Cong. & Admin. News at 3390-3391, 3400; *Lavin*, 942 F.2d at 185 (*bona fide* purchaser provisions designed to require protection previously left to discretion of Attorney General). If the tax lien-holder fails to establish that he or she is protected by one of these defenses to forfeiture, there can be no "valid lien" for taxes to be paid and no forfeited interest (in the form of tax liabilities) for the Attorney General to "remi[t] or mitigat[e]." Because ownership of the property will have vested in the United States as of the commission of the offense, state and local authorities cannot (absent a congressional waiver of immunity from state and local taxation that we do not find in 28 U.S.C. § 524 or elsewhere) levy taxes on such property after the date of the offense any more than they could levy taxes on a federal courthouse or post office.

[15] The following is a reprint of the Attorney General's Order No. 1860-94, dated March 19, 1994.

In: U.S. Department of Justice Asset Forfeiture ...
Editor: Onni Nieminen
ISBN: 978-1-62808-226-5

Chapter 2

GUIDE TO EQUITABLE SHARING FOR STATE AND LOCAL LAW ENFORCEMENT AGENCIES*

U.S. Department of Justice

FOREWORD

In the nearly 25 years since the Comprehensive Crime Control Act of 1984 authorized federal officials to implement a national asset forfeiture program, asset forfeiture has become one of the most powerful tools for targeting criminals—including drug dealers and white collar criminals— who prey on the vulnerable for financial gain. Forfeiture statutes are now prevalent throughout the federal legal code and their use, along with other important anti-crime measures, has had a significant impact on crime.

One of the most important provisions of asset forfeiture is the authorization to share federal forfeiture proceeds with cooperating state and local law enforcement agencies. The Department of Justice Asset Forfeiture Program serves not only to deter crime but also to provide valuable additional resources to state and local law enforcement agencies. As this is written, the Department of Justice has shared over $4.5 billion in forfeited assets with more than 8,000 state and local law enforcement agencies.

A Guide to Equitable Sharing for State and Local Law Enforcement Agencies serves to promote and maintain the integrity of the equitable sharing program so that it can continue to merit public confidence and support. For this reason it is supplemented with the National Code of Professional Conduct for Asset Forfeiture (*see* Appendix B). All seizing and prosecutorial agencies should ensure compliance with this Code.

Most importantly, this *Guide* seeks to assist state and local law enforcement agencies participating in the program by clarifying the directives they must follow to obtain and use equitably shared funds. The goal is to make the process as clear as possible so that local communities and the nation can thrive from reduced crime and from quality law enforcement.

---

* This is an edited, reformatted and augmented version of U.S. Department of Justice, Criminal Division, Asset Forfeiture and Money Laundering Section, dated April 2009.

Richard Weber, Chief
Asset Forfeiture and Money Laundering Section
Criminal Division; Department of Justice

I. What Is the Department of Justice Asset Forfeiture Program?

The Department of Justice Asset Forfeiture Program (the Program) is a nationwide law enforcement initiative that removes the tools of crime from criminal organizations, deprives wrongdoers of the proceeds of their crimes, recovers property that may be used to compensate victims, and deters crime. The most important objective of the Program is law enforcement. Equitable sharing further enhances this law enforcement objective by fostering cooperation among federal, state, and local law enforcement agencies.

Federal law authorizes the Attorney General to share federally forfeited property with participating state and local law enforcement agencies.[1] The exercise of this authority is discretionary and limited by statute. The Attorney General is not required to share property in any case.

The Controlled Substances Act most fully states the intent of Congress in the sharing of forfeited property. Section 881(e)(3) of Title 21, United States Code, provides that:

> The Attorney General shall assure that any property transferred to a State or local law enforcement agency...
>
> (A) has a value that bears a reasonable relationship to the degree of direct participation of the State or local agency in the law enforcement effort resulting in the forfeiture, taking into account the total value of all property forfeited and the total law enforcement effort as a whole; and with respect to the violation of law on which the forfeiture is based; and
>
> (B) will serve to encourage further cooperation between the recipient State or local agency and Federal law enforcement agencies.[2]

A Guide to Equitable Sharing for State and Local Law Enforcement Agencies applies only to the sharing of assets that were seized by Department of Justice investigative agencies and federal agencies participating in the Department of Justice Asset Forfeiture Program and that were forfeited judicially or administratively to the United States by the United States Attorney's Offices or Forfeiture Program participants. Participating agencies and components currently approved include:

U.S. Department of Justice agencies and components:

- Criminal Division, Asset Forfeiture and Money Laundering Section (AFMLS)
- Justice Management Division, Asset Forfeiture Management Staff (AFMS)
- Bureau of Alcohol, Tobacco, Firearms and Explosives (ATF)
- Drug Enforcement Administration (DEA)
- Federal Bureau of Investigation (FBI)
- U.S. Attorney's Offices (USAO)
- U.S. Marshals Service (USMS)

Components outside of the U.S. Department of Justice:

- U.S. Department of Agriculture, Office of Inspector General (USDA-OIG)
- U.S. Department of Defense, Criminal Investigative Service (DCIS)
- U.S. Department of State, Bureau of Diplomatic Security (DSS)
- U.S. Food and Drug Administration, Office of Criminal Investigations (FDA-OCI)
- U.S. Postal Inspection Service (USPIS)

The FBI, DEA, ATF, and USPIS are the only agencies participating in the Department of Justice Program that directly adopt seizures by state or local law enforcement agencies. Under limited circumstances, the USAOs may directly adopt such seizures.[3]

As soon as assets are identified for seizure/forfeiture in a federal investigation or an adoptive forfeiture, the USAO or seizing agency handling the case should contact the USMS to discuss pre-seizure planning to determine the necessary resources for property management and disposal requirements.[4] Pre-seizure planning is required to seize real property, businesses, or any unusual, complex, or unique assets (e.g., animals, property contaminated with hazardous material, leasehold agreements, partnership interests, valuable arts and antiques, or a large quantity of assets posing potential storage problems).

The U.S. Department of the Treasury administers its own Asset Forfeiture Program.[5] For policies and participating agencies, please visit the Treasury Executive Office for Asset Forfeiture website at www.treas.gov/offices/enforcement/teoaf/.

II. Which Non-federal Agencies Are Eligible to Participate in the Justice Equitable Sharing Program?

A. State or Local Law Enforcement Agencies

Any state or local law enforcement agency that directly participates in an investigation or prosecution that results in a federal forfeiture may request an equitable share of the net proceeds of the forfeiture.[6]

For purposes of equitable sharing, the Department of Justice defines *law enforcement agency* as a state or local government organization authorized to engage in as its primary function the investigation and apprehension, or the prosecution of individuals suspected or convicted of offenses against the criminal laws of the United States or of any state, county, municipality, or territory of the United States. Furthermore, a law enforcement agency is primarily composed of or employs individuals designated or qualified under state statutes as peace officers or those who are authorized to prosecute criminal violations or to exercise police powers such as making arrests, seizing property, executing warrants and court orders, and carrying firearms.

A *primary function* is one that: (1) occupies a clear majority of the agency's working time over a typical work cycle; and (2) is performed on a regular and recurring basis by the agency and a majority of its officers, employees, and agents. Functions that are of an emergency, incidental, or temporary nature are not considered primary even if they should amount to a majority of an agency's working time.

Typically, a law enforcement agency will include city, district, local, county, or state police, sheriff, or highway patrol departments, and state or local prosecutors' offices. Determinations of agency eligibility are solely within the discretion of the Department of Justice, Criminal Division.

Department of Justice policy requires shared monies and property to be used for law enforcement purposes. Sharing will be withheld from any state or local law enforcement agency where state or local law, regulation, or policy requires federal equitable sharing funds to be transferred to non-law enforcement agencies or expended for non-law enforcement purposes.

No sharing request or recommendation, including shares negotiated in a task force or other agreement, is final until approved by the federal deciding authority.

In accordance with the Crime Victims' Rights Act and the Attorney General's authority, the Department of Justice gives priority in the distribution of forfeited assets to valid owners, lienholders, federal financial regulatory agencies, and victims (in that order) through petitions for remission or mitigation or requests for restoration.[7] After losses to the above parties have been satisfied, any remaining net proceeds can be shared with state and local law enforcement agencies.[8]

B. State National Guard agency or unit

A state National Guard generally does not meet the law enforcement agency criteria for participation in the Department of Justice Equitable Sharing Program because its primary mission serves a military or other non-law enforcement purpose. An individual National Guard unit, however, may qualify for sharing if:

1) It is a distinct unit of a state National Guard that has counterdrug activities as its primary mission and receives funding solely for this purpose; or
2) It is a military police or similar state National Guard unit that provides support to federal law enforcement agencies in counterdrug activities.

In determining whether a National Guard unit qualifies to participate in the sharing program, the Department of Justice will consider the following:

1) The unit directly performs or operationally supports law enforcement functions, e.g., marijuana eradication, surveillance, air transport, or field communications, as opposed to clerical assistance;
2) Direct or supporting law enforcement functions occupy a clear majority of the unit's working time over a typical work cycle and are performed on a regular and recurring basis;
3) State law vests the unit with peace officer authority, i.e., to investigate criminal activity and conduct searches, seizures, or arrests; and
4) State law permits the unit to receive equitably shared funds to finance law enforcement functions.

The Department of Justice will determine whether individual National Guard units are eligible to participate in the Equitable Sharing Program on a case-by-case basis. Once a state National Guard unit has been determined to be eligible, it will participate in the program in the same manner as any other state or local law enforcement agency, including adherence to reporting and compliance requirements, procedures to apply for shares of forfeiture properties, and all equitable sharing policies.

C. State and Local Prosecutorial Agencies

State and local prosecutorial agencies are eligible to receive equitable sharing for assistance they provide in federal forfeiture cases. The following are examples of ways prosecutorial agencies may qualify for an equitable share:

1) Providing assistance in the preparation of search and seizure warrants and other documents relating to the seizure and forfeiture. (Sharing percentage will be based on the degree of participation in the investigation, usually calculated by the work hours expended.)
2) Providing a key informant or substantially assisting throughout the investigation that leads to a federal forfeiture. (Sharing percentage will be based on the degree of participation in the investigation, usually calculated by the work hours expended.)
3) Cross-designating state or local attorneys to handle the federal forfeiture or related criminal cases in federal court. (The Department will authorize sharing of up to five percent of the total net forfeiture proceeds with local prosecutors who cross-designate attorneys to handle adoptive and/or joint forfeiture cases in federal court as Special Assistant United States Attorneys. That sharing amount will be deducted from the Federal Government's share.)
4) Prosecuting criminal cases under state law directly related to a federal forfeiture. (Sharing percentage will be determined on a case-by-case basis.)

III. How Do Agencies Participate in the Equitable Sharing Program?

A. Joint Investigation

Joint investigations are those in which federal agencies work with state or local law enforcement agencies or foreign countries to enforce federal criminal laws. Joint investigations may originate from participation on a federal task force or a formal task force comprised of state and local agencies or from state or local investigations that are developed into federal cases.

B. Adoption of a State or Local Seizure

An adoption occurs when a state or local law enforcement agency seizes property and requests one of the federal seizing agencies[9] to adopt the seizure and proceed with federal forfeiture. Federal agencies may adopt such seized property for forfeiture where the conduct giving rise to the seizure is in violation of federal law and where federal law provides for forfeiture.

A state or local law enforcement agency requesting federal adoption of a state or local seizure must comply with all applicable state laws and regulations pertaining to the transfer of seized property to a federal law enforcement agency, including any requirement for a state judicial order or prosecutorial consent (e.g., declination letter) for such transfer. When required by state law, a state transfer order should be obtained for assets seized pursuant to a state search warrant or a warrantless search to which state jurisdiction has attached. Federal officials should consult with appropriate state or local authorities in adoption situations.

State and local agencies have **30 calendar days** from the date the property is seized to request a federal adoption. The adopting federal agency may waive the 30-day deadline where the state or local law enforcement agency requests a waiver in writing, which must include a written explanation of exceptional circumstances that justify the delay. The lack of personnel to process paperwork will not be considered an exceptional circumstance that would justify an untimely request for federal adoption.

IV. What Are the Minimum Monetary Thresholds for Adoptive Forfeitures?

Generally, seized property will not be adopted for federal forfeiture unless the equity in the property exceeds the following thresholds:

Minimum Adoption Thresholds

Conveyances	Vehicles	$5,000
	Vessels	$10,000
	Aircraft	$10,000
Real Property	Land and Improvements	$20,000 or 20 percent of the appraised value, whichever is greater
All Other Property	Currency Bank Accounts Monetary Instruments Jewelry, etc.	$2,000
	Firearms	May be forfeited regardless of value

The United States Attorneys, in consultation with federal seizing agencies and state and local law enforcement, may institute higher or lower district-wide thresholds for judicial forfeiture cases as law enforcement or management needs require. Department of Justice Asset Forfeiture Program participating agencies and the Department of the Treasury may set their own thresholds.

Exceptions may be made in individual cases where an overriding law enforcement benefit requires the seizure of an asset that does not meet the thresholds. In such cases, the thresholds may be waived when forfeiture will serve a compelling law enforcement interest, such as the forfeiture of a crack house, a conveyance with hidden compartments, or a vehicle used in alien smuggling that is seized at an international border. Any downward departure from the monetary thresholds in individual cases must be approved in writing by a supervisory level official, and an explanation of the reason for the departure must be noted in the case file. For example, an appropriate basis for a downward departure is that the owner or person in possession of the property has been arrested or will be criminally prosecuted.

Lower thresholds may not necessarily result in increased sharing with state and local law enforcement agencies. Because sharing is always based on net proceeds, forfeiture of property with a lower value may result in no net proceeds to share.[10]

V. How Is Property Federally Forfeited?

Forfeiture is the taking of property derived from a crime, involved in a crime, or that which makes a crime easier to commit or harder to detect without compensating the owner.

A. Administrative forfeiture

Administrative forfeiture is the process by which federal seizing agencies may declare property forfeited to the United States without judicial involvement.[11] Seizures must be based on probable cause. Federal law authorizes the seizing or adopting federal agency to administratively forfeit:

Maximum Administrative Forfeiture Thresholds

Monetary Instruments	(e.g., cash, checks, stocks, bonds)	Unlimited Value
Hauling Conveyances	(e.g., vehicles, vessels, and aircraft used to transport illegal drugs)	Unlimited Value
Other Property	(e.g., bank accounts, jewelry, etc.)	$500,000 or less

B. Judicial Forfeiture

Judicial forfeiture, both civil and criminal, is the process by which property is declared forfeited to the United States by a court.[12] It is required for any property other than monetary instruments and hauling conveyances if:

1) the value of the other property exceeds $500,000;
2) a valid, timely claim has been filed in an administrative forfeiture; or
3) the property is real estate.

VI. How Do Agencies Apply for an Equitable Share?

After the seizure in a joint investigation or adoption in an adoptive case, a state or local agency may request a share of the property by submitting a Form DAG-71, Application for Transfer of Federally Forfeited Property, to the federal seizing agency.[13] A separate Form DAG-71 must be completed for each asset to be shared.[14]

A. Completing the Form DAG-71

1. In the upper right-hand corner of the Form DAG-71, enter the date, the name of the federal agency handling the seizure, and the federal agency case number.
2. Leave Part I of the Form DAG-71 blank. It is for federal use only.
3. In Part II, provide the state or local law enforcement agency's name, address, and the National Crime Information Center (NCIC) code or ORI tracking number. Enter the agency's name exactly as listed on the NCIC registration or the Equitable Sharing Agreement and Certification form.
4. The contact person is the person who has knowledge of the case and will be able to answer questions about the investigation.
5. In Part III under "Asset Requested" and "Property Requested," provide a complete description of the asset. If the asset is a vehicle, include the VIN, make, model, and type. If the asset is real property, include the full address and the block and lot number.
6. Place a check in the "Item" block if the agency requests an asset for official use, or place a check in the "Cash/Proceeds" block if requesting cash or proceeds and include the requested percentage.
7. In Part IV, state how the shared funds are intended to be used. Check all blocks that are appropriate and complete "Other" if the intended use is not listed.
8. In Part V, provide all pertinent information about the agency's contribution to the investigation. Include work hours spent by law enforcement officers on the seizure or subsequent hours expended in support of the forfeiture. For cases involving multiple assets, a separate Form DAG-71 needs to be submitted for each asset. Work hours must be stated for each seizure, not the total number of hours worked on the investigation.
9. Complete Part VI by providing a brief description of the case and a thorough explanation of the agency's contribution to the investigation. Never assume the deciding authority knows the details of the case or the agency's role.
10. In Part VII.B, the county attorney, city attorney, district attorney, state attorney, or law enforcement agency counsel can sign as legal counsel.

Sharing requests must be submitted within 60 days after the seizure or within 60 days after the federal adoption of a state or local seizure. The 60-day rule may be waived by the federal seizing agency in exceptional circumstances upon a written request stating the reasons for the late submission of the equitable sharing request which would justify the waiver. The waiver request must accompany the Form DAG-71. In judicial forfeitures, an agency may amend its Form DAG-71 within 60 days after forfeiture to reflect any continued participation in the case.

No sharing request will be considered after the forfeited property has been distributed, deposited into the Assets Forfeiture Fund, or otherwise disposed of according to law.

B. Common Causes of Delay

Forfeiture, like all legal proceedings, takes time. Equitable sharing may occur only after the federal forfeiture has been completed, the United States has taken clear title to the property, the property has been sold or otherwise disposed of as provided by law, and a final sharing decision has been made by the appropriate federal official. Listed below are some factors that may delay sharing:

1. If the forfeiture involves victims of crime who may be entitled to remission or restitution, sharing cannot occur until the victims' claims are resolved. All available funds must be used to compensate victims before any sharing payments are made.
2. If the forfeiture involves property that must be sold, the sale must be completed and the net proceeds determined before sharing may occur.
3. If the agency submits an incomplete Form DAG-71, the missing information must be provided before sharing can occur. For example, if the form does not contain complete or specific information about the contribution of the local law enforcement agency, such as the number of hours expended and any unique or indispensable contribution by the local law enforcement agency, then that information must be provided before sharing will be authorized. Federal agencies submitting equitable sharing packets must also include federal agency work hours. Federal investigative work hours are always required in joint cases so that the relative degree of participation of the agencies can be determined. The equitable sharing deciding authority cannot evaluate the sharing request without this information.
4. Distribution in equitable sharing cases involving forfeited assets with a total value of $1 million or more requires the approval of the Deputy Attorney General. Equitable sharing packages forwarded to AFMLS must include all assets listed in the forfeiture order. For example, where a forfeiture order includes cash in the amount of $1.5 million, a bank account containing $500,000, and six other assets such as automobiles and pieces of jewelry worth $30,000, the Deputy Attorney General is the equitable sharing decision-maker for all eight assets.
5. The USMS electronically transfers equitable sharing payments to a participating state or local law enforcement agency's bank account. If the USMS does not have an agency's banking information, the funds cannot be transferred. To facilitate wire transfers, all participating agencies must complete and submit an Automated Clearing House (ACH) Vendor form to the USMS. If an agency's banking information changes, an updated ACH Vendor form must be submitted. The ACH Vendor form may be downloaded from www.usdoj.gov/criminal/afmls/forms or www.usmarshals.gov/assets
6. In cases involving both domestic and international sharing, international sharing must be completed before domestic sharing can occur. International sharing, which

requires both Department of Justice and Department of State approval and concurrence by the Department of the Treasury, often takes additional time to complete.

VII. How Is an Agency's Equitable Share Determined?

A. Adoptive Seizures

The federal share in adoptive cases where 100 percent of pre-seizure activity was performed by a state or local agency will generally be 20 percent of the net proceeds.

B. Joint Investigations with Federal Agencies

Equitable shares allocated to a law enforcement agency must bear a reasonable relationship to the agency's direct participation in the investigation or law enforcement effort resulting in the forfeiture. The deciding authority ordinarily determines equitable shares by comparing the number of work hours expended by each agency participating in the seizure. Where the work hours alone do not reflect the contribution of a law enforcement agency, the deciding authority considers qualitative factors in making a sharing allocation. In determining the amount of an adjustment based on qualitative factors, the deciding authority will consider such factors as:

- the inherent importance of the activity;
- the length of the investigation;
- whether the agency otherwise entitled to an adjustment would already receive a comparatively large share based on reported work hours;
- whether an agency originated the information leading to the seizure;
- whether an agency provided unique and indispensable assistance;
- whether an agency initially identified the assets for seizure;
- whether an agency seized one or more assets that were forfeited in non-federal proceedings during the same investigation; or
- whether the agency could have achieved forfeiture under state law but instead joined forces with the United States to conduct a more effective investigation or prosecution.

The presence of any of the above qualitative factors may warrant an adjustment in the percentage awarded to an agency. If, and to what extent, an adjustment is warranted is within the discretion of the deciding authority and will be done on a case-by-case basis.

If certain criteria are satisfied, state and local law enforcement agencies that are members of a task force may receive equitable sharing based upon the task force written sharing agreement. In no case will the federal share be less than 20 percent.

1. Spin-Off Investigations

In a case where assets are seized in an investigation that is a spin-off of a larger multi-agency investigation, the deciding authority may approve sharing with an agency that contributed work hours to both the initial investigation and the spin-off seizure. In limited instances, the deciding authority may determine that an agency which did not participate in the subsequent seizure but provided indispensable assistance in the initial investigation that aided investigators in the spin-off investigation is eligible for a share of the asset from that spin-off case. The determination of an agency's eligibility to share in assets seized in spin-off investigations will be made on a case-by-case basis.

C. Sharing in Task Force Cases

Many task forces involving federal, state, and local law enforcement agencies have pre-arranged, written equitable sharing agreements based upon relative numbers of personnel and other contributions to the task force operation. The following criteria apply to both formal and informal task forces and these pre-arranged percentages will be honored only when:

- the agreement is in writing, signed, and dated by all participating agencies, and reviewed and updated annually;
- the pre-arranged sharing percentages fairly reflect overall agency contributions to the task force, including accounting for any participation by a federal agency;
- the deciding authority is satisfied that the pre-arranged percentages continue to reflect the true overall agency contributions to the task force, including accounting for any participation by a federal agency;
- the task force has a well-defined subject area or organization target as its focus, and the specific seizures are part of the overall investigative function of the task force (e.g., an airport seizure by an airport interdiction task force is part of an investigation of airport drug smuggling, not simply an investigation of a particular smuggler); and
- the agreement is made before or at the onset of an investigation; the deciding authority will not honor informal sharing agreements agreed upon following the conclusion of an investigation.

If the total appraised value of all assets in a single administrative or judicial forfeiture order is $1 million or greater, a copy of the task force agreement must be submitted along with the completed Form DAG-71.

1. Formally Chartered Task Forces

The Department of Justice will generally honor written sharing agreements by formal task forces that are legal entities entitled to receive and spend money. A formal task force may receive a sharing disbursement by indicating its NCIC/ORI tracking number or equitable sharing tracking number assigned by AFMLS on the Form DAG-71. Alternatively, separate disbursements may be made to the members of a formally chartered task force based on its agreed sharing percentages.

2. Informal Task Forces

The Department of Justice will generally honor written sharing agreements by informal task forces when the informal task force itself is a permanent or semi-permanent entity established to conduct a long-term investigation of multiple targets committing similar violations in a particular location or of a single target engaged in multiple criminal activities over a lengthy period of time such that multiple forfeiture cases over the life of the task force are likely. If the informal task force and its pre-arranged percentages are acceptable, separate sharing amounts will be disbursed to each individual law enforcement agency in the task force. No funds will be disbursed to the informal task force itself. A joint investigation of a specific target or organization does not constitute an informal task force simply because it is labeled as such. So-called task force agreements based merely on jurisdictional boundaries will not be honored.

For example, an acceptable investigation of multiple targets includes a long-term interdiction operation at a local airport. An acceptable investigation of a single-target might be a long-term investigation of a major drug trafficking organization where participating agencies work on different aspects of the investigation.

D. Equitable Sharing Deciding Authorities

1. Investigative Agency

If the total appraised value of all the assets forfeited in a single *administrative* forfeiture order is less than $1 million, the investigative agency determines the appropriate equitable share for each asset and requesting agency.

2. United States Attorney

If the total appraised value of all the assets forfeited in a single *judicial* forfeiture order is less than $1 million, the United States Attorney determines the appropriate equitable share for each asset and requesting agency.

3. Deputy Attorney General[15]

In either multi-district cases, cases involving the equitable transfer of real property, or cases where the total appraised value of all the assets forfeited in a single administrative or judicial forfeiture order is $1 million or more, the Deputy Attorney General determines the appropriate equitable share of each asset. In determining whether the $1 million threshold has been reached, the federal seizing agency and the United States Attorney processing a sharing request must combine the current "Asset Value" listed in the Consolidated Asset Tracking System (CATS) of each of the assets included in the forfeiture order or declaration of forfeiture. If the total value for all of the assets is $ 1 million or greater, the Deputy Attorney General is the equitable sharing decision-maker for all of the assets. Property forfeited under a single judicial order cannot be split up or separated so that only those individual pieces of property with values greater than $1 million are sent to the Deputy Attorney General for sharing decisions.

E. Sharing Always Based on Net Proceeds

Equitable sharing is based on the net proceeds of the forfeiture, which is calculated as follows:

Gross receipts	From forfeiture or the sale of forfeited property
Less	Qualified third-party interests (e.g., valid liens or mortgages)
	Money paid to victims (persons who incurred a monetary loss of a specific amount as a direct result of the offense underlying the forfeiture, or a related offense)
	Federal case-related expenses (e.g., advertising costs, out-of-pocket investigative or litigation expenses)
	Federal property management and disposition expenses (e.g., appraisal, storage, security, sale)
	Any award paid to a federal informant
	Payments for the services of experts and consultants with whom the
	Department of Justice has contracted to assist in asset identification, seizure, management, forfeiture, or disposition, wherever it is feasible and economically practicable to directly trace such costs and allocate them on a reasonable and consistent basis among the assets subject to forfeiture
	International sharing
	Any reimbursements relating to the seizure from the Assets Forfeiture
	Fund to the requesting agency (e.g., overtime, leased space)
Equals	Net Proceeds of the Forfeiture

Federal law mandates that sharing is discretionary. Therefore, any equitable sharing payments to be disbursed to state and local law enforcement agencies that amount to less than $50.00 after all expenses are paid will be extinguished and the funds will remain in the Assets Forfeiture Fund.

VIII. What Are the Uses of Equitably Shared Property?

A. Law Enforcement Uses

Except as noted in this *Guide*, equitably shared funds shall be used by law enforcement agencies for law enforcement purposes only. Subject to laws, rules, regulations, and orders of the state or local jurisdiction governing the use of public funds available for law enforcement purposes, the expenses noted below are pre-approved as permissible uses of shared funds and property. To avoid a conflict of interest or the appearance of a conflict of interest, any employee of any federal, state, or local governmental agency (or members of his or her immediate family or those residing in his or her household) who was involved in the investigation which led to the forfeiture of the property to be sold by the USMS contractor is prohibited from purchasing, either directly or indirectly, forfeited property. Additionally, Department of Justice employees and contractors may not, without prior written approval of a designated agency official, directly or indirectly purchase property that has been forfeited to the United States; or personally use such property that has been directly or indirectly purchased from the United States by a member of his or her immediate family. The fact that shared property was forfeited as a result of a particular federal violation does not limit its use. For example, when an agency receives a share of property that was forfeited for a federal drug violation, the recipient is not limited in its use of the property in the recipient agency's drug enforcement program. Among the following uses, priority should be given to supporting community policing activities, training, and law enforcement operations:

1. Permissible Uses

a) **Law enforcement investigations**—the support of investigations and operations that may result in furthering the law enforcement goals and mission, e.g., payment of overtime for officers and investigators; payments to informants; "buy," "flash," or reward money; and the purchase of evidence.

b) **Law enforcement training**—the training of officers, investigators, prosecutors, and law enforcement support personnel in any area that is necessary to perform official law enforcement duties. Priority consideration should be given to training in: (1) asset forfeiture in general (statutory requirements, policies, procedures, case law); (2) the Fourth Amendment (search and seizure, probable cause, drafting affidavits, confidential informant reliability); (3) ethics and the National Code of Professional Conduct for Asset Forfeiture,[16] (4) due process; (5) protecting the rights of innocent third parties (individuals and lienholders); (6) use of computers and other equipment in support of law enforcement duties; and (7) this *Guide*.

c) **Law enforcement and detention facilities**—the costs associated with the purchase, lease, construction, expansion, improvement, or operation of law enforcement or detention facilities used or managed by the recipient agency. For example, the costs of leasing, operating, and furnishing an off-site undercover narcotics facility is a permissible use of shared funds. Capital improvements should not be made on leased property or space since the law enforcement agency will not benefit from the improvements upon termination of the lease; improvement costs are generally covered in the terms of the lease. Approval from AFMLS is required prior to making such capital expenditures.

d) **Law enforcement equipment**—the costs associated with the purchase, lease, maintenance, or operation of law enforcement equipment for use by law enforcement personnel that supports law enforcement activities. For example, furniture, file cabinets, office supplies, telecommunications equipment, copiers, safes, fitness equipment, computers, computer accessories and software, body armor, uniforms, firearms, radios, cellular telephones, electronic surveillance equipment, and vehicles (e.g., patrol cars and surveillance vehicles).

e) **Law enforcement travel and transportation**—the costs associated with travel and transportation to perform or in support of law enforcement duties and activities. All related costs must be in accordance with the agency's state per diem and must not create the appearance of extravagance or impropriety.

f) **Law enforcement awards and memorials**—the cost of award plaques and certificates for law enforcement personnel, provided that the plaque or certificate is in recognition of a law enforcement achievement, activity, or the completion of law enforcement training, and the cost does not create the appearance of extravagance or impropriety. Shared funds may not be used to pay cash awards.

   Shared funds may be used to pay the costs for modest commemorative plaques, displays, or memorials that serve to recognize or memorialize a law enforcement officer's contributions, such as a memorial plaque or stone at a police department facility in honor of officers killed in the line of duty.

g) **Drug and gang education and awareness programs**—the costs associated with conducting drug or gang education and awareness programs by law enforcement agencies. Such costs include meeting costs, anti-drug abuse literature costs, travel expenses, and salaries for officers working in a drug education program such as DARE.

h) **Matching funds**—the costs associated with paying a state or local law enforcement agency's matching contribution or share in a federal grant program, provided that the grant funds are used for a permissible law enforcement purpose in accordance with this *Guide* or where such use is authorized by federal law.

i) **Pro rata funding**—a law enforcement agency's percentage of the costs associated with supporting multi-agency items or facilities. For example, if a town purchases a new computerized payroll system, and the police department payroll represents 20 percent of the total use of the payroll system, then the police department may use shared money to fund its pro rata share (20 percent) of the operating and maintenance expenses of the system.

j) **Asset accounting and tracking**—the costs associated with the accounting, auditing, and tracking of expenditures for federally shared cash, proceeds, and tangible property. For example, the use of shared funds to pay the fees associated with the contracting of a bookkeeper is permissible.
The OMB Single Audit Act requires any agency that expends more than $500,000 in federal funds in an agency's fiscal year to complete an external audit. The use of forfeiture funds to perform this audit is permissible.

k) **Language assistance services**— In connection with their law enforcement activities and operations, recipient agencies are encouraged to consider the need for language services for persons with limited English proficiency and, consistent with the provisions of this *Guide*, may use shared funds to provide such services. Examples of such permissible uses include the costs of language training for law enforcement personnel and 911 operators, contracting for interpretation services, and printing law enforcement documents in foreign languages.

l) **Transfers to other law enforcement agencies**—Cash transfers of shared funds from one state or local law enforcement agency to another are permitted. In order to receive a cash transfer of shared funds, the law enforcement agency must be in compliance with the Agreement, Certification and Audit provisions of this *Guide* (*see* part X*)*. All cash transfers must be used in accordance with the permissible use provisions of this *Guide*. The agency transferring the funds is responsible for verifying that the recipient agency is eligible to receive sharing. The transfer must be reported on the Equitable Sharing Agreement and Certification form filed by both the donor and recipient agencies.

m) **Support of community-based programs**—A state or local law enforcement agency or prosecutor's office may use up to 15 percent of the total of shared monies received by that agency in the last two fiscal years for the costs associated with drug abuse treatment, drug and crime prevention education, housing and job skills programs, or other nonprofit community-based programs or activities that are formally approved by the chief law enforcement officer (e.g., chief, sheriff, prosecutor). All expenditures must be supportive of and consistent with a law enforcement effort, policy, and/or initiative.

Cash transfers to community-based programs are not permitted. State and local law enforcement agencies are prohibited from making cash transfers or donations to support community-based programs. Instead, agencies may directly purchase supplies, equipment, and/or services for eligible community-based programs, or reimburse such programs for eligible expenditures with a valid, itemized receipt. *See* Appendix C for guidelines to determine a community-based program's eligibility.

n) **Windfall situations**—Where the total amount of federal equitable sharing received within one fiscal year represents over 25 percent of a state or local law enforcement agency's annual budget, recipient agencies may utilize the amount over 25 percent to provide additional support to community-based programs as referenced in letter m above. For example, if an agency's annual appropriated budget is $1 million and the agency receives a total of $300,000 in equitable sharing funds during the fiscal year, the amount above $250,000 (25 percent of the agency's budget), or $50,000, is considered a "windfall." The agency, in its discretion, may use all or part of this money in addition to the 15 percent permitted under section m above. In windfall situations, AFMLS may require additional auditing and/or reporting regarding the agency's handling and expenditure of funds.

2. Impermissible Uses

a. Salaries—Equitable sharing monies may not be used to pay the salaries and benefits of current, permanent law enforcement personnel, except in limited circumstances. The purpose of this rule is to protect the integrity of the asset forfeiture and equitable sharing programs so that the prospect of receiving equitable sharing monies does not influence, or appear to influence, law enforcement decisions.
Exception: Equitable sharing funds may be used to pay the salaries and benefits of law enforcement officers in the following limited situations:

1. **Express statutory authorization**—When federal law expressly permits state and local law enforcement agencies to use equitably shared funds to pay the salaries and benefits of local law enforcement officers or as matching funds in federal grant programs, such use is permissible. For example, the Community Oriented Policing Services (COPS) program established by the Violent Crime Control and Law Enforcement Act of 1994, allows state and local law enforcement agencies to use equitably shared funds to meet the local match requirements of that program, including grants for salaries and benefits.
2. **Overtime of officers and investigators**—Shared funds may be used to pay the overtime of officers and investigators involved in law enforcement operations. This policy is applicable to all officers and is not limited to those working on drug-related investigations.
3. **New positions and temporary or not-to-exceed one year appointments**—Shared funds may be used to pay the first year's salary and benefits of an individual hired for a new sworn law enforcement position that supplements the current law enforcement work force. After the first year, the salary and benefits for that position must be paid entirely from the agency's appropriated funds. Shared funds may also be used to pay the salaries of temporary (less than one year) positions or not-to-exceed one year appointments. This exception applies

strictly to sworn law enforcement positions. Shared funds may not be used to provide funding for unsworn, support personnel (e.g., administrative, secretarial, or clerical positions).

4. **Salary of an officer hired to replace an officer assigned to a task force**—When a law enforcement agency assigns a law enforcement officer to a task force[17] for a period of at least one year or the life of the task force and hires a new law enforcement officer to replace the officer so assigned, the agency may pay the salary and benefits of the replacement officer from equitably shared funds so long as the replacement officer does not engage in the seizure of assets or narcotics law enforcement as a principal duty.[18]

A principal duty is a duty that the officer is expected to perform regularly. In order to pay the replacement officer's salary with equitably shared funds, the task force must be a law enforcement entity constituted under federal, state, or local law that is primarily engaged in specific and targeted law enforcement activities involving more than one law enforcement agency. In addition, the chief administrative officer of the law enforcement agency assigning an officer must not maintain direct day-to-day operational control of the task force although he or she may participate in the policy-level control of such task force.

When a law enforcement agency has assigned an officer and paid for the replacement as specified above, and it becomes necessary to return the officer from the task force, the law enforcement agency may continue to use forfeited funds to pay for the salary and benefits of the replacement officer for a period not to exceed six months.[19]

5. **Specialized programs**—A law enforcement agency may pay the salary and benefits of a law enforcement officer assigned to specific approved specialized programs which do not generally involve traditional law enforcement functions. Officers assigned to programs such as DARE do not routinely perform narcotics law enforcement or seizure duties. Accordingly, there is little risk that their conduct will actually influence law enforcement priorities or create a conflict of interest.

b. **Use of forfeited property by non-law enforcement personnel**—Non-law enforcement agency personnel are not permitted to use shared vehicles, forfeited property, or items purchased with shared funds.

c. **Payment of education-related costs**—Shared funds may not be used for scholarships, financial aid, or non-law enforcement classes. Only tuition for law enforcement classes necessary to the performance of an officer's official duties is permitted.

d. **Uses contrary to the laws of the state or local jurisdiction**—Shared funds and property may not be used for any purpose that would constitute an illegal or improper use of state or local law enforcement funds or property under the laws, rules, regulations, and orders of the state or local jurisdiction of which the agency is a part.

e. **Non-official government use of shared assets**—Any use that creates the appearance that shared funds are being used for political or personal purposes is not permitted. For example, the use of shared funds for a sheriff's campaign paraphernalia is impermissible.

f. **Purchase of food and beverages**—Shared funds generally may not be used to pay for food and beverages (alcoholic and non-alcoholic) for consumption by law enforcement personnel or their guests, except for the limited circumstances listed below:
   1. **Conference package policy**—Shared funds may be used to purchase food and beverages provided as part of a conference package. For example, a hotel provides complimentary coffee and bagels for breakfast with the rental of its conference room for an authorized training event. The same conference package rule applies to food or beverages served at a banquet or party to recognize law enforcement achievements.
   2. **Meals during local operations**—Shared funds may also be used to purchase food and beverages if state or local law or rules governing reimbursement of expenses permit officers to be reimbursed for such expenses, e.g., meals purchased while an officer is on official travel, attending a training conference, or engaged in a disaster operation, such as earthquake or hurricane relief.

g. **Extravagant expenditures**—Receiving agencies should use federal sharing monies prudently and in such a manner as to avoid any appearance of extravagance, waste, or impropriety. For example, tickets to social events, hospitality suites at conferences, or meals outside of the per diem are impermissible uses of shared funds.

3. General Guidance Concerning Use

a) **Windfall situation**—In a windfall situation, where an agency receives equitable sharing funds totaling more than 25 percent of its budget in a fiscal year, the agency may be subject to additional audit and reporting requirements.

b) **Use of interest income**—Interest earned on forfeited cash or proceeds must be deposited into the agency's equitable sharing revenue account and used for law enforcement purposes and is subject to the same use restrictions as shared cash or proceeds.

c) **Anticipated shared property should not be budgeted**—Agencies should not "spend it before you get it" or budget anticipated receipts. Receiving agencies may not commit to the spending of sharing monies for a certain purpose in advance. For example, if a local law enforcement agency files a Form DAG-71 to request a 50 percent share of $100,000, the $50,000 should not be obligated or budgeted for two reasons: (1) the completion of the forfeiture is uncertain; and (2) the amount of the sharing that will ultimately be approved is also uncertain.

d) **Shared monies should not be retained unnecessarily**—Shared monies normally should be expended for their designated use or other permissible law enforcement purpose as they are received. Shared monies may be retained in a holding account for up to three years to satisfy future needs or retained longer for major long-term expenditures such as capital improvements.

e) **Use of proceeds from sale of shared property**—Proceeds from the sale of shared property, facilities, equipment, and other items acquired with shared funds must be deposited into the agency's equitable sharing revenue account and are subject to the same permissible use restrictions and reporting requirements as shared cash or proceeds, in accordance with the provisions of this *Guide*.

B. Increase and Not Replace

Sharing must be used to increase or supplement the resources of the receiving state or local law enforcement agency or any other ultimate recipient agency. Shared resources **shall not be used** to replace or supplant the appropriated resources of the recipient. The recipient agency must benefit directly from the sharing. In determining whether supplantation has occurred, the Department of Justice will examine the law enforcement agency's budget as a whole and allow agencies to use equitable sharing funds for any permissible purpose as long as shared funds **increase** the **entire law enforcement budget**. The Department of Justice may terminate sharing with law enforcement agencies that are not permitted by their governing authorities to benefit directly from equitable sharing.

Example of Improper Supplantation: A police department receives $100,000 in federal sharing money only to have its budget cut $100,000 by the city council. In this instance, the police department has received no direct benefit from equitable sharing whatsoever. Rather, the city as a whole has received the benefit of the sharing.

C. Transfer of Forfeited Real Property

The transfer of federally forfeited real property is permitted only in the following three situations:

1. Through the equitable sharing process, real property may be transferred to a state or local agency which substantially participated in the investigation that led to the seizure of the property. The agency must demonstrate a compelling law enforcement need for the property and outline its intended use on the DAG-71 form. The agency must also sign a memorandum of understanding with regard to the use of the property and agree to pay any federal costs/ expenses as well as the federal share before the transfer will be approved.

Example: A state police department assists in the seizure of a farm where drugs were grown. The agency may request the property instead of the proceeds from its sale if the agency has a compelling need, such as a law enforcement training facility or a police substation.

2. The Weed and Seed Initiative[20] authorizes the transfer of federally forfeited real property through state or local law enforcement agencies to private, nonprofit organizations to support drug abuse treatment, drug and crime prevention and education, housing, and job skills programs, or other community-based programs. The requirements of the Weed and Seed Initiative are as follows:

a) The initial recipient of the property must be a state or local law enforcement agency which participated in the investigation that resulted in the forfeiture;
b) The ultimate recipient must be an appropriate nonprofit organization, which agrees to use the property in compliance with the initiative and agrees that if the property ceases to be used for its intended purposes for a specified time period, title may revert back to the United States.
c) Any state or local agency with a claim to an equitable share of the property must agree to waive the claim.

d) A Form DAG-71 must be submitted by the initial recipient to the USAO identifying the property to be transferred to the nonprofit organization pursuant to the Weed and Seed Initiative.
e) The USAO must submit a "Request for Transfer of Real Property Pursuant to the Weed and Seed Initiative" and a draft Memorandum of Understanding along with the Form DAG-71 to AFMLS.
f) AFMLS will submit the completed package to the Deputy Attorney General for approval of the transfer.

Generally, title to real property will be transferred to the state or local law enforcement agency. If the initial recipient state or local law enforcement agency is not authorized to take title to the real property, then either the state or local government agency authorized to accept title on behalf of the law enforcement agency will receive title, or under certain circumstances, the Department of Housing and Urban Development may be able to take title to the property for re-transfer to the Weed and Seed recipient.

Questions on transfers pursuant to the Weed and Seed Initiative should be directed to AFMLS.

3. A governor of a state in which a forfeited property is located may request that the property be transferred to that state for recreational or historic purposes or for the preservation of natural conditions. *See* 21 U.S.C. § 881(e)(4)(B). The Deputy Attorney General must approve these transfers.

D. Transfer of Forfeited Tangible Personal Property

1. Any forfeited tangible property (any property other than real estate) transferred to a state or local agency for official use must be used for law enforcement purposes only. Moreover, such transferred property is subject to the rules applicable to similar property purchased by a state or local agency with appropriated funds. Finally, forfeited luxury motor vehicles—an automobile with a National Automotive Dealers Association (NADA) wholesale value of $50,000 or more—may be placed in official use only for undercover law enforcement purposes.
   Example: A federally forfeited SUV is assigned to a state or local law enforcement official who is not authorized to use a government vehicle under local rule. This is impermissible because the forfeited SUV would be subject to the same use restrictions as purchased vehicles.
   Example: A federally forfeited luxury car worth more than $50,000 is assigned to a law enforcement official who is authorized to use a government vehicle, but the luxury vehicle is used for routine law enforcement work. This is impermissible because a luxury vehicle is being used for purposes other than undercover work, thereby misusing government resources and creating an appearance of impropriety.
2. The recipient law enforcement agency may, at its discretion, transfer the tangible property to another governmental department or agency to support drug abuse treatment, drug and crime prevention and education, housing, and job skills

programs, or other community-based programs. Such governmental department or agency may, in turn, transfer any tangible property so received to a private, nonprofit community organization to be used for such purposes.

> Tangible property transferred for official law enforcement use must be used for at least two years. If, however, the property becomes unsuitable for the stated purpose before the end of the two-year period, it may be sold with approval from AFMLS and the proceeds deposited in the agency's federal equitable sharing revenue account and used in compliance with this *Guide*.

E. Reimbursement of Federal Costs

State and local law enforcement agencies that receive real property or tangible personal property must pay the Department of Justice Assets Forfeiture Fund for any liens, costs related to storage or maintenance, costs of shares to other agencies, and the federal share. If the agency is unable to pay these expenses with appropriated or equitably shared funds, these costs can be charged against the agency's equitable share of other assets in the case. If the requesting agency is unable to pay the federal share, costs, and the shares of other agencies, the property will be sold and the proceeds equitably distributed to participating agencies.

F. Return of Equitably Shared Funds

On occasion, a criminal conviction, forfeiture order, or equitable sharing decision may be reversed after the equitable sharing payments have been disbursed to state and local law enforcement agencies. In such cases, it may be necessary for the shared funds to be returned to the United States. The state and local agency recipients will be notified of the reversal by the Department of Justice component that rendered the equitable sharing decision. When such a return of funds is necessary, the recipient state or local agency will have the option of either: (A) returning the funds via a check to the USMS or (B) having an equivalent amount off-set against future equitable sharing. When an agency elects to have the funds off-set against future sharing, it must contact the USMS District Office in writing.

IX. What Are the Accounting Procedures and Requirements for Shared Cash, Proceeds, and Tangible Property?

All participating state and local law enforcement agencies must implement standard accounting procedures and internal controls (e.g., tracking share requests and receipts, electronically depositing shares into a separate revenue account or accounting code) to track equitably shared monies and tangible property. Those procedures must be consistent with those set forth below.

A. Bookkeeping Procedures and Internal Controls

The state or local participating law enforcement agency must:

1. Establish a separate revenue account or accounting code through the agency's finance department for the proceeds from the Department of Justice Equitable Sharing Program. This account or accounting code will be used solely for funds from the Department of Justice Equitable Sharing Program. No other funds may be included in this account or with this accounting code.
   This bank account information must be provided to the USMS on the ACH Vendor form. The process of electronic payments, known as E-Share, provides a fast, efficient, and secure method of making equitable sharing payments. Participation in the program is mandatory. The form may be downloaded from www.usmarshals.gov/assets or www.usdoj.gov/criminal.afmls.
2. Not commingle Department of Justice equitable sharing funds with funds from any other source. Corrective measures must be taken if this occurs.
3. Deposit any interest income earned on equitably shared funds in the same revenue account or under the accounting code established solely for the shared funds.
4. Maintain a log and copies of all Forms DAG-71 forwarded to the Department of Justice. A consecutive numbering system should be used for control purposes. The log should contain seizure type (property or currency), amount, share amount requested, amount received, and date received.
5. Update the log when an E-Share notification is received. The amount received may differ from the amount requested.
6. Establish an internal procedure to recommend expenditures from the revenue account. In many small agencies, the chief of police determines the purposes for which the funds are used. In larger agencies, committees have been formed to make recommendations for expenditures to the agency head. The agency head must authorize all expenditures from the federal sharing revenue account.
7. Use tangible property placed into official use for a law enforcement purpose for at least two years following the transfer. After two years, the property may be sold for the benefit of the law enforcement agency. All proceeds from the sale of such property must be deposited into the agency's equitable sharing account. Agencies requesting to sell property prior to two years must obtain approval from AFMLS.
8. Use purchased or acquired luxury automobiles only for undercover assignments.
9. Obtain approval for expenditures from the governing body, such as the town council or city manager's office, if appropriate.
10. Upon final approval, issue contracts or purchase orders to formally disburse deposited assets for goods or services. Deduct purchase orders and contracts from the account balance.
11. Maintain a record of all expenditures from the revenue account or accounting code. These expenditures must be in accordance with this *Guide*.
12. Issue quarterly and yearly reports that detail the actual amounts and uses of the federal asset sharing funds and property within their jurisdiction, if appropriate.

X. What Are the Reporting and Audit Requirements?

To ensure effective management, promote public confidence in the integrity of the Equitable Sharing Program, and protect the Asset Forfeiture Program against potential waste, fraud, and abuse, the Department of Justice has established for participating law enforcement agencies reporting requirements that include the annual submission of the Equitable Sharing Agreement and Certification form and, if applicable, an audit report. A state or local law enforcement agency must be in compliance with the reporting requirements set forth in this *Guide* to receive any distribution of money or property under the Equitable Sharing Program. An agency is considered to be in compliance once the Equitable Sharing Agreement and Certification form is submitted electronically and the signed Affidavit/ Signature page is received within the required deadlines.

A. Federal Equitable Sharing Agreement and Certification Form

As a prerequisite to participating in the Department of Justice Equitable Sharing Program, a state or local law enforcement agency must annually submit to AFMLS a signed Equitable Sharing Agreement and Certification form. (*See* Appendix E.) The agreement must be signed by the head of the law enforcement agency and a designated official of the governing body.[21] By signing the Affidavit, the signatories agree to be bound by the statutes and guidelines that regulate the equitable sharing program and certify that the law enforcement agency will comply with these guidelines and statutes.

State and local law enforcement agencies must submit this form within 60 days after the end of an agency's fiscal year, regardless of whether funds were received or maintained during the fiscal year. The report must be completed electronically and emailed to aca.submit@usdoj.gov.

Once the agency has emailed the form, the Affidavit/Signature page must be printed, signed, and faxed to AFMLS.

New participants will check the "New Participant" button on the form, enter the agency's fiscal year end date, current fiscal year budget information, and proceed to the Affidavit/Signature page. Existing participants will check the "Existing Participant" button on the form and complete the Annual Certification Report and the Affidavit/Signature page. Participating agencies must notify AFMLS of any change in administration at the law enforcement agency and/or its governing body by checking the "Change in Administration" button and resubmitting the Agreement and Certification form electronically.

Where the agency or organization submitting the Agreement is a multi-agency task force, Table A of the Equitable Sharing Agreement and Certification form must be completed providing a list of the task force members or participating law enforcement agencies. If the task force distributes or transfers any equitably shared monies or property to any member or participating state or local law enforcement agency, it must ensure that each such recipient agency has a valid Equitable Sharing Agreement and Certification form on file with AFMLS.

If equitable sharing receipts are deposited in an interest bearing account, interest income must be reported on the certification section of the form. Agencies are not required to use interest bearing accounts. If an agency enters a zero in the "interest income accrued," it must check the non-interestbearing account box. If the reporting law enforcement agency uses any funds for "other law enforcement expenses," "transfers to other law enforcement agencies," "permissible use transfers," or "matching grants," the tables in the certification section of the form must be completed with all requested information. The total values will auto-populate into the certification section of the form. Agencies that do not receive federal equitable sharing funds or property during a fiscal year must submit the Equitable Sharing Agreement and Certification form listing "0" receipts. The head of the law enforcement agency and a designated official of the governing body must sign the Affidavit page of the Equitable Sharing Agreement and Certification form.

B. Annual Audit

State and local law enforcement agencies that receive federally shared cash, proceeds, or tangible property are required to perform an audit consistent with the Single Audit Act Amendments of 1996 and OMB Circular A-133, *Audits of States, Local Governments and Non-Profit Organizations*. Per those guidelines, agencies that expend more than $500,000 in federal funds (e.g., Justice and/or Treasury forfeiture funds, grants, cooperative agreements) per fiscal year are required to conduct an external audit. In such circumstances, an independent accounting firm may be contracted to perform the required audit. Copies of this audit must be retained by the law enforcement agency. Forfeiture funds may be used to pay the fees associated with conducting such audits.

The *Government Auditing Standards*, issued by the U.S. General Accounting Office, must be followed by auditors and audit organizations conducting the required independent financial audit. These standards pertain to the auditor's professional qualifications, the quality of the audit effort, and the characteristics of professional and meaningful audit reports.

C. Record Retention

State and local law enforcement agencies shall retain for a period of at least five years all documents and records pertaining to their participation in the Department of Justice Equitable Sharing Program and their receipt and expenditure or use of shared cash, proceeds, real property, or tangible personal property, including but not limited to Forms DAG-71, Equitable Sharing Agreement and Certification forms, accounting and bookkeeping documents, logs and records, bank records and statements, and audit reports.

XI. What If Agencies Do Not Fulfill the Compliance Requirements?

This *Guide* describes the sharing process and is binding upon all state and local agencies seeking federal sharing transfers. At the time agencies receive shared funds, they will be asked to certify that the cash or property shared will be used consistent with the Form DAG-71 or as otherwise authorized and consistent with the policies set forth in this *Guide*.

Noncompliance with the policies of this *Guide* may subject recipient agencies to one or more of the following sanctions:

1. Denial of an agency's sharing request;
2. Temporary or permanent exclusion from further participation in the equitable sharing program;
3. Offsets from future sharing in amounts equal to impermissible uses;
4. Civil enforcement actions in U.S. District Court for breach of contract; or
5. Where warranted, federal criminal prosecution for false statements under 18 U.S.C. § 1001, fraud involving theft of federal program funds under 18 U.S.C. § 666, or other sections of the criminal code, as applicable.

No equitable sharing funds or property will be distributed to any state or local law enforcement agency that is not in compliance with the annual reporting requirements outlined in this *Guide*. A law enforcement agency that has requested an equitable share of federally forfeited money or property in accordance with the provisions of the *Guide* but is not in compliance with the reporting requirements will be notified in writing by AFMLS and will be given 60 calendar days to come into compliance. If the requesting agency comes into compliance within the 60-day period, it will receive any withheld sharing funds or property.

Additional time to comply may be granted upon request. However, if the agency fails to become compliant within one year, the agency's sharing requests will be denied and extinguished, and any equitable sharing money and/or property being held will be deposited into the Department of Justice Assets Forfeiture Fund. Any such denial and the deposit of money and/or property into the Assets Forfeiture Fund shall be final and irrevocable. Any sharing requests for money and/or property not yet forfeited are not affected.

APPENDIX A: WHAT ARE THE TYPES OF FEDERAL FORFEITURE?

Forfeiture is the taking of property derived from a crime, involved in a crime, or that which makes a crime easier to commit or harder to detect.

A. Administrative Forfeiture

Administrative forfeiture is the process by which property may be forfeited to the United States without judicial involvement. Federal seizing agencies perform administrative forfeitures. Seizures must be based on probable cause. The authority for a seizing agency to start an administrative forfeiture action is found in 19 U.S.C. § 1607.

Administrative forfeiture can be used to seize and forfeit the following:

- any amount of currency;
- personal property valued at $500,000 or less, including cars, guns, and boats;
- hauling conveyances of unlimited value.

Real property cannot be forfeited administratively.

If the property owner files a claim, the administrative forfeiture process stops and the Government must bring a forfeiture action in federal court or return the property to the claimant. The seizing agency forwards the claim to the United States Attorney's Office for action.

B. Judicial Forfeiture

Judicial forfeiture, civil and criminal, is the process by which property may be forfeited to the United States by filing a forfeiture action in federal court.

- Criminal Forfeiture

Criminal forfeiture is an action brought as part of the criminal prosecution of a defendant that includes the forfeiture of property used or derived from the crime. If the defendant is convicted, the judge or the jury may find that the property is forfeitable. Forfeiture is limited to the property interests of the defendant and only to property involved in the particular counts on which the defendant is convicted. Only the defendant's interest can be forfeited in a criminal case because criminal forfeiture is part of the sentence in the criminal case. For example, if the defendant used someone else's car to commit a crime and the owner of the car was not indicted for the crime in which the car was used, the car cannot be forfeited in the criminal case. Instead, a civil forfeiture case can be filed against the car.

If a third party claims an interest in the property that the Government seeks to forfeit criminally, the issue is determined in an ancillary hearing before the court only after the criminal trial is completed, the defendant convicted, and a preliminary order of forfeiture is entered. Once the interests of third parties are resolved, the court issues a final order of forfeiture. The order of forfeiture might not happen for months or years, even if the forfeiture is uncontested, resulting in a delay in the disposal of the property.

If the property subject to forfeiture is no longer available, the court can enter a money judgment or order the forfeiture of substitute assets.

- Civil Forfeiture

Civil forfeiture is a proceeding brought against the property rather than against the person who committed the offense. Civil forfeiture does not require either criminal charges against the owner of the property or a criminal conviction.

To obtain a federal forfeiture, the Government must prove the forfeiture and the connection between the property and the crime by a preponderance of the evidence. Forfeiture may be applicable to property that is traceable as proceeds of the offense, that facilitated the offense, or that was involved in money laundering. All claims of interest or ownership in the property, such as property owned by third parties, are resolved in a single trial.

APPENDIX B: NATIONAL CODE OF PROFESSIONAL CONDUCT FOR ASSET FORFEITURE

1. Law enforcement is the principal objective of forfeiture. Potential revenue must not be allowed to jeopardize the effective investigation and prosecution of criminal offenses, officer safety, the integrity of ongoing investigations, or the due process rights of citizens.
2. The Constitution and Federal Statutes prohibit the improper use of personal characteristics such as race, color, national origin, gender, or religion to target individuals for law enforcement action.
3. No prosecutor's or sworn law enforcement officer's employment or salary shall be made to depend upon the level of seizures or forfeitures he or she achieves.
4. Whenever practicable, and in all cases involving real property, a judicial finding or probable cause shall be secured when property is seized for forfeiture. Seizing agencies shall strictly comply with all applicable legal requirements governing seizure practice and procedures.
5. If no judicial finding of probable cause is secured, the seizure shall be approved in writing by a prosecuting or agency attorney or by a supervisory-level official.
6. Seizing entities shall have a manual detailing the statutory grounds for forfeiture. This manual will include procedures for prompt notice to interest holders, the expeditious release of seized property where appropriate, and the prompt resolution of claims of innocent ownership.
7. Seizing entities retaining forfeited property for official law enforcement use shall ensure that the property is subject to internal controls consistent with those applicable to property acquired through the normal appropriations processes of that entity.
8. Unless otherwise provided by law, forfeiture proceeds shall be maintained in a separate fund or account subject to appropriate accounting controls and annual financial audits of all deposits and expenditures.
9. Seizing agencies shall strive to ensure that seized property is protected and its value preserved.
10. Seizing entities shall avoid any appearance of impropriety in the sale or acquisition of forfeited property.

APPENDIX C: GUIDELINES FOR DETERMINING A COMMUNITY-BASED PROGRAM'S ELIGIBILITY

To ensure that recipient law enforcement agencies administer these guidelines for determining a community-based program's eligibility in accordance with the federal law and Department of Justice policy, an agency's chief law enforcement officer must ensure his or her agency's adherence to the following requirements governing eligibility, background, and compliance of applicants to be eligible to benefit from shared funds. The federal investigating agencies and the United States Attorney's Offices also are tasked with helping to ensure applicants' suitability to receive guidelines for shared funds use expenditures. Once completed, the chief law enforcement officer's certification that an applicant is eligible to benefit from shared funds will remain effective for one year.

I. Eligibility

For an applicant to benefit from permissible use expenditures, the chief law enforcement officer shall determine that the applicant fulfills the following eligibility requirements:

A. Type of Entity

The applicant must be either:

1. a state, county, or local governmental department or agency; or
2. a private, nonprofit organization, pursuant to 26 U.S.C. § 501(c)(3) or (4).

B. Activity of Entity

The applicant also must be primarily engaged in providing a program that is both:

1. community-based; and
2. supportive of and consistent with a law enforcement effort, policy, or initiative.

Such programs include, but are not limited to, the following:

1. drug abuse treatment;
2. drug and crime prevention education;
3. providing housing; or
4. providing job skills.

In order to assist chief law enforcement officers in determining whether a potential recipient of benefits under the guidelines for supporting community-based programs with shared funds is eligible, the Department of Justice provides the following non-exclusive list of examples of activities that it has approved in the past as qualifying to benefit from equitable sharing:

1. establish a detoxification center;
2. fund a Police Athletic League's "Summer Playstreets" program for crime and drug prevention;
3. fund a city parks department's anti-gang initiative;
4. fund "Law Enforcement Explorer Posts," a Boy Scouts program promoting law enforcement training and community service;
5. fund a "Crime Stoppers" program providing reward money and assistance to neighborhood watch groups including training on observance and effective witness skills:
6. purchase a computer for teaching job skills and drug and alcohol awareness to probationers;

7. fund programs for incarcerated youth, parents of murdered children, and domestic violence victims; and
8. fund a methadone clinic.

Considering each of these approved activities, the Department of Justice based its approval on the activity's nexus to a law enforcement interest, whether:

1. direct (e.g., paying rewards for key information);
2. preventative (e.g., funding a methadone clinic, drug awareness program, anti-gang initiative, and probationer training); or
3. developmental in promoting community policing (e.g., incorporating law enforcement awareness in a Boy Scout program).

II. Background and Compliance with Law and Policy

A. Certification by Applicant

An applicant for benefits to support community-based programs with shared funds must certify in writing the following aspects of its background and compliance with federal law and Department of Justice guidelines:

(1) The applicant fulfills the basic eligibility requirements set forth in parts I.A and B above.

(2) The applicant agrees:

a. to account separately for all guidelines for shared funds use benefits received; and

b. to subject such accounting to the standard accounting requirements and practices employed under state or local law for recipients of federal, state, or local funds.

(3) The applicant is in compliance with the federal civil rights laws.

(4) The applicant is in compliance with federal laws that apply to the applicant.

(5) No officer, director, trustee, or fiduciary of the applicant has been:

a. convicted of a felony offense under federal or state law; or

b. convicted of any drug offense.

(6) No shared benefits will be used for political or personal purposes.

(7) No shared benefits will be used for any purpose that would constitute an improper or illegal use under the laws, rules, regulations, or orders of the state or local jurisdiction in which the applicant is located or operates.

The applicant's certification must be signed by the head of the applicant entity and must be submitted to the chief law enforcement officer who will approve expenditures on the applicant's behalf. The chief law enforcement officer shall maintain this certification as a record as long as the applicant may benefit from shared funds, and thereafter, for as long as the chief law enforcement officer is required to maintain records under applicable state or local laws or regulations. Any applicant that cannot certify its compliance with number 5 above (criminal record of principals) should provide the chief law enforcement officer with a detailed explanation of the aspects in which, and the reasons why, certification is not possible. A chief law enforcement officer who wishes to provide support to an applicant that cannot certify compliance with number 5 above shall provide an explanation for his or her position, along with a copy of the applicant's explanation, as an attachment to the law enforcement agency's Form DAG-71 (Application of Transfer of Federally Forfeited Property) to the Asset Forfeiture and Money Laundering Section (AFMLS), Criminal Division, Department of Justice. AFMLS will make the final decision on whether the provision of guidelines for shared funds use benefits is appropriate. An applicant for benefits under these guidelines that cannot certify the other aspects of its background and compliance with federal law and Department of Justice guidelines (numbers 1–4, 6 and 7 above) will be denied guidelines for shared funds use benefits.

B. Statement by Chief Law Enforcement Officer

The chief law enforcement officer shall explain in writing why the applicant's receipt of permissible use benefits for the particular activity or use is supportive of and consistent with a law enforcement effort, policy, and/or initiative within the guidelines to support community-based programs. The chief law enforcement officer also shall maintain this written statement as a record as specified in section II.A above.

C. Inquiry by the Chief Law Enforcement Officer

A chief law enforcement officer is also responsible for determining whether an applicant for benefits under these guidelines or its principals (e.g., officer, director, trustee, or fiduciary) currently is the subject of federal, state, or local criminal investigation. Accordingly, a chief law enforcement officer shall:

1. utilize all investigative resources available (e.g., National Crime Information Computer) to determine the applicant's status and provide the findings to the federal investigative agency on the Form DAG-71; and
2. fully identify the applicant and its principals on the Form DAG·71.

D. Inquiry by the Federal Investigating Agency

The federal investigative agency that receives the Form DAG·71 shall use the information identifying the applicant and its principals to conduct further checks of whether the applicant or its principals currently are the subject of a federal, state, or local criminal investigation. The federal investigative agency also shall provide this identifying information to the United States Attorney in the district where the applicant is located, and where the applicant is operating, and to the chief law enforcement officer involved (unless non-disclosure is required to safeguard a federal investigation in progress).

E. Inquiry by the United States Attorney

The United States Attorney in the district where an applicant or one of its principals is located, or where it or one of its principals is operating, shall determine whether the applicant or principal currently is the subject of grand jury proceedings or other prosecutorial scrutiny in that district, and the United States Attorney shall notify the federal investigative agency of the findings, and also shall notify the chief law enforcement officer involved (unless non-disclosure is required by federal law or to safeguard a federal investigation in progress).

Appendix D: Form DAG-71: Application for Transfer of Federally Forfeited Property

Date: ☐☐ ☐☐ ☐☐
Investigative Agency: ☐☐☐
Case Number: ________

U.S. Department of Justice

Application for Transfer of Federally Forfeited Property
(For Use By United States Law Enforcement Agencies Only)

I.

For Federal Use Only

Asset #: ________
Seizure Date: ________
Judicial District: ________
Case Type: Adoption: ☐ Joint: ☐
(Check One)

(For Additional Information - See Instructions)

- All assets transferred must be used for the law enforcement purpose stated in the request.
- Deadline for submission of this request is sixty (60) days following the seizure.
- The requesting agency will be responsible for reimbursing the Federal Government its costs and may be responsible, in a single-asset case, for reimbursing the federal share.

II. Requesting Agency Name:
Address: ________
NCIC Code: Date: ☐☐☐☐☐☐☐☐☐
Contact Person: ________ Telephone Number: (____) ________

III. Asset Requested: ________ ☐ Other assets in this case *(Attach list)*
Property Description: ________
Request Type:
☐ Item ☐ Cash/Proceeds ____%

IV. Specific Intended Law Enforcement Use:
☐ Salaries ☐ Purchase of Equipment ☐ Other (Please explain): ________
☐ Purchase of Vehicles ☐ Place into Official Use *(If other than cash)*

V. Contribution (If any answer to A thru E is yes, provide details in Part VI):

		Yes	No
A.	Did your agency originate the information leading to the seizure?	☐	☐
B.	Were any other assets seized under state law?	☐	☐
C.	Were extraordinary expenses incurred?	☐	☐
D.	Did your agency supply any unique or indispensable assistance?	☐	☐
E.	Are there any assets located in foreign countries associated with this case?	☐	☐
F.	How many hours were expended? ________ hours	☐	☐

FORM DAG-71
DEC.92

Case Number: ____________

U.S. Department of Justice

Application for Transfer of Federally Forfeited Property
(Page 2)

VI. Additional space for detailed answers (Indicate Part to which answer(s) apply)

(If more space is required, use a separate sheet of paper and attach.) Attachment: ☐ Yes ☐ No

VII. Certifications:

A. The requester certifies that the above information is true and accurate, that the property transferred will be used for the law enforcement purpose stated, and that all monies received pursuant to this request will be deposited and accounted for consistent with applicable state laws, regulations, and orders. The requester agrees to report on the actual use of equitably transferred property upon request. The requester agrees to pay fees and expenses necessary to effect transfer of title not later than the time of transfer. The requester understands that if it is unable to pay the necessary fees and expenses at the time of transfer, the asset will be sold and the maximum percent of net sale proceeds will be forwarded in lieu of the asset.

Signature/Title ____________ Date ____________

B. As legal counsel, I have reviewed this Application for Transfer of Federally Forfeited Property and I certify that the contract person identified in Part II has the authority to accept forfeited property and is the official to whom transfer documents and/or money should be delivered.

Signature/Title ____________ Date ____________

Address: ____________

Telephone Number: (____) ____________

U.S. DEPARTMENT OF JUSTICE
Instructions for Completing Form DAG-71
Application for Transfer of Federally Forfeited Property

General Instructions

- Transfer of federally forfeited property is governed by the Department of Justice Attorney General's Guidelines on Seized and Forfeited Property (Guidelines).
- Requesting **state or local** law enforcement agency (Agency) head or designee must complete the DAG-71. (**Note:** Incomplete or inaccurate information is the most common cause of delay in processing.)
- For international transfer of federally forfeited property, contact the Asset Forfeiture Office, Criminal Division, Department of Justice, Washington D.C.
- A **separate** DAG-71 must be completed for **each** asset (or proceeds) requested.
- The **deadline** for submitting the DAG-71 to the federal investigative agency processing the forfeiture (federal agency) is **60 days from the date of the last seizure in the case**. No DAG-71 will be considered if submitted after the deadline.
- In a one-asset case where the Agency requests the tangible property in lieu of proceeds, the Agency must return costs and the appropriate federal equitable share to the United States. If the Agency is unable to return the costs and federal share, the property will be liquidated and the proceeds distributed proportionally. (Upon adequate justification, exceptions may be granted by the deciding official.)

DAG-71

Part I: For federal use only. (**Note:** Asset Number refers to federal investigative agency case number or uniform identifier.)

Part II: Provide information requested. If **NCIC code** is not known, contact the federal agency responsible for processing this forfeiture. **Contact person** is the person who has authority to accept property and transfer documents, and/or money.

Part III: Provide as complete a property description as possible. Include serial or vehicle identification number. You must check either **"Item"** (if requesting the asset) or **"Cash/Proceeds"** (if requesting a percentage of the asset). Attach list of any other assets in this case.

By law, **percentage requested** must be based on the "degree of direct law enforcement effort by the state or local agency resulting in the forfeiture, taking into account the total value of all property forfeited and total law enforcement effort, including any related criminal prosecution with respect to the violation of law on which the forfeiture is based." (21 U.S.C. 881(e)(3)).

Part IV: Indicate specific intended law enforcement purpose(s) for requested cash, proceeds or tangible property. Pursuant to the Guidelines, all property, including cash and proceeds, must be used for the specific law enforcement purpose(s) approved.

Part V: Answer all items A-F. If an answer to A thru E is yes, provide details in Block VI.

Part VI: Space for additional information.

Part VII: Agency head or his designee and appropriate legal office must certify that information provided in Blocks I-VI is true and accurate.

SUPPLEMENTAL INSTRUCTIONS FOR MULTIPLE ASSETS

Where multiple assets are seized on the same date, in the same case, and the same request is made for each asset, preparation of paperwork can be simplified by using the following method:

(1) Complete one original of the DAG-71. In Block III, Asset Requested, enter "See asset marked by an 'x' on the attached list."

(2) Prepare a list of all assets seized in the case, as shown in the sample below.

(3) Photocopy the DAG-71 and the list as many times as needed. You will need one copy for each asset.

(4) Enter an "x" in the appropriate place next to one asset on each copy of the list. That copy will serve as the original DAG-71 for the asset marked with an "x."

(5) Provide original signatures on all DAG-71s.

Below is a sample of such a list:

LISTING OF ASSETS SEIZED
CASE NO.: ______

	Asset ID No. (Fed. Use Only)	Asset Description	Serial Number
_	93DEA000789	$32,000 U.S. currency	n/a
_	93DEA000790	1993 Lexus 4 dr sedan, metallic gold	345YG89FE9332
_	93DEA000791	One Panasonic cellular phone	678954321
X	93DEA000792	1992 Jeep Cherokee, red	777HG90QRW772
_	93DEA000793	Electronic Equipment:	
		IBM PS/1 computer	8833IBM76321
		60 MB hard drive	954673021
		Okidata printer	785432976

Note: This list can also fulfill the requirement to provide a list of all assets seized in a case.

APPENDIX E: EQUITABLE SHARING AND AGREEMENT ANNUAL CERTIFICATION REPORT

OMB Number 1123-0011
Expires 7-31-2011

Equitable Sharing Agreement and Certification

○ Police Department ○ Sheriff's Office ○ Task Force (Complete Table A, page2)
○ Prosecutor's Office ○ Other (specify) ____________

Agency Name: ____________

NCIC/ORI/Tracking Number: ☐☐☐☐☐☐☐☐☐

Street Address: ____________

City: ____________ **State:** ______ **Zip:** ______

Contact: Title: ______ First: ______ Last: ______

Contact Phone: ______ **Contact Fax:** ______

Contact e-mail: ____________

Last Fiscal Year End (mm/dd/yyyy): ☐

○ **New Participant:** Read the Equitable Sharing Agreement (page 4) and sign the Affidavit (page 5)

○ **Existing Participant:** Complete the Annual Certification Report, read the Equitable Sharing Agreement (page 4), and sign the Affidavit (page 5)

○ **Change in Administration:** Select to report change to Agency or Governing Body head DURING the current fisca year. Read the Equitable Sharing Agreement (page 4) and sign the Affidavit (page 5).

○ **Amended Form:** Revise the Annual Certification Report, read the Equitable Sharing Agreement (page 4), and sign the Affidavit (page 5).

Annual Certification Report

	Summary of Equitable Sharing Activity	Justice Funds	Treasury Funds
1	Beginning Equitable Sharing Fund Balance (must match Ending Equitable Sharing Fund Balance from prior FY)		
2	Federal Sharing Funds Received		
3	Federal Sharing Funds Received from Other Law Enforcement Agencies and Task Forces (complete Table B, page 2)		
4	Other Income		
5	Interest Income Accrued ☐ Check box if non-interest-bearing account.		
6	Total Equitable Sharing Funds (total of lines 1 - 5)	$0.00	$0.00
7	Federal Sharing Funds Spent (total of lines a - n below)	$0.00	$0.00
8	Ending Balance (subtract line 7 from line 6)	$0.00	$0.00

Page 1 of 5

January 2009
Version 1.5

	Summary of Shared Monies Spent	Justice Funds	Treasury Funds
a	Total spent on salaries for new, temporary, not-to-exceed one year, employees		
b	Total spent on overtime		
c	Total spent on informant and "buy money"		
d	Total spent on travel and training		
e	Total spent on communications and computers		
f	Total spent on firearms and weapons		
g	Total spent on body armor and protective gear		
h	Total spent on electronic surveillance equipment		
i	Total spent on building and improvements		
j	Total spent on other law enforcement expenses (complete Table C, page 3)		
k	Total transfers to other state and local law enforcement agencies (complete Table D, page 3)		
l	Total 15% Expenditures in Support of Community-based Programs (complete Table E, page 3)		
m	Total 25% Windfall Transfers to Other Government Agencies (complete Table F, page 3)		
n	Total spent on matching grants (complete Table G, page 3)		
	Total	$0.00	$0.00

Miscellaneous Data

o	Agency's budget for current fiscal year		
p	Jurisdiction's budget for current fiscal year		
q	Appraised Value of Other Assets Received		

Table A: Members of Task Force

Agency Name	Address

Table B: Equitable Sharing Funds Received from other Agencies

Transferring Agency Name, City, and State	Justice Funds	Treasury Funds
Agency Name Agency Address		

January 2009
Version 1.5

Table C: Other Law Enforcement Expenses

Description of Expense	Justice Funds	Treasury Funds

Table D: Equitable Sharing Funds Transferred to Other Agencies

Receiving Agency Name, City, and State	Justice Funds	Treasury Funds
Agency Name		
Agency Address		

Table E: 15% Expenditures in Support of Community-based Programs

Recipient	Justice Funds

Table F: 25% Windfall Transfers to Other Government Agencies

Recipient	Justice Funds	Treasury Funds

Table G: Matching Grants

Matching Grant Name	Justice Funds	Treasury Funds

Table H: Civil Rights Cases

Name of Case	Type of Discrimination Alleged				Status
	☐ Race	☐ Color	☐ National Origin	☐ Gender	○ Settled ○ Pending
	☐ Disability	☐ Age	☐ Other		

Paperwork Reduction Act Notice

Under the Paperwork Reduction Act, a person is not required to respond to a collection of information unless it displays a valid OMB control number. We try to create accurate and easily understood forms that impose the least possible burden on you to complete. The estimated average time to complete this form is 30 minutes. If you have comments regarding the accuracy of this estimate, or suggestions for making this form simpler, please write to the Asset Forfeiture and Money Laundering Section, Program Unit, 1400 New York Avenue, N.W., Second Floor, Washington, DC 20005.

January 2009
Version 1.5

Equitable Sharing Agreement

This Federal Equitable Sharing Agreement, entered into among (1) the Federal Government, (2) the above-stated law enforcement agency ("Agency"), and (3) the governing body, sets forth the requirements for participation in the federal equitable sharing program and the restrictions upon the use of federally forfeited cash, property, proceeds, and any interest earned thereon, which are equitably shared with participating law enforcement agencies. By its signatures, the Agency agrees that it will be bound by the statutes and guidelines that regulate shared assets and the following requirements for participation in the federal equitable sharing program. Receipt of the signed Equitable Sharing Agreement and Certification (this "Document") is a prerequisite to receiving any equitably shared cash, property, or proceeds.

1. **Submission.** This Document must be submitted to aca.submit@usdoj.gov within 60 days of the end of the Agency's fiscal year. This Document must be submitted electronically with the Affidavit/Signature page (page 5) submitted by fax. This will constitute submission to the Department of Justice and the Department of Treasury.

2. **Signatories.** This agreement must be signed by the head of the Agency and the head of the governing body. Examples of Agency heads include police chief, sheriff, director, commissioner, superintendent, administrator, chairperson, secretary, city attorney, county attorney, district attorney, prosecuting attorney, state attorney, commonwealth attorney, and attorney general. The governing body's head is the person who allocates funds or approves the budget for the Agency. Examples of governing body heads include city manager, mayor, city council chairperson, county executive, county council chairperson, director, secretary, administrator, commissioner, and governor.

3. **Uses.** Any shared asset shall be used for law enforcement purposes in accordance with the statutes and guidelines that govern the federal equitable sharing program as set forth in the current edition of the Department of Justice's *Guide to Equitable Sharing (Justice Guide)*, and the Department of the Treasury's *Guide to Equitable Sharing for Foreign Countries and Federal, State, and Local Law Enforcement Agencies (Treasury Guide).*

4. **Transfers.** Before the Agency transfers cash, property, or proceeds to other state or local law enforcement agencies, it must first verify with the Department of Justice or the Department of Treasury, depending on the source of the funds, that the receiving agency is a federal equitable sharing program participant and has a current Equitable Sharing Agreement and Certification on file.

5. **Internal Controls.** The Agency agrees to account separately for federal equitable sharing funds received from the Department of Justice and the Department of the Treasury. Funds from state and local forfeitures and other sources must not be commingled with federal equitable sharing funds. The Agency shall establish a separate revenue account or accounting code for state, local, Department of Justice, and Department of the Treasury forfeiture funds. Interest income generated must be accounted for in the appropriate federal forfeiture fund account.

The Agency agrees that such accounting will be subject to the standard accounting requirements and practices employed for other public monies as supplemented by requirements set forth in the current edition of the *Justice Guide* and the *Treasury Guide.*

The misuse or misapplication of shared resources or the supplantation of existing resources with shared assets is prohibited. Failure to comply with any provision of this agreement shall subject the recipient agency to the sanctions stipulated in the current edition of the *Justice* or *Treasury Guides*, depending on the source of the funds/property.

6. **Audit Report.** Audits will be conducted as provided by the Single Audit Act Amendments of 1996 and OMB Circular A-133. The Department of Justice and Department of the Treasury reserve the right to conduct periodic random audits.

Affidavit

Under penalty of perjury, the undersigned officials certify that **they have read and understand their obligations under the Equitable Sharing Agreement** and that the information submitted in conjunction with this Document is an accurate accounting of funds received and spent by the Agency under the *Justice and/or Treasury Guides* during the reporting period and that the recipient Agency is in compliance with the National Code of Professional Conduct for Asset Forfeiture.

The undersigned certify that the recipient agency is in compliance with the nondiscrimination requirements of the following laws and their Department of Justice implementing regulations: Title VI of the Civil Rights Act of 1964 (42 U.S.C. § 2000d et seq.), Title IX of the Education Amendments of 1972 (20 U.S.C. § 1681 et seq.), Section 504 of the Rehabilitation Act of 1973 (29 U.S.C. § 794), and the Age Discrimination Act of 1975 (42 U.S.C. § 6101 et seq.), which prohibit discrimination on the basis of race, color, national origin, disability, or age in any federally assisted program or activity, or on the basis of sex in any federally assisted education program or activity.

During the past fiscal year, has the Agency been part of any proceedings alleging discrimination by the Agency? ○ Yes ○ No

If you answered yes, complete Table H. Please disclose (1) all proceedings pending before any court or administrative agency, (2) any nondiscrimination laws the Agency has been found in violation of, and (3) any settlement agreements the Agency has entered into during the last fiscal year.

Agency Head		**Governing Body Head**	
Signature:		Signature:	
Name:		Name:	
Title:		Title:	
Date:		Date:	

Final Instructions:

Step 1: Click button to save in PDF format for your records [Save as PDF]
Step 2: Click button to save in XML format [Save as XML]
Step 3: E-mail the XML file as attachment to aca.submit@usdoj.gov
Step 4: Fax a signed copy of THIS PAGE ONLY to (202) 616-1344

Note: The Agency will not be in compliance until the e-mail and the fax of this page are received.

FOR AGENCY USE ONLY
Entered by ________
Entered on ________
FY End:
NCIC: Agency: Phone:
State: Contact: E-mail:

Page 5 of 5

January 2009
Version 1.5

End Notes

[1] 21 U.S.C. § 881(e)(1)(A) and (e)(3), 18 U.S.C. § 981(e)(2), and 19 U.S.C. § 1616a.
[2] 21 U.S.C. § 881(e)(3).
[3] In accordance with *Asset Forfeiture Policy Manual* (2008), Chap. 1, Sec. VIII.G.

[4] *See* Pre-Seizure Planning Guide, USMS Pub. No. 106 (June 2000) for further information regarding pre-seizure planning.

[5] Participating agencies in the Treasury Asset Forfeiture Program include the Internal Revenue Service (IRS), U.S. Immigration and Customs Enforcement (ICE), U.S. Customs and Border Protection (CBP), U.S. Secret Service (USSS), and U.S. Coast Guard.

[6] *See* part VII on how to calculate sharing percentages for participating agencies.

[7] Remission or mitigation is the return of forfeited property to an owner or lienholder of the property or to a victim of the crime underlying the forfeiture. *See* 28 C.F.R. § 9.8 (2008). Restoration is the use of forfeited funds to pay restitution to the victim of a criminal offense in accordance with a restoration order entered as part of a criminal judgment.

[8] Sharing is always based on net proceeds. *See* part III.E.

[10] *See* part VII.E for a definition of *net proceeds*.

[11] *See* Appendix A for additional information on the different types of federal forfeiture.

[12] *Id.*

[13] *See* Appendix D for a copy of the Form DAG-71 and other supplemental instructions.

[14] The Form DAG-71 (*see* Appendix D) and the Equitable Sharing Agreement and Certification (*see* Appendix E) are current as of the date of the printing of this *Guide*. The most current versions of these forms are available on the Department of Justice Web site at www.usdoj.gov/criminal/afmls/forms.

[15] By order dated June 5, 1995, the Deputy Attorney General delegated his authority to make final equitable sharing decisions to the Assistant Attorney General for the Criminal Division in cases where the seizing agency, the United States Attorney, and AFMLS agree on the allocation of forfeited property.

[16] *See* Appendix B for a copy of the National Code of Professional Conduct for Asset Forfeiture.

[17] For example, groups of state and local law enforcement agencies frequently establish separate units under the command of an experienced officer. All assigned agents have full law enforcement power within the combined area of the constituent agencies. The chief of police of any one constituent agency does not exercise day-to-day individual command authority over the task force but may sit as a member of a Steering Committee, Board of Directors, or other supervisory authority which sets general task force policies.

[18] For example, Officer Y is assigned to a task force. The agency may then hire Officer Z and may pay Officer Z's salary from asset forfeiture funds. Officer Z may not be assigned to a narcotics unit and he may not be assigned to a unit that identifies assets for seizure. If during Officer Z's routine patrol duties, he stops a vehicle found to contain narcotics and cash, the agency may continue to pay Officer Z's salary from asset forfeiture funds.

[19] This provision is designed to afford law enforcement agencies the opportunity to rearrange staffing assignments without suffering severe financial hardships and also recognizes that the hiring process can take time.

[20] *See Asset Forfeiture Policy Manual* (2008), Chap. 6, Sec. VIII.

[21] For purposes of the Equitable Sharing Agreement and Certification form, a governing body is an institution or organization that has budgetary oversight over the law enforcement agency. A law enforcement official should not sign for the governing body unless the official has budgetary oversight over the agency.

INDEX

D

E

F

G

H

I

N

O

P

Q

R

S